T0180089

Lecture Notes in Information Systems and Organisation

Volume 11

More information about this series at http://www.springer.com/series/11237

Teresina Torre · Alessio Maria Braccini
Riccardo Spinelli
Editors

Empowering Organizations

Enabling Platforms and Artefacts

 Springer

Editors
Teresina Torre
University of Genoa
Genoa
Italy

Riccardo Spinelli
University of Genoa
Genoa
Italy

Alessio Maria Braccini
Department of Economics and Business
Tuscia University
Viterbo
Italy

ISSN 2195-4968   ISSN 2195-4976   (electronic)
Lecture Notes in Information Systems and Organisation
ISBN 978-3-319-23783-1   ISBN 978-3-319-23784-8   (eBook)
DOI 10.1007/978-3-319-23784-8

Library of Congress Control Number: 2015949457

Springer Cham Heidelberg New York Dordrecht London
© Springer International Publishing Switzerland 2016

Printed on acid-free paper

Springer International Publishing AG Switzerland is part of Springer Science+Business Media
(www.springer.com)

Contents

Introduction

Teresina Torre, Alessio Maria Braccini and Riccardo Spinelli

Abstract The socio-technical approach to the study of the relations between people and technology in organizations has a long standing tradition in the managerial research. The increased adoption of information and communication technologies in organizations contributed to offer new empowerment opportunities for organizations, as well as opened new avenues for research. ICTs offer different, peculiar, organizational and individual affordances if compared to process technologies. ICTs are also continuously evolving at a quick pace. As a result the literature has seen, throughout the years, the growth and the evolution of different conceptualizations of the socio-technical relationship between technology and organization. On this specific topic this book contains a selection of the best papers presented and accepted at the XI edition of the ItAIS conference, held in Genova in November 2014. Papers included in the books discuss the role of empowerment potential for organization of IT artifacts and IT platforms, providing the results of cutting-edge research projects in the Italian and international scientific community.

Keywords Technology and Empowerment · IT Artefacts · IT Platforms · Socio-Technical Systems

T. Torre (✉) · R. Spinelli
Università degli Studi di Genova, Genoa, Italy
e-mail: teresina.torre@economia.unige.it

R. Spinelli
e-mail: riccardo.spinelli@economia.unige.it

A.M. Braccini
Università degli Studi della Tuscia, Viterbo, Italy
e-mail: abraccini@unitus.it

© Springer International Publishing Switzerland 2016
T. Torre et al. (eds.), *Empowering Organizations*, Lecture Notes in Information
Systems and Organisation 11, DOI 10.1007/978-3-319-23784-8_1

1

1 Empowering Organization: A Continuous Challenge

When Rosabeth Moss Kanter (in 1977) first introduced the concept of empowerment in working contexts, she suggested workers would require some discretion to emancipate themselves from the hitherto dominant hierarchical structure, and that it would be really positive for organizations and their capacity to develop.

Born in social and political context in the 1960s, the term empowerment defined a growing process based on an increasing in self-esteem, in self efficacy, and self-determination aimed to bring out the potential of each person, thereby producing a more inclusive society through everybody's active participation in public life. Quickly, the concept has been introduced in managerial and organizational studies, underlying that development is real and effective if organizational actors, human resources, and workers have the opportunity to grow first. Their knowledge, experience and motivation—usually underused—can increase, through empowerment processes, while their favourite responsible behaviours remain coherent with the demand for more participation in the strategies and activities of an enterprise.

In more recent time, organizational empowerment is considered an effective tool for management to confer responsibility of all employees and support their engagement and motivation [1]. Indeed, an empowering organization allows to its members to have a better control on their work and on their working conditions [2]. Hence, an organization wishing to create an empowering context has to begin with individual empowerment.

Someone considers empowerment a cutting-edge technology ensuring both strategic advantage that enterprises are looking for and opportunities that people seek [3]: so, organizational empowerment is presented with a positive connotation, just for this implication.

This orientation finds its proper contextualization into the socio-technical approach, in which the role of workers is evaluated just for their capability in managing technologies and technical context. In this perspective empowerment become an interpretative key to understand the logic of social-technical system.

As known, the concept of socio-technical system emerged from the observation that the way in which people worked did not follow the mechanistic view of procedures, which emphasized specialization and division of labor minimizing the role of each worker, his respective competences and ability in using working tools and instruments. Relations among workers were found to be important [4]: workers cooperate and collaborate to use the available technologies. The performance of a productive system was strictly connected with the interaction between two coessential dimensions: social dimension, which is created by people all together and their particular organization; and technical one, which is represented by materials, machinery and plants with task and interrelations among such tasks. Both are open, organic systems that regularly interact with external environment, producing feedback and adaptive actions in order to face with required changes.

Since the first analysis, the concept of socio-technical system emerged as a useful basis to describe and understand any kind of organization. This is because it underlines the strong relationship between technology and human being and social aspects, and explains the need to consider both the components for an effective organizational design. Central is the idea of joint optimization, that summarizes the necessary dynamic equilibrium between key variances of technical system for the organizational purposes and the variance control analysis developed by workers and the job satisfaction need, pure expression of workers' behavior in working context [5].

In this perspective it is evident the relation with an empowering organization, whose aim is essentially the evaluation of a proactive role played by workers. Intrinsic job satisfaction and individual preferences become the starting point to analyze the organizational system and to build it according to job redesign orientation more finalized to satisfy the requisites of technical system [6]. At the same time innovative and free behaviors aimed to facilitate the goals of the organization more than the rigorous application of role prescription, but moreover this appears directly connected with high level of intrinsic satisfaction.

This approach can be helpful in understanding the relation between *organization* and *technology* because its nature is structurally adaptive, considering as basic the complementary between social aspect and technical content [7]. A socio-technical system is based on a rich interplay of human actors, introduced in multi-agent systems, that use different and heterogeneous interfaces, with a certain degree of discretion by worker and an operational environment in which technology evolution assumes an increasing intensity [8].

2 Organization and Technology

The debate on the relation between *organization* and *technology* has a long standing tradition in the managerial literature [9, 10], and saw different perspectives across the years [10, 11]. In the organizational mainstream literature three milestones characterized the study of this duality: the contributions on technological complexity by Woodward [12–14], the studies on complex and routine activities by Perrow [15, 16], and the work on interdependences and on supporting technologies by Thompson [17].

The advent of digital technologies (ICTs) enriched this debate with the discussion of new affordance for organizations [18]. ICTs embeds a great empowerment potential for organizations, allowing both individuals and organizations to achieve changes and to pursues innovation and improvements [19–24]. The adoption of ICTs interested a large part of human activities, and continuously change the way people live and work [25].

ICTs afford people and organizations to easily create, manage, store, and transmit information. Doing so they support all the main organizational processes [26]: sense-making, decision-making, and knowing. For this characteristic ICTs deeply differ from process and automation technologies that were traditionally studied by the technology and organization debate in the literature [24, 27, 28]. ICTs empower organization, as they allow them to resort to new and different organizational forms or control instruments, which in the end foster and promote organizational change and performance improvements.

In the study of the relation between organization and digital technology a pivotal element is the ICT artefact, being it the main manifestation of the ICT with which individuals and organizations relate. Different ways to investigate the mutual influence between organization and technology have been used in the literature, mainly following different conceptualization of the ICT artefact [29]. In the recent years technology innovation contributed to change the nature of the ICT artefact. The diffusion of mobile technologies and social media produced new organizational affordances, enriching the socio-technical nature of the ICT artefact, and giving rise to the concept of ICT platform.

2.1 *The ICT* Artefact

The ICT artefact can be seen just as a *tool*, a "computing resource (that) is best conceptualized as a particular piece of equipment, application or technique which provides specifiable information processing capabilities" [30]. Under this perspective what ICT affords organization is mainly seen under a technical perspective, sometimes in an uncorrelated manner to the social and organizational surroundings. Under this perspective ICT is usually seen as a tool to substitute human labour, to enhance productivity, to process and exchange information, and to change social relations [29].

The ICT artefact can be seen as a *proxy*, i.e. a set of properties or key elements shared by different pieces of ICT. This perspective focuses more on the technology in action, assuming that different ICT artefacts can be described by common measures or values. ICT artefacts are then intended either as perceptions (i.e. how they are understood by people using them), or as diffusion trends or adoption rates, or as capital/value/benefits [29].

The *computational* perspective neglects instead the social side of technology focusing only on the technical capabilities and performance of these artefacts in manipulating, storing, and transferring information. Under this perspective ICT artefacts are studied jus either as a collection of algorithms to build new or improve existing systems to support human activities, or as mathematical models used to represent and simulate processes or events [29].

A final perspective on ICT artefacts does not only considers the artefact as the single important element, but takes it as a part of a larger ensemble which includes all the other elements which are necessary to use the specific artefact to support human activities. This is part of an effort to un-black box the technology, to directly include in the object of study the human agency that underpins the work of the ICTs, to better understand both how the technology empowers the organization. Following this perspective ICT artefacts can be seen [29] as development projects (i.e. the set of design, development and implementation processes of an ICT artefact.), as production networks (i.e. as an ensemble of different ICT artefacts at a national or industry level), as a system embedded in another system, or as a an artefacts which embeds social structures [31, 32].

2.2 *The ICT* **Platform**

Recent developments of digital technologies called for an enlarged perspective of the conceptualization of the ICT artefact. Considering the diffusion of the Internet, more and more often ICT resources are used by organizations as a collection of different interconnected elements, forming a *platform*. Some author include in the definition of platform just a set of ICT features (mainly software based) that provide shared functionalities trough which an ICT artefact interoperates with another one [33]. To this perspective some see in this just a novel and more complex conceptualization of an ICT artefact [34].

ICT platforms do not only involve pieces of technical artefacts (i.e. pieces of software and hardware), but they also encompass a more rich set of different actors, involving both final uses, owners, and developers, and work on a basis of a set of shared resources designed and organized to allow, at the same time, both control by the owner, and evolution and diffusion by the final user [33–35].

ICT platforms can therefore be seen as complex socio-technical systems that are not stable over time, evolving trough the enlargement of the use base, and of the enrichment of the features offered to users [36, 37]. Going through an evolutionary approach these systems are not designed from scratch, but grow "conservatively through mutation and hybridization, rather than outright break with the past" [38].

The study of the technology and organization problem under this perspective calls for a more complex understanding of the mutual influences among the different components of this *assemblage* [39]. Seen from this perspective the capabilities of a platform are not only those of the components (i.e. there are not just a sum of the former), but emerge also by the intra-action of the components [40], i.e. by the co-joint action of the different components which, by the very fact of being part of such a system, show new and different properties and capabilities.

3 Contents of the Book

Within this reference framework this book presents a selection of the best peer reviewed articles presented at the XI Edition of the annual conference of the Italian Chapter of AIS (ItAIS) which took place on November 21st–22nd in Genova, hosted by the Department of Economic and Business Studies of the University of Genova. The book is composed by 22 original chapters. Each chapter studies the empowerment potential of ICTs artefacts and platforms adopting different perspectives within the two socio-technical and technical extremes.

A first set of papers adopts a sociotechnical perspective on information systems, with particular attention to management practices and to specific artefacts. Benevolo et al. [41] draw the attention to a novel but rapidly flourishing topic, that is Smart City initiatives. By studying Smart Mobility projects as part of wider Smart City initiatives, they investigate the role of ICT in supporting smart mobility actions, influencing their impact on the citizens' quality of life and on the public value created for the city as a whole. The "public" dimension is in common with Romanelli's [42] paper too. In this case, the unit of analysis are Parliaments, viewed as organizations seeking legitimacy by engaging citizens in the policy process thanks to Internet technologies; the model of e-sustainable Parliament is discussed, together with a review of Parliamentary e-participation initiatives.

Moving towards a more business-oriented context, Agrifoglio et al. [43] address the so-called "sailing ship" effect, that is the strategic reaction of new-comers that enter into a new market for adopting and improving old technology although technological change occurs and innovative solutions are available. By introducing a case study based on the instant photo industry after Polaroid leaving it, they demonstrate how this apparently inconsistent strategy can be successful.

Halfway between business practice and management education is Bednar and Sadok's [44] chapter, where they describe a teaching experience of information systems analysis and design unit. A sociotechnical toolbox is introduced and the application made by students in a real life business is described. The benefits from this project are twofold, as students experience of real world business and the entrepreneurs develop new insights and understandings of key features of their own work practices.

The second group of papers in the book keeps the sociotechnical perspective but shifts the focus to platform-based solutions and topics. Again, two sub-groups may be identified, according to a more "public"or "business" orientation.

To the first one certainly belongs the contribution of Ribaudo et al. [45], which analyses the emerging role of Universities as democratic intermediaries in e-Participation. Some experiences that recently took place in the city of Genoa are presented, where the local University played a core role as guarantors of the public dialogue in the design of democratic deliberative digital environments. Paletti and Za's [46] chapter too addresses a topic of public interest, when they design a new Disaster Management System that, while following the most recent United Nations' suggestions, includes citizens and volunteers in the disaster management organization in order to decrease vulnerabilities and to develop resilient communities.

The contribution of Mancini and Ferruzzi [47] has a hybrid nature, as Authors face a business topic—the use of collaboration platforms for management control—but in a no-profit context, that is a research institute. With an Italian-based case study, they show how this platform has become an important support device for management control processes and represents an opportunity for a higher integration among the components of the control process itself.

Far more business-oriented are the other three papers in this group. Firstly, Iannotta and Gatti [48] investigate the evolution and the new trends in the e-recruitment services, by introducing an Italian case study of e-recruiting platform and showing innovative solutions in order to more efficiently match the requests of employers and job seekers. Secondly, Testa et al. [49] explore the relationship between human actors and technology in the context of a social media platform. Moving from Pickering's "mangle" theory and Jones' subsequent metaphor of "double dance of agency", they present a case study of a social-media platform run by a leading Italian firm in the food industry. A series of interrelated emergent phenomena arise, entangling managers, customers, and the social media platform, introducing further dimensions in the "dancing" metaphor. Lastly, Mola and Russo [50] investigate the influence of pervasive use of ICT-based platforms such as electronic marketplaces on the evolution of inter-organizational relationships. They analyse two Internet platforms specialized in outsourcing the e-commerce related processes in the fashion industry. Their results confirm that such platforms are deeply changing the system of relationships between clients and suppliers, affecting the processes performances, and requiring a new conceptualization of the traditional supply chain.

The remaining chapters of the books include contributions where the adopted perspective is mainly technical, and the attention is greatly concentrated on the technical characteristics of a given artefact or platform.

Beginning with those contributions presenting artefacts, a couple of papers introduce art-related solutions. Deufemia et al. [51] present a mobile application, named PetroSketch, for supporting archaeologists in the classification and recognition of petroglyph symbols; it uses a flexible image-matching algorithm, which compare the sample image with a set of references taken from archaeological archives. Calandra et al. [52], instead, design E.Y.E. C. U., a modular eye tracking system that supports art galleries fruition; every time a visitor lingers on a painting detail, a hidden camera detects her gaze and the framework beams, in real time, the related illustrative contents on the wall region around it.

A large group of papers deals with network and software related artefacts. Two chapters of this section are dedicated to app design. Caruccio et al. [53] propose a wizard-based development process that guides the users towards the construction of Web applications: a pilot application to student information management in Universities is discussed. Similarly, Vitiello et al. [54] propose MIDE, a Java-written tool that devises patterns in the form of ready-to-use application templates and interface snippets targeted at the Android platform, which could be particularly useful for novel users and programmers. Instead, Deufemia et al. [55] present several experiments aiming to compare the performances of classifiers of user intent on search engine pages; they also propose a metric to evaluate them and detect the most promising features for deriving a better classifier. Imrie and Bednar [56] address the problem of managing and controlling data stored on devices in a distributed technologies environment. They categorize and compare different approaches to controlling data on distributed devices, from the perspective of their effects on the usefulness to the end user. Finally Cassino and Vozella [57] propose the integration of a paradigm borrowed by risk theory, within a tool for the evaluation of software systems through the analysis of visual components of its interface; their tool could support organizations to define and properly allocate liability among system actors in order to identify recurring errors in view of a potential reengineering of the system.

Although still focused on an artefact, McGrath's [58] contribution differs from the previous ones as it addresses a more abstract topic: the Author investigates through an experiment the idea generation process of ad hoc pairs using external visualizations for divergent thought. The objective is to examine whether the perceived possibility to change visual representations of ideas impacts the cognitive persistence of pairs.

The final chapters of the book adopt a technological point of view to explore platforms.

Di Mascio et al. [59] move from social dynamics in the aftermath of the earthquake in L'Aquila (Italy) and discuss how IT solutions may support social recovery. They introduce the Emepolis + project, a kind of social network available as a mobile app which aims to help local citizens in the reconstruction of their city and in the recovery of their community: differently from traditional social networks, the focus of Emepolis + is not on user profiles, but rather on the issues posted by the users themselves.

The contribution of Ruggieri et al. [60] returns instead to a business context, as it explores the role of cloud working platforms in reshaping the job market. While in Iannotta and Gatti's [48] the focus was on e-recruitment services, in this chapter the Authors explore the crowdsourcing phenomenon, presenting three international platforms. They conclude that cloud working offers the employers an opportunity to externalize their activities via web and represents for the employees the chance to better manage their working life.

Finally, Bolici and Della Rosa's [61] contribution focuses on virtual currency markets. They analyse the rise and fall of Mt. Gox, a leading virtual currency exchange platform, in order to understand the value and the risks associated to the system and the consequences of the breakdown of one of the most important player in the market.

The volume ends with the contribution of Ricciardi and Rossignoli [62], which stands out from the others due to its theoretical and methodological nature. In their paper, in fact, the Authors propose a classification framework for Management and Information Systems studies, and apply it to a set of itAIS 2011 selected papers. Their results cast light on the extreme methodological variability in MIS research, necessary to cope with the complexity of the technology and organization relationships, confirming the value of complementary approaches and methods and allowing for an easier orientation in the increasingly wide spectrum of MIS studies.

References

1. Johnson, R., Redmond, D.: L'arte dell'empowerment. Come realizzare un'organizzazione snella più competitiva coinvolgendo e responsabilizzando il personale. Franco Angeli, Milano (1999)
2. Zimmerman, M.A.: Empowerment theory. In: Rappaport, J., Seidman, E. (eds.) Handbook of commnity psychology, pp. 43–63. Springer, US (2000)
3. Cherns, A.E.: Principles of sociotechnical design revisited. Hum. Relat. **40**, 153–162 (1987)

4. Emery, F.E., Trist, E.L.: The causal texture of organizational environments. Hum. Relat. **18**, 21–32 (1965)
5. Emery, F.E., Trist, E.L.: Analytical model for sociotechnical systems. In: Pasmore, W.A., Sherwood, J.J. (eds.) Sociotechnical systems: a sourcebook, pp. 120–133 (1978)
6. Marchiori, M.: L'approccio socio-tecnico. L'organizzazione: concetti e metodi, pp. 92–121. Carocci, Roma (2010)
7. Mumford, E.: Designing human systems for new technology—the ethics method. Manchester business school (1983)
8. Dalpiaz, F., Giorgini, P., Mylopoulos, J.: Adaptive socio-technical systems: a requirements-based approach. Requir. Eng. **18**, 1–24 (2013)
9. Orlikowski, W.J., Robey, D.: Information technology and the structuring of organizations. Inf. Syst. Res. **2**, 143–169 (1992)
10. Orlikowski, W.J.: Using technology and constituting structures: a practice lens for studying technology in organizations. Organ. Sci. **11**, 404–428 (2000)
11. Styhre, A.: Organizing technologies of vision: making the invisible visible in media-laden observations. Inf. Organ. **20**, 64–78 (2010)
12. Woodward, J.: Management and technology. Her Majesty's Stationery Office, London (1958)
13. Woodward, J.: Industrial organization: theory and practice. Oxford University Press, New York (1965)
14. Woodward, J.: Industrial organization: behavior and control. Oxford University Press, New York (1970)
15. Perrow, C.: A framework for the comparative analysis of organizations. Am. Sociol. Rev. **32**, 194–208 (1967)
16. Perrow, C.: Organizational analysis: a sociological view. Wadsworth, Belmont (1970)
17. Thompson, J.D.: Organizations in action. McGraw-Hill, New York (1967)
18. Zammuto, R.F., Griffith, T.L., Majchrzak, A., Dougherty, D.J., Faraj, S., Dogherty, D.J.: Information technology and the changing fabric of organization. Organ. Sci. **18**, 749–762 (2007)
19. Henderson, J.C., Venkatraman, N.: Strategic alignment: a model for organizational transformation through information technology. In: Kochan, T.A., Useem, M. (eds.) Transforming organizations. Oxford University Press, New York (1992)
20. Davenport, T.: Process innovation: reengineering work through information technology. Harvard Business School Press, Boston (1993)
21. Orlikowski, W.J.: Improvising organizational transformation over time: a situated change perspective. Inf. Syst. Res. **7**, 63–92 (1996)
22. Dedrick, D., Gurbaxani, V., Kraemer, K.L.: Information technology and economic performance: a critical review of the empirical evidence. ACM Comput. Surv. **35**, 1–28 (2003)
23. Markus, L.M.: Technochange management: using IT to drive organizational change. J. Inf. Technol. **19**, 4–20 (2004)
24. Leonardi, P.M.: Activating the informational capabilities of information technology for organizational change. Organ. Sci. **18**, 813–831 (2007)
25. Orlikowski, W.J.: Technology and institutions: what can research on information technology and research on organizations learn from each other? MIS Q. **25**, 145–165 (2001)
26. Martinez, M.: Organizzazione, informazioni e tecnologie. (2004)
27. Lucas, H.C.: Performance and the use of an information system. Manage. Sci. **21**, 908–919 (1975)
28. Rice, R.E.: Computer-mediated communication and organizational innovation. J. Commun. **37**, 65–94 (1987)
29. Orlikowski, W.J., Jacono, C.S.: Desperately seeking the "IT" in IT research—a call to theorizing the IT artifcat. Inf. Syst. Res. **12**, 121–134 (2001)
30. Kling, R.: Defining the boundaries of computing across complex organizations. In: Boland, R. J., Ruby Hirschheim (eds.) Critical issues in information systems research, pp. 207–262. John Wiley & Sons, New York (1987)
31. Giddens, A.: The constitution of soceity. University of California Press, Berkeley, CA (1984)

32. Jones, M.R., Karsten, H.: Gidden's structuration theory and information systems research. MIS Q. **32**, 127–157 (2008)
33. Tiwana, A., Konsynski, B., Bush, A.A.: Platform evolution: coevolution of platform architecture, governance, and environmental dynamics. Inf. Syst. Res. **21**, 675–687 (2010)
34. Tilson, D., Lyytinen, K., Sørensen, C.: Digital infrastructures: the missing IS research agenda. Inf. Syst. Res. **21**, 748–759 (2010)
35. Tilson, D., Sørensen, C., Lyytinen, K.: Change and control paradoxes in mobile infrastructure innovation: the android and iOS mobile operating systems cases. Proc. Annu. Hawaii Int. Conf. Syst. Sci. pp. 1324–1333 (2011)
36. Grisot, M., Hanseth, O., Thorseng, A.A.: Innovation of, in, on infrastructures: articulating the role of architecture in information infrastructure evolution. J. Assoc. Inf. Syst. **15**, 197–219 (2014)
37. Hanseth, O., Lyytinen, K.: Design theory for dynamic complexity in information infrastructures: the case of building Internet. J. Inf. Technol. **25**, 1–19 (2010)
38. Blanchette, J.: Viewpoint: computing as if infrastructure mattered. Commun. ACM **55**, 32–34 (2012)
39. De Landa, M.: A new philosphy of society: assemblage theory and social complexity. A&C black (2006)
40. Barad, K.M.: Meeting the universe halfway: quantum physics and the entanglement of matter and meaning. Duke University Press (2007)
41. Benevolo, C., Dameri, R.P., D'Auria, B.: Smart mobility in smart city. In: Torre, T., Braccini, A. M., Spinelli, R. (eds) Empowering organizations: enabling platforms and artifacts, LNISO, pp. 13–28. Springer, Heidelberg (2015)
42. Romanelli, M.: Designing e-sustainable parliaments. In: Torre, T., Braccini, A. M., Spinelli, R. (eds) Empowering organizations: enabling platforms and artifacts, LNISO, pp. 29–38. Springer, Heidelberg (2015)
43. Agrifoglio, R., Schiavone, R., Metallo, C.: Investigating the sailing ship effect as newcomers' stategic reaction to technological change. In: Torre, T., Braccini, A. M., Spinelli, R. (eds) Empowering organizations: enabling platforms and artifacts, LNISO, pp. 39–49. Springer, Heidelberg (2015)
44. Bednar, P., Sadok, M.: Bridging the gap between theory and practice: socio-technical toolbox. In: Torre, T., Braccini, A. M., Spinelli, R. (eds) Empowering organizations: enabling platforms and artifacts, LNISO, pp. 51–62. Springer, Heidelberg (2015)
45. Ribaudo, M., Torrigiani, C., De Cindio, F., Palumbo, M.: The university in the polis: an emerging role of democratic intermediary in e-participation?. In: Torre, T., Braccini, A. M., Spinelli, R. (eds) Empowering organizations: enabling platforms and artifacts, LNISO, pp. 63–76. Springer, Heidelberg (2015)
46. Paletti, A., Za, S.: Designing a new model of DMS for developing a resilient community. In: Torre, T., Braccini, A. M., Spinelli, R. (eds) Empowering organizations: enabling platforms and artifacts, LNISO, pp. 77–90. Springer, Heidelberg (2015)
47. Mancini, M., Ferruzzi, C.: Using collaboration platforms for management control processes: new opportunities for integration. In: Torre, T., Braccini, A. M., Spinelli, R. (eds) Empowering organizations: enabling platforms and artifacts, LNISO, pp. 91–101. Springer, Heidelberg (2015)
48. Iannotta, M., Gatti, M.: Innovating e-recruitment services: an italian case study. In: Torre, T., Braccini, A. M., Spinelli, R. (eds) Empowering organizations: enabling platforms and artifacts, LNISO, pp. 103–114. Springer, Heidelberg (2015)
49. Testa, S., Massa, S., Martini, A.: The inextricable intertwining of the firm, the platform and the customer: the case of a social media platform for innovation. In Torre T., Braccini A. M., Spinelli R. (eds) Empowering Organizations: Enabling Platforms and Artifacts, LNISO, pp. 115–131. Springer, Heidelberg (2015)
50. Mola, L., Russo, I.: From e-marketplace to e-supply chain: re-conceptualising the relationship between virtual and physical processes. In Torre T., Braccini A. M., Spinelli R. (eds) Empowering Organizations: Enabling Platforms and Artifacts, LNISO, pp. 133–145. Springer, Heidelberg (2015)

51. Deufemia, V., Granatello, M., Merola, A., Pesce, E., Polese, G.: Comparing classifiers for web user intent understanding. In: Torre, T., Braccini, A. M., Spinelli, R. (eds) Empowering organizations: enabling platforms and artifacts, LNISO, pp. 147–159. Springer, Heidelberg (2015)

52. Calandra, D.M., Di Mauro, D., D'Auria, D., Cutugno, F.: E.Y.E. C. U.: Emotional eYe trackEr for Cultural heritage support. In: Torre, T., Braccini, A. M., Spinelli, R. (eds) Empowering organizations: enabling platforms and artifacts, LNISO, pp. 161–172. Springer, Heidelberg (2015)

53. Caruccio, L., Deufemia, V., Polese, G.: A wizard-based environment for EUDWeb development process. In: Torre, T., Braccini, A. M., Spinelli, R. (eds) Empowering organizations: enabling platforms and artifacts, LNISO, pp. 173–185. Springer, Heidelberg (2015)

54. Vitiello, G., Tortora, G., Di Giovanni, P., Sebillo, M.: Practicing mobile interface design principles through the use of HCI design patterns—an education strategy. In: Torre, T., Braccini, A. M., Spinelli, R. (eds) Empowering organizations: enabling platforms and artifacts, LNISO, pp. 187–198. Springer, Heidelberg (2015)

55. Deufemia, V., Indelli Pisano, V., Paolino, L., De Roberto, P.: A mobile application for supporting archaeologists in the classification and recognition of petroglyphs. In: Torre, T., Braccini, A. M., Spinelli, R. (eds) Empowering organizations: enabling platforms and artifacts, LNISO, pp. 199–211. Springer, Heidelberg (2015)

56. Imrie, P., Bednar, P.: End user effects of centralised data control. In: Torre, T., Braccini, A. M., Spinelli, R. (eds) Empowering organizations: enabling platforms and artifacts, LNISO, pp. 213–225. Springer, Heidelberg (2015)

57. Cassino, R., Vozella, A.: Risk assessment to support liability allocation performed by the system GUI analysis. In: Torre, T., Braccini, A. M., Spinelli, R. (eds) Empowering organizations: enabling platforms and artifacts, LNISO, pp. 227–239. Springer, Heidelberg (2015)

58. McGrath, L.: Cognitive antifreeze: the visual inception of fluid sociomaterial interactions for knowledge creation. In: Torre, T., Braccini, A. M., Spinelli, R. (eds) Empowering organizations: enabling platforms and artifacts, LNISO, pp. 241–256. Springer, Heidelberg (2015)

59. Di Mascio, T., Gobbo, F., Tarantino, L.: Requirements and open issues for ISs supporting dynamic community bonding in emergency situations. In: Torre, T., Braccini, A. M., Spinelli, R. (eds) Empowering organizations: enabling platforms and artifacts, LNISO, pp. 257–271. Springer, Heidelberg (2015)

60. Ruggieri, A., Mosconi, E.M., Poponi, S., Silvestri, C.: Digital innovation in the job market: an explorative study on cloud working platforms. In: Torre, T., Braccini, A. M., Spinelli, R. (eds) Empowering organizations: enabling platforms and artifacts, LNISO, pp. 273–283. Springer, Heidelberg (2015)

61. Bolici, F., Della Rosa, S.: Mt.Gox is dead, long live Bitcoin! analysis of the rise and fall of the leading virtual currency exchange platform. In: Torre, T., Braccini, A. M., Spinelli, R. (eds) Empowering organizations: enabling platforms and artifacts, LNISO, pp. 285–296. Springer, Heidelberg (2015)

62. Ricciardi, F., Rossignoli, C.: Research methods in the itAIS community: building a classification framework for management and information systems studies. In: Torre, T., Braccini, A. M., Spinelli, R. (eds) Empowering organizations: enabling platforms and artifacts, LNISO, pp. 297–315. Springer, Heidelberg (2015)

Smart Mobility in Smart City

Action Taxonomy, ICT Intensity and Public Benefits

Clara Benevolo, Renata Paola Dameri and Beatrice D'Auria

Abstract Smart City is a recent topic, but it is spreading very fast, as it is perceived like a winning strategy to cope with some severe urban problems such as traffic, pollution, energy consumption, waste treatment. Smart City ideas are the merge of some other more ancient urban policies such as digital city, green city, knowledge city. A Smart City is therefore a complex, long-term vision of a better urban area, aiming at reducing its environmental footprint and at creating better quality of life for citizens. Mobility is one of the most difficult topic to face in metropolitan large areas. It involves both environmental and economic aspects, and needs both high technologies and virtuous people behaviours. Smart Mobility is largely permeated by ICT, used in both backward and forward applications, to support the optimization of traffic fluxes, but also to collect citizens' opinions about liveability in cities or quality of local public transport services. The aim of this paper is to analyse the Smart Mobility initiatives like part of a larger Smart City initiative portfolio, and to investigate about the role of ICT in supporting smart mobility actions, influencing their impact on the citizens' quality of life and on the public value created for the city as a whole.

Keywords Smart city · Smart mobility · Digital city · Benefits · ITS

1 Introduction

During the latest 50 years, city dimensions have been increasing more and more, all over the world. By 2050, 70 % of population will live in cities [1]. Cities are both places of opportunities and places of diseases. Opportunities, because cities are

C. Benevolo · R.P. Dameri (✉) · B. D'Auria
Department of Economics and Business Studies, University of Genova, Genoa, Italy
e-mail: dameri@economia.unige.it

C. Benevolo
e-mail: benevolo@economia.unige.it

B. D'Auria
e-mail: beatricedauria.dauria@gmail.com

© Springer International Publishing Switzerland 2016
T. Torre et al. (eds.), *Empowering Organizations*, Lecture Notes in Information
Systems and Organisation 11, DOI 10.1007/978-3-319-23784-8_2

places where people live and meet, where companies are settled and schools and universities are most present. Diseases, because in city traffic, pollution and waste production are worse than elsewhere and the cost of living is very high.

Public Administration and Municipalities are facing a challenging task, to harmonize a sustainable urban development taking into account the need of both creating job opportunities and preserving the environment, offering to people in city the best living conditions. Moreover, cities are looking for competitive advantage in attracting and retaining the best, more educated and skilled human resources for innovative and performing companies, and high touristic fluxes, also thanks to the perceived quality of life, to have the best performance in public value creation.

Smart City is considered like a winning urban strategy using technology to increase the quality of life in urban space, both improving the environmental quality and delivering better services to the citizens [2]. Several academic papers have been written about smart city, smart strategies and smart initiatives, interesting a very large set of topics: from waste treatment to air quality, from green energy production to buildings energetic efficiency, from open data to e-government in smart city. However, few works till now have been reasoning about more complex aspects, such as how all these topics—also very different each others—interact reciprocally, which benefits they could produce, how they impact on the quality of life of citizens, how much they are able to effectively solve the urban problems and how well the smart projects perform.

To respond to this questions, this paper introduces a deep analysis focalised on one of the most important topics in smart city, that is, smart mobility. Mobility is one of the most important facilities to support the functioning of the urban area [3]. However, transport produces several severe negative impacts and problems for the quality of life in cities, such as: pollution; traffic; street congestion; long time to cross the city and therefore a negative impact on work and life balance; high cost of public local transport services; and so on. Therefore, Smart Mobility is one of the most promising topics in Smart City, as it could produce high benefits for the quality of life of almost all the city stakeholders.

Smart Mobility is not a unique initiative, but a complex set of projects and actions, different in goals, contents and technology intensity. Especially ICT could be the pivot of a Smart Mobility initiative or completely lack. Our paper aims to analyse and classify Smart Mobility actions, considering their ICT content and their goals and trying to answer to the following Research Questions: are Smart Mobility initiatives necessarily ICT-intensive? Which are the main goals of the Smart Mobility initiatives? Which benefits could they produce?

In the further chapters, our analysis faces the Smart Mobility topic taking into consideration several aspects. In Sect. 2, Smart Mobility is rooted in the international literature about urban development, Smart City, smart actions impact on quality of life and stakeholders' expectations. In Sect. 3 the most recurrent Smart Mobility initiatives implemented in smart city strategies all over the world are analysed and a taxonomy is suggested. In Sect. 4 the role of ICT in Smart Mobility and the benefits of Smart Mobility for citizens' quality of life is described. In Sect. 5 we outline reached results, research limits and further works.

2 Smart City and Smart Mobility: Some Reference Models

The Smart City topic, even if recent, has its roots in more consolidated urban strategies, deriving from different streams of study and finally merged into the Smart City vision. Thanks to a deep literature survey and analysis about the definitions and labels attributed to cities [4], we grouped the topics in three streams:

1. Digital city: it regards the use of ICT to support the creation of a wired, ubiquitous, interconnected network of citizens and organizations, sharing data and information and joining online services, supported by public policies such as e-government and e-democracy [5];
2. Green city: it regards an ecological vision of the urban space, based on the concept of sustainable development. Green policies in city regard both reducing the city footprint on the environment, reducing pollution waste and energy consumption, and preserving or creating public green areas like parks and gardens [6];
3. Knowledge city: it regards the policies aiming at enforcing and valuing data, information and knowledge available and produced in city, especially through its cultural institutions, but also produced and used by companies, innovative districts, technological parks [7].

Giffinger et al. [8] define Smart City as "a city well performing in a forward-looking way in economy, people, governance, mobility, environment, and living, built on the smart combination of activities of self-decisive, independent and aware citizens". (See also [9].) It emerges that technology and ICT—the Digital City components—are necessary, even if they are not the goal but the instrument, as the final aims are to improve the citizens' quality of life and to well manage natural resources (Green City), involving citizens thanks to a participated city governance (Smart City). Therefore, depending on the authors, each city is smart as far as it is committed into the implementation of smart economy (competitiveness), smart environment (natural resources preservation), smart governance (participation), smart living (quality of life), smart mobility (transport and ICT) and smart people (social and human capital).

Smart Mobility is therefore only one of the topics regarding the Smart City implementation [10]. It is however a crucial topic, impacting on several dimensions of the smart city, on numerous aspects composing the citizens' quality of life and regarding all the potential stakeholders expecting benefits from the smart city implementation [11]. Smart Mobility is seen like a slice of the Smart City, crossing all the components listed above [12].

From the literature analysis, we can gather the most important Smart Mobility objectives [13, 14]. They are summarized in the following six categories:

1. reducing pollution;
2. reducing traffic congestion;

3. increasing people safety;
4. reducing noise pollution;
5. improving transfer speed;
6. reducing transfer costs.

Moreover, a successful, smarter mobility system in city uses all the paradigms composing the smart city, that is: digital city, green city, knowledge city.

- Digital city, because the traffic system could use ICT and software applications for a lot of different aims, such as optimizing traffic fluxes, support effective public transport routes, collect citizens' opinions and suggestion about urban mobility, and so on [15].
- Green city, because the environmental impact of transport in city is one of the main causes of city pollution [16].
- Knowledge city, because the smartness of transport depends also on the sharing of civic values and on the citizens' smart behaviours [17].

Smart Mobility is therefore a multifaceted topic, involving all the smart city paradigms and generating a set of heterogeneous benefits for all the smart city stakeholders. They can act like agents of the Smart Mobility initiatives, that is, to be the movers of the actions, or gain the resulting benefits, or the both.

3   The IT Governance and Service Model: Basic Principles

Because of the enormous potential adverse impact of a poorly managed mobility system on the quality of life, Smart Mobility is often presented as one of the main options to seek more sustainable transport systems [3]. It could also be seen as a set of coordinated actions addressed at improving the efficiency, the effectiveness and the environmental sustainability of cities. In other words Smart Mobility could consist of a hypothetically infinite number of initiatives often (but not always) characterized by the use of ICT. As pointed out by Staricco (2013) there are two meanings of Smart Mobility respect to the use of ICT: the first one refers to an efficient and effective mobility system and is independent from the role played by ICT, but it is rather connected to the use of appropriate technologies;[1] while the second one relates to a mobility system characterized by a consistent and systematic use of ICT.

The Smart Mobility sector presents a remarkable breadth of contents and implications because of the large number of variables to which is connected. It is possible to identify several studies focused on individual applications, while it is

---

[1]The author reports the case of Curitiba, in Brazile, where efficient transport solutions have been taken but very low-tech and low-investment.

more difficult to find studies that provide an holistic and interrelated vision of these actions. Due to the complexity of the urban mobility scenario, the aim of this paper, which operates a multiple level classification of a large number of Smart Mobility initiatives due to a deep literature review, is trying to provide an overview of this area through the proposal of an action taxonomy considering three aspects:

1. Smart Mobility actors: who are the main agents moving the smart initiatives;
2. Use and intensity of ICT in Smart Mobility initiatives;
3. Goals and benefits of Smart Mobility actions on smart goals.

The suggested taxonomy is based on a literature review; the survey regards economic papers regarding policies and technologies for urban mobility and smart mobility, especially in European cities.[2]

First of all the initiatives are classified into four main groups respect to the different key actors, such as:

- public transport companies and organizations;
- private companies and citizens;
- public bodies and local governments;
- the combination of all of them, when all these actors realize together integrated initiatives (for example, Integrated Transport Systems—ITS).

Each action is then related to a major, minor or non-existent incidence of ICT technology and finally is connected to the most important and recurrent Smart Mobility goals. This study wants, in fact, deeply explore the interrelations between initiatives, aims and enabling technologies. The final results of this taxonomy is summarised in Table 1. Below there is a description of each group, a brief illustration of the actions composing each one, the intensity of ICT involved and the benefits of each action on the Smart Mobility goals described above.

3.1 Public Mobility: Vehicles and Innovative Transport Solutions

This group includes all the initiatives carried out by the companies or organizations suppling the local public transport services in the city. It is composed by actions of different nature but characterised by a common factor, that is, they aim to positively change the quality of public transport under different points of view. As shown in Table 1, this set collects either solutions involving a change in the fleet of transport vehicles and fuels (such as the adoption of electric vehicles, vehicles EUR 5, vehicles with automated driving or CNG vehicles) or interventions which improve

---

[2]The most innovative Intelligent Transport System have also been collected from the offer of the main international vendors.

Table 1 Smart mobility taxonomy, ICT intensity and targets

	Intensity of ICT adopted	Benefits in Smart Mobility					
		Reduction of pollution	Reduction of congestion	Increased safety	Reduction noise pollution	Improving transfer speed	Reducing transfer costs
1. Public mobility: vehicles and innovative transport solutions							
Electric vehicles	L	*			*		
Vehicles EUR 5	L	*			*		
Use of alternative fuels (LPG, methane, hydrogen, bio-diesel, fuel cell)	M	*					*
Vehicles with automated driving	M			*			
Integrated management of public transport vehicles	M	*	*	*	*		*
Collective taxis	L		*	*	*	*	
Integrated ticketing system	M		*			*	*
2. Private and commercial mobility: vehicles and innovative transport solutions							
Electric vehicles	L	*			*		
Vehicles EUR 5	L	*			*		
Use of alternative fuels (LPG, methane, hydrogen, bio-diesel, fuel cell)	L	*					
Vehicles with automated driving	M			*			
Car sharing (with georeferencing and geotagging)	L		*				*
Car pooling	L		*				*
Hire and ridesharing services	M		*				*
Bike sharing (with georeferencing and geotagging)		*	*		*		*

(continued)

Table 1 (continued)

	Intensity of ICT adopted	Benefits in Smart Mobility					
		Reduction of pollution	Reduction of congestion	Increased safety	Reduction noise pollution	Improving transfer speed	Reducing transfer costs
Piedibus	L		*	*	*		
Automotive navigation system	M			*			*
Eco-driving	L	*		*	*		
3. Infrastructure and policies to support mobility							
Infrastructure, changes and addressing mobility							
Parking	L						
Park and ride	L	*	*		*		
Bicycle lanes	L	*	*	*	*		
Columns recharge electric vehicles	L	*					
Message signs about mobility	M		*				*
Integrated traffic lights	M	*	*		*		*
Pedestrian zones or auto-free zones	L	*		*	*		
Restricted (or limited) traffic zones	L	*		*	*		
Bus lane or bus only lane	L	*	*	*			*
Parking guidance system	M	*	*				
Systems for speed control and management	M		*				*
Mobility management based on the level of pollutant emissions	L	*					
Integrated policies to support smart mobility initiatives							
Traffic flows division (private, public, commercial)	L	*	*	*	*		
Integrated ticketing	M						*

(continued)

Table 1 (continued)

	Intensity of ICT adopted	Benefits in Smart Mobility					
		Reduction of pollution	Reduction of congestion	Increased safety	Reduction noise pollution	Improving transfer speed	Reducing transfer costs
tariff integration between public and private transport	M						*
Incentives for the use of less polluting fuels	L	*					
Control of emissions	L	*					
Speed limit sign	L			*			
Economic incentives and/or higher taxation measures (congestion pricing, ecopass, cordon pricing, road pricing, park pricing)	L	*	*				
Tax incentives and/or measures such as higher taxation on polluting fuels	L	*					*
Regulation of access (pedestrian areas, time bands, ZSL, STL)	M		*		*		
Redesign of city times (public schedules, school schedule etc.)	M	*	*	*			
Redesign of the city and its spaces (residential and industrial areas, integrated neighborhoods etc.)	M	*	*	*			*
4. Systems for collecting, storing and processing data, information and knowledge aimed to design, implement and evaluate policies and integrated initiatives of SM							
Demand control systems for access to reserved areas (cordon pricing, congestion pricing, electronic tolling, electronic tolling with GPS, pay as you drive)	H	*	*	*		*	
Integrated parking guidance systems	M | H	*	*	*	*	*	*

(continued)

Table 1 (continued)

	Intensity of ICT adopted		Benefits in Smart Mobility					
			Reduction of pollution	Reduction of congestion	Increased safety	Reduction noise pollution	Improving transfer speed	Reducing transfer costs
Variable Message Signs (VMS)	M	H	*	*	*		*	
Urban Traffic Control (UTC)	M	H	*	*			*	*
Video surveillance systems for area and environment security	M	H			*	*		
Integrated systems for mobility management		H		*	*	*	*	*
Traffic data collection systems (section control, variable speed limit control, ramp metering etc.)	M	H		*	*			
Expert systems for the correlation and filtering of events (Automatic Incident Detection—AID)	M	H		*	*		*	
addressing and control systems of urban and suburban traffic (section control, ramp metering, variable speed limit, activation of the emergency lane for congestion)	M			*	*		*	
Systems for the management of fleets and logistic	M	H	*	*			*	*
Systems for managing fleets of vehicles of public transport adapted to UTC (system of planning, monitoring and reporting of public transport service, integrated electronic ticketing system, information system for users of public transport)	M		*	*			*	*

the quality of public service without however impinging on vehicles (such as the introduction of an integrated ticketing system or the provision of collective taxis).

Analizing the ICT intensity in these smart initiatives, it is possible to notice a heterogeneous picture. The actions range from low to medium ICT intensity. In the case of interventions on vehicles, they can involve different technologies than ICT, such as the use of electric motors, or may be ICT intensive, as in the case of driveless vehicles. Regarding the integrating ticketing, ICT intensity is high only if this policy is based on a set of applications requiring the use of smart devices such as the mobile phone. In this case, the SMS-based solutions do not require large investments but it needs citizens involvement and readiness in terms of techno-logical literacy and their willingness to use this system. For this reason ICT, when introduced into an environment ready to accept it, is able to determine a significant step forward for the creation of a modern and sustainable urban transport system [18].

3.2   Private and Commercial Mobility: Vehicles and Innovative Transport Solutions

This group regards initiatives carried out by private citizens and companies, even if supported and stimulated by public policies. It includes a range of interventions that can include both the introduction of vehicles with certain characteristics, and actions regarding the mode of transport which affect the citizens' behaviours.

Among the solutions most frequently cited in the Smart Mobility literature, we can find some actions belonging to this group such hybrid cars and car-sharing. Hybrid vehicles would allow a pronounced reduction of pollutant emissions without requiring, as a primary need, the development of new technologies.

Car sharing is a service that allows you to use a car reservation, picking it up and bringing it back in a parking lot, and paying due to the use made. It allows reduction of urban congestion, reduction of polluting emissions (gas and noise), reduction in employment of public space and, in general, a new push towards the use of public transport [19]. Findings also show, following the adoption of car-sharing, one modal shift to other alternative modes of transport respect to the private car, such as walking or cycling [20, 21]. Nevertheless, there are possible disadvantages. According to Mariotti [22] the strong importance related to the possession of the car may partly explain the lack of role played today by most of the active car-sharing initiatives.

As evidenced in Table 1, many of the initiatives of private mobility are low ICT intensity, as bike sharing, another very frequent initiative. It is because almost all these initiatives depend on the behaviour of single citizens and it does not involve the role of ICT.

3.3 Infrastructure and Policies Supporting Mobility

The third set includes two sub-groups of actions: infrastructure and policies supporting Smart Mobility.

The first sub-group includes infrastructural projects which, in different ways, affect urban mobility: for example, the creation of bicycle lanes or interventions aiming at changing mobility as the creation of restricted traffic zones. The expansion or creation of bicycle lanes is an intervention that is closely linked to the use of the bicycle as a mean of private transport and could have positive effects on the spread of bike-sharing; initiative that, despite the difficulties linked to the topography of each city and the possibility of theft, led to a modal shift from car to bike from 2 to 10 % in cities like Paris, Montreal and Lyon [23]. The closure to traffic of certain urban areas for time zones or periods of the day in order to reduce pollution and congestion represents an other interesting solution adopted by municipalities. As highlighted by De Ciutiis [24] among the major objectives sought by the LTZ (Limited Traffic Zone in Italy), there may be safety compliance, particularly in the city centre, especially in the peak hours of pedestrians, the reduction of pollution levels and the increase in revenue administration where it is expected to pay a congestion charging.

The second sub-group is represented by a series of integrated policies that can be implemented to change the mobility system, in particular by the public decision maker (for example: incentives for the use of less polluting fuels, tax incentives or measures such as higher taxation on polluting fuels). Other interventions that may alter the urban mobility may be the redesign of the city and its spaces (residential and industrial areas, integrated neighborhoods etc.).

The two sub-groups contain actions which range from low to medium intensity of ICT: for example a low-intensity ICT initiative is represented by an intervention amending, introducing or expanding a pedestrian zone. An intervention to medium intensity ICT is, however, the introduction of a control system of the speed that is supported by sensors, cameras and devices based on Information Technology devices.

3.4 Intelligent Transport Systems

The fourth group consists of a large number of Smart Mobility solutions characterized by a medium-high intensity of ICT.

Intelligent Transport Systems (ITS) are advanced applications to collect, storage and process data, information and knowledge aiming at planning, implementing ad evaluating integrated initiatives and policies of Smart Mobility. They are a large and heterogeneous set of applications, including:

- Demand control systems for access to reserved areas (cordon pricing, congestion pricing, electronic tolling, with GPS, pay as you drive);
- Integrated parking guidance systems;

- Variable Message Signs (VMS);
- Urban Traffic Control (UTC);
- Video surveillance systems for area and environment security;
- Integrated systems for mobility management;
- Traffic data collection systems;
- Expert systems for the correlation and filtering of events; etc.

In this set the role of ICT is essential in supporting applications and systems of detection and processing of data and information. These systems can be very sophisticated and are designed to handle different kinds of information in respect of various activities related to mobility: you can then treat systems designed to detect and drive traffic, video surveillance systems, systems addressing the parking and so on.

According to ENEA [25] experiences made so far in the EU countries, USA and Japan show that the introduction of ITS technologies has significantly contributed to improve the efficiency, safety, environmental impact and overall productivity of the transportation system. These applications, as pointed out by the European Commission, are an attractive solution to many of the problems of the transport sector: in the road sector it is possible to record reductions in journey times (15–20 %), in energy consumption (12 %) and in emissions of pollutants (10 %), as well as increases in network capacity (5–10 %) and decreases in the number of accidents (10–15 %). Significant results have also been achieved in the fleet management and logistics processes of goods and in the exercise of public passenger transport.

This category is perhaps the most advanced frontier in terms of Smart Mobility solutions. It is a series of possible actions that can be implemented only under certain conditions: it is necessary, first of all, that the use of ICT is adopted in an integrated manner and to cover not only a few number of projects. The adoption of these solutions requires a holistic view, the presence of previous policies and an integrated vision across different dimensions of urban living. The rapid development of ITS technologies should be subject to reflections weighted with respect to purchasing decisions because decisions not taking into account the already started innovations can lead to unsolvable errors. In fact, many solutions are not expensive in the introduction phase, but they run the risk of poor acceptability by the community [9].

4   Smart Mobility Actions and Smart Goals

The different groups shown in Table 1 and the actions composing them, highlighted in the first column, are related to two other macro-variables evidenced in the second and third columns: the intensity of ICT for each action and the goals pursued by such actions. As already pointed out previously, the first macro-column, titled "Intensity of ICT adopted", has three sub-columns, indicating a low, medium and high level of intensity of ICT. From the intersection between these columns and the rows corresponding to different actions you can then observe the level of intensity of ICT. It is a systematization of a large number of initiatives discussed in the literature, with an emphasis on ICT. As can be seen from this classification, it can be state that the wide range of initiatives analyzed is often but not strictly and necessarily tied to high intensity of ICT. Although the new frontier of innovation is certainly linked to the adoption of mobility solutions for ITS, we can say it is possible to adopt solutions and changes in the system of mobility without the need for large investments or sophisticated technologies. We can therefore argue that ICT is a pivotal, but not necessary technology to start the implementation of Smart Mobility initiatives; its importance however increases when the complexity and the maturity of Smart Mobility projects become higher. In ITS or other integrated Smart Mobility policies, ICT plays a crucial and fundamental role.

The second column Benefits is composed by six sub-columns, regarding the six smart goals as listed in Sect. 3. The goals highlighted are those pursued through the examined actions. As evidenced in the table, not all cells are complete because not all actions can be associated with a target, while some of them contribute to the achievement of more objectives.

Several findings derive from the analysis of Table 1 respect to the benefits associated to the Smart Mobility actions. First of all, an interesting evidence is the fact that certain actions contribute to the achievement of these objectives more pervasively than others. Looking, for example, at some integrated systems based on ICT such as ramp metering or urban traffic control systems, it is possible to observe a positive effect that affects almost all the objectives underlined. In this case it is possible to say that the ICT, if properly directed, would seem to have a greater positive benefit than other initiatives.

Finally, observing the listed objectives it is also possible to note that these are closely related to those of a smart city as well as to the concept of well-being expressed by the OECD. In its "Better Life Index", in fact, the OECD underlines the most important areas that a society has to improve in order to enhance its quality of life. The concept of well-being is wide but it is possible to individuate some common targets to look at: the safeguard of the environment is strictly related to the reduction of PM10 concentrations in the air and green house gas emission and is one of the most important. Also personal safety and a good balance between work and life time are shared goals between well-being and Smart Mobility. It is possible therefore to argue that Smart Mobility directly impacts on the quality of life of people living in cities and to design a link between Smart Mobility actions and well-being indicators. This could be very useful to better support Smart Mobility implementation, especially choosing the most effective actions and prioritizing the ones better impacting on citizens' well-being.

5 Conclusions: Results, Limits and Further Work

Several interesting findings emerge from the analysis of Smart Mobility actions rooted into the stream of studies regarding the Smart City and also its more consolidated components, that is, Digital City and Green City.

The main contribution of this paper is the proposal of an action taxonomy regarding a comprehensive approach about Smart Mobility; it deeply differs from the analysis founded in literature, generally focused on specific Smart Mobility subjects.

Smart Mobility emerges from the survey like a pivotal component of Smart City strategies and Smart Mobility and Smart City goals are often overlapped. Smart Mobility contributes to Smart City aims with its specific but harmonised goals, impacting on the most important Smart City objectives such as reducing the environmental footprint of the city or improving the citizens' quality of life. The six Smart Mobility specific goals we suggest are fully linked with the broader Smart City ones.

ICT is not a must-to-have technology to implement Smart Mobility actions; several of them are based on other technologies (regarding vehicles or fuels for example) or on no technology at all but it depends only on a better, more virtuous citizens' behaviour, such as using public transport or bike instead of private car. However, the role of ICT becomes fundamental when complexity, integration and extension of Smart Mobility programs increase. Therefore we can argue a positive correlation between the Smart Mobility maturity and the use of ICT.

From the survey an evolving path in Smart Mobility actions and programs emerges; it includes three phases, that we can call: Starting, Intermediate and Mature. The Starting phase regards smart actions belonging to the first three groups showed in Table 1. Actions are often immature, not spatially coordinated, regarding only a small portion of the urban area, difficult to replicate elsewhere. It specially regards pilot initiatives implemented in European smart cities at the beginning of this smart wave. The Intermediate phase includes several Smart Mobility governance actions, such as pilot projects repetition, integrated mobility plans, measuring benefits and negative impacts. The Mature phase is characterised by the use of ITSs, collecting, processing and sharing data, information and knowledge above a complex and integrated Mobility System. This fourth set of initiatives is successfully implementable in cities only if they have already realized an implementation readiness, based on a large knowledge about Smart Mobility in city and a good level of citizens' involvement and awareness about Smart Mobility opportunities and potential benefits.

Finally, smart people are the winning card to implement sustainable, successful and effective Smart Mobility Systems, including both high technology applications and virtuous and aware behaviours. Especially in the most mature phases of the Smart Mobility implementation, each citizen is a proactive actor, accepting a limitation in its own transfer freedom (reducing the use of private car, for example) and embracing the pursuing of shared smart aims.

Despite the largeness of this analysis, it is possible to find some weaknesses and elements to be consolidated. The main weakness is represented by the need to move from a theoretical to an empirical analysis in order to validate the proposed classification. At present, only few initiatives are already fully implemented, the more of them are in the start phases and it is therefore imossibile to evaluate the real benefits produced by Smart Mobility, regarding both single initiatives and a whole Smart Mobility portfolio.

As soon as the maturity of Smart Mobility acrions will increase, the validation of our model would be stronger; it should especially regards:

- The validation of the suggested taxonomy, that is, the classification of Smart Mobility actions in the four sets described in Table 1;
- The analysis of produced benefits especially for the citizens' quality of life;
- The definition of a set of indicators to measure the benefits.

References

1. Dameri, R.P.: Comparing smart and digital city: initiatives and strategies in Amsterdam and Genoa. Are they digital and/or smart? In: Dameri, R.P., Rosenthal-Sabroux, C. (eds.) Smart City. How to Create Public and Economic Value with High Technology in Urban Space, pp. 45–88. Springer, Heidelberg (2014)
2. Hall, P.: Creative cities and economic development. Urban Stud. **37**, 633–649 (2000)
3. Staricco, L.: Smart Mobility, opportunità e condizioni. J. Land Use Mob. Environ. **3**, 289–354 (2013)
4. Dameri, R.P., Cocchia, A.: Smart city and digital city: twenty years of terminology evolution. In: ItAIS 2013, X Conference of the Italian Chapter of AIS, 14 Dec 2013, Milano, Italy (2013)
5. Ishida, T., Isbister, F., (eds.): Digital Cities: Technologies, Experiences, and Future Perspectives. No. 1765. Springer (2000)
6. Benevolo, C., Dameri, R.P.: La smart city come strumento di green development. Il caso di Genova Smart City. Impresa Progetto **3**, 1–30 (2013)
7. Fontana, F.: Il capitale intellettuale nella pianificazione strategica urbana. In: XXXII conferenza italiana di scienze regionali (2011)
8. Giffinger, R., Fertner, C., Kramar, H., Kalasek, R., Pichler-Milanović, N., Meijers, E.: Smart Cities: Ranking of European Medium-Sized Cities. Centre of Regional Science (SRF). Vienna University of Technology (2007)
9. Caragliu, A., de Bo, C., Nijkamp, P.: Smart cities in Europe. J. Urban Technol. **18**(2), 65–82 (2011)
10. Nam, T., Pardo, T.A.: Smart city as urban innovation: focusing on management, policy, and context. In: Proceedings of the 5th International Conference on Theory and Practice of Electronic Governance. ACM (2011)
11. Arena, M., Cheli, F., Zaninelli, D., Capasso, A., Lamedica, R., Piccolo, A.: Smart mobility for sustainability. In: AEIT Annual Conference 2013: Innovation and Scientific and Technical Culture for Development, AEIT (2013)
12. Sciullo, A., Occelli, S.: Collecting distributed knowledge for community's smart changes. TeMA. J. Land Use Mob. Environ. **6**(3), 293–309 (2013)
13. Lawrence, F., Kavage, S., Litman, T.: Promoting public health through smart growth: building healthier communities through transportation and land use policies and practices. APA (2006)

14. Bencardino, M., Greco, I.: Smart communities. Social innovation at the service of the smart cities. TeMA. J. Land Use Mob. Environ. (2014)
15. Mechant, P., Stevens, I., Evens, T., Verdegem, P.: E–deliberation 2.0 for smart cities: a critical assessment of two 'idea generation' cases. Int. J. Electron. Govern. 5(1), 82–98 (2012)
16. Zygiaris, S.: Smart city reference model: Assisting planners to conceptualize the building of smart city innovation ecosystems. J. Knowl. Econ. 4(2), 217–231 (2013)
17. Nam, T., Pardo, T.A.: Conceptualizing smart city with dimensions of technology, people, and institutions. In: Proceedings of the 12th Annual International Digital Government Research Conference: Digital Government Innovation in Challenging Times. ACM (2011)
18. Amoroso, S., Caruso, L., Enea, B.: I sistemi di trasporto intelligenti per il successo dei servizi in ambito urbano. In: Atti 14° Conferenza Nazionale ASITA-Brescia 9–12 novembre, pp. 51–57 (2010)
19. Fistola, R.: Gestione innovative della mobilità urbana: car sharing e ICT. Tema-J. Land Use Mob. Environ. 0, 51–58 (2007)
20. Katzev, R.: Car sharing: A new approach to urban transportation problems. Anal. Soc. Iss. Public Policy 3(1), 65–86 (2003)
21. Burlando, C., Arduino, G., Nobile, D.: Il car sharing come business development area: analisi del settore, strategie d'impresa e ricadute socio-economiche. In: IX Riunione Scientifica Società Italiana di Economia dei Trasporti e della Logistica, Napoli, 3–5 ottobre (2007)
22. Mariotti, I., Beria, P., Laurino, A.: Car sharing peer to peer: un'analisi emprica sulla città di Milano. Rivista di Economia e Politica dei Trasporti 3, 1–16 (2013)
23. Midgley, P.: Bicycle-sharing schemes: enhancing sustainable mobility in urban areas. Commission on Sustainable Development Nineteenth Session, New York, 2–13 May 2011
24. De Ciutiis, F.: Pratiche urbanistiche. Vantaggi e Criticità della ZTL: alcuni casi studio. Tema-J. Land Use Mob. Environ. 4, 133–136 (2011)
25. ENEA: http://old.enea.it/produzione_scientifica/pdf_brief/Valenti_ITStrasporti.pdf

Designing e-Sustainable Parliaments

Mauro Romanelli

Abstract Parliaments are seeking legitimacy as responsive and sustainable institutions engaging citizens in the policy process by embracing Internet technologies. Social sustainability relies on participation of citizens and knowledge emerging through interaction. Parliaments as information and knowledge based organizations select different choices for sustainability structuring the e-parliament along a continuum between improving processes and engaging citizens from information provision to active citizenship.

Keywords e-parliament · e-participation · Social sustainability

1 Parliaments as Organizations Seeking Legitimacy

Internet technologies (IT) lead parliamentary institutions to behave as open, transparent and accessible organizations by structuring the e-parliament for making available documents and information to be viewed and discussed by citizens. Parliaments are managing new technologies to restore the relationship of confidence with citizens distrusted by politics coherently with values of social sustainability which relies on citizens participation in the policy processes as result of knowledge sharing and dialogue [1, 2]. Organizations embrace ideas, values and beliefs conforming to the expectations of the key stakeholders for achieving greater legitimacy than better performance [3]. Parliaments seeking legitimacy under conditions of uncertainty [4] tend to enhance stability and comprehensibility of organizational activities fostering continuity and credibility, pursuing active or passive support [5]. International organizations as the Global Centre for ICT in Parliament, a joint venture between the United Nations Department of Economic and Social Affairs

M. Romanelli (✉)
Università degli Studi di Napoli Parthenope, Dipartimento di
Studi Aziendali ed Economici, Naples, Italy
e-mail: mauro.romanelli@uniparthenope.it

© Springer International Publishing Switzerland 2016
T. Torre et al. (eds.), *Empowering Organizations*, Lecture Notes in Information
Systems and Organisation 11, DOI 10.1007/978-3-319-23784-8_3

(Undesa) and the Inter Parliamentary Union (IPU), promote the development of information and communication technologies (ICTs) in order to modernize processes and parliamentary core functions (oversight, legislation and representative roles). The IPU recommended the guidelines (2009) for building the contents of parliamentary websites bridging the provision of information and participatory democracy [6]. Parliaments as public institutions have to encourage the participation of citizens by the use of ICTs for improving the acceptance and legitimacy of democratic processes [7]. Parliaments as complex, information intensive and knowledge based organizations are embracing new technologies to reinforce representative democracy [8], ensuring the legitimacy of parliamentary institution and policies, moving toward a participatory democracy [9, 10]. Thereby, only few parliaments have developed an adequate and strategic ICT capacity leveraging the capabilities in the staff for using and sharing knowledge [11], stimulating a two-way dialogue with citizens [12]. Parliaments may follow a different design for e-sustainability by managing information, knowledge and technologies along a continuum between enhancing internal workings and connecting with people by engaging citizens from information provision to active participation in the public life. This study is based on archival and qualitative data drawn by analysis and review of the literature on the introduction of ICTs within parliamentary institutions.

2 Parliaments as Complex Organizations: The Role of Parliamentary Staff

Parliaments are the institutions through which governments are held accountable to the electorate by overseeing the executive authority, performing lawmaking and policymaking activities, and representing the interest of citizens [9]. Parliaments qualify as complex organizations facing uncertainty and complexity as fundamental problem [4]. Parliamentarians as representatives, legislators and scrutinizers of the government, constitute the operating core acting as knowledge workers and develop their expertise in particular areas to contribute to policy formulation [13]. Parliaments could not perform their functions without support of parliamentary staff. Parliaments need their own source of information and expertise to remain independent from government. Ratifying parliament does not exert any influence on policy-making. It is aided by a registration staff able to ensure merely administrative support and transcript of debates. Decisional parliament is able to play a proactive, powerful and more independent role in policy formulation and overseeing its implementation. It is supported by a consulting staff knowledge oriented able to provide professional and technical support for drafting on lawmaking processes. Mixed models of parliament and staff develop over time [14]. ICTs make parliamentary staff as a gate-keeper able to play a relevant role in the process of gathering, selecting and interpreting information, taking the most of the day-to-day decisions on managing parliamentary affairs [15].

3   Defining the e-Sustainable Parliament

Parliaments as media infrastructure re-presenting source of information and knowledge coherently with usage and adoption of new technologies [16] need to appear as transparent, open and accessible institutions connecting with citizens by encouraging political participation [15]. Social sustainability implies the development of models of democratic engagement inclusive of the effective public participation in every policy area [1, 17]. E-democracy implies the use of ICTs to support democratic decision-making processes and relates to e-participation as knowledge, interactive and collaborative process for consultation, dialogue and confrontation [18]. The e-parliament is defined as an efficient organization where stakeholders use information and communication technologies to perform their primary functions of lawmaking, representation, and oversight more effectively. The concept of e-parliament is related to a legislature that is empowered to be more open, transparent and accountable through ICTs encouraging people to be more engaged in the public life by providing higher quality of information and greater access to documents and activities of the legislative body fostering the development of an equitable and inclusive information society [19]. Increasingly, technological developments enhance and strengthen participation to develop the policy process as result of dialogue and shared values [2], knowledge sharing and creation through interaction between public institutions and people [20]. Parliaments behave as e-sustainable representative institutions improving internal workings and developing policies as result of citizens participation based on knowledge sharing, dialogue and consensus in order to sustain public trust promoting citizenship and accountability [10].

3.1   Revitalizing Parliaments Through New Technologies

Parliaments have to cope with the advent of an increasing disengagement and distrust of citizens feeling disaffected and unheard of democratic institutions [21]. Parliaments as symbols of political integration and sources of coherent policy [22] are becoming aware in using digital technologies to support engagement with citizens and reinvigorate both traditional representative arrangements [23], reinforcing legitimacy of new parliamentary institutions [24]. Parliaments are embracing new technologies under increasing pressure to present themselves as accountable legislative institutions avoiding to become marginalized institutions [25]. Thereby, technological modernization seems not to lead automatically to new forms of democracy. Trends toward electronic democracy tend to vary with political context [26]. ICTs applications contribute to support legitimacy function played by parliaments as the reassurance of working for meeting the needs of citizens [15]. Internet Technologies as a digital bridge between parliaments and citizens enhance the quality of democratic governance making available for citizens a growing amount of information about legislative process providing a means of seeking the views of constituents on public policy. Parliaments tend to develop new technologies for a direct channel of communication with constituencies bypassing traditional parties in order to legitimize public policies and values of representative democracy [10]. Parliaments could embrace new technologies in order to improve the image of representative institutions seeking legitimacy and consensus, performing their functions only to a better level (modernization and reform) or reinforcing representative institutions engaging people to participate in the political system (reinvigoration) [27]. Parliaments should adopt ICTs in order to focus on discussion and public debate improving participation and involvement of citizens to be included in decision-making processes (deliberative democracy) [28].

3.2 Towards an Information or Knowledge Approach for e-Parliament Design

Parliaments as information intensive organizations [15] producing knowledge policy making related by documents, laws, acts [29] should be able to develop transparent processes facilitating a two-way transfer of knowledge between public institution and stakeholders for building a successful partnership in order to better develop and implement sustainable policies [30]. Information and knowledge require different tools and concepts to be developed by technology [31]. Managing information, as outcome of a knowledge process as stored and transmitted in digital form, may support knowledge as resource that exists only within an intelligent system [32]. Parliaments have integrated into their work new ICTs to enhance parliamentary functions (representative, legislative, scrutiny, oversight, legitimacy, education, conflict resolution) in terms of communication possibilities, dissemination and management of information [15]. The concept of e-parliament is related to the use of ICTs for strengthening parliamentary core functions and enhancing the interface between government and the public. E-parliament services enable citizens to be actively included in decision making processes reinforcing participatory democracy [33]. The e-parliament becomes an opportunity for making functional and effective parliamentary affairs through the automation of parliamentary information by overcoming bureaucratic obstacles that facilitate information exchange and sharing [24, 25, 34]. ICTs significantly make the legislators as transparent and accountable actors by designing efficient processes as tool of control and evaluation on public policy and reinforcing the lawmaking functions [35]. Digital document management systems support transparency and efficiency of parliamentary operations. Parliaments managing legislative documents and internal information by technologies are able to build a knowledge resource in order to legislate effectively providing the public with relevant and accountable information [11]. Managing knowledge, competence and expertise should enhance parliamentary routine work efficiency. ICTs support extensively parliamentary basic functions by developing and sharing data, information and knowledge as significant resource providing new opportunities for knowledge management [13].

3.3 Building the e-Participation Within Parliaments

E-participation initiatives should facilitate a way of communication between citizens and politicians [36] as stakeholders responsible for civic engagement, deliberative and democratic effects [7]. Technological strategic design does not ensure effective deliberative participation without engagement and inclusion of citizens in the political decision making [37]. Parliaments may use the Internet for educating and informing people, encouraging feedback and public participation in policy formulation [38]. Parliaments are using advanced ICTs as computer supported arguments visualization and structured e-forums to increase the quality and quantity of public participation on legislation under formation [29]. Parliaments should ensure the sustainability of e-participation initiatives moving towards more participatory approaches than unidirectional information dissemination by designing organizational policies and capacity building programs [39]. The age of parliament, the structure of parliamentary business and staff organization, the constitutional parliamentary system may affect the efforts of parliaments in developing and improving parliamentary core functions coherently with ICTs processes and new technologies [15, 26]. Information availability and accessibility, infrastructure and technologies, government organization and policy issues exert influence on the effective design of e-participation activities [7]. Parliaments seem able to provide transparency in the provision of data and information making a limited use of interactive features leading citizens to comment and deliberate on policy and legislation issues [40, 41]. Views and opinions of citizens should be considered by listening and learning representative institutions [25] for engendering an effective political transformation [34]. Parliaments should facilitate and summarize public inputs into the policy process and gather the feedback of citizens by searching a dialogue with people [42].

4 Parliamentary e-Participation Initiatives: Lights and Shadows

New technologies make available parliamentary records to be viewed and discussed by citizens acting petitions, communicating with committees, submitting enquiries [43]. According to Macintosh [18] e-enabling (to support the access to the internet taking advantage of information available), e-engaging (to enable contributions and support debate on policy issues) and e-empowering (to support active participation of citizens as producers of policy) are identified as levels of participation according to a growing scale over time in relation to OECD framework [44] to take part in the decision-making and influence the policy agenda: *information* as a one-way relationship in which government makes available information for citizens; in the *consultation* level citizens are encouraged to contribute their views on a particular issue; In the *active participation* citizens are empowered by actively participating in the policy making process (partnership). ICT tools (ranging from web portals to consultation platforms, e-petitioning systems as examples) can be implemented to change or reinforce parliamentary institutions governed by path depth processes, support more participatory forms of citizenship and facilitate a two way dialogue. Web portals help to bridge representation and communication functions. E-petitioning systems are citizenship oriented and focus on interaction between citizens and public institutions like e-consultations (representation oriented) [45]. Tambouris et al. [46] identify five levels of participation between one-way or two-way channels: e-informing as prerequisite for citizens willing to contribute and e-involving as the one-way channel for providing information on policies ensuring that public concerns are considered; e-consulting and e-collaborating as two-way channels for collecting public feedback, for a partnership with citizens actively participating in the developing alternatives and preferred solutions; e-empowering for implementing what citizens decide. Thereby, few parliaments have actively developed a two-way dialogue with their citizens to identify better the needs and problems of the society and to acquire approval by constituency [11, 47].

Parliamentary websites as public face of the representative institution and accountable voice in front of the executive authority permit to the decision-making to be more publicly visible [23]. Parliamentary websites provide the citizens with detailed information on parliamentary work, committees actions and legislative activity, plenary debates increasing the chances of ex ante and ex post public scrutiny of legislatures [48]. Most of parliaments are advanced in managing social media to meet internationally recognized standards and best practices. Only in few cases quality, completeness and availability of information can be positively judged in terms of accessibility and transparency [10]. Websites can be used as a platform to conduct polls on policy matters via online-surveys and equipped with e-mail addresses and discussion boards to deliberate with citizens strengthening the committee's role with regard to information, consultation and dialogue [15]. The Brazilian House of Representatives launched the *e-Democracia* project (in 2009) aiming to engage citizens in lawmaking process providing through website multiple participatory mechanisms: citizens can share information about a problem to be addressed by law, identify and discuss possible solutions, draft the bill itself [18]. Thereby, websites seem not to open up to consultation and participation of citizens as partners of legislative and policy processes [23, 44, 48], failing to provide a realistic account of decision-making procedures [49]. Parliaments are still in the phase where one-way access of information is the main use of parliamentary websites. Parliaments should facilitate a two-way interaction in terms of information and communication meaningful and relevant for citizens [11, 48].

On line consultations influence policy but do not solve the disconnection between politicians and citizens; e-consultations enable participants to interact and learn over an extended period of discussion and raise aspects of policies under discussion, enable legislators to participate in the discussion and understand policy issues, raising questions and responding to citizens' comments. Thereby, citizens seem to inform policy and law makers than make policy expecting representatives to be responsive to their input [50].

Petitions systems inform policy development and executive scrutiny as to affect policy change. Parliaments permit policy to be debated enhancing the relationship with citizens without solving the disengagement of citizens for politics [51]. The Scottish Parliament (February 2004) established an e-petition system enabling citizens to voice their concerns to be used in many stages of policy-life cycle to amend new policy being debated by the legislature and empower level of citizen participation, permit to create, view, sign and submit petitions, add background information, join a discussion forum [18]. The e-petitioning system makes parliament to be seen by citizens as more responsive institution to the public encouraging public involvement in policy making setting. Thereby, e-petitions do not yet permit an effective way of talking to their representatives for citizens [52]. People can obtain background information, make a comment about the issue, sign on-line, and receive feedback about the progress of a petition. E-petitioner seems to be as useful tool in influencing politicians making an informed choice about whether or not to support and sign the petition [53].The e-petitioning system may help to increase the legitimacy and functioning of representative institutions [54] and legitimize the founding of a new legislature because of moderate transformative potential [55]. The introduction of the e-petition pilot scheme as launched in the September 2005 was an important step for modernizing the petition procedures in the German *Bundestag*. New technologies have introduced new forms of interaction broadening the public relations of the parliament for citizens, enhancing the accessibility and transparence of the legislature by enriching the information acquired [56]. Thereby, the decline of trust in the *Bundestag* has grown over time despite of technological advances for strengthening the communication between parliamentarians and citizens [57].

5 Discussion and Conclusions

Parliaments are embracing new technologies in order to restore trust of citizens in democratic institutions. Thereby, the development of the e-parliament coherently with values of sustainable citizen participation seems to be still in infancy [10, 47]. Parliaments may redesign staff structure and capabilities coherently with the nature and independence of legislature from the executive authority in order to incorporate new technologies in the reengineering of lawmaking processes [15, 23]. Parliaments as democratic and sustainable institutions should incorporate new technologies in their workings in order to design the e-parliament as resource for modernizing processes, creating, managing and sharing knowledge by interacting with citizens and fostering their active participation and contribution into the policy process. Thereby, there are no clear guidelines that are able to address and implement effectively a sustainable participatory process [58]. Democratic values and strategic orientations of political actors influence the adoption of new technologies for extending public participation [55]. Making available information electronically does not enough encourage citizen participation without changing the culture of representation in mindset of both parliaments and the citizens. Parliaments are seeking a coherent behavior towards e-sustainability by bridging direct and mediate forms of democracy in a mixed polity [22]. Parliaments may behave as decisional or ratifying legislatures developing a participatory democracy managing new technologies, information and knowledge. Parliaments may select a different approach to e-parliament design along a continuum between modernizing or improving processes and connecting with people by engaging effectively citizens as partners of policy formulation in decision-making processes and consultation ranging from information to active participation. Parliaments tend to follow an information approach by embracing new technologies for merely modernizing internal processes without ensuring an effective participation and contribution of citizens in the policy process. Parliaments are developing e-participation initiatives seeking legitimacy as institutions open and close to citizens. Parliaments connecting with citizens by managing and sharing knowledge may redesign work organization structuring a professional staff knowledge oriented and improving processes. Parliaments tend to follow a knowledge approach and behave as sustainable and accountable institutions managing people contribution for creating new knowledge useful for designing better policy solutions by encouraging and fostering the active participation of citizens.

References

1. McKenzie, S.: Social sustainability: toward some definitions. Hawke Research Institute Working Paper Series No. 27, Hawke Research Institute, Magill (2004)
2. Denhardt, R.B., Denhardt, V.J.: The new public service: putting democracy first. Nat. Civic Rev. **90**, 391–400 (2001)
3. DiMaggio, P.J., Powell, W.W.: The iron cage revisited: institutional isomorphism and collective rationality in organizational fields. Am. Sociol. Rev. **48**, 147–160 (1983)
4. Fox, H.W., Hammond, S.W.: Congressional Staffs: Invisible Force in American lawmaking. The Free Press, New York (1977)
5. Suchmann, M.C.: Managing legitimacy; strategic and institutional approaches. Acad. Manag. Rev. **20**, 571–610 (1995)
6. IPU: Guidelines for Parliamentary Websites (2009)
7. Sæbø, Ø., Rose, J., Flak, L.S.: The shape of eParticipation: characterizing an emerging research area. Gov. Inf. Q. **25**, 400–428 (2008)
8. Leston Bandeira, C.: Are ICTs changing parliamentary activity in the portuguese parliament? J. Legislative Stud. **13**, 403–421 (2007)
9. Smith, C., Webster, W.R.: The emergent ICT culture of parliamentarians: the case of the Scottish parliament. Information Polity. **13**, 249–273 (2004)

10. Griffith, J., Leston-Bandeira, C.: How are parliaments using new media to engage with citizens? J Legislative Stud. **18**, 496–513 (2012)
11. Oppd: Information and Communication Technologies in Parliament. Tools for democracy, European Parliament, Bruxelles (2010)
12. AA, VV.: World Parliamentary Report. NU (2012)
13. Suurla, R., Mustajarvi, O., Markkula, M.: Developing and Implementing Knowledge Management in the Parliament of Finland. Oy Edita Ab, Helsinki (2002)
14. Chimenti, C.: Gli apparati delle camere. Quad. Costituzionali **3**, 573–580 (1981)
15. Leston-Bandeira, C.: The impact of the internet on Parliaments: a legislative studies framework. Parliamentary Aff. **60**, 255–274 (2007)
16. Mulder, B.: Parliamentary Futures: re-presenting the issue information, technology and dynamics of information. Parliamentary Aff. **52**, 553–556 (1999)
17. Geczi, E.: Sustainability and public participation: toward an inclusive model of democracy. Adm. Theor. Prax. **29**, 375–393 (2007)
18. Macintosh, A.: characterizing e-participation in policy-making. In: Proceedings of the 37th Hawaiii International Conference on System Sciences, pp. 1–10 (2004)
19. AA, VV.: World Parliamentary Report. NU (2008)
20. Al-Sudairy, M.A.T., Vasista, T.G.K.: Fostering Knowledge Management and Citizen Participation via E-Governance for Achieving Sustainable Balanced Development, pp. 52–64 (2012)
21. Lusoli, W., Ward, S., Gibson, R.: (Re)connecting politics? Parliament, the public and the internet. Parliamentary Aff. **59**, 24–42 (2006)
22. Raab, C.D., Bellamy, C.: Electronic democracy and the 'mixed polity'. Symbiosis or conflict? In: Gibson, R., Römmele, A., Ward, S. (eds.) Electronic Democracy. Mobilisation, Organization and Participation Via New ICTs, pp. 17–42. Routledge, London (2004)
23. Dai, X., Norton, Ph.: The internet and parliamentary democracy in Europe. J. Legislative Stud. **13**, 343–353 (2007)
24. Coleman, S., Taylor, J.A., Van De Donk, W.: Parliament in the age of internet. Parliamentary Aff. **52**, 365–370 (1999)
25. Coleman, S., Spiller, J.: Exploring new media effects on representative democracy. J. Legislative Stud. **9**, 1–16 (2003)
26. Zittel, T.A.: Digital parliaments and electronic democracy: a comparison between the US House, Swedish Riksdag and the German Bundestag. In: Gibson R., Römmele A., Ward S. (eds.) Electronic Democracy. Mobilisation, Organization and Participation Via New ICTs, pp. 70–95. Routledge, London (2004)
27. Gibson, R., Römmele, A., Ward, S.: Introduction. Representative democracy and the Internet. In: Gibson, R., Römmele, A., Ward, S. (eds.) Electronic Democracy. Mobilisation, Organization and Participation Via New ICTs, pp. 1–16. Routledge, London (2004)
28. Päivärinta, T., Sæbø, Ø.: Models of e-democracy. Commun. Assoc. Inf. Syst. **17**, 818–840 (2006)
29. Loukis, E.: Using advanced information technologies for increasing public participation in the Greek parliament. J. Balkan Near Eastern Stud. **13**, 14–28 (2011)
30. Riege, A., Linsday, N.: Knowledge management in public sector. J. Knowl. Manage. **10**, 24–39 (2006)
31. McDermott, R.: Why information technology inspired but cannot deliver knowledge management. Calif. Manage. Rev. **41**, 103–117 (1999)
32. Blumentritt, R., Johnston, R.: Towards a strategy for knowledge management. Technol. Anal. Strateg. Manage. **11**, 287–300 (1999)
33. Kingham, T.: e-Parliaments. The use of information and communication technologies to improve parliamentary processes. WBI, Working Papers (2003)
34. Papaloi, A., Gouscos, D.: E-parliaments and novel parliament-to-citizens services. JeDEM **3**, 80–98 (2011)
35. De Rosa, R.: Il Parlamento Italiano alla prova tecnologica. Politica del Diritto. **3**, 545–569

36. Trechsel, A.H., Kies, R., Mendez, R., Schmitter, Ph. C.: Evaluation of the Use of New Technologies in Order to Facilitate Democracy in Europe, EP, (2003)
37. Rose, J., Sanford, C.: Mapping eParticipation research: four central challenges. Commun. AIS **20**, 909–943 (2007)
38. Taylor, J.A., Burt, E.: Parliaments on the web: learning through innovation. Parliamentary Aff. **52**, 503–517 (1999)
39. Ona, S.: Exploring the use of new technologies in participation practices in legislation. J. E-Gov. **36**, 79–91 (2013)
40. Berntzen, L., Healy, M., Hahamis, P., Dunville, D., Esteves, J.: Parliamentary web presence: a comparative review. In: Proceedings of 2nd International Conference on e-Government, pp. 17–25. (ICEG 2006) Pittsburgh (2006)
41. Loukis, E., Xenakis, A.: Evaluating parliamentary e-participation. In: Proceedings of IEEE Third International Conference on Digital Information Management (ICDIM), London (2008)
42. Papaloi, A., Ravekka Staiou, E., Gouscos, D.: Blending social media with parliamentary websites: just a trend, or a promising approach to e-participation? In: Reddick, Ch. G., Aikins, S.K. (eds.) Web 2.0 Technologies and Democratic Governance: Political, Policy and Management Implications, pp. 259–275. Springer, New York (2012)
43. Missingham, R.: E-parliament: opening the door. Gov. Inf. Q. **28**, 426–434 (2001)
44. OECD: Promise and problems of E-Democracy: Challenges of Online Citizen Engagement. Oecd, Paris (2003)
45. Pratchett, L.: Comparing local e-democracy in europe: a preliminary report. In: DESA: E-Participation and E-Government: Understanding the Present and Creating the Future, pp. 128–146. UN, New York (2007)
46. Tambouris, E., Liotas, N., Tarabanis, K.: A framework for assessing eparticipation projects and tools. In: Proceedings of 40th Hawaii International Conference on System Science, pp. 1–10. (HICCS-40), Hawaii (2007)
47. Marcella, R., Baxter, G., Moore, N.: An exploration of the effectiveness for the citizen of Web-based systems of communicating UK parliamentary and devolved assembly information. J. Gov. Inf. **29**, 371–391 (2002)
48. Sobaci, Z.: What the Turkish parliamentary web site offers to citizens in terms of e-participation: a content analysis. Inf. Polity **15**, 227–241 (2010)
49. Setälä, M., Grönlund, K.: Parliamentary websites: theoretical and comparative perspectives. Inf. Polity **11**, 149–162 (2006)
50. Coleman, S.: Connecting Parliament to the public via the internet: two case studies of online consultations. Inf. Commun. Soc. **7**, 1–22 (2004)
51. Hough, R.: Do legislative petitions systems enhance the relationship between parliament and citizens? J. Legislative Stud. **18**, 479–495 (2012)
52. Miller, L.: E-petitions at Westminster: the way forward for democracy? Parliamentary Aff. **62**, 162–177 (2009)
53. Malina, A., Macintosh, A., Farrell, S.: Digital democracy through electronic petitioning. Adv. Digit. Gov. **26**, 137–148 (2002)
54. Bochel, C.: Petition systems. contributing to representative democracy? Parliamentary Aff. **66**, 798–815 (2013)
55. Lindner, R., Riehm, U.: Electronic petitions and institutional modernization. JeDEM **1**, 1–11 (2009)
56. Mambrey, P., Neumann, H.-P., Sieverdingbeck, K.: Bridging the gap between parliament and citizen? the internet services of the german Bundestag. Parliamentary Aff. **52**, 480–492 (1999)
57. Saalfeld, T., Dobmeier, R.: The Bundestag and german citizens: more communication growing distance. J. Legislative Stud. **18**, 314–333 (2012)
58. Islam, M.S.: Towards a sustainable e-Participation implementation model. Eur. J. ePractice **5**, 1–12 (2008)

Investigating the Sailing Ship Effect as Newcomers' Strategic Reaction to Technological Change

Rocco Agrifoglio, Francesco Schiavone and Concetta Metallo

Abstract This paper is aimed at investigating the sailing ship effect as strategic reaction of newcomers that enter into a new market for adopting and improving old technology than new one when technological change occurs. Based on the case-study method, we conducted a qualitative analysis for collect data on a peculiar company, The Impossible Project, was born to meet the instant photo amateur needs after Polaroid stopped producing instant cameras. Unlike most of the incumbents' and newcomers' behaviors, the Impossible Project is a rare case of a company that entry into a new market niche for focusing on the old technology, than other one, when technological change occurs. This empirical evidence has shown an opposite strategic behavior to technological change, providing interesting insights for research and practice.

Keywords Technological change · Sailing ship effect · Newcomer · Old technology-based newcomer

R. Agrifoglio (✉)
Department of Management and Economics, "Parthenope" University, Naples, Italy
e-mail: agrifoglio@uniparthenope.it

F. Schiavone
Department of Management Studies and Quantitative Methods, "Parthenope" University, Naples, Italy
e-mail: schiavone@uniparthenope.it

C. Metallo
Department of Science and Technology Studies, "Parthenope" University, Naples, Italy
e-mail: metallo@uniparthenope.it

© Springer International Publishing Switzerland 2016
T. Torre et al. (eds.), *Empowering Organizations*, Lecture Notes in Information Systems and Organisation 11, DOI 10.1007/978-3-319-23784-8_4

1   Introduction

Everyday technology affects and plays some role in our lives. We continuously need and use technology to perform some action or achieve some goal. Technology refers to the knowledge and/or subcomponents and machineries used by firms in order to develop and assembly their own technological products (or artifacts) for customers. Products differ by technological knowledge as they are commercialized by firms in order to satisfy market needs [1].

The evolution of technology and technological products is a typical phenomenon in every industry. Rapid technological change affects and shapes the dynamics of competition and structure of industries over time. Technological change is the social and economic process by which an invention becomes a novel technology (innovation) which diffuses within an industry [2]. Technology evolves over time within specific technological trajectories and depends on the organizational routines (capabilities) of firms and on their continuous search of new technological solution to offer to the market. Evolutionary economics scholars were the first to explain why old technologies survive for some time after a new technology starts diffusing into a market (e.g., [3–5]).

The shift towards a new technological paradigm starts when a technological discontinuity emerges [6] and new technological trajectories, technically more advanced and based on different scientific notions, stem from it. Technological discontinuity is based on any breakthrough that advances an industry prices versus performance frontier (in other words, the industry technical progress) [6, p. 604], and shapes a new technological cycle. Every cycle starts with a ferment era in which emerging technological formats compete in order to become the new dominant design. A dominant design changes the characteristics of innovation and competition within an industry as it establishes new architecture specifications within its product category. The predominance of one technology over its competitors starts an era of incremental change over which firms focus on the improvement of the dominant technology's performance. This phase lasts until a new breakthrough occurs and a new technology, competing with and winning against the incumbent one, emerges. Afterwards, a new technological cycle with a new ferment era restarts and a new "standard war" for the identification of its new dominant design is launched.

Analysis of the strategic alternatives incumbent firms can implement when technological change occurs is a popular topic in the existing literature on technology competition [7, 8]. Howells [7][1] proposes three main strategic alternatives when incumbent firms, manufacturing the old technology, face technological change: (a) exit from the old market; (b) switch towards new technology; (c) the sailing ship effect.

---

[1]Unlike Howell research, other scholars have also identified a fourth type of strategic reaction: a combination of sailing ship effect and switch [13]. In this way, companies both keep their presence in the old market and enter in the new market.

Exit from the old market is the most drastic reaction possible for technological change. In some cases, exit is the most appropriate reaction following drastic market shrinkage. Otherwise, this strategic reaction may reflect the disinterest (or incapability) of the firm to face competition under new market conditions and technological standards. The adoption of this reaction implies that the firm needs to search for one or more new markets in which to enter and re-invest the resources dismissed from the old one. In their study on the effects of technological change on the structure of the American tire industry, Klepper and Simons [9, 10] found that small and young firms tend to exit from the market when a new technology emerges. So while in some cases it may be a small firm that leads technological innovation in a market, Suarez and Utterback [11] note that firms entering into an industry many years before the emergence of the dominant design are likely to face and survive technological change better than younger organizations. Suarez and Utterback explain this evidence by arguing that older firms have more resources to experiment with during periods of fast change.

The switch toward new technology is a strategic reaction more frequently followed than exit. In this case, the firm renews its product portfolio by developing and commercializing new products based on the emerging technology and its paradigm. In this way, the firm contributes to the Creative Destruction of the former market equilibriums. The switch is a complex process based on several decisions concerning corporate strategy, the organizational structure of the firm, and the psychology and perceptions of its managers. Even with superior resources, large and established firms may fail in the implementation of this strategy.

While exit from the old market and switch towards new technology are two strategic reactions more obvious and most widely investigated by the literature, the sailing ship effect is less followed than other ones, but more interesting for practitioner implications and academic research. The sailing ship effect is the acceleration of innovation in the old technology in response to the threat from the new and occurs when firms attempt to preserve their own technological competencies from a decline due to technological change. Some academic research has investigated the sailing ship effect focusing on the strategic reaction of the old technology-based firm that continues to perform its activity when technological change occur (e.g., [7, 12–15]). On the other hand, when technological change occurs, new business opportunities for firms from outside industry (well-known as newcomers) could be created too. This is the rare case of which newcomers entry into new market niches when technological change occurs, so deciding to adopt the old technology rather than switch towards new one. We define these firms as old technology-based newcomers.

Our paper is aimed to investigate the sailing ship effect focusing on the strategic behaviors of the old technology-based newcomers that enter into a new market niche for adopting and improving old technology. Therefore, the research question that guided this study is "What lead old technology-based newcomers to entry into new market niches when technological change occurs?". Based on the case-study method, we conducted a qualitative analysis for collect data on a peculiar company, The Impossible Project, was born to meet the instant photo amateur needs.

2 Literature Review

A review of the literature about the main strategic reactions of incumbent firms during or after technological change outlines different behaviors for preserving and/or renewing their business processes. Adner and Snow [8] analyzed old technology firms that do not want to exit from the market or switch to a new technology. This strategy of maintaining the focus on the old technology and therewith the creation of the coexistence of "obsolete and superior technologies" [16] was often observed and seen as a real alternative. In this context it can be differentiated between mainly two strategies called racing and retreat strategies. In the former case firms behave in a way that is called sailing ship effect [7, 17, 18].

The sailing ship effect is the "acceleration of innovation in the old technology in response to the threat from the new" [7, p. 887]. Its name derives from what happened in the naval industry in the second half of 1800s: an increase of the innovation and performance of sailing ships occurred after the introduction of steam ships. The explanation of Gilfillan [17] was that sailing ships producers perceived the steam ships as a threat by which their competitors were able to surpass them. Such firms responded by revitalizing and repositioning their older technology within the broader product market. The product is no longer commercialized in the mass market, but instead is positioned as a niche product for those groups of users not interested in adopting the new technology. The sailing ship effect, thus, occurs when an old technology is revitalized and experiences a "last gasp" due to the risk of replacement by a new substituting one.

The model of competing technology S curves goes back to Foster [19] and describes an established, now old, technology (T_O) that has secured its position over other available technologies (T_{OX}) and from a certain time on was confronted with a new technology (T_N) with a technology which was superior from time t^* [16]. However, in our case, the old technology improved (T_{O+1}) with the introduction of the new technology. This effect is a "process whereby the advent of a new technology engenders a response aimed at improving the incumbent technology" [16, p. 593]. The sailing ship producers perceived the steam ships as a threat and, thus, improved the performance and innovated their traditional products. The sailing ship effect can be seen as a strategic reaction opposite to technological retreat [8]. Technological retreat is a strategic approach by which old technology companies retrench their products in niche position within their traditional market and/or search for new market applications. Hence the goal is not growth and expansion but rather survival and contraction which is "contrary to traditionally assumed firm objectives" [16].

If an old technology loses the mainstream this does not necessarily means that it loses the entire market. Even though it is possible that all customers uniformly prefer the new technology it is a matter of evaluation criteria. Indeed, as De Liso and Filatrella [16] suggested, there exist "several drivers for variance that may lead parts of the market to continue to prefer the old technology to the new" such as budget constraints, heterogeneity of preferences over attribute bundles or emotional/nostalgic elements of the old technology.

Overall, this type of reactions implies changes on both the production-side and the demand-side and deep strategic reactions for companies within and outside industry (e.g., [14, 15]). Within industry, the repositioning of old technology products from mass to niche market could affect incumbents' behaviors, as well as the relationships with suppliers, partners and channels. Incumbents could react to changes developing internally or by integration new and necessary capabilities despite they keep focusing on the old technology. On the other hand, general purpose technologies might introduce new technological competencies and distribution channels or partners into the industry which affect old technology and its (retrofitted or not) products. Outside industry, newcomers might decide to entry into an industry whereby technological change occurred, focusing on the old technology rather than new one. Empirical evidences have shown newcomers entry into new market niches due to technological changes aimed at improving and innovating old technology rather than dominant design. Like incumbents, the strategic reactions of newcomers to technological change due to new business opportunities stemming from the repositioning of old technology products from mass to niche market. A depth analysis of how newcomers react to technological change due to dominant design occurred still lacks in the literature.

3 Methodology

We conducted a qualitative analysis based on case-study method in order to collect data on a peculiar company: The Impossible Project. According to Benbasat and colleagues [20], "case methodology is clearly useful when a natural setting or a focus on contemporary events is needed" (p. 372). Furthermore, our decision to select just one case is agree with Yin research [21], who assumed "to confirm, challenge or extend a theory, there may exist a single case" (p. 42). As suggested by the qualitative research literature [20, 21], the analysis was conducted using online archives, interviews, and observations. Online archives, available on The Impossible Project's website and web, were analyzed by using document analysis techniques. Furthermore, we also conducted some semi-structural interviews to mangers of the Impossible Project and observed the social media usage by firm and customers, as well as their interaction and communication ways.

The case study approach allows us to better understanding firm's behaviors, with particular reference to communication and interaction with their customers, due to technological change.

4 The Case of the Impossible Project

Founded in 1937 by Edwin H. Land, Polaroid Corporation is an American company become very popular for its instant film and cameras. Despite photographic film was invented by Agfa, Polaroid was the first company to develop and launch on market the commercial instant camera, Polaroid Land Camera Model 95 and Type 40 Land film, in 1948. The initial system was essentially a black and white print system, but this was the beginning of instant photography as we know it today. In 1963, Polaroid launched the Automatic 100, the most popular instant camera and film that produced instant color pictures changing from the existing black and white technology. Despite the instant photography had proven to be an attractive and growing new segment of the amateur photographic market, the market started declining in 1982. In October 2001, Polaroid filed for Chapter 11 bankruptcy protection and restructuring in the US. Finally, in February 2008—after 60 years of production—, when digital technology had made the mobile phone most people's instant camera of choice, Polaroid stopped producing instant film changing from instant photography to digital photography products.[2] From that moment, instant film amateurs could no longer use their Polaroid instant cameras.

After Polaroid announced that it would stop producing instant film for Polaroid cameras, two people, Dr. Florian Kaps (Polaroid fans) and André Bosman (a former of the Polaroid company since 1980 at Enschede), decided to found a company to produce materials for Polaroid cameras, the Impossible Project. The main aim of the company was to reinvent instant film based on materials that no longer existed (instant films) for a product that was no longer on the market (Polaroid Cameras).

In October 2008, the Impossible Project saved the last Polaroid production plant by buying the last factory the world manufacturing Polaroid instant film in Enschede, the Netherlands, as well as production equipment. According to Dave Bias, vice president of Impossible America, states "when we started, it was literally impossible to make instant film for Polaroid cameras. All the infrastructure, factories, and distribution systems had been dismantled by Polaroid, and we had nothing but one factory where all the final assembly took place." Thus, they took ten of their very best former employees of Polaroid in order to form the Impossible team [22]. The Polaroid employers were a crucial resource for company because possess knowledge and skills for that products and business. As Bosman suggested, "We have a total of about 300 years of experience here; that is the key to reinventing this process."

Before starting the business, founders decided to conduct two research for understanding consumer base and market trend [23]. Primary research was conducted with a focus group at a rotary club and interviews with four owners of Polaroid cameras aimed to establish the current and potential consumer base.

---

[2]The company had already stopped producing instant cameras for consumers the year before. Its global warehouses have only enough film to last until the end of 2009.

Secondary research looked at market trends, focusing on the instant camera market niche and consumer's attitude towards technology. Research results are shown in Table 1.

In April 2010, the Impossible Project started to invent and produce totally new instant film materials for traditional Polaroid cameras: Impossible Silver Shade Film (monochromatic) and Impossible Color Shade Film. Thanks to the Impossible Project, the analog instant photography has been saved from extinction by preventing more than 200 million perfectly functioning Polaroid cameras from becoming obsolete.

Then, the company continues to invest in instant films and cameras improvement. In October 2012, the company and Polaroid have launched a range of collectible products, called The Polaroid Classic range, that originate from different periods of Polaroid's history. Among the various products of the company, one of the most innovative and popular is the Impossible Instant Lab. It is a device designed to transform any digital image via iOS phones into a real Polaroid-style instant photos that can be shared, exhibited and preserved. The idea derived from a passionate team of instant photography practitioners and professionals in fine mechanics, optics, and design who built the first prototype of Instant Lab. Using kickstarter platform, the project was successfully funded by 2,509 backers who donated $559,232 of $250,000 goal.

In October 2012, moreover, a private investment company takes majority control of Impossible and André Bosman, one of The Impossible Project's founders, retires from the company. In July 2013, Impossible develops its first iOS app, a part of the operational system of the Instant Lab that scans digital iPhone images to analog instant film. Finally, in October 2013, the firm appoints the Teenage Engineering Jesper Kouthoofd, of a Swedish company, to design its first analogue instant camera. It is the first Polaroid-type camera to be developed in a decade.

As the Impossible Project website points out, "today, Impossible is no longer a 'project' but a fast-growing company with around 130 employees in Austria, Germany, the Netherlands, Britain, France, the USA, Japan and China. Its core products are analog instant film, refurbished Polaroid cameras, and its own-designed range of analog instant cameras. But the Impossible Project's ambitions are bigger: from its new creative headquarters in Berlin, Germany, Impossible is intent on creating the future of analog instant photography" [22].

Figure 1 shows the numbers of The Impossible Project.

Table 1 Research results on instant photo and cameras consumers and market

Consumer	Market
Users are primarily aged between 15 and 35	Instant film and cameras is a niche market
Generation (45+) are embracing the digital market and see no point in going backwards	There is a growing trend for software that emulates the style of film photography
User is young, experimental, and creative	Digital photography is now more accessible than ever before
UK users are more available to use Instant film and cameras	The digital market is growing and getting cheaper each year

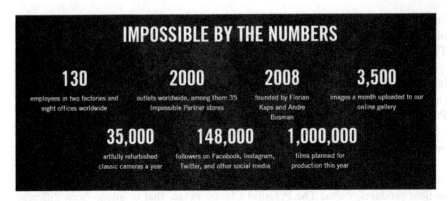

Fig. 1 Numbers of The Impossible Project. *Source* https://www.the-impossible-project.com/about/

4.1 The Impossible Project and the Future of Analog Instant Photography

Although the Impossible Project is an old technology-based firm, the technology is considered as crucial for encouraging young and creative instant film amateurs to become involved with the brand. In particular, the Impossible Project uses various technologies for supporting the interaction and communication among customers such as both traditional, such as website, and social media, such as blog, Facebook, and Twitter.

The website of The Impossible Project's is the first way for people to collect information on the company, such as the business idea, history and shops, on its products, such as films and cameras, as well as to access gallery section, blog and social media. The Gallery [24] is a collection of silver and color shade photos posted around the world by Polaroid's professional and amateur photographers and easily available for comments and sharing by famous social media. The blog of that website [25], instead, is a virtual place where Polaroid lovers posted specific articles about photography, events and new company products and for leaving comments, tips or impressions on them. Today, blog contains the 954 items divided for various categories such as photography (471), products (21), tutorials (69), events (180), factory (11), and miscellanea.

With refer to social media, The Impossible Project uses Facebook, Twitter, Tumblr, Pinterest, and Flickr to communicate and interact with fans. In particular, Facebook, Twitter, and Flickr are mainly administered at both Global level, whilst Tumblr and Pinterest are only administered at Local level by company stores. The company considers social media as very important for its communication strategy because they allow Polaroid amateurs to perform practice and, thus, encouraging the reaching of new customers and loyalty of the old one. Furthermore, social media

Table 2 Numbers of The Impossible Project's social media

Social media/impacts	Facebook	Twitter	Pinterest	Flickr
Likes/followers	66,452	4,394	3,065	>8,000
Talking about/tweets	1,167	13,848	–	–
Photos/pins	1,254	–	859	125,165

shows customer's tastes and beliefs, allowing company to understanding attitudes and predict their behaviors. Table 2 shows the numbers of The Impossible Project's social media.

In particular, The Impossible Project's Facebook Fanpage [26] has more than 66,452 likes, of which 1,167 people talking about this, and 1,254 photos. At local level, The Impossible Project's ASIA Fanpage [27] has more than 3,529 likes, of which 591 talking about this, and more than 1,500 photos uploaded. On the contrary, The Impossible Project's Twitter Fanpage [28] has more than 4,394 followers and 13,848 Tweets. Like Facebook, Twitter is also used at Local level by the The Impossible Project's USA [29] and The Impossible Project's ASIA [30]. The first has 28,873 followers and 35,832 tweets, while the second has 1,629 followers and 10,558 tweets. Furthermore, The Impossible Project's USA Pinterest Fanpage [31] has more than 3,065 followers, with 25 bacheches and 859 pins. Finally, The Impossible Project's Flickr Fanpage [32] has more than 8,000 members and 125,165 photos uploaded.

5 Conclusions

This paper was aimed to investigate the sailing ship effect as strategic reaction of newcomers entry into a new market for adopting and improving old technology when technological change occurs. Based on the case-study method, we focused on a peculiar company, The Impossible Project, was born to meet the instant photo amateur needs after Polaroid stopped producing instant cameras. Unlike most of the incumbents' and newcomers' behaviors, the Impossible Project is a rare case of a company that entry into a new market niche for focusing on the old technology, than other one, when technological change occurs.

This empirical evidence has shown an opposite strategic behavior to technological change, providing interesting insights for research and practice. In particular, this study contributes to the literature about the technological change by focusing on strategic reactions of newcomers, than incumbent firms, when new technological paradigm emerges. Through The Impossible Project's analysis, our research contributes to expand the boundaries of Howells' [7] taxonomy by showing the sailing ship effect due to newcomer's strategic reaction than incumbents. Moreover, the Impossible Project case shows as the decision to stay with the old technology is a rational choice that favored business success, because this decision is focused on demand context in which the technology is deployed (Adner and Snow, 2009). With the arrival of the digital photography products, Impossible Project was able to capture qualitative changes in the composition of the customers that constituted the market for the old technology (see Table 1. Research results on instant photo and cameras consumers and market). The company has based its successes on existence of a nostalgia value dimension or emotional attachment for old technology succeeding into carve out a niche sustainable (Adner and Snow 2009). As Adner and Snow (2009, p. 12) highlighted: "the introduction of the new technology exposes new lines of segmentation—niche opportunities within a market that previously had been regarded as homogenous. Within these niches, the old technology can maintain a sustainable advantage over the new technology." In such circumstances, the rise of the digital photography products (new technology) created a new opportunity for the instant photo (old technology), positioning as a specific product in a niche market rather than as an inferior substitute in the old market. Another aspect that has favored Impossible Project's success has been the first-mover advantage, because the niche's smaller size compared to the original market means that it can support a lower number of producers (Adner and Snow 2009). In fact, after Polaroid announced that it would stop producing instant film for Polaroid cameras, Impossible Project has been able to perceive the needs of instant film amateurs, offering them materials for Polaroid cameras. Finally, this study also contributes to practice because provides additional and different strategic alternatives for companies when technological change occurs. Technological change could provide firms new business opportunities due to a series of improvements in the older technology that augment its capacity and prolong its economic life.

References

1. Pavitt, K.: Technologies, products and organization in the innovating firm: what Adam Smith tells us and Joseph Schumpeter doesn't. Ind. Corp. Change **7**(3), 433–452 (1998)
2. Schumpeter, J.A.: Capitalism, Socialism and Democracy. Harper and Brothers, New York (1942)
3. Dosi, G.: Technological paradigms and technological trajectories. Res. Policy **11**(3), 147–162 (1982)
4. Nelson, R.R., Winter, S.G.: An Evolutionary Theory of Economic Change. Harvard University Press, Cambridge (1982)
5. Rosenberg, N.: Inside the Black Box: Technology and Economics. Cambridge University Press, Cambridge (1982)
6. Anderson, P., Tushman, M.L.: Technological discontinuities and dominant designs—a cyclical model of technological change. Adm. Sci. Q. **35**, 604–633 (1990)
7. Howells, J.: The response of old technology incumbents to technological competition: does the sailing ship effect exist? J. Manage. Stud. **39**(7), 887–906 (2002)
8. Adner, R., Snow, D.: Old technology responses to new technology threats: demand heterogeneity and graceful technology retreats. Ind. Corp. Change **19**(5), 1655–1675 (2010)
9. Klepper, S., Simons, K.L.: The making of an oligopoly: firm survival and technological change in the evolution of the U.S. tire industry. J. Polit. Econ. **108**(4), 728–760 (2000)

10. Klepper, S., Simons, K.L.: Dominance by birthright: entry of prior radio producers and competitive ramifications in the U.S. television receiver industry. Strateg. Manag. J. **21**(10–11), 997–1016 (2000)
11. Suarez, F., Utterback, J.: Dominant designs and the survival of firms. Strateg. Manag. J. **16**, 415–430 (1995)
12. Snow, D.C.: Beware of Old Technologies' Last Gasps, pp. 17–18. Harvard Business Review (2008)
13. Schiavone, F.: Strategic reactions to technology competition: a decision-making model. Manag. Dec. **49**(5), 801–809 (2011)
14. Schiavone, F., Agrifoglio, R.: Information technology and the survival of old declining products: a case study. AWERProcedia Inf. Technol. Comput. Sci. **3**, 895–899 (2013)
15. Schiavone, F.: Communities of Practice and Vintage Innovation. A Strategic Reaction to Technological Change. Springer, New York (2013)
16. De Liso, N., Filatrella, G.: On technology competition: a formal analysis of the sailing ship effect. Econ. Innov. New Technol. **17**, 593–610 (2008)
17. Gilfillan, S.C.: Inventing the Ship. Follett Publishing Co., Chicago (1935)
18. Mendonça, S.: The "sailing ship effect": reassessing history as a source of insight on technological change. Res. Policy **42**, 1724–1738 (2013)
19. Foster, R.N.: Innovation: The Attacker's Advantage. Summit Books, New York (1986)
20. Benbasat, I., Goldstein, D.K., Mead, M.: The case research strategy in studies of information systems. MIS Q. **11**(3), 369–386 (1987)
21. Yin, R.: Case Study Research: Design and Methods. Sage, Beverly Hills (1994)
22. https://www.the-impossible-project.com/about/
23. http://cargocolletive.com/nicolawillison/The-Impossible-Project-Strategy
24. https://shop.the-impossible-project.com/gallery/
25. https://blog.the-impossible-project.com/
26. https://www.facebook.com/ImpossibleGlobal?fref=ts
27. https://www.facebook.com/pages/Impossible-Tokyo-KK/151195978278650
28. https://twitter.com/impossible_HQ
29. https://twitter.com/ImpossibleUSA
30. https://twitter.com/impossibletokio
31. http://www.pinterest.com/impossibleusa/
32. https://www.flickr.com/groups/polapremium/

Bridging the Gap Between Theory and Practice: Socio-Technical Toolbox

Peter Bednar and Moufida Sadok

Abstract This paper describes a teaching experience of information systems (IS) analysis and design unit. In this unit every student applies a socio-technical (ST) toolbox in a real life business. These projects give students experience of real world business practices, issues and processes and provide opportunities to create a stimulating learning environment. At the same time the projects help involved businesses to develop new insights and understandings of key features of their own work practices, in support of their business development.

Keywords Socio-Technical analysis · Systems practice · Organizational change · Work related learning

1 Introduction

The primary focus of this paper lies in the description of a teaching experience of information systems (IS) analysis and design unit through two selected students' projects (out of 22) using a socio-technical (ST) toolbox in practice. The toolbox, which consists of 27 different analytical tools for organization analysis, was used by the students over a period of 6 months. The involvement and commitment to the ST practice was about almost weekly sessions for companies. Mostly sessions would be between one and 2 h. Additional to these sessions a number of observations have been conducted in order to understand the business practices as well as a number of

P. Bednar (✉)
School of Computing, University of Portsmouth, Portsmouth, UK
e-mail: peter.bednar@port.ac.uk

P. Bednar
Department of Informatics, Lund University, Lund, Sweden

M. Sadok
Higher Institute of Technological Studies in Communications in Tunis, Tunis, Tunisia
e-mail: moufida.sadok@port.ac.uk

© Springer International Publishing Switzerland 2016
T. Torre et al. (eds.), *Empowering Organizations*, Lecture Notes in Information
Systems and Organisation 11, DOI 10.1007/978-3-319-23784-8_5

interviews and questionnaires have been used. The use in practice of ST toolbox brings with it opportunities for future graduates to more engage with the practical and complex problems of everyday organizational life. The contribution of this paper is to highlight and extend the debate as to why dialogue between companies and academia subsequently impact on the practice and theory of IS. Indicating that, upon reflection, there is a need to revise curricula design and IS research methodologies.

In fact, the starting point of reflection in this paper is an agreement with the key findings of Besson and Rowe [1] work which has identified a lack of description and conceptualization of the transformation process in the main stream of IS research. The authors have particularly noticed a lack of description of the construction and the routinization phases. This phenomenon may be attributed to a variety of reasons but it is relevant to include among them the education of the future practitioners and academics which is influencing their view and understanding of IS as a discipline and IS as a practice. Kawalek [2] has argued that IS as a discipline provides little guidance on the process and practice of organizational change. Therefore, students might be unprepared to deal with the complexity and requirements of real world businesses. It is argued in this paper that the distinction between IS as a data processing system and IS as a human activity system provides a frame of reference to explain the reasons why the gaps in understanding the transformation process continue to be relevant issues to explore in the IS research. In view of IS as a data processing system, efforts for developing IS have been oriented to the design of effective artifacts and a number of structured and formal methods in IS methodologies have been developed. Hard systems approaches have been applied with a focus on the efficacy and internal consistency of systems specifications and their development. In this perspective, the development and implementation of IS are considered as a driven and results of organizational change. This stream of IS research is pervasive and prevalent in the higher education of future practitioners and academics as well as in the highly ranked IS journals.

Considering IS as human organized activity, the transformation process is de-scribed as an emergent learning process based on the exploration and understanding of contextual dependencies and supported by a number of methods and techniques. This bears out the analysis of [3] when the author pointed out that a technological change involves a trade-off between exploration of new possibilities and exploration of old certainties in organizational learning. The ST systems design literature equally put forward evidence of the relevance of contextual analysis within which emphasis is placed on human and technical dependencies in the context of an evolving organizational environment. Holistic IS methodologies such as Effective Technical and Human Implementation of Computer supported Systems (ETHICS) by Mumford [4], Soft Systems Methodology (SSM) by Checkland [5], Client-Led Design by Stowell and West [6], Object Oriented Analysis and Design (OOAD) by Mathiassen et al. [7] and approaches such as the Strategic Systemic Thinking (SST) framework by Bednar [8] support analysis into any relevant aspect of IS analysis and development and deal with complex organizational issues. This stream of IS research continue to be poorly referenced and ignored even though the pioneers of this stream have been active and contrarian researchers since the first era of IS history. Despite the considerable number of publications from the sixties to currently, the ST and soft systems approaches continue to be marginalized and underestimated in the higher education of future IS practitioners and academics. The ST toolbox introduced in this paper draws up and extends methods and techniques from a collection of a number of contemporary ST methodologies. It has been developed and used in practice in many different types of organizations over a period of approximately 10 years [9]. Over the years previous versions of the ST toolbox has been used to support analysis of many business processes such as in warehouses belonging to supermarkets, pharmacies, news agencies and doctor practices.

Thus this paper is structured as follows. The first section sets up a stream of IS re-search which have addressed the description of the organization transformation process but continue to be poorly referenced or ignored. The second section provides examples addressing the process of transformation in ST literature. The third section introduces a ST toolbox as an example to support teaching systems analysis in order to enable students to keep up with the requirement of practice. The outcomes of two selected students' projects are also underlined in this section. Finally, conclusive remarks are presented in Sect. 4.

2 Considering Human Activity in IS Design and Analysis

The definition of an IS as a system in which data is processed to achieve efficiently organizational goals is commonly accepted. Where there is less agreement, however, in the elicitation and relevance of these goals to different stakeholder' perspectives as well as in the ways the systems have been designed and implemented. Efforts for developing IS have been oriented to the design of effective artifacts that meet the information needs and requirements of top management. Orlikowski and Iacono [10] make a case that IT should be viewed as the core of IS as a discipline and as a practice. Waterfall, prototyping and prescriptive approaches for IS design have been proposed and applied. A number of structured and formal methods in IS methodologies such as SSADM (Structured Systems Analysis and Design Method and Business Development Method) have been widely advertised. Hard systems approaches have been harnessed based on the hypothesis that systems exist in the real world and can be identified and "engineered". Consequently, the system objectives can be defined in advance and alternative means of achieving them can be modeled. Considering only one point of view as objective and correct, the focus is more on how to do things in certain and precise situations. Alter [11] however emphasizes a need for IS field to address the whole context within which IT-reliant work system is designed, developed, implemented and maintained. He states that the use of IT to support IS activities does not require IT artifact to be the primary subject focus of IS field. In the IS academic field ever since its official inception as a specific area of interest at the IFIP (International Federation for Information Processing) conference in New York in 1965, questions in multidisciplinary contexts—such as systems thinking, structuring uncertainty, defining and managing wicked problem spaces, ST systems, human activity systems, inquiry systems [12–15] have been addressed. Langefors [16] discusses the role of organizational IS. He considered that, in order to manage an organization, it would be necessary to know something about the current state and behavior of its different parts and also the environment within which it was interacting. These parts would need to be coordinated and inter-related, i.e. to form a system. Thus, means to obtain information from the different parts of a business would be essential and these means (information units) would also need to be inter-related. Since the effectiveness of the organization would depend upon the effectiveness of the information units, an organization could be seen as crucially 'tied-together' by information. For [16], therefore, the organization and its IS could be viewed as one and the same. In this perspective, the consequences of any IT reliant IS development efforts are very contextually dependent. The IS universe is more and more characterized by the growth in number of stakeholders, the quality and the quantity of the different users influencing the design and implementation of IS projects as well as the successes and failures of such projects [17]. IS development process as an ongoing contextual inquiry [8] is characterized as an emergent ST change process conducted through sense making and negotiations among stakeholders [18]. As [19] point out, organizational change is only likely to result in success if the individual actors are engaged with that change. It is thus likely that any change imposed from above is likely to result in failure.

3   Socio-Technical Methods Use and Implementation

By way of a narrative and storytelling that draws on the author's own experiences applying ETHICS in many companies in Europe and the United States, [7] discussed how her research perspective in relation to ST philosophy can be applied in managing change with the introduction of a new work systems or a new technology as a part of the change process. The case studies described in her book offer examples of organizational design activities and assessments to illustrate how the suggested method, based on a participative design, can provide support to problem solving and change process management. One case study for example addresses the design and implementation of an expert system to assist the sales force of a large American enterprise. The sales force is skilled in sales and business knowledge but they had low computer confidence. The new project manager for the development of the expert system, who also will play the role of a facilitator, decided to use the ETHICS methodology to involve the future users in the design process of the software. He created a design group from the technical project team and from the sales staff to integrate organizational, human, technical and task-related factors into the development process. The sales force identifies their needs and requirements and the technical group translates these needs in a working system. It is for example necessary to understand according to a sale force perspective the meaning of a helpful and/or useful system. Mumford describes the stress and anxiety of the project manager before the start of design process, because he had doubts about the adhesion of the sales force to the use of the new system since it might be in dissonance with the principle of "selling". He also had concerns about the use of ETHICS methodology as it might be perceived as complicated. Mumford also provides details about the whole experience of the project development including the multiple meetings of the design group, the enthusiastic and difficult steps of a participative design experience and the successful implementation of the new expert system. She describes how during the different meetings the involved team discusses the problems of existing system, future needs and potential benefits of a new system. Questions about the reasons of change, system sustainability and boundaries are also addressed. The routinization meetings cover the implementation diagnosis, the realization of benefit management analysis and the evaluation and self-reflective element in terms of improved efficiency and job satisfaction. In [20], the authors use creation rather than design to describe the process of IS development. Such process requires a deep understanding of how a particular actors attribute meanings to their perceived world and how the purposes assigned to the IS are perceived to be "truly" relevant within this world. It follows that a dialogue in which management can explore the values, goals and preferences of individuals during the process of IS development must be desired. The application of SSM in the UK's National Health Service (NHS) is a particular case study where techniques such as CATWOE (Customers, Actors, Transformation process, Worldview, Owners, Environmental constraints) analysis and rich pictures are deployed to support the participation of all stakeholders in complex problem situations. One of the main features of this organization is the absence of unitary power structure because the provision of health care in the UK is based on a complicated network of autonomous and semi-autonomous groups. This leads to consideration of further key problems in NHS projects: identification of relationships in the network subject of change, exploration of the impact of change on existing relationships according to multiple perspectives. In Client led IS Design, [21] put the client(s) in control of the whole IS Development process and apply a set of techniques to support the appreciation process of a problem situation and to enable communication between IS professional and client(s). A case study of a medium sized manufacturing company is given to display the practical use of the aforementioned framework. To cope with increasingly competitive dynamics the reappraisal of the commercial activities has been achieved to consider how the use of IT could help to improve the operating efficiency. The board of this company decided to employ a consultant with multidisciplinary background (combination of business and IT) capable to deal with transversal problems within the Commercial Department uttered by the managing group. A number of techniques and diagrams such as spray diagrams, system map, decision tree, Black box diagrams, Rich pictures, and activity models have been used to consider and represent the IS processes and activities in the clients' perspectives. These techniques used as a mean of communications support a learning process through which the involved group develops a contextual under-standing and awareness of the potential changes and related problems in working practices implied by the developing IS. In this case study, such discussion has revealed the use of a parallel and personal IS by some sales staff to process orders bypassing the formal working procedures. The involvement and commitment of clients is also pursued in the technical specification and implementation phases (e.g. change) of the "new" IS. From a routinization perspective, the clients agree about the implementation of the changes arising from the incorporation of IT into the IS which might induce new needs in training and skills development as well as the setup of new working practices.

4 Students' Projects Realization

The ST toolbox deals with 8 themes supporting the application of ST tools for systems analysis in practice and organized in a particular order for pedagogical purposes. They are: change analysis, system structure definition, system purpose, system perspectives, system priorities, desirable system, system action and system for evaluation and engagement. ST toolbox places great emphasis on developing understanding of the business systems design. Every student applies ST toolbox in a real life business in the setting of the realization of a second year project. Mainly the involved organizations are small and local businesses but at times they can also be smaller departments or sections within large organizations (not necessarily always local). These projects give students real world experience of real world business practices, issues and processes. At the same time the projects help involved businesses to develop new insights and understandings of key features of their own work practices, in support of their business development. The two pro-jects described here are part of the core in an undergraduate degree in Business IS. Given the complexity of business analysis, students require analytical and problem-solving techniques for identifying and evaluating organizational and technical consequences of design and implementation of the proposed system. The work can be described as a form of action research. The analyst (investigator/researcher) engages with a real world problem situation in a business. The project would normally involve three employees per case organization, typi-cally representing three different jobs in the same section or department. The engagement is based on reflection and the methods used include observation, participatory observation, interviews and questionnaires. Typically for dialogue and reflection purposes techniques such as Mind-Mapping and Rich Pictures (as described in [6]) would be used regularly by the analyst both to support a dialogue about understanding the problem situation between the analyst and the interviewee and as a tool for reflection by the analyst (and the interviewee). This is in line with [22] where the conclusion is that "engaged actors need support to surface their contextually-dependent understandings, individual and collectively and engage in a 'dance of change'". The typical inquiry would consist of at least six main interviews per employee (semi-structured, with additional complementary interviews mostly open-ended and flexible), regular observation of work activities (typically twice a month) and questionnaires (initially one ST questionnaire with sixty questions per employee). One key feature of the project approach is to support employees in their reflection over their change potential. The agenda could be described with the following: "Change is endemic in organizational life. When engaging with change activity that attempts to address complexity (as opposed to complicatedness), contextual experts need to be the key decision-takers. This means redistribution not only of responsibility and action but also decision-taking power [22]. Additionally to this there would also be a small number (usually four or five) of open ended conversations and meetings with relevant line managers. The analyst would normally keep a research journal from which excerpts were used to support the analyst description and documentation of conclusions of the inquiry itself. The main aspects of the analysis and inquiry practice were documented in specific templates which are part of the ST Toolbox. At the end of each case project a report consisting mainly of the ST templates were transcribed, printed out by the analyst and then signed off by the respective organizational departmental manager (who had given permission for the project in the first place). After which the results were evaluated by the same manager.

The first project is related to an UK retailer providing a wide range of electrical goods and houses wares. The marketing strategy of the company includes a high interest to how effectively satisfy customers' needs. In one of 96 standalone shops, the student identified a need for improvement of business processes and jobs and proposed an IT based solution to overcome some of the management difficulties related to stock control. The analysis has involved three relevant stakeholders: store manager, supervisor and sales assistant. The different stakeholders have discussed existing problems, future demands, opportunities that new business process plus a new technology could bring. They also have achieved a holistic multi-criteria benefit analysis to set up the positives and negatives of the current and future system. In the input-output analysis, the student used a work-flow diagram to show how inputs are linked to which part of the process and where in the process specific outcomes are originating. In benefit management analysis, the student described how each potential benefit would be managed to mention exactly what the benefit is supposed to be and how it could be made happen in the real world and recognizable by the experiences of the stakeholders involved. Table 1 is an extract of financial benefit (cost-benefit) analysis.

Table 2 is an extract of quantifiable benefit analysis in other words what makes sense to be counted (but not necessarily measured).

Table 3 is an extract of measurable benefit analysis in other words what makes sense to be measured.

Table 1 Cost-benefit analysis

Type of change	Description
Do new things	Income from goods ordered and sold for individual customers
	Lower staff costs from automating processes of stock availability checks and ordering goods for customers (not much human input and time not required)
Do things better	Increased sales due to improved sales analysis
	Lowered storage costs as less stock is being held due to better forecasting resulting in coordination of deliveries and quantities of products being delivered
Stop doing things	By stopping certain jobs such as gathering feed-back manually, management can concentrate purely on analysing the information instead and using it to boost sales
Notes	Saving money on payroll as less staff input required due to more automated processes and technology being used
	Lower storage costs
	Coordination of deliveries

Table 2 Quantifiable benefit analysis

Type of change	Description
Do new things	Staff checking weekly rotas more frequently
	Reduced queue times due to faster, contactless payment method
	Less mistakes made when adding new stock to stock control system due to teamwork and ability to verify
Do things better	More relevant trends and patterns spotted in sales analysis
	Less tasks put on the supervisor when manager absent
	Lower number of denied card payments
	Reduced time needed to locate products in the stockroom because of better organisation and automation of the system
	Reduced number of tasks assigned to supervisor when manager absent, making daily tasks list more realistic to complete
Stop doing things	Less customer queries about ordering goods to store as click and collect self-ordering available
	Less distraction by eliminating product availability enquires from managers of other branches as stock control system integrated across all branches electronically
Notes	Rotas available electronically
	Click and collect in store
	Sales monitoring and analysis software
	Card readers connected via wires, not wireless, enable contactless payment
	Customer service checking
	More organised stock and automated inventory management system

Table 3 Measurable benefit analysis

Type of change	Description
Do new things	Customer service and sales targets met and exceeded more often
	More accurate stock levels due to automated stock control system
	More accurate quality control with received deliveries thanks to verification
Do things better	Improved sales analysis due to better tools
	Customer service levels increased due the fact sales assistants are working more effectively and have more access to information and authority
	Faster response time to customer queries
Stop doing things	Equal share of tasks between manager and supervisor, supervisor able to work on the same or similar level when manager is in store, giving supervisor more status, responsibility and sense of achievement
Notes	Sales monitoring and analysis software
	More realistic targets

Table 4 Observable benefit analysis

Type of change	Description
Do new things	Sales assistants feeling more secure about their jobs with permanent part-time contracts
	Improved job satisfaction for assistants and supervisor from more authority and access to information
Do things better	Employees more aware of the shifts they are assigned to and any arising updates and changes
	Less stress from using the software over the manual sales analysis system
	Sales assistants happier to take role of CSR during busy times thanks to supporting technology
	Better relationships between work colleagues from increased teamwork
Stop doing things	Sales assistants and supervisor feeling more relaxed and less under pressure due to reduced supervision
Notes	Rotas availability and access to staff
	Supervision
	Part-time contracts instead of zero-hour
	Increased teamwork—relationship forming

Table 4 is an extract of observable benefit analysis in other words what makes sense to be noticed (but not necessarily to be quantified or measured).

The second student project is about a well-known international retailer of shoes for different age groups (Fig. 1).

In the stakeholder analysis, the student has discussed with the Manager, Sales assistant, and customer. A rich picture is used to develop his understanding of business practices in this company. The system change analysis is done together

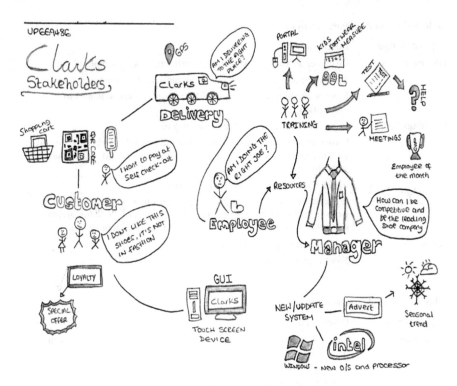

Fig. 1 Change analysis

with system boundary analysis and analysis of existing and future system. For the manager, the use of an "archaic" computerized system has two consequences on his job. Firstly, he has to manually calculate daily, weekly and monthly sales. Secondly, he does not have the possibility to achieve an online stock availability checking. Therefore, the implementation of an advanced check-out system could potentially improve the efficacy and effectiveness of the shop management. Figure 1 illustrates a rich picture as a result of change analysis conducted by the student to understand existing job practices and to outline the potential improvements and problems of the new system.

Table 5 is an extract of holistic multi-criteria benefit analysis realized by the student where there is a description of the pro's and con's of existing job practices and the pro's and con's of the potential future practices.

Table 5 Holistic multi-criteria benefit analysis

	Change in Behaviour/Potential Future System		
Negative impact and influence benefit	*Negatives of the future system* May take time for the manager to learn the new system properly. Customers that lack in IT may find the self-checkout difficult to use—therefore extra staff may be required to help out the customers. Can be costly and may not be satisfactory. If system fails will require further assistance (i.e. engineers/technicians)	*Positives of the future system* The self-checkout will speed up the process and reduce the workload for the manager, as he can manage other responsibilities. Having a new database system will minimise the duplication of data, so less work for the manager. New operating and processer will speed up work. Also the online portal will save manager time as employees can refer to instead of asking the manager for guidance	Positive impact and influence benefit
	Negatives of the current system The current system is not touch screen therefore it requires using the mouse a lot, which isn't really effective in a retail shop. Calculating the sales cost is manual therefore possibility of getting errors in figures when the manager does he calculations manually. The manager cannot order product from another store electronically for the customer	*Positives of the current system* Manager finds the current system simple to use, as he's been using it for many years. The stock control is automated, so the manager knows the system will automatically pick it up when more than three products of one item is sold, and order it automatically, therefore it saves manager time. Kids feet are automatically measured using the iPad system, which gives an accurate value	
	No change in behaviour/current system		

5 Conclusion

The use in practice of ST toolbox supports constructive learning and develops critical analysis skills of the students who will be future systems analysts or designers. The overall intention is to encourage critical analysis and reflection alongside development of understanding of business processes. The two examples provided in this paper illustrate how the ST toolbox can benefit student learning about the exploration of multiple perspectives associated with systems design and organizational change as well as support the development of work related skills.

References

1. Besson, P., Rowe, F.: Strategizing information systems-enabled organizational transformation: a transdisciplinary review and new directions. J. Strateg. Inf. Syst. **21**, 103–124 (2012)
2. Kawalek, J.P.: Rethinking Information Systems in Organizations: Integrating Or-ganizational Problem Solving. Routledge, London (2008)
3. March, J.G.: Exploration and exploitation in organizational learning. Organ. Sci. **2**(1), 71–87 (1991)
4. Mumford, E.: Redesigning Human Systems. IRM Press, London (2003)
5. Checkland, P.: Systems Thinking, Systems Practice. Wiley, Chichester (1981)
6. Bednar, P.M., Day, L.: Systemic combinatory use of brainstorming, mind-maps and rich pictures for analysis of complex problem spaces. In: Proceedings of ECRM 2009. The 8th European Conference on Research Methods in Business and Management, pp. 38–47. Valetta, (2009). (22–23 June 2009)
7. Mathiassen, L., Munk-Madsen, A., Nielsen, P.A., Stage, J.: Object Oriented Anal-ysis and Design. Marko, Aalborg (2000)
8. Bednar, P.M.: A contextual integration of individual and organizational learning perspectives as part of IS analysis. Informing Sci. J. **3**(3), 145–156 (2000)
9. Bednar, P.M., Sadok, M., Shiderova, V.: Socio-Technical toolbox for business analysis in practice. In: Caporarello, L., Di Martino, B., Martinez, M. (eds.) Smart Organizations and Smart Artifacts: Fostering Interaction Between People, Technologies and Processes. Lecture Notes in Information Systems and Organization, vol. 7. pp. 219–228. Springer (2014)
10. Orlikowski, W.J., Iacono, C.S.: Research commentary: desperately seeking the "IT" in IT research—a call to theorizing the IT artifact? Inf. Syst. Res. **12**(2), 121–134 (2001)
11. Alter, S.: 18 reasons why it-reliant work systems should replace "the it artifact" as the core subject matter of the is field. Commun. Assoc. Inf. Syst. **12**, 365–394 (2003)
12. Checkland, P.: Towards a systems-based methodology for real-world problem-solving. J. Appl. Syst. Eng. **3**(2), 87–116 (1972)
13. Churchman, C.W.: The design of inquiring systems. Basis Books, New York (1971)
14. Langefors, B.: Theoretical Analysis of Information Systems. Studentlitteratur, Lund (1966)
15. Mumford, E., Henshall, D.: A Participative Approach to the Design of Computer Systems. Associated Business Press, London (1978)
16. Langefors, B.: Essays on Infology,—Summing up and Planning for the Future. Studentlitteratur, Lund (1995)
17. D'Atri, A., De Marco, M.: Interdisciplinary Aspects of Information Systems Studies. Springer, Heidelberg (2008). ISBN 978-3-7908-2009-6
18. Luna-Reyes, L.F., Zhang, J., Gil-Garcia, J.R., Cresswell, A.M.: Information system development as emergent socio-technical change: a practice approach. Eur. J. Inf. Syst. **14**, 93–105 (2005)
19. Checkland, P., Holwell, S.: Information, Systems and Information Systems. Wiley, Chichester (1998)
20. Checkland, P., Scholes, J.: Soft Systems Methodology in Action. Wiley, Chich-ester (1990)
21. Stowell, F., West, D.: Client-led Design: A Systemic Approach to Information Systems Definition. McGraw-Hill, London (1994)
22. Bednar, P.M., Welch, C.: Contextual inquiry and socio-technical practice. Kybernetes **43** (9/10) (2014)

The University in the Polis: An Emerging Role of Democratic Intermediary in e-Participation?

Marina Ribaudo, Claudio Torrigiani, Fiorella De Cindio
and Mauro Palumbo

Abstract e-participation enables citizens' voices to be heard more clearly and frequently, but does not self-implement. Strategies should be planned, models should be followed, the public actor should encourage administrative and political changes. In this paper the well established OECD levels of engagement (information, consultation, public participation) are described, with reference to enabling digital technologies: a need of trustworthy intermediaries emerges. This conceptual framework drives the presentation of some experiences that recently took place in the city of Genoa, highlighting the emerging role of the university as a democratic intermediary.

Keywords Democratic intermediary · Participation levels · e-participation

1 Introduction

The crisis of representative democracy is now quite evident and involves both political parties, as organizations representing citizens, and institutions, legitimized by vote to govern. The concentration of power in global players, far beyond the control of nation states, reduces the real power of democracy. The growth of inequalities beyond a certain limit erodes trust in the formal equality of citizens and

M. Ribaudo (✉) · C. Torrigiani · M. Palumbo
University of Genoa, Genoa, Italy
e-mail: ribaudo@unige.it

C. Torrigiani
e-mail: torrigiani@unige.it

M. Palumbo
e-mail: palumbo@unige.it

F. De Cindio
University of Milan, Milan, Italy
e-mail: fiorella.decindio@unimi.it

© Springer International Publishing Switzerland 2016
T. Torre et al. (eds.), *Empowering Organizations*, Lecture Notes in Information
Systems and Organisation 11, DOI 10.1007/978-3-319-23784-8_6

the employment crisis pushes citizens towards non-conventional forms of production and consumption. Hence, a crisis of governance is added to that of democratic institutions: less entitled to govern, they cannot always have an impact on the real determinants of people's lives. Along with a growing sense of apathy and impotence, a demand for bottom-up participation is also growing: therefore, institutions seek for new forms of citizens' inclusion in decision-making processes to give voice to the needs of direct democracy and to restore confidence and legitimacy.

Participation trust offered by ICTs fits into this framework. This paper aims to show that, without solid theoretical assumptions, it is not possible to design appropriate modalities of participation of citizens in decision-making processes, that make use of the ICTs as a fundamental element. In the digital era, participatory processes that do not integrate online and offline modalities are not sustainable; by reflecting on how these opportunities are configured and how they can be adapted to the requirements of participation, it is possible to propose concrete and appropriate solutions.

While a frequent role assigned to the Internet is disintermediation, in the public sector a new role for intermediaries emerges in the literature. Edwards [12] suggests to consider moderators of public forums as *democratic intermediaries* between citizens and public institutions. Taking inspiration from experiences such as MySociety,[1] and its pioneering activities with projects such as FixMyStreet, TheyWorkForYou, etc., [6] call for "an entirely new kind of public agency, designed to forge fresh links between communication and politics and to connect the voice of the people more meaningfully to the daily activities of democratic institutions". Also [2] identify the need for new, third millennium bodies to lend stability to various cultural initiatives: although they do not refer to the digital world, the kind of body they outline, called Participatory Foundation, inspired the statute of the RCM[2] Participatory Foundation, promoted by the Civic Informatics Laboratory at the University of Milan to provide continuity to the RCM initiative, one of the first community network in Europe [10]. Reflecting on these experiences, [8] points out the need of identifying such third party bodies as guarantors of the public dialogue in the design of democratic deliberative digital environments.

This paper pursues these considerations by applying them at the case of the city of Genoa, where the municipality undertook some initiatives of e-government and e-participation. In some of them the University of Genoa already played a role that somehow corresponds to the pattern sketched above. From the discussion of these cases, we envisage the great potential that the university, in its role of third-party, can play in the public sphere. The balance of the paper is as follows. Section 2 presents different levels of participation, also discussing how new technologies can help to bridge the increasing gap between citizens and political institutions. Section 3 introduces some of the initiatives that took place in the city of Genoa, and Sect. 4 concludes this work discussing the role universities can play in this context.

---

[1]http://www.mysociety.org.

[2]www.fondazionercm.it.

2 Levels of Participation

One key issue in relation to participation—that certainly involves participation processes supported by ICTs—is the transposition of these processes into decisions. The possibility for participation processes of directly influencing decisions, attaining the deliberative level [14], depends on the role they have with respect to the formal decision-making processes. This role is not defined once and for all, but is object of regulation processes and progressive institutionalization, that may lead to:

- The definition of behavioral codes in the context of a specific participation process, like for example the subscription of a "participatory contract" in the initiatives promoted by the RCM Foundation [8].
- The enactment of specific laws or rules binding at the territorial or thematic level.

The influence of these processes on the decisions arises however, in different ways, depending on whether the participation:

- Is promoted "from above" by the public actor which, for institutional role, holds the decision-making power (the so-called *top-down* participation). In this case, the participation should have already defined its status within the decision-making process and the rules pre-define the mode and the space given to it at the deliberative level. There is therefore a level of meta-participation within which the public actor decides who will participate, what matters, when and how, and, above all, with what degree of decision-making power.
- Is promoted "from below", thanks to the initiative of citizens who hold a stake but do not have decision-making power on the issue under consideration (the so-called *bottom-up* participation). In this case, the participation attempts to create spaces within a decision-making process that had not solicited nor foresaw rules or space for participatory decision-making instances. This second mode is to be distinguished based on the fact that it has local character or not: citizens may be activated by a particularistic question about "their backyard"[3] or, conversely, as a matter of general interest. Whatever the level concerned, we can say positively that "democracy is substantial (real) when people can participate in, and influence, the choices that are relevant to their life".[4]

In top-down participation usually the public actor makes the rules and enforces them, while in the bottom-up case, the rules are normally the result of a negotiation process between the citizens who have decided to take action. In this second case, compliance with the rules is more easily subject to spontaneous sanctioning of deviant behaviors since the rules are not defined ex ante, but are the result of negotiation processes.

---

[3]To echo the Not In My Back Yard syndrome.
[4]Mary Kaldor, Opening Speech World Forum for Democracy, Council of Europe, Strasbourg, November 2013.

Bottom-up participation may be more susceptible to conflicts *among participants*, which could be called "regulatory" because somehow functional to define the "rules of game"; bottom-up participation is also the subject of a greater social control from the bottom and spread, which can contain in a spontaneous way such conflict. Moreover, conflicts may arise *between participants and decision-makers* too, depending on the way in which the participation result is incorporated or not in the decision. Also in this case, becomes therefore essential the support of a participatory contract that governs the interaction between the citizens and the decision-maker.

By contrast, top-down participation is generally regulated a priori, then apparently less prone to "regulatory conflict", since there are rules and they are clear. But just because it is stimulated by the decision-maker, the more difficult it benefits from wide-ranging social control from below, while it remains in charge to those who have promoted to mediate and manage conflicts and emerging instances. When promoting a top-down participation process, the decision-maker must therefore adjust and operate it with much forethought and awareness or, easily, it will result in highly conflictual situations. A problem that arises in this case is that the decision-maker often organizes the participation using implicit assumptions on the behavior of the participants, inspired by instrumental rationality. However, usually among the participants instrumental and expressive instances are much more interrelated (see in this regard the contribution of [19] in response to the paradox of free riders highlighted by [15].

In both cases, the participatory process will succeed if there is clarity on the following two key issues [8]:

- The "stakes", with a balance between commitment and expected return. Participants (citizens, politicians, civil servants) should clearly know "what will I gain?" from their commitments. Along with the rules of the game, the participatory contract must explain this point. This applies, even if in a different way, also in bottom-up processes: "I participate if it can change things".
- The "actor" who enforces the rules, namely the participatory contract negotiated between the social actors involved. As already observed in Sect. 1, in the literature on the topic the figure of the *democratic intermediary* [12] has emerged, generalizable to the role of a third-party, and we claim that, in several cases, universities (or their expressions, such as the RCM Foundation) can play this role of democratic intermediary, being meeting places for multidisciplinary languages and cultures, and guarantors of participation processes, thus preventing them degenerating into demagogic and manipulator processes.

Let us now look at *e-participation* and at the role that ICTs play in the two modes of activation of the process. Different levels of participation can be identified and this issue has been extensively treated in the literature, where different classifications have been proposed. In this paper we refer to the model introduced in [5] that suggests three main levels of involvement (information, consultation, and public participation), based on the direction of information flow (one-way, two-ways) and on the intensity of the relationship between citizens and institutions. Other classifications exist, and the interested reader can check the literature for more details (see for example [1, 17, 22]).

2.1 Information Level

Today, governments feel with a greater urgency a duty of transparency, which is actually enshrined in the law for many years. On the technological level, ICTs facilitate access to information to those citizens who spontaneously activate, but only to the extent that the public administration (PA) is sufficiently transparent and provides access to such information. A government that wants to inform the citizens —also in view of a subsequent involvement at higher levels (consultation, public participation)—is potentially facilitated by ICTs but, in this respect, there is a problem of inequality among citizens' access to ICTs and then to the processes of e-participation. The existence of the digital divide, of course, does not absolve the government from using the full potential of ICTs for citizens' participation. Rather, the gap in terms of civic participation is one more reason to reduce the digital divide itself. We can frame this problem from different perspectives:

- If we consider the presence of the *supporting infrastructure*, different situations emerge, with not covered specific areas in which it is impossible or very hard for citizens to access the information[5] conveyed by the government.
- If we consider the differences in *socio-economic status* and the availability of economic resources, the disadvantaged segments of the population are easily excluded from access to the network and participatory processes channeled through it.
- If we consider the *generational differences*, we realize that large segments of the population—particularly the elderly less educated people—could be excluded from these processes since they are not accustomed to the use of ICTs although, potentially, they are more active and involved than the younger. Conversely, the young and very young people (the so-called "digital natives"), are certainly facilitated with respect to the medium but often less interested in active engagement.

In this regard, the increasing tendency of the political class to use rhetorically ICTs and especially social media to promote and expand the participation of (younger) citizens in political life, seems designed to easily obtain legitimacy and presumed consent (the "I like") rather than democratization of decision-making

---

[5]This is not dissimilar from a participatory process in presence, taking place in areas which are difficult to reach by citizens; in this case it would be possible to introduce the idea of a *physical divide* for in presence participatory processes.

processes. The use of social media such as Facebook and Twitter for the management of public dialogue with citizens is more and more widespread [3, 18] but another possible choice is that of implementing dedicated platforms that use the social media as a vehicle for advertising participatory initiatives to make them as inclusive as possible [20]. Environments such as Facebook and Twitter, born for social interaction, can be used by public agencies as an additional channel for the dissemination of information one-way (broadcasting) with occasional and ephemeral two-ways interaction/dialogue. In Sect. 3, the Facebook pages which are presented show that this channel is appropriate to broadcast information easily accessible and shareable by the public, much less to encourage their active participation, except in the case of emergency management.

3 Consultation Level

If we consider consultation, ICTs can facilitate both top-down and bottom-up participation but have a potentially more ambiguous role, at least for three reasons:

- The first reason is due to a problem of *user identity*, namely the fact that in online communication we cannot be certain of the identity of the person we interact with.
- The second reason is related to the fact that, by involving substantial numbers of citizens, communication processes at the base of the participatory process will most often be *asynchronous* and subject to the typical characteristics of online communication. The meaning of the sentences written by another person is less immediate since it is not supported by non-verbal communication[6] but it has the advantage of forcing those who want to be included to explain clearly and unambiguously their message, also allowing them to combine/attach written references and links to the sources used, making messages potentially less ideological.
- The third reason is related to the *interpretation* of the messages conveyed in these participatory processes. Here come into play, as intermediaries of communication processes, actors who play a key role and may moderate, reformulate or aggregate what expressed by citizens, facilitate discussion and bring a number of instances, suggestions or opinions to the next (deliberative) level. The moderator-facilitator of the process, in analogy to what should be done in presence, must ensure that those who have expressed a position recognize themselves in the interpretation and synthesis made and returned as part of the result of the process. This process of interpretation and synthesis of the positions

---

[6]The conventional symbols (e.g. emoticons) used to substitute for this deficiency have limited efficacy compared to non-verbal communication in presence.

expressed by the citizens is transparent only to the extent that it is *public* and *accessible to stakeholders*. This allows the control of the facilitators from the participants. Under these accessibility conditions, online participation may present less risk of manipulation than offline participation, where the processes of interpretation are more elusive and less easily controlled. For both online and offline participation mediation transparent rules are necessary as well as a code of ethics of the facilitator [21].

3.1 Public Participation Level

At this level, the involved citizens share decision-making power with the actor who, institutionally, should take decisions on the considered issue. It is worth noting that to some extent top-down and bottom-up participation patterns must converge at this level, otherwise the decision might have a political weight (depending on the size of the movement that expresses it) but without cogency legislation.

Many of the limitations and advantages mentioned for the previous levels also apply to this one, with different shades. Certainly ICTs can facilitate and reinforce participation, but this possibility depends on the way in which this level is linked with information and consultation. While in offline participation the actor may have strong difficulties in accessing information and debates when called to contribute in decision-making, in online participation this can be much easier. Imagine a citizen who should express his position on one issue, going to an offline consultation and selecting one alternative on a white paper: even if he has some doubts, he does not have the possibility of coming back to the debates he heard or the articles he read. In an online consultation the same citizen could connect to an online platform and select one alternative among several possibilities: it is easy to provide him with links to all related information, and these materials are rapidly sortable and accessible with few clicks on the same platform. While in offline participation informing citizens is costly, time consuming and usually time bounded, in online participation these limits can be easily overcome.

Finally, we emphasize the following two aspects. Firstly, there is a specific phase of the participatory process, the definition of the possible decision alternatives, which is placed in between the consultation and public participation levels, which can take advantage of software and tools for idea gathering, which offer a powerful technological answer to be combined with the most adequate management of the participatory processes. These tools, thanks to their tagging and ranking features, prompt the emergence of decision alternatives among different proposals on the same subject. Secondly, at this stage and at all considered levels, it is convenient to adopt in a balanced way online and offline modes of participation and qualitative and quantitative research techniques [16].

4 Online Participation Examples in Genoa

This section introduces some e-participation initiatives that took place in the municipality of Genoa, with a special attention to those in which the university played an active role. The first four experiences show different examples of top-down processes, the last two are bottom-up processes, promoted directly by citizens.

1. Urban Center. One of the first experience of top-down participation is the Urban Center,[7] whose development started in 2006 thanks to project funded by the Italian Government in a call for e-democracy. The aim of the project was the design and the development of a virtual Urban Center (i.e., a web portal) for Genoa, since the town was witnessing a significant urban transformation phase. Hence the idea of proposing an online space that could (1) help the administration sharing with citizens information on urban planning and territorial policies; (2) promote new urban projects; (3) gather suggestions from stakeholders and citizens; (4) promote people's participation in the municipality decision-making process.

Discussions involving citizens and experts were carried out during the project, the most significant being probably the one taking place in 2009 on the project of a motorway by-pass of the city [4]. In that case, most of the activities were organized in presence (offline), in form of public meetings with experts, an independent board of faculty members of the University of Turin, and local communities. The online Urban Center has been mostly used to distribute material (institutional acts, different projects proposals, FAQs,…), to broadcast news and collect questions from the citizens in thematic forums, in a *mixture* of offline and online phases. The University of Genoa has been involved in the project as a technology partner while the University of Turin played the role of the democratic intermediary.

2. Facebook pages. In 2009, following the experience of many others, the municipality of Genoa launched its Facebook pages[8] to broadcast news (bus strike, weather information,…) and events (concerts, workshops and conferences,…), and to promote the interaction between the administration and the citizens. These pages enriched the institutional websites, offering citizens the opportunity to share their opinions via (moderated) comments and express their preferences through the "I like" button. However, there was not much space for active engagement: in this case Facebook pages offered another information/advertising channel with minor room for citizens' feedback.

3. Authority for Public Local Services. A third top-down e-participation initiative is the one promoted by the Authority for Public Local Services,[9] an independent body responsible for the monitoring of the services provided by the municipality. Among the participatory activities of the Authority we recall the online space allowing citizens to report the inefficiencies encountered when using

---

[7]http://www.urbancenter.comune.genova.it/.

[8]https://it-it.facebook.com/citta.genova.

[9]http://www.asplgenova.it/.

the services offered by the municipality through a web form, whose content is forwarded to the competent office; best practices can be reported too, the most interesting ones being filtered and published on the website. The Authority also encourages the notification of citizens' alerts about problems to be fixed, in the style of the popular FixMyStreet service already replicated in several cities in Italy.[10]

4. ComunaliGenova2012. The examples discussed so far see the PA as *the subject* promoting citizens' engagement, in a pure top-down approach, placing at the first level, the information level, in some cases with (moderate) interaction with citizens.

A different experience is the one carried out during the municipal election of 2012 with the goal of stimulating a stronger involvement of citizens. This time, a democratic intermediary[11] has opened a website, called ComunaliGenova2012[12] (CG2012), based on the open source platform openDCN, where DCN stands for Deliberative Community Networks. CG2012 is a participative platform, set up by the University of Genoa as an independent body not engaged in the campaign, where the different social actors play on a neutral ground, in the style of the analogous initiatives undertaken during the Milan municipal elections in 2006 [9] and 2011 [11].

In that period, users could enroll to the platform and introduce themselves as candidates in a dedicated area where they could post information on their curriculum vitae and their electoral program. 291 users enrolled to CG2012, 73 of them as candidates, who considered it as yet another form of advertising for their political candidature. Problems have been reported by citizens in the Problem&Proposal space, many on them accompanied by possible solutions. Among the suggested topics we recall the water purifier, the difficult access to the sea, the role of ICTs in a smart city, the lack of libraries and green areas, and mobility issues.

As discussed in [11], the municipal elections are an effective opportunity for promoting online dialogue among citizens and between citizens and local institutions at the urban level. The electoral period is especially suitable for triggering participation of the political actors, especially of the candidates who, if elected, will become citizens' representatives.

Although the website was intended to survive after the elections this was not the case. Indeed, despite the initial enthusiasm, and even though some requests to the institutional actors, the municipality has not embraced the initiative and the website has slowly lost its visitors. Candidates who have been elected, once reached their goal, disappeared; some of them have also asked to the administrator of the

---

[10]Let us recall for example the early initiative on road safety held in Milan in 2008 (http://www.sicurezzastradale.partecipami.it), the Internet Reporting System launched in Venice in May 2008 (http://iris.comune.venezia.it) which collected since then 20392 reports, and the experience of Udine (http://www.epart.it/udine) based on the custom technology ePart for urban maintenance, well integrated in the website of the municipality.

[11]The University of Genoa, with he help of the Civic Informatics Laboratory of the University of Milan and of the RCM Foundation.

[12]http://www.comunaligenova2012.it, now archived at http://comunaligenova2012.opendcn.org/.

platform to remove their online presence, probably willing to delete the "digital traces" of their political experience.

The lack of interest of the municipality for this experience is quite surprising if we consider the role of Genoa as a smart city. Indeed, Genoa is probably still closer to the technological view of a smart city rather then to the more recent idea of a "human" smart city populated by smart communities [13], although some experiences exist, documented as results of European projects [7].

Summarizing, the case of the Urban Center was a good example of how difficult is moving from information to consultation of citizens, especially in cases where the decision that should be taken closely affects their lives and their properties. The greater success achieved by the platform ComunaliGenova 2012 in listening and dialogue with citizens was limited to the election period, while the period after revealed the utilitarian use by candidates who have opted not to continue the confrontation. The initiative promoted by the Authority for Local Public Services— although apparently little known—is interesting both for the presence of an independent body that plays the role of mediator with the municipal administration, and because the focus on the inefficiencies of municipal services suggests more a function of signaling that of listening with a potential direct impact on concrete decisions that affect the lives of citizens.

5. OpenGenova. Moving to the third level of Sect. 2, public participation, it is worth mentioning the *bottom-up* experience which started in 2013 thanks to a group of citizens who have launched the group OpenGenova. This is a community of citizens, who meet mostly online on the group's website,[13] discuss about the problems of the town, propose possible solutions. Members of the community can also publish online calls for *offline laboratories* on a given subject and try to involve in the activities other members or new participants. One of the first laboratory, for example, promoted co-working trying to aggregate young people in a shared place where they can exchange ideas and collaboratively develop innovative projects. Another one suggested to transform a street in Genoa into a new "promenade" with the elimination of some parking spaces, the widening of the existing pavement, and the installation of kiosks for public exercises.

Interestingly, this group has recently involved the Centro Est municipality[14] and organized a context called *Partecip@*. A call for projects has been advertised asking groups of citizens to suggest improvements for buildings and other public spaces to be renewed. On its side, the municipality has allocated a monetary budget for the winners of the context. Citizens were not only asked for contribution with ideas and projects, but residents in the area were also involved in the selection of the best proposals: voting has been organized through a polling, opened on the Urban Center website, in a short circuit between bottom-up and top-down

---

[13]http://www.opengenova.org/.

[14]From the administrative point of view, the city of Genoa is divided into nine municipalities, each one corresponding to a different area in the town.

participation, whose convergence has been suggested in Sect. 2 for the public participation to become effective.

OpenGenova, is a case of bottom-up public participation that illustrates, on the one hand, the need for the right mix of online and offline participation moments, which have different functions in the activation process of the citizens, on the other hand, the need for these initiatives to be recognized by those who have formal decision-making power so that the direct initiatives of the citizens can take effect.

6. Angeli del fango. Finally, another bottom-up participation process which is worth mentioning is the one known as "Angeli del fango" which has seen the mobilization of citizens in the case of the two floods that have hurt the city in 2011 and 2014. In both cases, groups of citizens, mainly students, auto-organized to help removing mud and debris in the areas affected by the flood. In these cases, the mobilization took place thanks to the use of Facebook and Twitter which show their power and immediacy in emergency management.

4.1   Online Survey

Do the recent experiences discussed so far mean that time is now mature for online participation? Probably yes, but with some care as we will discuss in the remaining part of this section.

At the beginning of 2014, an online survey on the quality of the municipality ICT services has been administered to citizens in an attempt to monitor the quality of the PA online support, and the results have been summarized in a report delivered to the managers responsible of these services. The survey, prepared by university experts, has been advertised through a link in the homepage of the website of the municipality, without any other action from the PA. Therefore it has been filled by citizens who—for any reason—landed on this web page and voluntarily decided to follow the link and answer. In addition to the questions on the online services, three multiple choice questions on e-participation have been added to understand the needs of the sample of respondents. During a period of 6 months (Jan–Jun 2014) 2023 questionnaires have been filled, but only 347 have been completed until the end and thus contain also the answers to the last questions on e-participation.

Due to a lack of space we cannot discuss here all the results of the survey, but we just stress that, when asked "Which tools do you consider more appropriate to facilitate citizens' participation in the municipality decision-making process?" respondents selected as their first option the answer "Consultation within an online platform for e-democracy" (with 168 answers out of 347 participants, about 48 % of the sample), immediately followed by "Public meeting" (96 answers, 28 %) and "Survey filled at the municipal office" (80 answers, 23 %).

Even though the first option has been selected by half of the respondents, the second and third options propose indeed offline activities and thus their popularity suggests a need for both forms of participation, online *and* offline, to guarantee everyone a chance for active engagement, somehow contrasting both digital *and* physical divide. This is particularly interesting if we consider the fact that most likely the respondents who completed the survey are those who are already familiar with the use of ICTs but, despite this, they suggest an associated use of online and in presence activities.

When asked "Which issues do you consider more interesting for citizens' participation in the municipality decision-making process?" respondents selected as their first two options "Mobility" (230 answers, 62 %) and "Ecology and environment" (173 answers, 50 %). The other options which received high scores are "Urban redevelopment" (149 answers, 43 %), "Security" (145 answers, 42 %), and "Education and culture" (136 answers, 39 %). This result shows citizens' interest in those aspects of daily life they would like to be able to discuss with the administration. Other choices, like for example the participatory budget or the city development planning did not get the same score, perhaps because the respondents did not feel competent enough in these fields. Top rated options seem to confirm that initiatives like the one supported by the Authority for Public Local Services might work well is sufficiently advertised and, above all, if followed by practical implementation.

Going back to the initial question, time seems mature for citizens' participation that should be implemented in different forms (with and without ICTs) and citizens are willing to get involved, specially for those decisions affecting their daily life.

5 Conclusions

The availability and dissemination of appropriate technologies and the desire of participation, top-down and bottom-up, converge in generating a large number of experiences of e-participation and e-democracy, which, however, have several limitations.

A first problem is the lack of clarity, except in some cases, on how the results of participation will be included in the decision-making process. This lack of clarity is both legal-administrative and methodological since it is not always completely clear how the official decision-making processes will take into account the results of participation: In what way? With which amplitude? Moreover, too little attention is given to the techniques used to collect citizens' views, summarize them, and put in relation with decision-making processes. If they are collected with qualitative methods, they leave room for interpretation of the decision-makers but, if they are standardized in a distorting way, they fail in respecting the spirit of participation.

The second limit is the way in which the processes of information and feedback are managed. What is the appropriate level of information to be disseminated to the public? Too much information is likely to create confusion and to involve only people sufficiently educated on the issue or with sufficient level of literacy; too little information is likely to simplify the problems and artificially produce biased opinions. Similarly, what feedback should be provided to those who participate?

Models of total transparency may be practiced only by those who have enough time and cultural resources. It is clear, however, that both in top-down and bottom-up participation processes, the presence of a democratic intermediary ensuring all participants in relation to the adopted method and the derived results should be guaranteed.

Among the cases described in Sect. 3, the Urban Center and ComunaliGenova2012 have seen the involvement of the University of Genoa, with different processes and outcomes in relation to the issues addressed by the participatory processes. These examples do not certainly provide a conclusive proof of a vocation of the university for this role, but lead us to reflect on the strengths and weaknesses of the academic institution in assuming the responsibilities of democratic intermediary. Indeed, the presence of such democratic intermediary opens, in our opinion, an ample room for active engagement of the university, which embodies the values and incorporates the competencies of merit, method and technology to play a facilitation-mediation role of participatory processes, ensuring in a transparent way its real independence.

Some well established examples of such democratic intermediaries already exist, for example the RCM Foundation which brings together—in different roles—local institutions, university, schools, private enterprises, and representatives of civil society. This is indeed a big challenge that should be urgently addressed, specially to foster a stronger integration between the universities and their urban territories, thus stimulating the third mission of the university to qualify the *Third Millennium University*.

References

1. Arnstein, S.R.: A ladder of citizen participation. J. Am. Plan. Assoc. **35**(4), 216–224 (1969)
2. Bellezza, E., Florian, F.: Le fondazioni del terzo millennio. Pubblico e privato per il non-profit. Passigli editori (1998) (in Italian)
3. Bertot, J., Jaeger, P., Hansen, D.: The impact of polices on government social media usage: issues, challenges, and recommendations. Govern. Inf. Q. **29**(1), 30–40 (2012)
4. Bobbio, L.: Prove di democrazia deliberativa. Parole chiave **43**,185–203 (2011) (in Italian)
5. Caddy, J., Vergez, C.: Citizens as Partners: Information, Consultation and Public Participation in Policy-Making. OECD Publishing, (2001)
6. Coleman, S., Blumer, J.: The Internet and Democratic Citizenship: Theory, Practice and Policy. Cambridge University Press (2009)
7. Concilio, G., De Bonis, L., Marsh, J., Trapani, F.: Urban smartness: perspectives arising in the Periphéria project. J.Knowl. Econ. **4**(2), 205–216 (2013)
8. De Cindio, F.: Guidelines for designing deliberative digital habitats: learning from e-participation for open data initiatives. J. Commun. Inf. **2**(8) (2012)
9. De Cindio, F., Di Loreto, I., Peraboni, C.: Moments and modes for triggering civic participation at the urban level, pp. 97–113. Information Science Reference, IGI Global, Hershey (2008)
10. De Cindio, F., Gentile, O., Grew, P., Redolfi, D.: Community networks: rules of behavior and social structure. Inf. Soc. **19**(5), 395–406 (2003)

11. De Cindio, F., Krzatala-Jaworska, E., Sonnante, L.: Problems&Proposals, a tool for collecting citizens' intelligence. In: CSCW2012 Workshop on Collective Intelligence as Community Discourse and Action, Seattle (2012)
12. Edwards, A.R.: The moderator as an emerging democratic intermediary: the role of the moderator in internet discussions about public issues. Info. Pol. 7(1) (2002)
13. Hollands, R.: Will the real smart city please standup? City Anal. Urban Trends Cult. Theory Policy Action 12(3), 303–320 (2008)
14. House, E., Howe, K.: Deliberative democratic evaluation. In: Ryan, E., De Stefano, L. (eds.) Evaluation as a Democratic Process, New Directions for Program Evaluation, vol. 85. Jossey Bass, San Francisco (2000)
15. Olson, M.: The Logic of Collective Action: Public Goods and the Theory of Groups. Harvard University Press (1971)
16. Palumbo, M., Torrigiani, C.: Participatory evaluation in the field of social policies: why, who, what, where, how and when. Working Paper Series, FPeV 25 (2013)
17. Pastore, V.: Si fa presto a dire valutazione. Una riflessione su attori, finalità, tecniche e strumenti. Rivista Trimestrale di Scienza dell'Amministrazione 4, 73–108 (2010). In Italian
18. Picazo-Vela, S., GutiÃ©rrez-MartÃ-nez, I., Luna-Reyes, L.: Understanding risks, benefits, and strategic alternatives of social media applications in the public sector. Govern. Inf. Q. 29 (4), 504–511 (2012)
19. Pizzorno, A.: (1978). Political exchange and collective identity in industrial conflict. In: Crouch, C., Pizzorno, A. (eds.) The resurgence of class conflict in Western Europe since 1968, vol. 2, pp. 277–298. London
20. Senato della Repubblica. I media civici in ambito parlamentare (2013) (in Italian). http://www.senato.it/service/PDF/PDFServer/BGT/00739736.pdf
21. Torrigiani, C.: Partecipazione e valutazione partecipata. In: Palumbo, M., Torrigiani, C. (eds.) La partecipazione tra ricerca e valutazione, pp. 112–134. Franco Angeli (2009) (in Italian)
22. Wiedemann, P., Femers, S.: Public participation in waste management decision making: analysis and management of conflicts. J. Hazard. Mater. 33(3), 355–368 (1993)

Designing a New Model of DMS for Developing a Resilient Community

Andrea Paletti and Stefano Za

Abstract The increasing number of people affected and the economic loss caused by disasters and daily emergencies need necessary a change in the disaster management approach. The Hyogo framework has introduced the concept of resilience underlining the importance of prevention and first aid in disaster management. However, after a first analysis, the existing models of disaster management systems (DMS) do not seem to follow this strategy. This paper seeks to design a new model that considers the Hyogo framework and that includes citizens and volunteers in the disaster management organization in order to decrease vulnerabilities and to develop resilient communities.

Keywords Volunteering · Active citizenship · Italian Civil Protection · Disaster management systems · Crowd sourcing

1 Introduction

Disasters are becoming more frequent and destructive than in the past [1]. From 2001 to 2010, the EM-DAT database (http://www.emdat.be/) registered 38,400 disasters in the world. The trends show that the number of people affected and the economic loss are increasing because of the vulnerable socio-economic conditions and of the lack of organization [2]. For the same reasons, the number of deaths and injured in daily emergencies is increasing. For example, the International

A. Paletti
London School of Economics (LSE), London, UK
e-mail: a.paletti@lse.ac.uk

S. Za (✉)
eCampus University, Novedrate, CO, Italy
e-mail: stefano.za@uniecampus.it; sza@luiss.it

S. Za
CeRSI – LUISS Guido Carli University, Rome, Italy

© Springer International Publishing Switzerland 2016
T. Torre et al. (eds.), *Empowering Organizations*, Lecture Notes in Information Systems and Organisation 11, DOI 10.1007/978-3-319-23784-8_7

Federation of the Red Cross (IFRC) has estimated that the number of deaths caused by car accidents will increase from 1 million per year of 2010 to 2 million per year in 2020 causing economic loss estimated between 1 to 3 % of the gross national product of the affected countries [3]. The UK Red Cross has calculated that the 41.4 % of accidents happen at home, the 19.5 % happen on roads, the 17.1 % during sport activities and the 15.2 % at work [4]. In addition, researches about the human behaviour during disasters and emergencies show that untrained people are more likely to have an inappropriate and risky behaviour [5]. Immediate first aid plus an appropriate behaviour are then crucial in daily emergencies as well as in disasters in order to reduce the number of deaths and of the economic loss [6]. For example, to save the life of somebody affected by a heart attack it is necessary to provide the cardiopulmonary resuscitation manoeuvre (CPR) in 4 min. Then the ambulance has to arrive in 12 min to provide early defibrillation [7]. The data of the American Hearth Foundation, show that the USA counts more than 424,000 people per year (more than 1000 per day) affected by a heart attack and the 90 % died. In addition, time and first aid are important also during natural disasters. During the tsunami of 2008 the 82 % of deaths was registered the first day and the remaining 18 % by the first week. [8]. Moreover, evidence has shown that also the most advance organization and countries are not able to provide an immediate first aid for temporal and spatial issues that cannot be overcome by the current emergency organizations. For example, it has been calculated that the 90 % of the ambulances in France arrive in 14 min in urban areas and in 18 min in rural areas [3]. For disasters like tsunami, floods and earthquakes, international and organized aids usually arrive after 72 h [9]. The only way to save victims of emergencies and disasters is to act immediately utilizing the people and the resources that are already in the place of the emergency or of the disasters [10]. This means to be a resilient community. Indeed, resiliency could be defined as "the capability of a system to maintain its functions and structure in the face of internal and external change and to degrade gracefully when it must" [11], hence it also implies a "system's capability to recover to normal operational state with all available resources" [12]. This revolutionary thought is mainly underlined in the Hyogo framework.

In 2005 in Kobe, Hyogo, Japan, the World Conference on Disaster Reduction was held and adopted the "Hyogo framework" that is part of the International Strategy for Disaster Reduction in order to make resilient and less vulnerable communities [13–16]. The UN has invited all the countries to sign this document and to recognize the importance of resilience, risk reduction, emergency preparedness and effective recovery programs (UN report, 2005).

The Hyogo framework stresses the importance of 5 main pillars: (1) an efficient organization where each bureau knows its role and its duties during an emergency, (2) a risk evaluation in order to understand which are the threats (3) appropriate infrastructures that can mitigate disaster (dam, channels, telecommunication systems, etc.) and can facilitate coordination and information, (4) effective services such as the police or firefighters that have the proper means and training to face disasters (5) healthy citizens that knows the risks and have the proper training to protect themselves or to rescue. Another important pillar to make a resilient community and to reduce the vulnerabilities is the citizen involvement through different forms of participation in order to mitigate or to prevent disasters or emergencies.

In this paper, the Hyogo framework will be used first to check if the different existing models of DMS help to develop a resilient community and then it is proposed a new model of DMS that based on the Italian case. Finally, conclusions and further steps are discussed.

2 Comparison Among Existent DMS

The TEC, the Tsunami Evaluation Coalition, a multiagency committee that evaluated the relief operation of 2004 Tsunami, declared in its report that IT can be the most driving innovation for disaster management [17]. Many international organizations and IT companies have recently developed a lot of IT, technological tools and DMS that support disaster managers [18]. In this work, DMSs are ICT-enhanced support tools, providing the infrastructure (sensors, telecommunication systems, dedicated software application, etc.) that supports one or more of the four main emergency management phases: prevention and mitigation, preparedness, response, and recovery [19]. Some of the most representative examples of DMS are: ReliefWeb (a platform developed by the UN agency OCHA), IRMA (a platform to make simulations and scientific evaluations), and Sahana (an open source software that helps organizing effective relief operations).

ReliefWeb (http://reliefweb.int/) is a platform that provides information, data and maps about disasters and crisis. The platform provides email alerts, latest updates, headlines in order to improve the knowledge and the evaluation of the worldwide disasters. The platforms has also a complete archive of information related to all the countries with additional maps that can be used to plan operations or projects according to precise and updated information. These functionalities helps to understand the risk and partially to improve the organization of the aids according to precise data and information. On the other hand, ReliefWeb does not provide or improve the efficiency of the infrastructures, it neither improves services in the affected countries to protect the community. Then it cannot be considered a fully resilient DMS [20, 21].

IRMA was a European Commission project of 2008 for managing disasters in Africa. It focused mainly on potentiating infrastructures (sensors, new telecommunication systems, etc.) to analyse many factors related to floods such as flood lines, digital elevation models and hydrology models that affect topography and terrains. IRMA tends to improve services, the management of the infrastructures, the organization and the risk evaluations through a major information and coordination. However, neither IRMA can be considered a complete resilient DMS [22].

Sahana (http://sahanafoundation.org/) is a platform that improves incredibly the capability of organization and of coordination of the actors involved in the disaster relief operations providing also important services to refugees and to rescues. On

Table 1 Looking at the existing DMS t through the Hyogo framework

DMS	Infrastructure/services	Training/health	Organization	Risks evaluation	Citizens involvement
ReliefWeb	No	No	Yes	Yes	No
IRMA	Yes	No	Yes	Yes	No
Sahana	Yes	No	Yes	No	No

the other hand, it does not provide any infrastructures or risk evaluation service. Then, also Sahana cannot be considered a fully resilient DMS [23–26].

However, the most important point is that all the DMSs existing today do not support first aid services, emergency training, preventive healthcare, and do not decrease the socio-economic vulnerabilities (see Table 1). In addition, the existing systems do not consider the relevant example of citizen participation during emergencies attested by Ushaidi and by the use of social network during disasters [27, 28]. Another significant point is that these DMSs do not fully exploit the potentialities of the new technologies to create new types of organization but simply digitalize existent organization and bureaucratic procedures.

It is therefore necessary to try to change the paradigm of DMS in order to establish an emergency organization and to alleviate the vulnerabilities, in the pre-disaster stage. All the actors in the community have to be trained in the pre-disaster stage to be part of the emergency organization. Then the change of paradigm is here.

3 Problems and Needs of Volunteering Organizations: The Case of the Italian Civil Protection Volunteers

From the previous examples and analysis it appears clear that is needed a new organization that involves all the actors and especially the citizens in order to individuate, to mitigate and to fight possible threats. In the world there are 1 billion volunteers and 13 million of them are from the Red Cross and their work corresponds to 1.4 trillion US dollars, more than the 2 % of the global GDP that according to a ILO research of 2011 corresponds to a value of 1.4 trillion US dollars [29]. This means that the design of innovative DMSs cannot neglect the extraordinary contribution of active citizens and volunteers in the development of resilient communities. Consequently, the first step of this research is focused on how to create a resilient emergency organization looking initially at volunteers as main actors involved in both preventing (ex-ante) and managing (ex-post) emergencies.

Then in order to have a better idea of the needs and the perspective of volunteers, this research concentrates its analysis on the Italian Civil Protection (http://www. protezionecivile.gov.it/) that counts 4000 volunteering associations with totally 800 thousands volunteers specialized in disaster and emergency relief operations and spread in all the Italian territory. For this aim, a survey was conducted among the members between December 2013 and February 2014. The questionnaire was sent to the chief association through an email utilizing SkyDrive a Microsoft free tool that guarantees anonymity and that collects all the data directly in an Excel spreadsheet. The respondents were 125. Cause of the limited support, resources this sample is still small to be statistically representative of the population however, these data provide a first insight and give us the possibility to reflect better about problems and needs of the volunteers that are already part of a well structured and homogenous volunteering organization such as the Civil Protection. The platform is built around volunteers and not around people rescued that today are just victims and the platform wants to make them potential rescues and more responsible citizens.

3.1 Data Collection

On the basis of the response, volunteers are mainly men (71 %) with an average age of 43 years old. On average, they spend from 5 to 10 h a month volunteering and the major factor that influences the number of hours of service is the availability of free time. In fact, the bigger number of volunteers is represented by freelance that usually can manage their free time as they prefer. Volunteers were initially introduced to volunteering by friends and family members that usually represents the first reference group of a person.

In addition, the 73 % teaches first aid and other important notions to friends and to their families and this can be considered as a multiplier effect to spread first aid knowledge in the community. Moreover, the volunteers of the Italian Civil Protection are well-educated. The 48 % has a high school diploma and the 38 % a university degree; this confirm the already known positive correlation between level education and volunteering [30, 31].

The 100 % of volunteers join the Civil Protection since they want to improve and to protect their territory because the majority (75 %) thinks that it is degraded or threatened. The 100 % of volunteers thinks that the experience as volunteer made them a better and more responsible citizens. On the other hand, volunteering associations have also several problems mainly related to the management of the volunteers (shifts, trainings, teams, etc.) and to the internal management (budgeting, bureaucratic procedures, management of the resources, etc.). In addition, the 97 % of volunteers wants more transparency in their associations in order to avoid waste of resources and lack of trust. The 93 % thinks that there is a high competition among volunteering associations and the 53 % do not completely trust in the training of the volunteers from other associations. This lack of trust and spirit of competition could represent a relevant problem in the volunteering sector.

About the possible change in the volunteering organization, the 69 % seems in favour to a hierarchic and meritocratic model based on different careers of specialization and grades, like in the military organizations, in order to guarantee common and certified trainings and rules. The volunteering should be also opened to young students as it happens in the Red Cross. In addition, volunteers would be happy to be awarded for their efforts with meaningful gifts such as additional training courses, free medical checks or free tickets for museums. All gifts that do not enrich volunteers but that are considered as a reward for their services. In fact volunteers cannot receive money because they might change their motivation and mind [29].

About the current level of digitalization of Civil Protection volunteers, the respondents declared that the 82 % of the associations have a website and the 72 % of the volunteers have a smartphone always connected to internet. To give an idea of how the DMS for the Civil Protection may appear, volunteers were invited to visit the website of GAIA project (https://gaia.cri.it/) managed by the Italian Red Cross. The 100 % of the volunteers welcomes the introduction of a platform like GAIA to improve the organization of the Civil Protection. The 96 % would like to use the digital platform also for additional functionalities such as managing shifts and communication with their association or contacting other volunteers following the model of a social network. Furthermore, the platform could be used to manage the bureaucratic procedures with the local office of the Civil Protection. All the volunteers would like to have a certified training, and the 83 % would be happy to be trained through e-learning courses.

4 A New Model of DMS for Developing a Resilient Community

This platform has been modelled according to the Italian case, however it can be implemented in all developed countries that have an high rate of volunteering among the population. In fact, many studies and researches confirm that the socio-economic development and education influence positively the number of volunteers, then Italy can be easily compared with many other developed countries [31]. The DMS has to drive the development of a resilient community adopting a new approach that focuses more on the pre-disaster stage and on the increasing of the citizen participation in order to establish a major cooperation between civil society and state [32]. The platform has to incentivize a common citizen to become an active citizen and then a volunteer (see Fig. 1). An active citizen knows first aid, follows a resilient behavior (donating blood, saving water and electricity, doing preventive medical checks, etc.), and helps the government in controlling the territory and in collecting data [33, 34].

Then, if an active citizen wants to contribute actively in making the community more resilient he can become a professional volunteer receiving additional trainings and collaborating directly with public institutions. Additionally, it is important to award the active citizens and volunteers in order to maintain long term cooperation and to discourage free riders and unpreparedness.

Fig. 1 The two role of a citizen in a resilient community

Fig. 2 A diffused emergency management based on the vertical subsidiarity

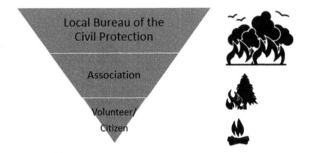

In addition, citizens and volunteers should be included in the organization according to the principles of vertical subsidiarity (Art.118 Italian Constitution) developing a diffused emergency management where each actor manages the projects and the operations according to its resources and competences (see Fig. 2).

Moreover, considering the current widespread use of digital technologies in our society, with their transformative role in linking and in recombining internal and external resources [35–37], and what arisen by the data collection, the new model of DMS should response to these three main requirements: (i) how to exploit and to combine information generated by people using digital technologies in their daily life (e.g. smartphone, social network, etc.), (ii) how to motivate and to stimulate people to be volunteer or active citizen, and (iii) how to support the monitoring and the coordination of volunteers and associations.

4.1 A DMS Based on Crowd Sourcing

In their daily life, citizens use smartphones and other devices that can be important tools for disaster management. Smartphones for example have many sensors integrated (magnetometers, accelerometers, passive infrared, acoustics, camera, GPS etc.) that if connected to internet can be useful to realize the "sensing participation" [38]. Existent crowd sourcing systems are usually integrated with social networks like Twitter, [38] and other less common systems consist in the integration of private sensors like cameras for surveillance, meteorological devices and others

Fig. 3 The functioning of a crowd sourcing system for a resilient community

sensors through the internet [39]. These systems have caused the collapse of the transaction costs making easier for a person to create a group or to reach and to coordinate thousands people [40].

Then crowd sourcing, already successfully used by Ushaidi [28], can be adopted as structural functionality of the platform where citizens and institutions can see the information (emergencies, incidents, traffics, obstruct drainage systems, etc.) that are categorized according to their competences on a shared map (see Fig. 3). This functionality is based on a network of integrated sensors and on the feedbacks of the citizens that creates "social collaboration" [38, 41]. The crowd sourcing functionality can be also described through a sociological framework that classifies the three level of organization of the IT community. The first level is *the sharing information* when citizen sends data and information by internet from his smartphone or domestic devices [42]. A citizen can for example inform about an accident sending a pre-made message with his GPS location to the platform [43]. With its smartphone he can also take pictures and register an audio message to report a damaged street [44]. The second level is *the collaboration* that implicates a responsibility and a duty for the actor, in fact the citizen can also receive alerts or request of aid according to its position and training [45]. Collaboration happens also among institutions and volunteers to manage some emergencies (bush fires, floods, highways accidents) or to satisfy some tasks (clean a park, monitor an area, save water, etc.). Offices and agencies could also share their data and files through the platform and can establish direct communication with the Civil Protection bureau or with the associations. The third level is *the collective action* that is the main purpose of the platform consisting in organizing and coordinating disperse and different resources to act as a unique body, under a unique strategy and to decrease vulnerabilities creating a resilient community [40, 46].

4.2 A Hierarchic and Meritocratic System for Volunteers and Active Citizens

This is the most important part of the platform, because it improves citizens' involvement and participation and incentivizes citizen to care more about their health and to be more responsible. In the proposed platform, the citizen is awarded every time he does something of good for the community (see Fig. 4). He is awarded with an amount of points based on the value of its action.

The platform has a sort of "market" with many gifts for its volunteers. Each gift requires a different amount of points according to the value. Each volunteer or citizen registered to the platform has a personal profile where he accumulates points. Once the volunteer has accumulated the amount of points he needs, he can take the gift he wants from the market of the platform. The market can be organized according to the structure of GroupOn (http://www.groupon.com/). Gifts are not money but awards that can enrich the culture, the health and the skills of the citizens. Both active citizens and volunteers can earn points. For example, an active citizen can earn points if he has a resilient behaviour: buying a seasonal ticket for public transporting, donating blood, recycling the waste, doing preventive medical checks, etc. Then if a citizen is also a volunteer he earns additional points according to the hours of services, to the trainings and to other related activities. Only active citizens and volunteers can join the platform and being awarded.

If a common citizen wants to become an active citizen, he has to attend and to pass a first aid course. Then, once he has passed the exam, he can join the platform and he can start supporting the community. If an active citizen wants to become a volunteer he can choose among four different tracks of specialization based on the current existing tasks of the Civil Protection volunteers. Each specialization has his careers and system of grades as in a military organization (see Fig. 5). The number

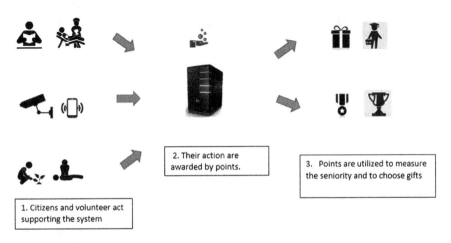

Fig. 4 The functioning of the awarding system for active citizens and volunteers

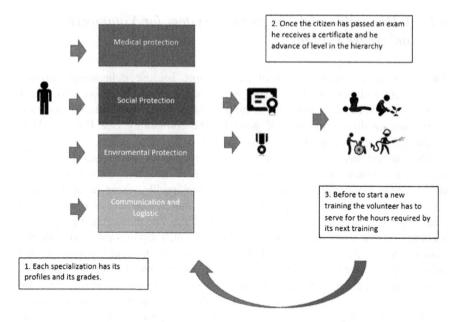

Fig. 5 The functioning of the training and career system

of hours of service and of trainings contributes to gain seniority and to the advancement of grade. Once the volunteer has passed his first specialized certification, he can start volunteering in an association that has his same specialization or that needs his profile.

Citizens and volunteers are trained through an e-learning platform inside the system. The e-learning platform is a suitable solution to guarantee a uniform training and flexibility to all the volunteers [47]. E-learning platforms are already used by many universities and there are also free e-learning platforms like Coursera (https://www.coursera.org/) that offers high quality academic courses to everybody for free. The proposed model of DMS has its own e-learning platform in which every volunteer or active citizen has his own user profile. It is possible to attend classes directly at home and to attend courses when the user prefers. The e-learning platform might be integrated with frontal classes to practice some maneuverers. All the exams are frontal exams and when a citizen passes an exam, he receives a certification and also points that are both registered in its profile.

4.3 A Platform that Improves the Organization and the Coordination

The proposed platform is structured on modules that can interact reciprocally. Then the system has several functionalities that can be developed and added. One of these

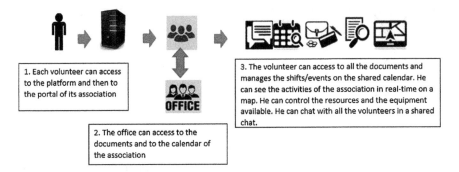

Fig. 6 Functioning of the module to manage the association

modules gives to each association its own website with many management and organizational tools (see Fig. 6). First of all, a shared calendar to put in order the activities and to organize the shifts among volunteers. Then, there is an internal "chat" to facilitate the internal communications. All the volunteers have the possibility to access to the documents and to the balance sheet of the association in order to control and to understand how the money are spent.

The module gives also the possibility to see the equipment and the vehicles available and their status. In addition, the office can communicate with the association and can access to its data and documents in order to facilitate the coordination and the communication.

Each association and volunteer can also have an application for tablet and smartphone that tracks the teams and the vehicles in order to understand the state of the operation, such as if a team is operating or not, if it needs help or not, and other useful information to plan strategies and to manage effectively the resources. Furthermore, this application allows the volunteers to communicate with the bureau during operations, giving also the possibility to monitor the situation in real time on a shared map.

5 Conclusion and Further Research

The Hyogo framework is the UN strategy for disaster reduction and it mainly invites countries to invest in prevention and in building a resilient community in the pre-disaster stage. On the other hand, the existing DMS do not follow the Hyogo framework. Hence, even though they contribute in saving lives, their effectiveness could be improved, increasing the number of saved people and also in reducing economic loss. In this research an innovative DMS platform is presented taking into account what emerged by the data collection and considering the transformative role of digital technology [48]. It seeks to fully respect the resilient framework in order to create a new organization where (i) citizens are trained and active part of the community and (ii) everybody contributes responsibly to individuate, to

Table 2 Looking at the new DMS and at the existing ones through the Hyogo framework

DMS	Infrastructure/services	Training/health	Organization	Risks evaluation	Citizens involvement
ReliefWeb	No	No	Yes	Yes	No
IRMA	Yes	No	Yes	Yes	No
Sahana	Yes	No	Yes	No	No
New DMS	Yes	Yes	Yes	Yes	Yes

mitigate and to fight possible threats under a unique strategy and organization (see Table 2). Contrary to the others, the proposed platform utilizes the existing IT infrastructures without adding new services or bureaus, that could reduce realization and maintenance cost. The platform is modular [36]. This characteristic could create an innovative ecosystem for open source sensors and applications that could be developed by the community and integrated to the platform. In addition, it proposes a new model of citizenship based on the collaboration with the institutions and on the empowerment of the citizen.

Since this paper presents only preliminary results of a research in progress, it is necessary to investigate more in deep on several aspects, such as on the potentialities of an open architecture based on crowd sourcing and open source contributions for disaster management, as well as on an awarding system based on points that could really influence the behaviour of citizens making them more responsible and active. Finally, the data collected through the questionnaire are indicative and seek to depict as a first step the needs and the problems of the volunteers. More resources and institutional collaboration are needed in order to extend the sample and to have statistically significant data that can be utilized to research organizational, sociological and psychological correlations among the volunteers of Civil Protection.

References

1. Williams, J., Nocera, M., Casteel, C.: The effectiveness of disaster training for health care workers: a systematic review. Ann. Emerg. Med. **52**, 211–22, 222.e1–2 (2008)
2. Zakour, M.J., Gillespie, D.F.: Community Disaster Vulnerability, pp. 1–15 (2013)
3. IFRC Report: First aid for a safer future (2010)
4. IFRC Health and Care Department: First aid for a safer future focus on Europe (2009)
5. Prati, G., Saccinto, E., Pietrantoni, L., Pérez-Testor, C.: The 2012 Northern Italy earthquakes: modelling human behaviour. Nat. Hazards (2013)
6. Schultz, C., Koenig, K., Noji, E.: A medical disaster response to reduce immediate mortality after an earthquake. N. Engl. J. Med. **334**, 438–444 (1996)
7. Cummins, R.O., Ornato, J.P., Thies, W.H., Pepe, P.E.: Improving survival from sudden cardiac arrest: the "chain of survival" concept. Circulation **83**, 1832–1847 (1991)
8. Johnson, J., Galea, S.: Disaster and Population Health. Springer, New York (2009)
9. Hou, L., Shi, P.: Haiti 2010 earthquake—how to explain such huge losses? Int. J. Disaster Risk Sci. **2**, 25–33 (2012)

10. Burstein, J.L.: The myths of disaster education. Ann. Emerg. Med. **47**, 50–52 (2006)
11. Allenby, B., Fink, J.: Toward inherently secure and resilient societies. Science **309**, 1034–1036 (2005)
12. Liu, D., Deters, R., Zhang, W.J.: Architectural design for resilience. Enterp. Inf. Syst. **4**, 137–152 (2010)
13. Innocenti, D., Albrito, P.: Reducing the risks posed by natural hazards and climate change: the need for a participatory dialogue between the scientific community and policy makers. Environ. Sci. Policy **14**, 730–733 (2011)
14. Stanganelli, M.: A new pattern of risk management: the Hyogo framework for action and Italian practise. Socioecon. Plann. Sci. **42**, 92–111 (2008)
15. Djalante, R., Holley, C., Thomalla, F.: Adaptive governance and managing resilience to natural hazards. Int. J. Disaster Risk Sci. **2**, 1–14 (2012)
16. Cutter, S.L., Barnes, L., Berry, M., Burton, C., Evans, E., Tate, E., Webb, J.: A place-based model for understanding community resilience to natural disasters. Glob. Environ. Change **18**, 598–606 (2008)
17. TEC: Joint evaluation of the international response to the Indian Ocean Tsunami (2007)
18. Magni, M., Provera, B., Proserpio, L.: Individual attitude toward improvisation in information systems development. Behav. Inf. Technol. **29**, 245–255 (2010)
19. Barbini, F.M., Atri, A.D., Tarantino, L., Za, S.: A new generation DMS for supporting social sensemaking. In: De Marco, M., Te'eni, D., Albano, V., Za, S. (eds.) Information Systems: Crossroads for Organization, Management, Accounting and Engineering, pp. 105–112. Physica-Verlag HD, Heidelberg (2012)
20. Wolz, C., Park, N.: Evaluation of ReliefWeb. (2006)
21. Mullen, I.C.: ReliefWeb: Vision & Strategy (2012)
22. Simonis, I., Anwar Vahed, D.M.: Integrated Risk Management in South Africa: Between Technological Features and Organizational Reality (2007)
23. De Silva, C., Prustalis, M.: The Sahana Free and Open Source Disaster Management System in Haiti (2010)
24. Isuru Samaraweera, S.C.: Sahana Victim Registries : Effectively Track Disaster Victims (2012)
25. Van De Walle, B., Van Den Eede, G., Muhren, W.: Humanitarian Information Management and Systems, pp. 12–21 (2009)
26. Silva, T., Wuwongse, V., Sharma, H.N.: Disaster mitigation and preparedness using linked open data. J. Ambient Intell. Humaniz. Comput. **4**, 591–602 (2012)
27. Huang, C.-M., Chan, E., Hyder, A.A: Web 2.0 and internet social networking: a new tool for disaster management?–lessons from Taiwan. BMC Med. Inform. Decis. Mak. **10**, 57 (2010)
28. Boccardo, P., Tonolo, F.G.: Remote sensing role in emergency mapping for disaster response. Eng. Geol. Soc. Territ. **5**, 17–24 (2015)
29. IFRC: Volunteering in Emergencies. IFRC Report (2011)
30. McClintock, N.: Understanding Canadian Volunteers, Toronto (2004)
31. Wilson, J., Musick, M.: Who cares? Toward an integrated theory of volunteer work. Am. Sociol. Rev. **62**, 694 (1997)
32. Ricciardi, F., Rossignoli, C., Marco, M.D.: Participatory networks for place safety and livability: organisational success factors. Int. J. Netw. Virtual Organ. **13**, 42–65 (2013)
33. Zardini, A., Rossignoli, C., Mola, L., De Marco, M.: Developing municipal e-Government in Italy: the city of Alfa case. In: Snene, M., Leonard, M. (eds.) Exploring Services Science, Lecture Notes in Business Information Processing, vol. 169, pp. 124–137. Springer International Publishing (2014)
34. Pennarola, F., Caporarello, L.: Enhanced class replay: will this turn into better learning? In: Wankel, C., Blessinger, P. (eds.) Increasing Student Engagement and Retention Using Classroom Technologies: Classroom Response Systems and Mediated Discourse Technologies, pp. 143–162. Emerald Group Publishing Limited (2013)

35. Resca, A., Za, S., Spagnoletti, P.: Digital platforms as sources for organizational and strategic transformation: a case study of the midblue project. J. Theor. Appl. Electron. Commer. Res. **8**, 71–84 (2013)
36. Yoo, Y., Henfridsson, O., Lyytinen, K.: Research commentary—the new organizing logic of digital innovation: an agenda for information systems research. Inf. Syst. Res. **21**, 724–735 (2010)
37. Basaglia, S., Caporarello, L., Magni, M., Pennarola, F.: Individual adoption of convergent mobile technologies in Italy. In: D'Atri, A., De Marco, M., Casalino, N. (eds.) Interdisciplinary Aspects of Information Systems Studies: The Italian Association for Information Systems, pp. 63–69. Physica-Verlag, Heidelberg (2008)
38. Demirbas, M., Ali Bayir, M., Akcora, C.G., Yilmaz, Y.S., Ferhatosmanoglu, H.: Crowd-sourced sensing and collaboration using twitter. In: Proceedings of 2010 IEEE International Symposium "A World Wireless, Mobile Multimedia Networks", pp. 1–9 (2010)
39. Schafer, B.: Crowdsourcing and cloudsourcing CCTV surveillance, vol. 01, pp. 434–439 (2013)
40. Shirky, Clay: Here comes everybody: how change happens when people come together. Penguin Group, London (2009)
41. Basaglia, S., Caporarello, L., Magni, M., Pennarola, F.: Team level antecedents of individual usage of a new technology. In: Proceeding of the 16th European Conference on Information Systems, Galway, Ireland (2008)
42. Federici, T., Braccini, A.M.: How Internet is upsetting the communication between organizations and their stakeholders: a tentative research agenda. In: De Marco, M., Te'eni, D., Albano, V., Za, S. (eds.) Information Systems: A Crossroad for Organization, Management, Accounting and Engineering, pp. 377–385. Physica-Verlag, A Springer Company, Berlin (2012)
43. Paredes, H., Fonseca, B., Cabo, M., Pereira, T., Fernandes, F.: SOSPhone: a mobile application for emergency calls. Univers. Access Inf. Soc. **13**, 277–290 (2013)
44. Yan, T., Marzilli, M., Holmes, R., Ganesan, D., Corner, M.: Demo Abstract : mCrowd—A Platform for Mobile Crowdsourcing (2010)
45. Banzato, A., Barbini, F., D'Atri, A., D'Atri, E., Za, S.: Social networks and information systems to handle emergency and reconstruction in natural disasters: the L'Aquila earthquake case study. Sprouts Work. Pap. Inf. Syst. **10**, Article 5 (2010)
46. Resca, A., Tozzi, M.L.: Designing organizational systems. Des. Organ. Syst. 301–318 (2013)
47. Caporarello, L., Sarchioni, G.: E-learning: the recipe of success. J. e-learn. Knowl. Soc. **10**, 117–128 (2014)
48. Sorrentino, M., Virili, F.: Web services and value generation in the public sector. In: Traunmüller, R. (ed.) Electronic Government. LNCS, vol. 3183, pp. 489–495. Springer, Berlin (2004)

Using Collaboration Platforms for Management Control Processes: New Opportunities for Integration

Daniela Mancini and Concetta Ferruzzi

Abstract Literature have analyzed the relationship between Management Control Systems (MCSs) and Information and Communication Technology (ICTs), with a particular focus on information integrated systems (transaction-oriented information systems as Enterprise Resource Planning software, analysis-oriented information tools as Business Intelligence software). During the latest decades, ICT has generated collaboration platforms, i.e. hardware/software solutions able to connect people in a 'social' and safe environment and to provide tools useful to create, organize, search, and share documents, information, ideas, calendars, and so on. Several studies have investigated the organizational implications of such platforms, especially for workgroups, as well as their impacts on sharing knowledge and information, especially in inter-organizational context. But the contribution of collaboration platforms to MCS remains little explored. This study analyses the use of collaboration platforms in research institutions (RIs). Based upon one Italian case study, the article provides a qualitative assessment regarding the introduction of a collaboration platform to support communication flows in the RI. We highlight how this platform has become an important support device for management control processes. We focus on the role of the collaboration platform in each control component and on the way in which it represents an opportunity for a more sophisticated level of integration among those components. The paper aims to contribute both to academia bridging the gap in studies regarding the relationship between MCSs and ICTs, and to practitioners by highlighting collaboration platform usage in a specific context.

Keywords Collaboration platform · Management control systems · Information sharing · SharePoint Workspace

D. Mancini (✉)
Parthenope University of Naples, Naples, Italy
e-mail: mancini@uniparthenope.it

C. Ferruzzi
Italian National Institute of Statistics - ISTAT, Rome, Italy
e-mail: ferruzzi@istat.it

© Springer International Publishing Switzerland 2016   91
T. Torre et al. (eds.), *Empowering Organizations*, Lecture Notes in Information
Systems and Organisation 11, DOI 10.1007/978-3-319-23784-8_8

1   Introduction

Companies are involved in searching new form of activities' coordination among organisational units to controlling the levers of processes efficiency and effectiveness, to guiding operations towards objectives and to aligning employees' goals to organization's ones. Information and communication technologies (ICTs) offer useful solutions to improve activities and processes coordination. In the latest decades, the spread of Internet and the ICTs development, especially office automation tools, have provided new solutions useful to share ideas, information, and documents, to manage complex projects and to find people and their personal details. These collaboration platforms, called also "digital platform" [1], "digital workspace" [2], "collaborative platform" [3], "groupware" [4], "virtual communities" [4, 5] are seen as useful tools to support collaborative work, especially in workgroups, virtual communities and inter-organizational relations (IORs). They are complex systems which include tools:

1. To sharing contents, with other employees, across the organization;
2. To organising information, documents and activities for a single person and for a team;
3. To searching information and people, and to analysing data from multiple sources by a graphic way.

ICTs do not produce relevant effects on value creation if they are considered as isolating systems [6], but it is important the way in which ICTs interact with other systems as information systems, activity systems and control systems [7]. Moreover ICTs affect not only data processing, but also organisation structure and processes, human resource management and style of management [8].

Organisational studies highlight positive implications of ICT adoption, in term of a better coordination among offices, a more efficient sharing of information and a greater increase of productivity [8, 9]. According to these considerations, literature on collaboration platforms examined how and why they can improve communication within groups [10], facilitate creativity [3], stimulate the generation of knowledge [1]. Scholars analysed collaboration platforms in different contexts such as project management [11], inter-organizational network [1], public administration [4, 5], and so on. Previous studies are essentially focused on organisational issues related to collaboration platforms usage, while little investigation is upon their implications on management control systems (MCSs).

To contribute to the extent literature on the relationship between ICTs and MCSs, we carried out a preliminary research to investigate this relationship in the Italian RIs. In particular, we investigate if and how a specific ICT tool, as a collaboration platform realised with Sharepoint Workspace, helps this company to better organise its MCSs.

We conducted a literature review and one case study analysis, to highlight if and how a collaboration platform, implemented to improve coordination and information sharing, affects other dimension as:

- Organisational control, in term of sharing of values and culture;
- Administrative control and information procedures, in term of their reconfiguration, transparency and compliance;
- Control and management processes, in term of enhance decisions effectiveness, integration of models, activities and tools.

The paper is structured as follows. Section 2 contains the literature review. Section 3 presents the research methodology, while Sect. 4 analyses the case study. The results are then presented in Sect. 5 with the conclusions of this study and its implications.

2 Literature Review

MCSs include a set of accounting models, information tools, decision making procedures to align employees behaviour with organisation's objectives and strategies [12] and to measure companies' performances [13].

Academic literature highlights the existence of a two-way relationship between MCSs and ICTs [14]. The implementation of ICT tools might affect MCSs, stimulating changes in their components; on the other hand, MCSs asset and characteristics might influence ICTs use and implementation.

Scholars analyse separately each MCS component and different ICT tools [14]. For the first aspect, studies consider management accounting systems [15], performance measurement systems [16], balanced scorecard scheme, activity based costing, etc. For the second aspect, literature considers office automation tools or integrated tools for management and control function such as ERP systems, BI systems, Internal Auditing Suite, CRM and SCM software and so on.

With regard to the influence of ICTs on MCSs, studies concern the relationship between ICT and different part of MCSs as human behaviors, tasks, techniques, and organisation. They examine ICT implementation in order to identify critical success factors in ERP or BI projects. They underline that social and organisational variables have to be carefully managed, taking in consideration the impacts of human behaviours on ICT, because of the employees' resistances to change.

Another stream of research considers ICT impacts on MCS tasks in term of information quality and effectiveness of decision making processes. These studies explore how IT acts on the relationship between cost and effectiveness of information processes. Information technology improves [17] the accuracy of information and the timeliness of information process, and reduces the cost of elaboration of data.

Another important research area regards the relation between ICTs and the organisation, with a focus on management accountants role [12, 18, 19] and administrative processes. Studies highlight that ICTs activate a hybridization of management accountant professionals [20]. Recently some studies examine how

ICTs affect the de-materialization of administrative and management processes and how they generate changes in organisational procedures [21].

ICT and MCS literature also investigate the integration and disintegration of information systems. It examines the level of integration that companies reach through different kind of ICT products and identify three steps of integration [22]:

- Data integration, which refers to the fact that "data are stored and maintained in one place only" [14, p. 43];
- Hardware/software integration, which concerns "network connectivity" and the communication among computers;
- Information integration, which concerns "the interchange of information between different departments".

The first two levels affect ICT, while the latter concerns MCS. We notice that integration is analysed inside different component of MCSs in term of data, information flows or procedures consistency. It is not clearly investigated how an ICT solution can support integration between MCS components [12, 23].

Moreover, the literature review highlights that studies are essentially concentrated on several ICT solutions (as ERP, BI), while there is a little consideration of collaboration platforms.

3 Methodology

This work is based on a qualitative case study methodology [24, 25] focused on an Italian RI which implemented a collaboration platform to support communication flows. The description of the case study is based on multiple information sources:

- Semi-structured interviews with key people involved in the project: director of the Business Unit, project leader, IT manager and content manager;
- Analysis of project memos, documents and reports produced by the work team, including presentations at the summit of the institute and users to explain the philosophy and objectives of the project, and teaching materials;
- Observation of the platform's operation and of the user's interaction.

In order to examine how and why collaboration tools affect MCSs, we refer to a revised version of the framework of Malmi et al. [12]. This model considers MCS composed of a systematic coordination of several mechanisms called [23]:

- Cultural control system based on value, beliefs and social norms (organizational or clan control);
- Cybernetic controls, that act on results through the definition of objectives, their measurement and the distribution of reward and compensation (management control);

- Administrative control system, that include control mechanisms able to monitor employee behaviour defining governance rules, organization structure and policies and procedures [25];
- Compliance control systems, that include a mix of mechanism able to assure transparency and compliance with law, regulation and internal standards.

The case examined is particular useful to investigate the implication of a collaboration platform on MCS because the activity of this kind of organization is mainly based on work team and on research projects founded by external financial sources. In this context each MCS component (administrative, cultural, results control) assumes a relevant role as well as the use of tools to sharing information, documents and ideas.

4 Case Study Description

The research concerns an Italian RI which introduced, in one of its business unit, a collaboration platform to support communication flows between offices and it illustrates how this platform has become more important as a support device for management control processes.

The business unit focus is the development of statistical literacy in Italian society and the promotion and dissemination of statistical knowledge through training projects delivered to its users and clients. Its goals are to develop human capital inside, to improve the statistical training of public administration personnel and to promote statistical literacy in the country.

This business unit, set up in 2011, meets the needs for quantitative literacy which society ever more clearly expresses: knowing how to interpret the data, learning to handle and use them to make and evaluate individual or political decisions, is part of the essential cultural baggage for fully experiencing the "information society". In this way, the institution offers all its experts' wealth of technical and professional skills to create projects in which three important elements interact: aptitude for research, knowledge of the statistical production processes and experience in training.

The business unit is organized in a Directorate, with independent decision making and budgeting process and it involves about 30 people.

The internal structure is as follows:

- A technical staff to support the Director in the coordinating activities, which takes care of strategic and management control, management and communication information systems, and manages relations with the administrative department;
- Five technical units, oriented to cope with a specific category of users and clients:

- National statistical system operators: the unit plans and organises training and professional qualification of European and national statistical system staff and the development of skills for National Statistical System operators;
- Other national and international institutions: the unit designs and implements training activities addressed to the Public Sector, Universities, private companies, foreign users (custom or standard courses);
- Dissemination of statistical literacy: the unit provides a training offer for the general public; defining and designing quantitative training initiatives dedicated to non-specialists (data journalism, data scientists, data business analysts), offers citizens tools for the interpretation of the national reality;
- Public and private school: the unit promotes statistical literacy especially for the younger generation to attract them to quantitative reasoning;
- International cooperation: the unit designs and implements training projects addressed to foreign users and foreign international organizations;

• Two projects team focused on:

- The development of a e-learning platform for training and knowledge sharing to promote the dissemination of the know how inside the Institute to create a learning environment for the growth and development of statistical literacy;
- The development of socio-economic research in collaboration with other institutions on issues of high national interest and the dissemination of knowledge and expertise through keynote, research grants and training.

Moreover, to manage specific projects and cross-sectional, involving also employees from other business units have been created specific working groups. Units and projects team also run activities on external funding: managing tenders and negotiations (strategic assessment and ex-ante evaluation, preparing administrative and technical documentation); managing contracts (organizational model, decision management system, planning and control system/auditing); managing performance and outcome (dissemination, ex-post evaluation, knowledge management).

The business unit in 2013 started a project to develop a collaboration platform to realise some main achievements: to enabling the business unit to communicate information about the offered services; to sharing tools and documents of public interest; to granting access to the documentation produced; to facilitating shared work asynchronously.

The project was carried out by a team consisting of: a project manager, a content coordinator and a technical one, two Sharepoint experts, a web editorial staff consisting of six people for managing and updating contents. Members of the IT Directorate also took part to the working group.

The collaboration platform was realised using "SharePoint Server 2010". The RI project team considered SharePoint as a powerful platform for document management and project collaboration. They had to share and exchange documents with internal and external units and partners. They viewed SharePoint as a solution for their engineering document management needs. Moreover they considered Share Point as a different way to see office automation because it is included into the Microsoft Office Suite, together with Ms Excel, Ms Access, and so on, and it can be used in an internet environment, and it also has a more social approach to information sharing than the other tools of the package.

The key problems were:

- Where to find documents and information: information generally was available but often lacked a point of reference that collect, file and classify them;
- How to organise information: information often were not structured and lacked of clear criteria and well-known classification;
- Why to share information: in the RI often people tended not to share the information that were viewed as an asset to be preserved rather than personal wealth to be shared;
- What key information to communicate within the organisation: often employees were inundated with a deluge of data from which they could not extract the relevant information.

The project has been accomplished by the following steps:

- Defining and design of the basic configuration:

  - Functionality and workflow;
  - Profiles, user groups and permission levels;
  - Organizational model for managing and updating content;
  - Information flows;
  - Criteria for the classification of documents managed and archived;
  - Content and tools to share information and documents;

- Implementation and testing of sections and workflow authorization;
- Information programs and training to support the start-up of the platform.

Several initiatives have been carried out in order to share the basic configuration with the top management and to organise training courses dedicated to users and administrators.

The collaboration platform automates the following processes:

- Submission of applications to courses, workflow management and authorization for attending courses (also through interaction with the platform MOODLE e-learning);
- Submission of applications to the database of teachers and experts, and management of the teaching assignments;
- Management of the information of the courses and other events (timetable, mailing, etc.);
- Monitoring agreements and their administrative, economic and financial issues (budget of the courses, expensive, fees, etc.);
- Planning and managing team meetings;
- Internal and organisational communication (achievements, awards, etc.).

The collaboration platform is organised as a website and structured in sections:

- An intranet area (visible from the entire staff of the RI) where information of general interest could be handled, documents and applications regarding courses and events were made available both for learners and for teachers;
- A reserved section where the business unit staff might share specific tools (calendars, planning meeting, standard forms, manual and procedures);
- Several thematic sections with reserved access to the working groups to share documents, working paper and support material.

The realisation of the platform allows the creation of shared workspaces to support:

- A more effective and integrated control process realised through: a document management system based on the digital dossiers of projects; the automation of the workflow of the budgeting and reporting;
- A more transparent and compliant information flow realised through the automation of the monitoring of administrative procedures and documentations in term of flows, steps and time expected;
- An higher level of integration between people and units realised through several tools to sharing information and to support the activity of the transversal working groups.

The results obtained, even though the project has not yet been completed, exceeded the expected outcomes, in fact in spite of the objectives of a more fluid communication and a more open sharing information, the platform has become an integrated environment, a unique place where manage coherently each dimension of MCS.

5 Conclusion

The paper analyses the relationship between ICT and MCS in an Italian IR considering a collaboration platform and each components of the control system. Control systems are organisational mechanisms used to guide companies towards their goals. These systems have some different components traditionally identified as: strategic control, organization control, management control, risk control, internal control system over financial reporting, compliance control [23, 26–30]. In general, automation provides tools able to manage individually these different sub-systems, as ERP or BI.

The implementation of a collaboration platform represents for the RI an opportunity to activate several changes in internal processes. In particular:

- A more effective realisation of the integration of control and management processes, of administrative procedures, of information flows and of management accounting processes;

- A more transparent and compliant information flow;
- A higher level of integration between different control mechanisms, based on results, behaviours and culture.

The case study shows that a collaboration platform is able to support simultaneously most MCS components. In other words, this ICT tool gives RI the opportunity to reach a higher level of integration. This integration is based on the convergence of different control sub systems in the same ICT platform and not only on data integration, hardware/software and information integration. This new level of integration is possible because that collaboration platform contains tools:

- To sharing information and managing information flows from an office to another, tracing every action and defining time and deadline for the execution of the activities. In this way the collaboration platform helps RI in its compliance and transparency purposes;
- To publishing and sharing ideas, objectives, information in a well-defined community, in order to create a control mechanism based on cultural and soft variables,
- To managing the budgetary process and the variances analysis, offering tools able to automatically match objectives and results formalised on a dashboard.
- To organising and managing digital documents and dossiers in order to improve efficiency in administrative processes.

This research contributes to study the relationship betwen ICTs and MCSs. According to the literature, it shows that collaboration platforms are useful in RI to improve the communication and information sharing between organisational units and project teams. The study also demonstrates that these platforms, related to MCSs, represent a relevant opportunity to improve simultaneously each component of the control systems and to reach higher level of their integration.

As this research is at an initial phase, the conclusion maybe applied basically to the case examined and to similar institutions. A possible direction for future research could be to extend this analysis to a larger number of cases took from different sectors.

References

1. Cremona, L., Lin, T., Ravarini, A.: The role of digital platform in interfirm collaborations. In: VIII Mediterranean Conference on Information Systems (2014)
2. Overbeek, S., van Middendorp, S., Rijsenbrij, D.: The digital workspace, in the financial sector. IT Manage. Select. 11, 38–51 (2005)
3. Agrifoglio, R., Metallo, C.: Virtual environment and collaborative work: the role of relation quality in facilitating individual creativity. In: D'Atri, A., Ferrara, M., George, J.F., Spagnoletti., P. (eds.) Information Technology and Innovation Trends in Organizations. Springer, Heidelberg (2011)

4. Capriglione, A., Casalino, N., Draoli, M.: Relational networks for the open innovation in the Italian public administration. In: D'Atri, A., Ferrara, M., George, J. F., Spagnoletti., P. (eds.) Information Technology and Innovation Trends in Organizations. Springer, Heidelberg (2011)
5. Alvino, F., Agrifoglio, R., Metallo, C., Lepore, L.: Learning and knowledge sharing in virtual communities of practices: a case study. In: D'Atri, A., Ferrara, M., George, J. F., Spagnoletti., P. (eds.) Information Technology and Innovation Trends in Organizations. Springer, Heidelberg (2011)
6. Baskerville, R., Meyers, M.: Information systems as a reference discipline. MIS Q. **26**, 1–14 (2002)
7. Beynon-Davies, P.: Formated technology and informated action: the nature of information technology. Int. J. Inf. Syst. **29**, 272–282 (2009)
8. Noble, F.: Implementation strategies for office systems. J. Strat. Inf. Syst. **4**, 239–253 (1995)
9. Law, D., Gorla, N.: Exploring factors underlying effective office information systems. Inf. Manag. **31**, 25–35 (2006)
10. Mansour, O.: Group intelligence: a distributed cognition perspective. In: Intelligent Networking and Collaborative Systems, INCOS '09, pp. 247–250 (2009)
11. Iacoviello, G., Lazzini, A.: IS to support project management: implication for managerial accounting. In: Mancini, D., Vaassen, E., Dameri, P. (eds.) Accounting Information Systems For Decision Making. Springer, Heidelberg (2013)
12. Malmi, T., Brown, D.A.: Management control systems as a package—opportunities, challenges and research directions. Manag. Acc. Res. **19** (2008)
13. Mancini, D.: Le Condizioni di Efficacia del Sistema di Controllo Aziendale. Qualità e Sicurezza del Sistema di Controllo, Giappichelli, Torino (2010)
14. Rom, A., Rohde, C.: Management accounting and integrated information systems: a literature review. Int. J. Acc. Inf. Syst. **8**, 40–68 (2007)
15. Chiucchi, M.S., Gatti, M., Marasca, S.: The Relationship Between Management Accounting Systems and ERP Systems in a Medium-Sized Firm: A Bidirectional Perspective. Management Control (2002)
16. Silvi, R., Bartolini, M., Raffoni, A., Visani, F.: Business Performance Analytics: Level of Adoption and Support Provided to Performance Measurement Systems. Management Control (2012)
17. Marchi, L.: Il Sistema Informativo Aziendale. Giuffrè, Milano (2003)
18. Granlund, M., Malmi, T.: Moderate impact of ERPs on management accounting: a lag or permanent outcome? Manag. Acc. Res. **13**, 299–321 (2002)
19. Scapens, R.W., Jazayeri, M.: ERP systems and management accounting change: opportunities or impact? A research note. Eur. Acc. Rev. **12**, 201–233 (2003)
20. Caglio, A.: Enterprise resource planning systems and accountants: towards hybridization? Eur. Acc. Rev. **12**, 123–153 (2003)
21. Ferruzzi, C.: Pubblica Amministrazione: Dematerializzazione del Sistema Documentario. Controllo di Gestione. **2**, 30–38 (2010)
22. Boot, P., Matolesy, Z., Wieder, B.: Integrated information systems (ERP systems) and accouting practice—the Australian experience. In: 3rd European Conference on Accounting Information Systems, Munich, Germany (2000)
23. D'Onza, G.: Il Sistema di Controllo Interno nella Prospettiva di Risk Management. Giuffrè, Milano (2008)
24. Eisenhardt, K.M.: Building theories from case study research. Acad. Manag. Rev. **14**, 532–550 (1989)
25. Yin, R.: Case Study Research. Design and Methods. Sage, London (1994)
26. Corsi, K.: Il Sistema di Controllo Amministrativo-Contabile. Prospettive e Dinamiche Evolutive alla Luce degli IAS/IFRS. Giuffrè, Milano (2008)
27. Mancini, D.: L'Azienda nella Rete di Imprese. la Prospettiva del Controllo Relazionale. Giuffrè, Milano (1999)
28. Corsi, K.: Il Controllo Organizzativo. Una Prospettiva Transazionale. Giuffrè, Milano (2003)

29. Lamboglia, R.: La Componente Immateriale e Organizzativa del Sistema di Controllo Aziendale. Giuffrè, Milano (2012)
30. Marasca, S., Riccaboni, A., Marchi, L.: Manuale Controllo di Gestione. Metodologie e Strumenti. Knowita, Arezzo (2013)

Innovating e-Recruitment Services:
An Italian Case Study

Michela Iannotta and Mauro Gatti

Abstract In a currently global, social and digital world, new challenges are coming to companies. The evolution of Information Technology and the rapid extension of the Internet have revolutionized the way of managing human resources. Nowadays, the real challenge for organizations is to achieve, hire and retain talents in order to enhance their competitive advantage. The paper aims to analyze the emerging trends in the e-recruitment services by investigating the case study of Face4Job, an innovative Italian start-up in this sector. The purpose is to explore why and how the problems related to traditional recruitment and e-recruitment models have led to an innovative solution of "talent hunting". Our findings show several innovative solutions in order to more efficiently match the requests of employers and job seekers and to make the search of talent much more qualified.

Keywords e-Recruiting services · Case study · Talent hunting

1 Introduction

The rapid diffusion of the Internet and Information Technology has greatly changed the way people interact both with and within organizations [1–5]. These changes provide new opportunities in Human Resources management in a currently global, social and digital world. According to the Resource-Based View [6–10], human resources are not simply instrumental in defining the firm's competitive advantage, but they are key elements in doing so. Nowadays, the real challenge for organizations is to achieve, hire and retain talents [11, 12] in order to enhance their

M. Iannotta (✉) · M. Gatti
Department of Management, Sapienza University of Rome,
Via del Castro Laurenziano, 9, 00161 Rome, Italy
e-mail: michela.iannotta@uniroma1.it

M. Gatti
e-mail: mauro.gatti@uniroma1.it

© Springer International Publishing Switzerland 2016
T. Torre et al. (eds.), *Empowering Organizations*, Lecture Notes in Information
Systems and Organisation 11, DOI 10.1007/978-3-319-23784-8_9

competitive advantage. Traditional recruiting systems have been gradually replaced by on-line recruitment, which represents the most widely used tool to hire people. That is because, on the one hand, on-line recruitment allows for consistent savings in time and resources than traditional one; on the other hand, it does not constrain organizations to search only for local candidates, but all over the world [11–13]. However, this kind of tool is not completely free of disadvantages.

This paper aims to analyze the new trends in the e-recruitment services. Our purpose is to investigate why and how the problems related to traditional recruitment and e-recruitment methods have led to an innovative solution of "talent hunting".

After the literature review, the research method is presented and the main findings are discussed. Conclusions, limitations and future research paths are provided in the last section.

2 Literature Review and Research Questions

2.1 Selection and Recruitment Process in Organizations

The importance of selection and recruitment processes for companies' competitiveness is clearly shown by the growing research on this topic in the last years [14–17]. The recruitment process is traditionally divided into two phases as it answers two main questions: "Whom to recruit?" and "Where to recruit?" [18, 19]. The first phase primarily requires a job description, in order to clarify what company wants from future employees, and then a person specification to define which competences and skills the company needs and looks for [20, 21]. For the "Where" question, companies can choose between internal and external recruitment according to their available resources.

After recruiting, the following steps are to screen and assess the candidates which are the stages of the selection process [19]. The employment interview is the most common and the most relevant tool for assessing the candidates [22–25]. Levashina et al. [25, p. 243] define employment interview as "a personally interactive process of one or more people asking questions orally to another person and evaluating the answers for the purpose of determining the qualifications of that person in order to make employment decisions". In this definition, interpersonal interaction is crucial, but it is not limited to face-to-face interaction, since the advancement of technology has enabled interaction through other media, such as telephone or computer video chat [e.g. 26]. With regard to recruitment outcomes, a large body of literature shows the higher validity of the structured rather than the unstructured interview, since it ensure a superior overlap between the candidate's profile and the job position and it can better predict job performance e.g. [23, 27–29]. Indeed, structured interviews require to ask the same questions to all the candidates, they are strictly linked to job requirement [30] and consequently, they particularly fit with the assumptions of procedural justice theory [31]. Finally, both behavioral and situational interviews allow for predicting the future behavior of employees in given circumstances on the basis of their past behavior or current intentions [32, 33]. More in detail, the former includes questions to assess both past and future behaviors and to evaluate their consistency [25]. The assumption is that past behaviors are the best predictors of future ones [19]. Similarly, the latter assumes that intentions can predict future behaviors [33]. Thus, situational interviews require asking candidate to describe what he would do in hypothetical job-related situations [25, p. 266].

The last step in the recruitment and selection process is the evaluation of its efficacy and efficiency. Generally, the efficiency is evaluated in relation with time and costs involved in both processes (number of involved HR professionals, costs for curricula management or for specialized service providers, and so on). For instance, the recruitment cost for each hired employee is made with the total amount of costs for recruitment process on the total number of applicants effectively hired. Instead, the selection cost for each candidate can be determined by the total amount of selection costs on the number of applicants under selection process [19]. On the efficacy side, we need to assess the ability of both processes to minimize false positives (when an applicant is hired for his seeming success, but he fails in results) as well as false negatives (when we not hire an applicant for his seeming failure, but he could have succeeded). In line with this remark, the screening ratio is usually used for evaluating the ability to attract candidates which possess the minimum requirements; and the selection ratios are the most frequent indicators for measuring the number of hired employees on the total number of candidates or post-screening candidates [19].

In the next section we will describe several recruiting tools and their evolution over time.

2.2   Evolution and New Trends in Recruiting Approaches

Traditional tools for searching candidates are typically: company databases and job posting for internal approaches; informal referrals, school and university placement office, job advertising, employment agencies for external approaches [34]. In line with our purposes, we mainly focus on external recruitment channels. More in depth, the development of Information Technology and the diffusion of the Internet have brought a revolution in recruiting methods by enabling online recruitment [11–13, 35–37]. Nowadays, the IT support is relevant for attracting, selecting and retaining talents [38, 39]. According to Cappelli [11, p. 140], in the new digital world, the hiring process is becoming similar to a marketing one because job candidates are approached by firms' recruiting units as customers to be "carefully identified and targeted, attracted to the company and its brand, and then sold on the job. In an environment with fierce competition for talent, companies that master the art and science of on-line recruiting will attract and keep the best people". Similarly,

Barber [40] argues that attracting applicants for a job position in a firm is one of the most critical steps in recruiting employees. By also taking into account the applicant's perspective, Thielsch, Träumer and Pytlik [41] note that the immediate feedback is the most appreciated aspect of e-recruiting by job seekers.

As described in Lee [13, p. 82], there are many e-recruiting sources: (1) general-purpose job board; (2) niche job board; (3) e-recruiting application service provider (ASP); (4) corporate web site; (5) e-recruiting consortium; (6) and hybrid (online and offline) recruiting service provider. Each one of these sources shows some advantages as well as disadvantages. Generally, e-recruitment has been appreciated for increased number of applicants, time and cost savings, improved employer image and independence of place and time [42, 43]. Furthermore it is considered to be particularly effective for talent hunting, since it allows for a strong interaction between recruiters and candidates and helps to find faster information [12]. More in detail, some authors [35, 36, 44] note that company's web sites are acknowledged as relevant cost-effective recruitment methods, but they require IT specialist and a high upfront development cost [13]. Job boards are considered helpful both for candidates and companies, by allowing job seekers to contact thousands of employers and reducing the cycle time of recruiting processes [37]. Unfortunately, they often provide too many and low quality applications, limited content control and very few relationships with candidates [37, 44]. Finally, there are so many job board sites on the Internet that companies can get very confused and spend a lot of time in deciding which job board suites better [37].

Regarding the identification of job board attributes, Koong, Liu and Williams [37] describe several primary attributes[1] that are provided to job seekers and corporate recruiters by the Internet Job Boards. On the job seekers side, they find out eight features: job database presence; career advice; allowing job seeker agents; job search by location; job search by category/type; job search by keyword; resuming deactivation controlled by job seeker; and allowing resume posting. On the corporate recruiters side, the primary attributes are: allowing targeted audience by level; offering jobs with varied skills at various levels; allowing direct/indirect online applications; paperless; allowing online resume management for recruiters; allowing access to candidates; allowing targeted audience by skill; allowing recruiter agents; allowing real-time postings; and international presence. In addition, they find three unique[2] attributes: allowing online screening; allowing online testing; and requiring job poster to use programming language.

Finally, through social media (blogs, wikis, email, text messaging, social networks) the barriers of social interaction are consistently reduced by activating at the same time some connections that otherwise could not take place. As underlined by Gravili [12], in this context, the social recruiting is a particularly effective method for time and cost savings, as well as for best talent hunting as it allows reaching both active and passive candidates. Despite this, some problems in recruiting

---

[1]These attributes were found in at least 75 % of the Internet Job Boards.

[2]These attributes were found in less than 50 % of the Internet Job Boards.

through social networks are still present, such as legal, ethical and privacy related issues [12].

By analyzing the main literature, certain items to deepen emerge. Online recruitment tools are relevant for businesses in order to hunt talents and to save time and costs. However, they still have a number of critical issues and they may be significantly improved. Despite this, there are relatively few contributions offering advice on how to improve e-recruiting services both in job seekers and in recruiter's perspective. To fill this gap, this paper aims to explore the case of an Italian job board (Face4Job) in order to add knowledge on the latest trends in this field. Our purpose is to investigate why and how the problems related to traditional recruitment and e-recruitment methods have led to an innovative solution of "talent hunting". In addition, we aim to better understand the strengths and the weaknesses of this innovative solution, how its effectiveness is measured and which are its possible future paths.

3   Research Methodology

To explore our research questions, the paper adopts a qualitative approach by presenting a case study according to Yin [45]. More specifically, we analyzed an Italian start-up in the e-recruiting sector. Face4Job was chosen for two main reasons. Firstly, its founder and CEO has been a professional recruiter for about 5 years. Secondly, it represents an innovative approach to e-recruitment services compared to the existing ones which were practiced by its founder. Especially, since its CEO was a direct user of digital and physical recruitment tools, Face4Job represents his innovative answer to save time and costs in recruiting process. Finally, the conceiving and the operational logic of Face4Job came from several meetings with international scholars particularly expert in human resources and from a careful analysis of what already exists, but not really convincing, in e-recruiting services.

Information was collected through documentary analyses, direct observations on the web site of Face4Job and an in depth semi-structured interview with its CEO.

With the documentary analysis [46–48] we studied several documents related to the gradual development of Face4Job, such as the CEO's presentations in several meetings, conferences and other events, articles in Italian newspapers and all the documents directly available by Face4Job website.

The exploration of the Face4Job website was guaranteed by using the login credentials of the CEO, both in the companies and in the candidates' areas. In this manner, a direct observation of the services offered by Face4Job was made possible.

The case analysis was made through a semi-structured interview, conducted with the founder of Face4Job, who is the person with the most thorough knowledge on Face4Job features and who oversaw its development since the beginning. The respondent was invited to participate to research by telephone and afterward the main research objectives and the interview outline was sent to him by email. The interview lasted approximately 30 min and it was carried out with the presence of both authors, in line with Arksey and Knight protocol [47]. The interview was divided into five sections: (1) Face4Job and e-recruitment services; (2) Using Face4Job; (3) Face4Job effectiveness; (4) Limitations and future paths for Face4Job; (5) Interviewee's structural data.

The interview was recorded and later fully transcribed from April 2014 and May 2014. Finally, a content analysis [49, 50] was made. Both descriptive and interpretative encoding was performed in order to identify recurring themes related to several relevant experiences and helpful in answering our research questions [51]. The analysis was first performed separately and then jointly by the authors in order to compare the results with the existing literature [52]. The results of the case study are presented in a narrative form [45] and they are emphasized in the discussion section.

In the next section, we disclose the results with regard to each part in which the interview was divided.

4   Case Study

4.1   Face4Job and e-Recruitment Services

Face4Job was founded on August 2013 and it was born from the intuition of its current CEO, who previously directed the R&D of a great American hi-tech start-up. Nowadays, the company is recognized among the Italian "Innovative Start-up" for the highly innovative and technological content of its project. In addition to the CEO, other five new shareholders with a solid international background were involved.

Face4Job represents an interesting case study, as it offers an innovative solution to several critical aspects in e-recruiting services. According to Face4Job CEO's experiences in the recruitment field, the most common problem related to traditional as well as to online recruiting is the large amount of time and costs that searching for candidates from job boards and others e-recruiting channels still requires.

The operating logic of Face4Job is the one which typically characterizes all the other job boards: the presence of a resume database and the online screening of curricula. Despite this, this logic presents so many innovative features in the way of matching between demand and offer of labor.

On the corporate recruiters side, the first element of discontinuity is represented by the replacement of the video CV, which involves spontaneous statements, with the video interviews. In other words, companies can submit some questions to the candidates in order to verify their skills and talent and in order to assessing their consistency with the job position. More in depth, these questions can be visible and the interviews are highly structured because they require the same items to all the applicants. In addition, to more efficiently match the requests of employers and job seekers, Face4Job uses a peer matching algorithm for overlapping the information in CV and talents of the candidates with the requirements provided by companies (skills, soft skills, training, experiences, and talents). This algorithm, developed in software house, accounts for 95 % of the information provided in CVs (studies, languages, previously experiences, hobbies) and only for 5 % of the talents which candidates declare they have. In this way, the algorithm allows for a fairly objective pre-assessment and automatic screening and the curriculum has the largest relevance.

On the job seekers side, Face4Job offers several services, such as a job database, job search by location/category/type, resume posting. When a job seeker submits his resume, he becomes a "player" and can immediately see the companies which are looking under his profile. Furthermore, the applicants can make a self-assessment by sorting their better talents. In this way, the candidates can also enable a self-branding mechanism, because their best skills are visible to all recruiters.

Face4Job proposes to the applicants ten talents which were chosen on the basis of an international study conducted in 2013 by Natasha Dalzell Martinez (Apollo Group Phoenix). These talents, to be ordered by the candidates, are particularly effective thanks to their objectivity. They are: adaptability, information management, communication skills, critical thinking, collaborativeness, entrepreneurship, cosmopolitanism, innovation, leadership, productivity and reliability. Finally, when an applicant submits a "video talent", he becomes a "facer" and he gains more visibility. A video talent can be spontaneously uploaded by applicants because standard questions of employment interviews are preset and they are always available in the candidates area. Otherwise, the candidate can upload the video talent when he is called by the recruiters to answer some specific questions.

4.2   Using Face4Job

Face4Job is actually operating for a few months. Most of the registered companies are those with a high employees turnover, such as call centers or tourist companies. A large number of companies also belong to the IT, Engineering, Financial, Manufacturing and non-profit sector. Face4Job is not just for large companies, but it also includes SMEs, such as a dental surgery or some franchise stores. According to the information collected, Face4Job is initially used more like a resume database, but afterwards the interaction between companies and applicants becomes intensive thanks to video talent. In Face4Job there are also many employment agencies which use it for preliminary employment interviews and for submitting a list of candidates to the client company. In this way, Face4Job promotes the direct match between work demand and offer as well as it may also represent a useful intermediary in recruitment. Instead, it is entirely excluded that it can replace the "head hunters" because the personal meeting is always important in this case.

Face4Job can overcome one of the most common problems of online recruiting: high amounts of curriculum, low quality of candidates and misrepresentations. This is possible thanks to "video talent" that allows company to verify candidates' declarations through strict controls by experienced people.

Using Face4Job is totally free for job seekers. Some promotions have been provided for companies until July 2014; now they can use Face4Job by paying for use with refills of different amounts. The costs include: using resume database, job posting, automated resume screening and twelve standard questions for video talent (ten questions for the basic talents, one for languages and one for any talent of the candidate).

4.3 Face4Job Effectiveness

The effectiveness of Face4Job as recruiting tool is measured through the evaluation of data related to accesses, actual use by businesses and candidates, requests and uploads of video talent. All this information is collected at the administrative level. Also, every time that a company closes its job posting, it have to justify its reason: in this way, it is possible to know if the employees have been chosen through Face4Job. Periodic surveys (weekly) are provided at entered companies and information relating to their use of Face4Job platform is periodically sent to them. Usually, every Sunday night a summary of new players and new facers is sent through preset formats. Monitoring and updating functions are carried out by an administrative supervisor. Monitoring is essential, as many job announcements remain open despite the worker has been hired. In such cases, Face4Job sees to contact companies and to close inactive job announcements.

Many feedbacks come also from candidates (for example, about the lack of some tasks or qualification titles) and this allows greatly improving the services offered beyond to increase the level of expertise of the main actors of Face4Job.

4.4 Some Limitations and Future Paths for Face4Job

One of the major limitations of Face4Job is the still low number of participants in the platform and the still weak brand. But these circumstances are quite normal in the early stages of a start up. Many critical issues also are related to the orientation of the website that should be graphically improved, according to the opinions of the main actors of Face4Job. Nowadays Face4Job doesn't have a social orientation and candidates don't communicate with each other. Face4Job is mainly characterized by the company-candidate relationship but many changes are planned for the future.

First of all, the CEO plans to strengthen the Face4Job's sociability and to encourage the interaction among the candidates by providing for group interviews or specific channels for developing entrepreneurial projects. Second, Face4Job will be launched at international level. Especially, the aim is to bring Face4Job in Middle East, Russia, Brazil, USA and Asia. This is because the business model of Face4Job is based on small prices, so it needs to have a large critical mass. Third, in the future Face4Job will allow a better personalization and customization of its services. Some examples could include: the personalization of the interview according to the company's needs, some agreements with universities for searching new graduates, the ability to optimize the algorithm by giving more weight to what matters most for a company. Finally, mobile app will be implemented and the insertion of a "room" virtual will be expected. Through the room companies can directly conduct employment interviews just from the Face4Job's platform, without using external software. According to the CEO, this is a great guarantee of privacy.

5 Discussion

By comparing the empirical evidences from interviews and the theoretical framework we have drawn, several reflections emerge. The presence of some problems in e-recruiting services is confirmed by our finding, especially the large amount of costs and time that are required for searching potential candidates. It is interesting to note that they were these problems to inspire a new business model in this sector because they have been directly tested from the founder of Face4Job.

Another interesting aspect concerns the logic underlying to the video talent. The introduction of a new form of employment interview, called "video talent", increases the interaction between recruiters and job seekers and it makes more efficient the "talent hunting", according with the intentions of Face4Job's CEO. Being able to directly verify the claims of a candidate (for example, with respect to the talents he claims to have), this confirms some research showing that individuals typically have an inflated view of their abilities and they frequently lack of self-insight [53]. Furthermore, this remark is confirmed by the fact that only 5 % of the peer matching algorithm takes into account the talents declared by the candidates. In this way, a more objective presentation is given to companies. Finally, the orientation of the video talent with standard questions underlines the relevance of the structured interviews for achieving a selection.

In conclusion, we emphasize another important issue. The future focus will be given to the orientation of Face4Job's website fits with the assumptions that the web site orientation can affect organizational attractiveness by influencing the perception of the website usability [54, p. 242]. If Face4Job will be able to attract more talents, this will be a guarantee of success for companies which seeking talents through Face4Job.

6 Conclusions, Limitations and Future Research

This paper analyzes the evolution and the new trends in the e-recruitment services, by investigating why and how the problems related to traditional recruitment and e-recruitment have led to an innovative solution of "talent hunting". This study contributes to the literature about e-recruiting in at least two ways. Firstly, it confirms the presence of some problems and disadvantages in e-recruiting practices. Secondly, it shows an innovative solution taken by an online recruitment service provider in order: (1) to more efficiently match the requests of employers and job seekers through specific algorithms and (2) to make the search of talent by a "video talent" system much more qualified.

At the same time, this work presents two main limitations. Firstly, it considers only the Face4Job's point of view, by relying especially on the interview with its founder/CEO, and secondly, it adopts a strictly qualitative methodology for analyzing and interpreting the results. Future research could replicate this analysis by involving also companies and candidates that are registered on Face4Job web site; integrate the qualitative research methods with quantitative one (such as surveys) in order to offer a more empirical contribution.

References

1. Wood, A.F., Smith, M.J.: Online Communication: Linking Technology, Identity, and Culture. Lowrence Erlbaum Associates, Mahwah (2001)
2. Wellman, B., Witte, J., Hampton, K.: Does the internet increase, decrease, or supplement social capital? Social networks, participation, and community commitment. Am. Behav. Sci. **45**(3), 436–455 (2001)
3. Markus, M.L., Robey, D.: Information technology and organizational change: casual structure in theory and research. Manage. Sci. **34**(5), 583–598 (1988)
4. Galliers, R.D., Baets, W.R.J.: Information Technology and Organizational Transformation: Innovation for the 21st Century Organization. Wiley, Chinchester (1998)
5. Stevens, P.M., Williams, K.P., Smith, M.C.: Organizational communication and information processes in an internet-enabled environment. Psychol. Mark. **17**(7), 607–632 (2000)
6. Penrose, E.: The theory of the growth of the firm. Wiley, New York (1959)
7. Barney, J.B.: Firm resources and sustained competitive advantage. J. Manag. **17**, 99–120 (1991)
8. Barney, J.B.: The resource-based theory of the firm. Organ. Sci. **7**(5), 469 (1996)
9. Barney, J.B.: Is the resource-based « view » a useful perspective for strategic management research ? Yes. Acad. Manage. Rev. **26**, 41–56 (2001)
10. Wernerfelt, B.: A resource-based view of the firm. Strateg. Manag. J. **5**(2), 171–180 (1984)
11. Cappelli, P.: Making the most of on-line recruiting. Harvard Bus. Rev. **79**(3), 139–146 (2001)
12. Gravili, G.: Il social recruiting. Cacucci Editore, Bari (2011)
13. Lee, I.: An architecture for a next-generation holistic e-recruiting system. Commun. ACM **50**(7), 81–85 (2007)
14. Boswell, W.R., Roehling, M.V., LePine, M.A., Moynihan, L.M.: Individual job-choice decisions and the impact of job attributes and recruitment practices: a longitudinal field study. Human Res. Manage. **42**, 23–37 (2003)

15. Breaugh, J.A., Starke, M.: Research on employee recruitment: so many studies, so many remaining questions. J. Manage. **26**, 405–434 (2000)
16. Dineen, B.R., Ash, S.R., Noe, R.A.: A web of applicant attraction: person–organization fit in the context of web-based recruitment. J. Appl. Psychol. **87**, 723–734 (2002)
17. Breaugh, J.A.: Employee recruitment: current knowledge and important areas for future research. Hum. Res. Manage. Rev. **18**, 103–118 (2008)
18. Breaugh, J.A., Macan, T.H., Grambow, D.M.: Employee recruitment: current knowledge and directions for future research. In: Hodgkinson, G.P., Ford, J.K. (eds.), International Review of Industrial and Organizational Psychology, vol. 23, pp. 45–82. Wiley, New York (2008)
19. Costa, G., Gianecchini, M.: Risorse Umane. Persone, Relazioni e Valore. McGraw-Hill, Milano (2009)
20. Cortese, C., Del Carlo, A.: La selezione del personale. Raffaello Cortina Editore, Milano (2008)
21. Martone, A. (ed): La selezione del personale. Nuovi strumenti. Guerini e Associati, Milano (2007)
22. Schneider, B., Schmitt, N.: Staffing organizations. Scott, Foresman, Glenview (1986)
23. Arvey, R.D., Campion, J.E.: The employment interview: a summary and review of recent research. Pers. Psychol. **35**, 231–322 (1982)
24. Macan, T.: The employment interview: a review of current studies and directions for future research. Hum. Res. Manage. Rev. **19**(3), 203–218 (2009)
25. Levashina, J., Hartwell, C.J., Morgeson, F.P., Campion, M.A.: The structured employment interview: narrative and quantitative review of the research literature. Pers. Psychol. **67**(1), 241–293 (2014)
26. Oliphant, G.C., Hansen, K., Oliphant, B.J.: A review of a telephone-administered behavior-based interview technique. Bus. Commun. Q. **71**(3), 383–386 (2008)
27. Schmidt, F.L., Zimmerman, R.D.: A counterintuitive hypothesis about employment interview validity and some supporting evidence. J. Appl. Psychol. **89**(3), 553–561 (2004)
28. Wiesner, C.S., Cronshaw, S.F.: A meta-analytic investigation of the impact of interview format and degree of structure on the validity of the employment interview. J. Occup. Psychol. **61**, 275–290 (1988)
29. Trentini, G. (ed): anuale del colloquio e dell'intervista. Utet, Torino (1995)
30. Campion, M.A., Pursell, E., Brown, B.K.: Structured interview: raising the psychometric properties of the employment interview. Pers. Psychol. **41**, 25–42 (1988)
31. Gilliland, S.W.: The perceived fairness of selection systems: an organizational justice perspective. Acad. Manag. Rev. **18**, 694–734 (1993)
32. Janz, T., Hellervik, L., Gilmore, D.C.: Behavior description interviewing. Allyn & Bacon, Boston (1986)
33. Latham, G.P., Saari, L.M., Pursell, E.D., Campion, M.A.: The situational interview. J. Appl. Psychol. **65**, 280–296 (1980)
34. Moser, K.: Recruitment sources and post-hire outcomes: the mediating role of unmet expectations. Int. J. Sel. Assess. **13**, 188–197 (2005)
35. Chapman, D.S., Webster, J.: The use of technologies in the recruiting, screening, and selection processes for job candidates. Int. J. Sel. Assess. **11**, 113–120 (2003)
36. Stone, D.L., Lukaszewski, K., Isenhour, L.C.: e-Recruiting: online strategies for attracting talent. In: Gueutal, H., Stone, D.L. (eds.) The Brave New World of EHR: Human Resources in the Digital Age, pp. 22–53. Wiley, New York (2005)
37. Koong, K.K., Liu, L.C., Williams, D.: An identification of internet job board attributes. Hum. Syst. Manage. **21**, 129–135 (2002)
38. Eckhardt, A., Laumer, S.: An IT-architecture to align e-recruiting and retention processes. Int. J. E-Serv. Mob. App. **1**(2), 38–61 (2009)
39. Weitzel, T., Eckhardt, A., Laumer, S.: A framework for recruiting it talent: lessons from siemens. MIS Quart. Executive (MISQE) **8**(4), 175–189 (2009)
40. Barber, A.: e Recruiting employees: individual and organizational perspectives. Sage Publications, Thousand Oaks (1998)

41. Thielsch, M., Träumer, L., Pytlik, L.: e-Recruiting and fairness: the applicant's point of view. Inf. Technol. Manage. **13**(2), 59–67 (2012)
42. Parry, E., Tyson, S.: An analysis of the use and success of online recruitment methods in the UK. Hum. Res. Manage. J. **18**(3), 257–274 (2008)
43. Sylva, H., Mol, S.T.: e-Recruitment: a study into applicant perceptions of an online application system. Int. J. Sel. Assess. **17**(3), 311–323 (2009)
44. Breaugh, J.A.: Employee recruitment: current knowledge and important areas for future research. Hum. Res. Manage. Rev. **18**, 103–118 (2008)
45. Yin, R.K.: Case study research: design and methods. Sage Publications, Beverly Hills (1984)
46. Mogalakwe, M.: The use of documentary research methods in social research. Afr. Sociol. Rev. **10**(1), 221–230 (2006)
47. Payne, G., Payne, J.: Key Concepts in Social Research. Sage Publications, London (2004)
48. Scott, J.: A Matter of Record, Documentary Sources in Social Research. Polity Press, Cambridge (1990)
49. Arksey, P., Knight, T.: Interviewing for Social Scientists. Sage Publication, London (1999)
50. Krippendorff, K.: Content Analysis. An Introduction to its Methodology. Sage, Thousand Oaks (2004)
51. King, N., Horrocks, C.: Interviews in Qualitative Research. Sage, London (2010)
52. Spiggle, S.: Analysis and interpretation of qualitative data in consumer research. J. Consum. Res. **21**, 491–503 (1994)
53. Baumeister, R.F., Schmeichel, B.J., Vohs, K.D.: Self-regulation and the executive function: the self as a controlling agent. In: Kruglanski, A.W., Higgings, E.T. (eds.) Social Psychology: A Handbook of Basic Principles, pp. 516–539. Guilford Press, New York (2007)
54. Ian, O., Williamson, I.O., Lepak, D.P., King, J.: The effect of company recruitment web site orientation on individuals perceptions of organizational attractiveness. J. Vocat. Behav. **63**, 242–263 (2003)

The Inextricable Intertwining of the Firm, the Platform and the Customer: The Case of a Social Media Platform for Innovation

Antonella Martini, Silvia Massa and Stefania Testa

Abstract The aim of this contribution is to explore the relationship between human actors and technology in the context of a social media platform, developed by a leading Italian firm in the food industry. In order to address these issues, we adopt a theoretical approach that is deeply rooted in Pickering's "mangle" theory, and Jones' subsequent metaphor of "double dance of agency". We developed a longitudinal case study with two rounds of interviews with marketing and R&D managers. The contribution provides three main theoretical contributions. It provides detailed attention to the co-evolution over time of human-material entanglement, an aspect that papers in this area often omit. It provides a clear picture of a series of inter-related emergent phenomena, entangling managers, users, and the social media platform. It introduces further dimensions in the dancing metaphor. On the practical side, the double dance of agency perspective on this platform's evolution also offers useful insight for practitioners.

Keywords Social software · Innovation · Double dance of agency model · Case study

1 Introduction

Common understanding of the innovation process today builds on the observation that firms rarely innovate alone and that the innovation process can be seen as an interactive relationship among producers, users and many other actors [1]. Based on

A. Martini
DESTEC, Università di Pisa, Pisa, Italy
e-mail: A.Martini@ing.unipi.it

S. Massa · S. Testa (✉)
DIME, Università degli Studi di Genova, Genova, Italy
e-mail: stefania.testa@unige.it

S. Massa
e-mail: silvia.massa@unige.it

© Springer International Publishing Switzerland 2016
T. Torre et al. (eds.), *Empowering Organizations*, Lecture Notes in Information Systems and Organisation 11, DOI 10.1007/978-3-319-23784-8_10

the idea that one of the fundamental sources of knowledge for innovation is the customer [2], coupled with drastic reductions in communication costs through the use of Web technologies, some firms have begun systematically involving users in their innovation processes by leveraging social media tools [3]. These tools rely on active content creation by users or members as a central distinguishing feature. Companies use social media to do what traditional advertising does: persuade consumers to buy a company's product or service. Some companies have recently become aware that social media is not simply another channel for distributing corporate information or an add-on to a firm's promotional media mix [4, 5]. These companies are experimenting with more advanced uses of social media [6]. The debate is open on the ability of consumers to develop ideas that can inspire product or brand managers to veer hugely from a chosen course of action [7]. Our focus is on the use of social media to gather innovative ideas from an online community. Other study perspectives have included incentives to contribution [8] and methods for idea screening and evaluation [9, 10]. The use by a firm of social media based tools raises several issues concerning the difficulty of conceptualizing the roles of the different actors involved, their capability to act, the impossibility to anticipate or control the consequences of their actions, among others. In order to address these issues, we adopt a theoretical approach rooted in Pickering's "mangle"[1] theory, and Jones' subsequent metaphor of "double dance of agency" i.e. human [11] and material agencies [12–14]. Drawing on actor network theory, Pickering suggests that technological systems need to be understood in terms of interaction between human and material agency and the two can be seen as constitutively intertwined. He describes the process of mutual adjustment by which human and material agency are interactively stabilized over time as a temporally emergent dialectic of resistance and accommodation represented by the mangle of practice. Resistance can be offered by any entity, including material objects and it can be defined as the occurrence of a block on the path to some goal [13]; accommodations are made by the user to overcome or avoid resistances, and Pickering calls the interplay of human and material agency, as they interactively stabilize each other, the "dance of agency" [14]. Jones introduced the concept of a temporally emergent double mangling where human agents seek to channel material agency to shape the actions of other human agents in a sort of "ongoing double dance of agency" [15]. This model considers different kinds of actors who influence one another in an ongoing dialectic of resistance and accommodation. This model is useful in studying the particularly complex interactions related to information technologies with their intangible products and extensive involvement in a diverse range of organizational work practices.

According to this theoretical approach, the process of information systems development and use is understood as an emergent process in which human and material agencies are inextricably intertwined. We adopt this approach to

---

[1]A mangle is an old fashioned device with two rollers and a crank used for pressing and wringing water out of wet laundry.

investigate a specific social media platform for innovation—In the Mill I Wish (MIW). MIW was developed by a leading Italian firm in the food industry to maintain contact with and gather innovative ideas from its customers. This case is particularly relevant because companies in the food sector are just beginning to experiment with social media [16]. We examine the ongoing functioning of MIW, and consider how the platform's material agency[2] (re)configures the practices and possibilities of different modes of engagement by multiple users and vice versa [14].

This chapter is organized as follows. In the next section we present the methodology. The case setting makes up section three, which is followed by the empirical evidence, both in terms of description and discussion, in section four. The chapter concludes with implications for researchers and practitioners.

2 Methodology

A single longitudinal case study (2009–2011) was developed: Barilla. The company is highly innovative and represents one of the most engaged companies experimenting with social media in Italy today. Data was collected primarily by means of semi-structured interviews inside the company and by observations of the social media under investigation. Interviews ranged between 40 min and 2 h involving key informants covering different roles. Full write-ups were done. Interviewees were given the opportunity to make comments on drafts. Secondary data were collected by using different sources of data and methods to validate one another [18]. In order to allow a more precise and nuanced description of MIW, a layered and modular view of the platform has been adopted. MIW platform is characterized by four layers—devices, networks, services and content [19–21]—two of which, i.e. services and contents, well describe MIW evolution over time.

The method for analyzing interview data (e.g., [22]) was intended as a process of progressive refinement, moving from raw transcribed interview text toward more general theoretical inferences. Collected data allowed the distinction and examination of two main developmental stages in MIW's life: the first stage (October 2009–November 2010) and the second stage (November 2010–November 2011). In each stage of the platform's evolution over time, frames of meaning for the different actors were derived from the analysis of interview data related the firm and of secondary data related to consumers/users. Such frames of meaning were confronted with the main elements of the mangle. The firm's and the users' agency were classified as human agency that intertwines in outer/inner entanglements

---

[2]As a reviewer noted, the usage of "material" in relation to a software platform could be counter-intuitive but the paper maintains the human/material dichotomy because literature referring to Pickering's work generally adopts this distinction, also when talking about a software tool (see e.g. [17]).

respectively, with the non-human, i.e. material, agency of the platform. The evolution of the platform is read as a continuous dialectic of resistance and accommodation.

3 The Social Platform

This contribution sheds light on the characteristics of the social media platform for innovation—MIW—that the brand Mulino Bianco of Barilla company implemented in 2009. Through this platform (http://www.nelmulinochevorrei.it/), customers can share ideas and suggestions about company's products, promotions, initiatives, social/environmental commitment and other aspects.

MIW provides the customers with the following main services: new idea submission, and voting on, commenting on and revising others' ideas. Ideas are collected in a structured manner, according to areas and thematic fields. Ideas are then voted on by the community and those ranked the highest (top ten) are considered for implementation by WM's marketing department. MIW includes a blog, which is also published in RSS (Really Simple Syndication) format, where WM employees write and discuss newly implemented projects or launched products, as well as about how ideas from customers are realized or how suggestions are used MIW also includes links to the official company web page and Facebook (FB). The "Contact tutor" button is available on the right side of the MIW home page to allow users to contact MIW staff in order to request support for posting a new idea. A counter is available with the number of ideas posted on the system with the number of total votes received. At the top of the page, there is a link to polls on issues of particular interest to the company.

4 Empirical Evidence: Presentation and Discussion

Figure 1 represents MIW's two main developmental stages described in Methodology section.

As it is shown in Fig. 1, we have identified two entanglements for each developmental stage. One, called inner entanglement, happens between the firm and the platform, while the other, called outer entanglement, is between the customers and the platform. Therefore, there are two kinds of human actors that intertwine with the same platform. The first is the firm, which has specific goals to be reached through the platform, intertwines with it to reach them and, last but not least, is responsible of the platform's initial design and subsequent modifications. The second is the customer, the final target of the firm's actions, whose behavior is entangled with the platform but that cannot directly modify its features. Moreover it is worth noting that the two entanglements are themselves deeply intertwined in that outcomes of the first. A detailed description of both developmental stages follows.

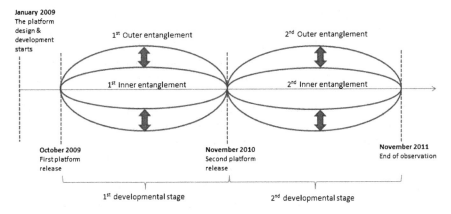

Fig. 1 MIW's main developmental stages

4.1 The 1st Developmental Stage

Figure 2 represents the two entanglements—inner and outer—we have identified in the first developmental stage. The inner entanglement includes: the firm's initial purposes and relevant features implemented on the platform; ongoing accommodations to emerging resistance; final assessment of resistance and the firm's decision to introduce significant adjustments of technology and organizational practices. The outer entanglement describes the intertwining between the human agency of customers and the material agency of the platform and how this may end, from time to time, into a resistance for the firm.

At the launch time in 2009, WM had the following main objectives for its digital strategy: gathering all brand lovers into an organized online community leveraging several examples of spontaneous online fan-clubs that arose for specific WM

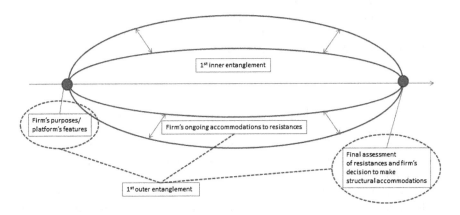

Fig. 2 The first developmental stage

products, such as "Pan di Stelle" biscuits or cult-like snack "Soldino", which is now out of production. In 2009, the FB page entitled "Give us back Soldino" had about 10,000 subscribers, while there were about 700,000 Pan di Stelle fans. To obtain feedback on WM initiatives and gain new insight from the online community, DCM spoke of a sort of "recruitment" of people to engage in a new relationship with the brand.

To this purpose, the firm decided to go "where the clients are". Then, the firm decided to monitor its fans meeting places (directly and indirectly), assigning each channel a specific task and maintaining a balanced relationship among them. Through its digital strategy, the firm wanted to have people experience its world by engaging them directly. MIW is part of WM's overall digital strategy, with the specific role of "engaging people and giving them a voice". MIW takes the concept of crowdsourcing and opens it up to any customer upon registration. MIW integrates and cross-promotes WM's web presence; MIW is bi-directionally linked to the official company web page and is also available as a FB application through which users can vote and comment on others' ideas. Users can also connect their MIW account with FB. In this way, any action they do on the MIW site or on MIW's FB application is visible on their FB bulletin boards. To reach the second objective, the main tools that WM activated were a blog and an application where people can put forward ideas and vote/comment/work on others' ideas. MIW's first year of activity recorded about 4,120 ideas; six of these were selected for implementation. MIW users are mainly WM customers and brand lovers, even though participation is open to anyone. From participation data after the first year of activity, users were 27 % men and 73 % women (98.6 % from Italy); the average age was 35. Women mainly using the platform have no children, are college educated and browse from home (these site demographics have been provided by Alexa.com at http://www.alexa.com/siteinfo/nelmulinochevorrei.it#). The community seems to be driven by people that strive to re-create the past, perhaps connected to their childhood, by proposing the re-edition of old products, old packaging, old gadgets. Several WM products have been on the market since the mid-seventies, so the community was formed prevalently by those who were children at that time. The mechanism of having the same users vote for their favorite ideas seemed to have a conservative effect that cut off the most potentially innovative ideas. Thus, in this first phase, MIW acted mainly as a generator of incrementally new ideas. Also, a couple of disruptive radically new ideas were proposed. They were not the most voted, but nevertheless the marketing unit selected them for implementation. In spring 2009, two users proposed that WM support protected WWF (World Wide Fund For Nature) sites in Italy. From this idea, three successful FB projects were started. Through one of them, the "count-a-tree" project, WM committed to planting one tree in a WWF site for each ten users that voted for their favorite WM product in the "Fruit histories" (milkshakes and fruit-cups) line, engaging in a sort of FB competition. Only 1 week from the application's launch date, 2,500 users had voted and 250 trees had been planted. After 20 days, the final target of a planting whole orchard had been reached and currently the competition continues on through new initiatives.

Through the mangle conceptual model, the story of MIW's first developmental stage can be read as a continuous dynamic of resistance and accommodation. Specifically, the online community's conservative nature can be read as resistance, while the marketing unit's direct intervention to select the most innovative ideas for implementation can be read as accommodation enacted by the company in response to the previously mentioned resistance. Several studies handle this issue considering both extrinsic (money, recognition, reputation) and intrinsic (social status, task fulfillment, altruism) benefits (see e.g. [10, 23–27]). At the same time, the material agency of the platform, which is entangled in the everyday practices of users, concretely participates in the production of output. As Scott and Orlikowski [28, p. 19] affirm, "social media are not neutral pipes through which knowledge is delivered but integrally and materially part of knowledge production". In line with the extant literature rooted on mangle theory we can say that the output of what we call inner entanglement is the unpredictable and emergent result of the mangle of practice between users and the platform. Such a result can be identified, from time to time, with the list of the 10 most voted ideas that WM takes into consideration for realization. This is a simplification, in that the result of entanglement between users and the platform is more rich and complex. We have narrowed the focus on the application to the gathering of ideas in order to exemplify our argument. The discussion on mangling could readily be extended to include all its features. In this case, the choice to produce limited editions of old products can be seen as accommodation by the firm. The winning idea was to start up production of a biscuit that was popular in the seventies. The firm carried out the idea of re-producing the biscuits and offered them as a free sample for customers who bought two packages of biscuits or snacks. In this way, the firm satisfied its most devoted customers, the "former children" community, without really returning to the past. In the same vein and in response to continuous calls for old surprises,[3] the firm activated a blog entirely dedicated to them and run by the person who has been managing WM surprises and promotions since 1978. As previously noted, another significant instance of resistance against the firm's purpose of gathering new ideas from customers was inherent in the mechanism of idea voting. The online community was conservative; therefore, the most innovative ideas risked being excluded. The accommodation chosen by the firm was to break the "rules of the game" by directly selecting the most promising ideas even though they were not the most voted by the community. At the end of the first developmental stage, the firm had identified the main forms of resistance to its original purposes, and once it had experienced the platform's potential, it identified new goals to be reached. The main forms of resistance involved both contents and methods and referred to the community's conservative tendency. Specifically, resistance can be identified as the tendency to suggest ideas repeatedly on the same issues, ideas frequently connected to a return to the past and the tendency to exclude the most radically new ideas by

---

[3]Some of WM's products contain small toys or gadgets in their packaging (e.g. small pie or cookie shaped erasers) which have become a cult phenomenon among adults.

simply not voting them. Another instance of resistance against the firm's dream to have a creative community working on innovative ideas for WM was that what the firm had was, at best, a community of "creative". In fact, the first year of MIW revealed that people tended to prefer suggesting their "original" ideas instead of working on someone else's ideas. The result was that suggested ideas were frequently replicated or were very similar to others, whereas promising ideas, which would have needed only slight adjustment to be considered for realization, remained untouched. The firm accommodated these instances of resistance through modification of technology and practices. At the same time, these mo would also facilitate the achievement of the new goals the firm identified for the platform.

4.2 The 2nd Developmental Stage

Figure 3 represents the two entanglements—inner and outer—that we have identified for the second developmental stage.

The second developmental stage starts with the revision and extension of the firm's initial goals. In particular, after the successful WWF initiative and receiving some unexpected, highly innovative ideas, the company interpreted these facts as signals of MIW's potential to gather not only incrementally new ideas, but also radically new ideas. This bias of a scarce innovative potential on the part of customers was also shared by DCM who declared at the launch of MIW that the firm's expectations were limited to incremental ideas, as reported in the first developmental stage.

As a result, in the second developmental stage, the company decided to pursue customer involvement in the innovation process with greater emphasis by fostering the proposal of radically new ideas and by improving the quality of proposals received. These new goals implied the implementation of new platform services,

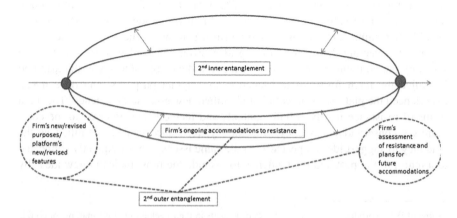

Fig. 3 The second developmental stage

such as a procedure called search-sift through-find, a tutor, and polls on specific issues.

The search-sift through-find procedure was introduced both to limit the conservative attitude of the online community and to foster more radically innovative ideas, therefore it represents both an accommodation to users' resistance and a mean to pursue the company's new innovation goals. This new service allows marketing staff and brand managers to choose an idea, independently from the success it garnered in the community. Several innovative ideas can be directly selected and developed. A set of ideas deemed interesting by WM staff but with few Community votes are resubmitted to the Community for reconsideration through the "Not to forget ideas" link. This new service impacts both the inner and outer entanglement. On one hand, it facilitates managers in identifying ideas with the most potential by means of a more advanced search and presentation system; on the other hand, it encourages users to go beyond easy suggestions while stimulating more challenging proposals. It is worth noting that ideas have to be analyzed by the firm's employees, which limits the applicability of automated information retrieval approaches. In this case, the platform mainly helps by providing an overview of large amounts of data, so that the marketing staff can gain insight from this information. Once an idea has been selected and developed, it appears on the list of developed ideas. It is clearly stated that the idea did not receive the highest ranking from the community, but that it was chosen directly by the company's management, thus contributing to a further reason for a sense of satisfaction by the contributor. The tutor was introduced to provide users with help in order to improve the quality of the proposals received, thereby reducing idea repetition and increasing recombination. It represents an accommodation to previously detected user resistance. The tutor provides suggestions on how to formulate ideas in order to make them clearer and have greater chances of being chosen by the community. However, the tutor does not provide any judgment on the quality of ideas. He/she also encourages users to check if their idea already exists in the community, avoiding resubmission of a previously existing idea. Repetition causes the idea to split votes, resulting in a low correlation between the quality of an idea and the number of votes it receives. In the case of great similarity with an existing idea, the tutor may encourage users to post their idea description as a comment instead of a new stand-alone idea. The tutor can also open new discussion threads and delete inappropriate posts to safeguard the company's reputation. Through a tutor, the company aims to be present, not to show off and to remain as neutral as possible.

Polls on specific issues of particular interest to the company were introduced to pursue the objective of getting new ideas from the community more effectively. It represents an accommodation to the users' resistance of proposing mainly conservative ideas, aimed at re-launching discontinued products. Each brand manager can launch a quantitative/qualitative poll and then the Marketing Research Unit identifies users to be involved in the poll in order to have a stratified sampling of the population under investigation. This procedure rewards customers with indirect financial incentives (free products) on the basis of the intensity of their participation in the polls.

In the second developmental stage, there was a revision of the professional figures involved in MIW. As a consequence of the new services, a more systematic involvement of managers in different units was enacted. In the first developmental stage, DCM acted as a sort of "idea-router", involving the relevant brand manager, the marketing unit or the platform innovation manager from time to time. In the second developmental stage, with the new "Search-sift through-find" service and the launch of specific polls, brand managers and the marketing unit were stimulated to interact directly with the tool and use it to look for new ideas on specific themes of interest. WM realized that only selected managers and experts in specific fields can usefully interact with customers and identify radical innovative ideas. New services were introduced in order to enlarge the commitment of the whole company; also, a carefully selected group of employees was chosen to directly interact with customers. The new professional figures involved are themselves a form of accommodation to the resistance that emerged both in the inner and outer entanglements. In the inner entanglement, the resistance addressed is represented by the above-mentioned conservative customer behavior. In fact, merely knowing that there were marketing and innovation experts behind the scenes with the task of observing and scouting "highly innovative" ideas had the effect of stimulating the most innovative wing of the online community. In the outer entanglement, the resistance addressed is represented by the risk of bias connected to the involvement of only one person (i.e. DCM), or one department (i.e. the digital communication department) in MIW. Moreover, in order to guarantee company engagement in MIW at all levels, firm's practices were revised introducing in the second developmental stage: a weekly review meeting involving Directors, the Business Development and Innovation Unit (BD&I) and the Digital Communication Unit; a monthly newsletter sent to BD&I, MKT, the Marketing Research Unit and Trade; and periodical review meetings involving the whole company.

In the following, some of the resistance-accommodation dynamics subsequent to the start of the second developmental stage—indicated in Fig. 3 as "Firm's ongoing accommodations to resistance"—will be described.

A first example of resistance regards a slowing down of participation in the online community and the subsequent accommodation of the company. In the first months after launching MIW, the number of new ideas as well as comments on others' ideas grew at a fast pace. Then, in the second developmental stage, this pace started to decrease and, for a certain time, the number of ideas remained almost unchanged. The company interpreted this resistance in MIW's evolution path as a result of the fact that, up to that moment, WM had not yet launched any product based on ideas collected from MIW. This lack of action most likely provoked dissatisfaction among contributors. The first accommodation introduced by the company was to provide users more information about work in progress by means of the "Under realization ideas" link. Afterwards, a re-design of the evaluation process was undertaken in order to shorten the time-to-market factor. Small and easy to implement projects were given priority in order to show the community that the company was true to its word. Handling the process in a timely manner was illustration that the company was not using MIW as a mere communication channel, but that it seriously considered MIW as a precious source of new ideas. For customers, it is highly important that their suggestions are actually used by the company to innovate. In this vein, the firm launched an idea diary in order to keep customers constantly informed on the path followed by ideas submitted to MIW. According to interview data, the scarce communication by the firm about the "life" of ideas after submission to MIW was recognized as a factor affecting participation slowdown. The idea diary openly informs customers about idea processing towards realization/rejection. The team explains why they appreciated and selected the idea. If it is eventually realized, they discuss how it was carried out. Otherwise, they discuss the reasons for rejection. The team frequently groups several ideas together through the diary and provides a solution intended to merge stimuli from several users. This kind of accommodations seemed to produce the desired result and the participation rate on MIW began to increase again.

The second example of resistance-accommodation dynamics that we will describe regards the role of the tutor, introduced to help customers in formulating new ideas. Interviews revealed that the use of a tutor turned out to be initially below company expectations. The community did not seem to appreciate this new service and scarcely used it. This customer behavior can be read as resistance towards the firm's aim of gathering better formulated ideas from the online community. A few months later, some comments were posted on the blog and forced the company to change the way the tutor was introduced to the community.

After this company accommodation, consisting of an adjustment of technology content, the message became more generic and better suited to MIW users who are not young Net surfers—as described above—and who, in fact, started to rely on the tutor more often and more readily. The language turned from a sort of official and political jargon—as noted by some users—to a more emotional and easy tone. Again, this is an example of how social media are not "neutral pipes" and a few words to introduce a new actor into a community can strongly influence users' behaviors. It is never known in advance which accommodations will be successful and if they will lead to the emergence of new resistance. As illustration that the resistance-accommodation dynamics are a never ending story, interviewees told us of a plan to start a third developmental stage introducing some structural changes in the platform's features. The changes will include features to help users explore the idea space by linking similar ideas more clearly on the site, therefore reducing the repetition of similar ideas while increasing recombination with other existing ideas. Table 1 summarizes main resistances-accommodation occurred along the first and the second developmental stages.

Table 1 Resistance—accommodation across stages

Stage	Resistance	Accommodation		
		Adjustment of technology	Revision of firm's practices related to the platform	Revision of firm's practices related to the real world
1st	Conservative attitude (return to old surprises)	Launch of a blog on old surprises (content and service)	Introduction of a new role for a long standing employee (the woman who has been managing WM surprises and promotions since 1978)	–
1st	Conservative attitude (return to old surprises)	Communication on the homepage of the organized meetings (content)	–	Organization of big meetings for surprise collectors
1st	Conservative attitude (return to old surprises)	Communication on the homepage of the new techno-surprises (content)	–	Introduction of a new version of surprises as applications for smartphone
1st	Conservative attitude (return to old products)	Communication on the homepage of the launch of limited editions, list of the stores where to find the products and the duration of the initiative (content)	–	Production and sale of discontinued products as limited editions
1st	Conservative attitude (disruptive ideas are not voted)	Communication on the homepage of the new informal procedure of idea selection (content)	Deep examination of all the ideas suggested by customers and direct selection of the most innovative ones independently from the number of received votes (informal procedure) + direct involvement of marketing staff and brand managers on an occasional basis	–

(continued)

Table 1 (continued)

Stage	Resistance	Accommodation		
		Adjustment of technology	Revision of firm's practices related to the platform	Revision of firm's practices related to the real world
2nd	Conservative attitude (disruptive ideas are not voted)	Introduction of a new formal procedure "search-sift through-find" (service) and relevant communication: "from now on the marketing staff will fix eyes on your ideas" (content)	Direct involvement of marketing staff and brand managers on a systematic basis	–
2nd	Conservative attitude (disruptive ideas are not voted)	Introduction of a new link "not to forget ideas": ideas that have received only a few votes, and are vice versa considered interesting by the marketing staff, are brought back to the users' attention to be re-considered (service)	Direct involvement of marketing staff and brand managers	–
2nd	Low quality of ideas/discussion	Introduction of "contact tutor" service via MSN messenger or Skype to support new idea submission (content + service)	Introduction of a new role—the tutor—dedicated to support/intervene in the community (provide suggestions to improve ideas, open new discussions and delete inappropriate posts...)	–
2nd	Monothematic ideas (customers tend to focus on a limited set of topics when suggesting new ideas)	Launch of polls on specific issues (of interest to the company) (content + service)	Direct involvement of the brand managers and marketing research unit to suggest the poll, select the sample that can participate and examine the submissions	–

(continued)

Table 1 (continued)

Stage	Resistance	Accommodation		
		Adjustment of technology	Revision of firm's practices related to the platform	Revision of firm's practices related to the real world
2nd	Bias due to the initial direct involvement of the digital department only	–	All the already mentioned government activities that include participation of other departments (new services, launch of polls, tutorship…)	–
2nd	Bias due to the initial direct involvement of the digital department only	–	–	Introduction of a weekly review meeting involving Directors, the BD&I Unit and the Digital Communication Unit
2nd	Bias due to the initial direct involvement of the digital department only	–	–	Launch of a monthly newsletter to BD&I, MKT, the Marketing Research Unit and Trade
2nd	Bias due to the initial direct involvement of the digital department only	–	–	Organization of periodical review meetings involving the whole company
2nd	Participation slowdown	Launch of the idea diary (content + service)	Direct involvement of marketing managers in communication activities related to the diary on the platform	–
2nd	Participation slowdown	Extended account on the blog of the launch-promotional events occurring in the real life, with interviews to the participants and comments by the winners (content)	–	Organization of big events around the country to launch winning initiatives: the customers who suggested the winning ideas are invited to participate to the launch and to post comments on the blog

5   Conclusions

The scope of this contribution includes exploring the mangling of an information system and its users in the context of a social media platform. We investigated the empirical case study of MIW, a social media platform developed by a leading Italian firm in the food industry, created to maintain contact with its customers and gather innovative ideas.

Theoretical and practical contributions emerged. On the theoretical side, it provides detailed attention to the co-evolution over time of human-material mangling, an aspect that papers in this area often omit. It also aims to provide a clear picture of a series of inter-related emergent phenomena, entangling managers, customers, and the social media platform. Social media are a sort of modeling clay, allowing humans agents to (re)configure its shape in a way precluded to other kinds of information systems. It suggests the existence of two kinds of accommodations, both proactive and passive in nature. By their means, the company attempts to disrupt the prevailing users' conservative needs by stimulating the most innovative wing of the online community and by revising firm practices. A single-loop learning [29] can be identified where the organization compares its performance to a set of pre-established goals and tries to make appropriate accommodations. In some cases, a double-loop learning emerges where the firm reassesses goals themselves. It introduces further dimensions in mangling. The double mangle can only partly explain MIW's evolution over time; other mangles should be considered. In fact, as it is well known in the literature [30], once a firm decides to develop social media strategies, the whole ecosystem of online social media is somewhat activated. Thus, other mangles on different, loosely interconnected platforms (i.e. FB, Twitter, blogs, consumer forums, etc.) may have considerable impact on its evolution.

On the practical side, the mangle perspective on MIW's evolution also offers useful insight for practitioners. Analysis of the firm's initial objectives for MIW and description of a tortuous path made of resistance and accommodation clearly indicate that the output of social media is unpredictable, as it depends on several factors and is temporally emergent. Firms that decide to use social media should clearly define their objectives, constantly monitor the outcome, be prepared to adjust their objectives over time.

Future studies should seek to extend our findings, specifically exploring social media platforms for innovation in different organizational settings and industries. In fact, we note that our findings are limited to the extent that we only examined the adoption of one specific digital innovation in a particular organizational context. It seems fruitful to explore the possibility of applying the mangle theory to the entire social media ecosystem, which is deeply interconnected. We could further investigate how the ecosystem may create blocks (i.e. resistance) in accommodation processes undertaken by the companies. Finally, elaborating on the existence of two kinds of accommodations seems promising. By means of theory-building procedures and techniques [31, 32], we could try to enrich the mangle theoretical framework of reference and suggest a more fine-grained classification of accommodations.

References

1. Piller, F.T., Ihl, C., Vossen, A.: A typology of customer co-creation in the innovation process (2010). Available at SSRN: http://ssrn.com/abstract=1732127 or http://dx.doi.org/10.2139/ssrn.1732127
2. Prahalad, C.K., Krishnan, M.S.: The new age of innovation: driving co-created value through global networks. McGraw Hill, New York (2008)
3. Bughin, J., Hung Byers, A., Chui, M.: How social technologies are extending the organization. McKinsey Q. 1–10 (2011)
4. Aula, P.: Social media, reputation risk and ambient publicity management. Strategy Leadersh. 38(6), 43–49 (2010)
5. Piller, F.T., Vossen, A., Ihl, C.: From social media to social product development: the impact of social media on co-creation of innovation. Die Unternehmung 66(1), 7–27 (2012)
6. Füller, J., Matzler, K.: Virtual product experience and customer participation: a chance for customer-centred, really new products. Technovation 27, 378–387 (2007)
7. Urbick, B.: Innovation through co-creation: consumers can be creative (2012). http://www.innovationmanagement.se/2012/03/26/innovation-through-co-creation-consumers-can-be-creative/. Accessed 30 March 2012
8. Piller, F.T., Walcher, D.: Toolkit for idea competitions: a novel method to integrate users in new product development. R&D Manag. 36(3), 307–318 (2006)
9. Toubia, O.: Idea generation, creativity, and incentives. Working Paper, Columbia Business School, New York (2005)
10. Terwiesch, C., Xu, Y.: Innovation contests, open innovation, and multi-agent problem solving. Manag. Sci. 54(9), 1529–1543 (2008)
11. Giddens, A.: The constitution of society. Polity, Cambridge (1984)
12. Leonardi, P.: When flexible routines meet flexible technologies: affordance, constraint, and the imbrication of human and material agencies. MIS Q. 35(1), 147–167 (2011)
13. Pickering, A.: The mangle of practice: agency and emergence in the sociology of science. Am. J. Sociol. 99(3), 559–589 (1993)
14. Pickering, A.: The mangle of practice: time, agency and science. University of Chicago Press (1995)
15. Jones, M.: Information systems and the double mangle: steering a course between the Scylla of embedded structure and the Charybdis of material agency. In: Larsen, T., L. Levine, L., DeGross, J. (eds.). Information Systems: current issues and future challenges. Proceedings of the IFIPWG 8.2 & 8.6 Joint Working Conference on Information Systems 1998, Helsinki, pp. 287–302 (1998)
16. Engagement DB report. The world's most valuable brands. who's most engaged? (2011). http://www.slideshare.net/PingElizabeth/engagementdb-social-media-engagement-study-of-the-top-100-global-brands
17. Olohan, M.: Translators and translation technology: the dance of agency. Transl. Stud. 4(3), 342–357 (2011)
18. Jick, T.D.: Mixing qualitative and quantitative methods: triangulation in action. Admin. Sci. Q. 24(4), 602–611 (1979)
19. Resca, A., Za, S., Spagnoletti, P.: Digital platforms as sources for organizational and strategic transformation: a case study of the Midblue project. J. Theor. Appl. E-Commerce Res. 8(2) (2013)

20. Spagnoletti, P., Resca, A.: A design theory for IT supporting online communities. In: Proceedings of the 45th Hawaii international conference on system sciences, pp. 4082–4091 (2012). doi:10.1109/HICSS.2012.54
21. Yoo, Y., Henfridsson, O., Lyytinen, K.: The new organizing logic of digital innovation: an agenda for information systems research. Inf. Syst. Res. **21**(4), 724–735 (2010)
22. Sahay, S., Robey, D.: Organizational context, social interpretation and the implementation and consequences of geographic information systems. Account. Manag. Inf. Technol. **6**(4), 255–282 (1996)
23. Jeppesen, L.K., Lakhani, K.R.: Marginality and problem solving effectiveness in broadcast search. Organ. Sci. **21**(5), 1016–1033 (2010)
24. Boudreau, K.J., Lakhani, K.R., Lacetera, N.: Incentives and problem uncertainty in innovation contests: an empirical analysis. Manag. Sci. **57**(5), 843–863 (2011)
25. Von Hippel, E., von Krogh, G.: Open source software and the private-collective innovation model: issues for organization science. Organ. Sci. **14**(2), 209–223 (2003)
26. Von Hippel, E., von Krogh, G.: Free revealing and the private-collective model for innovation incentives. R&D Manag. **36**(3), 205–306 (2006)
27. Harhoff, D., Henkel, J., von Hippel, E.: Profiting from voluntary information spillovers: how users benefit by freely revealing their innovations. Res. Policy **32**(10), 1753–1769 (2003)
28. Scott, S.V., Orlikowski, W.J.: Getting the truth': exploring the material grounds of institutional dynamics in social media. Working paper series, 177. Information Systems group, London School of Economics and Political Science, London (2009)
29. Argyris, C., Schon, D.: Organizational learning. Addison-Wesley, Reading (1978)
30. Hanna, R., Rohm, A., Crittenden, V.L.: We're all connected: the power of the social media ecosystem. Bus. Horiz. **54**(3), 265–273 (2011)
31. Glaser, B., Strauss, A.: The discovery of grounded theory. Weidenfield and Nicolson, London (1967)
32. Strauss, A., Corbin, J.M.: Basics of qualitative research: grounded theory procedures and techniques. Sage Publications, Inc. (1990)

From e-Marketplace to e-Supply Chain: Re-conceptualizing the Relationship Between Virtual and Physical Processes

Lapo Mola and Ivan Russo

Abstract In this research in progress paper, we seek to understand how pervasive use of ICT based platform such as electronic marketplaces influences the evolution of novel inter-organizational relationship. We focus on selling and distribution processes in fashion industry analysing the emerging phenomena from the perspective of the services provider. We chose two Internet platforms specialized in outsourcing the e-commerce related processes in the fashion industry, as exemplary cases. Our preliminary results suggest that such as platforms are deeply changing the system of relationships between clients and suppliers, affecting the processes performances, requiring a new conceptualization of the main attributes of the traditional supply chain.

Keywords eBusiness · Electronic marketplace · Electronic supply chain

1 Introduction

In a time of economic recession, all organizations are trying to improve their performances reconfiguring their supply chain in order to achieve better results in term of total cost reduction, better time to market, improving the performance of the entire value chain, enhance customer satisfaction and loyalty.

Today's distribution channel systems are increasingly complex with producers serving end-user markets through multiple channels [1]. Scholars have discussed that with increasing competition, retailers tend to move towards channel proliferation [2]. Consequently, with growing competition in the marketplace and the increasing reach

L. Mola (✉)
SKEMA Business School, LSMRC, Lille Nord de, Lille, France
e-mail: lapo.mola@skema.edu

I. Russo
Dipartimento di Management, Facoltà di Economia, Università degli Studi di Verona, Verona, Italy

© Springer International Publishing Switzerland 2016
T. Torre et al. (eds.), *Empowering Organizations*, Lecture Notes in Information Systems and Organisation 11, DOI 10.1007/978-3-319-23784-8_11

of the internet, several retailers are moving from being purely single- to multi-channel, with the internet representing the most common multi-channel complement to an existing physical store strategy [3].

In the last few years, it became clear that, especially in mature markets, e-commerce strategies have represented one of the more effective strategies able to support such as reconfigurations. The potential strategies available to manage sales and marketing activities have changed radically in recent years. Faced with the technical, logistics, and communication challenges of e-commerce, many firms chose not to develop this capability (entirely) in-house; as a consequence, demand for e-commerce intermediation and outsourcing has increased dramatically [4, 5]. However, the choice of a e-commerce strategy is not a pure technological choice. Interactive technologies affects retailers capabilities and strategies, requiring the development of new business models and new marketing channels with the need to revamp the supply chain organization to be more competitive in the e-commerce channel. Consequently, those elements dramatically changes operations, communication and marketing strategy, relationships between suppliers and customers and the way to serve the consumers [6]. In each industrial sector and every market niche, a few players have emerged as top e-commerce intermediaries, such as Amazon, Opodo, Zalando and eBay. Nowadays companies no longer compete as independent organizations, but rather as integral parts of supply chain links and nodes [7], and the superior performance of a firm will depend on its managerial ability to integrate and coordinate its supply network as a whole [8–10].

If the extent literature provides several contribution on outsourcing practices and models, what is missing is an in depth investigation on what happened when organizations decide to outsources activities or processes never managed internally before. In fact, previous research do not separate outsourcing existing functions from new functions (i.e., functions that have never been part of a firm's business model) to external suppliers [11]; however with the advent of the Internet, many firms that have never adopted e-commerce in their business models may now consider doing so by outsourcing IT to external suppliers.

With this research project, we therefore aim at investigating how those external suppliers organize and align strategies and behaviors with their customer developing new business model and new challenge for inter-organization relationships along the supply chain. Thus our units of analysis are two global internet provider and how they organize their business model in serving e-channel for their customer. This can help managers to show the main opportunities in outsourced e-commerce activities based on different relational settings, resources and capabilities to improve their outcomes. To do so we compare two cases that represent a growing trend where organizations tend to externalize the e-commerce activities. In doing so many they externalize not only the technological part of the business. On the contrary, what emerges by the two cases is a need of continuous alignment between the traditional channels and the new ones.

In sum up, the study will try to answer to the following research questions:

1. What level of integration between physical and information flow will need in the new e-marketplace business model in the B2B context?
2. How does the integration between physical and information flow affect the e-commerce intermediary's strategy in the B2B context?

The paper is organized as follow: we first introduce the theoretical background on e-markets and supply chain, then we introduce the two cases. The data analysis and the preliminary results will conclude the paper.

2 Theoretical Background

2.1 E-marketplaces

Over the last two decades information and communication technologies have remarkably affected the traditional patterns of production and distribution thus restructuring the industrial organization of Western firms and reshaping firms' existing boundaries.

Across industries and product types, services using the Internet as basic infrastructure promised to bring down any type of boundary to collaboration [12–14]. New players—now known as electronic marketplaces or e-marketplaces—entered the scene as the mediators of virtually any type of transaction [15–17]. The main aim of the first generation of electronic marketplaces was the reduction of buyers' search and selection costs, increasing transparency, and increasing market efficiency, thus reducing prices [4, 16].

Despite the existing knowledge regarding the nature, functions and rules that regulate markets, there is not yet a dominant theory to explain the change brought about by electronic marketplaces in affecting global collaborations. Electronic marketplaces influence the traditional organizational form of hierarchy and market prompting new forms of collaborative business processes, which are fundamental to companies' operations and strategies [17–19].

Although inter-organizational dynamism thus goes far beyond a mere make-or-buy choice [20, 21] extant literature often concentrates solely on how new e-marketplaces, empowered by information and communication technologies (ICTs), influence make-or-buy strategies. Management choices get framed as pairs of opposites [22].

E-marketplaces as eBay or Amazon are not only virtual places where transactions take place. They are an independent actor able to reconfigure the relationships among the different players involved in the supply chain [18].

Moreover, B2B e-marketplaces are generally considered as "spaces" where potential buyers can find out about products and prices through electronic catalogs, auction and exchange methods and more in general through information technology capabilities supporting price negotiation. In this case, the e-marketplace acts as an intermediary between a buyer and a seller. However, in recent years, B2B e-marketplaces rather than acting as intermediaries in the buying process, act as process facilitators, i.e., they tend to foster integration of interorganizational systems and provide specific capabilities in view of cooperation along the supply chains [17].

As a consequence of the grow of the diffusion of e-marketplace, we are witnessing the shifting from a client-supplier relationship to a partner relationship allowing the choice among different approach of collaboration models [23].

2.2 Supply Chain and Inter-Organizational Relationships

An efficient supply chain helps companies to reduce costs but also to deliver better services to the final customers. Thus the functionality of an e-marketplace would be expected to deliver a strategic type of supply chain services and the success of electronic markets on the functionality and practicality of the applications for business to business trading especially for managing supply chain processes [24]. E-marketplaces may be beneficial to suppliers in order to increase sales channel, to reduce inventory requirements, to improve market reputation. Outsourcing strategy is part and parcel of the value chain of corporate activities. As the use of outsourcing has grown and changed significantly over the past years and is expected to do so in the future [25, 26] relationships between customer firms and their outsourcers denote an increasingly key interface in supply networks [27]. Some of the business functions that are commonly outsourced include sourcing, production, IT, logistics, marketing, and customer support functions [3, 28]. The extent to which these functions will get outsourced may differ between web-only and multi-channel retailers and it create new challenge in inter-organizational relationship in the customer-supplier relationships, particularly with the advent of e-commerce. Inter-organizational relationships have received significant attention in the marketing channels literature [29]. More recently, the supply chain literature has highlighted the relevance of cooperative inter-firm relationships for achieving competitive advantage [30, 31]. Consequently a large part of managing supply chains consists of managing multiple relationships among the member organizations [32], thus in that business context, inter-organizational relationships are usually reflected through partnerships or buyer–seller relationships where connections among these organizations range from single transactions to complex interdependent relationships.

The Internet technology has enabled companies to create a new market space that facilitates electronic interactions among multiple buyers and sellers. The supply chain is the term by which the business system represented by an industrial network of Inter Organizational Relationships (IOR) set up to support the buying and selling of goods has come to be known [33, p. 306]. Several studies in the literature search for factors that examine the importance of inter-organizational relationships

(IOR) in supply chains and their potential impact [34]. Historically, much of the extant research on inter-firm relationships has focused on how the characteristics of a particular dyad influence relationship effectiveness [35]. The magnitude between two or more organizations helps determine the type of relationship they will pursue [36]. Supply chain integration is a result of human interactions which can be supported, but not replaced by IT [37, 38].

Within the scope of RBV, outsourcing is a strategic decision about which activities must be performed in-house and which must be outsourced by a company, through means of agreements contracts with more capable firms to undertake activities as e-commerce in order to increase its performance. An extension of RBV is the Relational View (RV) theory, that it assumes that firms can benefit from inter-firm integration and strategic partnerships to get valuable resources they lack in-house [39].

The resource-based model of competitive advantage suggests that competitive advantage maybe sustained by harnessing resources and capabilities that are valuable, rare, imperfectly, imitable and non-substitutable [40]. Resources are tangible assets like labor, capital and equipment while capabilities are intangible assets like management skills, organizational processes, and knowledge sharing routines [41].

2.3 Methodology

In order to answer our research question, we undertook a multiple case study of two companies in the fashion market. With this case study method, we can analyze data in a specific context in depth and thereby investigate a phenomenon in its natural [42] through a detailed analysis of a few events and their relationships [43]. Furthermore, a case study offers a unique method to observe natural phenomena in the data [40], because unlike quantitative analysis, it considers data on a micro level [42, 44, 45].

We choose two different marketplaces different in size and governance in order to reduce the bias represented by the analysis of one single case, were the phenomena of the reconfiguration of the client suppliers relationship could be affected by the size of the marketplace in the fashion market. That market basically get four characteristics of fashion markets: short life cycles, high volatility, low predictability and high level of impulse purchasing [46, 47].

To carry out our study we collected 12 interviews, in two rounds of interview in both companies. We interviewed the CEOs, the COOs and the main key managers involved.

2.4   Case1: Portal.com

Portal.com is a global Internet retail partner for multiple fashion and design brands. Its market leadership steps from its multibrand stores combined with many online, single-brand flagship stores developed by Portal Service.

Portal.com is a virtual fashion boutique and multi-brand design firm created in 2000. With direct relationships with designers, manufacturers, and authorized dealers, the founder was able to make Portal.com an archive of designs and styles that otherwise would rarely be found in online stores. The site continuously scouts creative contributions in the exclusive collections of the most well-known designers; it also provides a selection of clothes and accessories off-season at discounted prices, as well as vintage clothing, original research books, and design texts.

Portal.com's new and innovative business model has helped establish it as an Italian pioneer in selling fashion and design products. Furthermore, its ability to "respect" and improve brand images has encouraged big fashion boutiques and international designer labels to view its development positively.

In 2008, Portal.com has opened a specialized website offering a virtual space filled with a selection of branded, cutting-edge, high-quality, handmade clothing for men and women. It also offers a sort of virtual shop window for vanguard designers. On the site, each brand has a dedicated mini-store, or corner, that features new collections through editorial content and exclusive videos, such that visitors gain access to the designers' world and inspirations..

Finally, in 2010 Portal.com has opened a website completely dedicated to women's shoes, including a mix of e-commerce, editorial content, and exclusive services. A wide and detailed assortment, from the top designers to very well-known brands, offers a vast selection of shoes, along with books about shoes, jewels for shoes, and products for shoe care.

Since 2006, Portal.comp has managed the online single-brand stores of several fashion brands that wanted to offer a collection already available in brick-and-mortar shops on the Internet too. The complete solution that Portal.com offers its brand partners includes:

- A reliable and flexible technological platform.
- Innovative design interfaces that reflect its mix of creative skills.
- Global logistics.
- Excellent customer care service that is always near the final client.
- International web marketing activity.
- Management of Internet retail activities by a team of professionals who provide unified knowledge of e-commerce dynamics and fashion which works in more than 100 countries and speaks 11 different languages.

Portal.com selects unsold goods from showrooms, shops, and distributors and posts it, photographed and cataloged, on its own website to reach a bigger, more heterogeneous market, including anyone in the world with Internet access. At the end of each fashion season, Portal.com also takes the unsold goods from different boutique collections and ships them to a warehouse in Italy, where they are subjected to quality control reviews. This control is additional to quality controls performed by the clothes manufacturers. After this process, the goods are classified and cataloged according to a series of characteristics, such as the manufacturer's code, model, size, and color. For each family of products, a "representative" item is chosen, photographed, and put on the website. After the photographic stage, the subsequent phase involves creating descriptions of the goods to add to the site. A seal also gets placed on the items, such that customers cannot return used garments.

Finally, each item receives a chip based on the most advanced RFID technology to enable easy scanning and greater control over the movements of the garments during handling and stocking, so the item can located and identified at each moment and in every place it has been. At this point, management of the items shifts to Due Torri Spa, a partner company that manages logistics. The delivery to end customers is managed by UPS. Not only is UPS responsible for the delivery of products throughout Italy and to hubs in the United States and Japan, but it also guarantees delivery times to customers.

2.5 Case2: Fashioncorp.com

Fashioncorp.com, founded in 2007, is a multicultural agency, based in Venice, specialised in the creation, management and promotion of top fashion brand e-commerce.

The Fashioncorp.com business model is to provide to their customers (brands) an e-commerce project that embrace managing logistics and inventory management, design and web marketing, information and financial flows and customer service.

The current organization is very lean due to the recent foundation of the company, basically it is structured in two main areas: the area of production and the management area. In the first area we have the graphics department, the creative department, the technical department and the editorial department. The task of these areas is to design and develop the e-commerce of the various brands, both from a creative point of view and visual. The area of management, however, is formed from the logistics department, customer care and the department of finance and administration. That area has to manage all transactions flow product, cash flow, information flow and customer service. Being the front end instead of the brand Fascioncorp.com must be highly integrated with the its customers, to constantly transmit data on inventories, order delivery, quality issue, sales trends and also consumer questions received from the customer service department.

Through the skills acquired over time, the team of Fashioncorp.com is used to study the customer history and every aspect's of marketing and communication, but it is not only that the core business of the company. The most important task that distinguishes Fashioncorp.com is to offer more than only website but it starts from the logistics management, to e-commerce strategy till customer care. Fashioncorp.com, in fact, looks like the suitable partner for the brand of the fashion world who do not have the skills and resources needed to open an online channel e-commerce.

The costs that a brand should approach to implement an internal department.

e-commerce are very high, because they require specific skills for visual creation of web design, technology development, logistics and customer care management. All these skills require a resource-intensive, from which it is difficult to get quick results. That's why giving rise to new business models, such as structured by Fashioncorp.com. First, it is interesting to see that Fascioncorp.com has two types of customers. The first is represented by the brand with which it establishes a partnership for the implementation of the e-commerce site, the coordination of all logistics activities and customer service; the second type of customer is the user who interacts with the web portal of e-commerce and from which Fascioncorp.com receives purchase orders, payments, and all requests for assistance provided by the customer service. There is a dual nature of the parties involved, which turns out to be both B2B and B2C. The part of e-commerce is aimed at the B2C relationship, but the primary nature of the relationship is in the relationship between Fashioncorp and B2B brand he works for. For Fascioncorp, in fact, is not very appear important to web users who buy on the web, but the way among the major fashion brands to which it can sell its know-how. Fascioncorp is working on behalf of the brand presenting itself as an integral part of the brand he works for. This determines the close relationship of partnership between Fascioncorp and its customers, although it is still too early to define these relationships as true partnerships and own.

3   Preliminary Findings

The first issue that emerged during the interview was related to the terminology in use. Word such as client and suppliers seems not fitting anymore to the needs of classification of the different players in the supply chain.

As pointed out by the COO of Fashioncorp.com: "the person who places the order on the website is not our client. He is our client's client. And our clients, the fashion maisons—we call them brand—are at the same time our client, because the pay for our services, but, at the same time our suppliers, as they provide the goods sold and delivered through the website".

It has been widely pointed out that the use of tools information technology is increasingly important to promote inter-organizational collaboration and improve performance [12, 17, 19, 21, 23]. From this we understand the importance of information technology as an aid to supply chain management, because it increases the ability to create collaborative relationships by encouraging the sharing of information, which in turn improves the visibility, reduce dependence on inventories, reduce costs, reduce total times lead and facilitate a quick response in logistics activities [13, 31, 38, 48].

As pointed out by the Portal.com sales manager: "The collaboration with the brands is the key factor. We are recognized not only as IT service provider but as business partners. This is the reason why have to design different type of agreement whit the producers, according to the level of collaboration needed".

We concentrated our study in the fashion industry on how two different e-commerce platform integrate and organize their business model respect their customers. But this integration cannot be taken for granted. The "fusion" of the different roles has some side effects. "Internet needs a sort of real time decision making process. And this seems not clear to the mangers of the brands. Sometimes some opportunities are missed because we cannot decide discount or promotion polices in time" (Fashioncorp Brand manager).

The data collected by interviews in Portal.com and in Fashioncorp.com enable us to understand deeper level of integration and collaboration between the company and its partners, in terms of technological integration and operational integration. Portal.com and Fashioncorp.com are not only outsourcer of well defined business processes. As those processes are not clearly know by the outsource, the Internet platform become a business partner of the company that at the same time is a supplier (when provide the goods that have to be sold on the website) and the client (of the e-commerce services) services of the web.

What seems to be relevant in the two cases is the governance of the relationship with the client. On one hand, Portal.com seems to be able to lead this relationship. Establishing the rules and designing the flows. On the other hand, Fashioncorp.com seems to be more affected by client's needs and reauests. Table 1 shows the main differences and similarities of the two organizations.

The level of collaboration needed, as highlighted in several interviews by the personnel of the two companies, become strategic. As pointed out by a the CEO of Fashioncorp.com: "What is done "on line" affects what happened "off line", as the good sold is traded non on the basis of the experience of the client in a face to face relationship within a shop but on the basis of the experience he has with the website in terms of speed of reaction, quality of the pictures shown reliability and completeness of the information provided. If something goes wrong, the client doesn't buy. So we must work with the brand in order to guarantee the correct alignment between the e-commerce side (from the technological and logistical point of view) and the off-line policies of the brand".

As represented in Fig. 1, once the IT is involved, the need of coordination and integration between the different actors become critical as the time of the action is the real-time. If in the off-line supply chain the interaction among the different actors involved in the processes follow a time lines that allow the separation of tasks and responsibilities as the transactions take place in different moment in time (t0, t1, t2, t3), in the on-line environment the transactions and the feedbacks take place almost immediately, without separation of roles and responsibilities.

Table 1 The two organizations

	Portal.com	Fashioncorp.com
Size	From medium to large	From Small to medium
Client's size	From small to large	From small to medium
Business model	Mix. Multi brand. Mono brand, on-line store	Mono brand
Client approach	With SME: captive	Relational
	With Large Ent. Relational	
Organization	Structured	Lean
Services	Designed by Portal	Taylor made

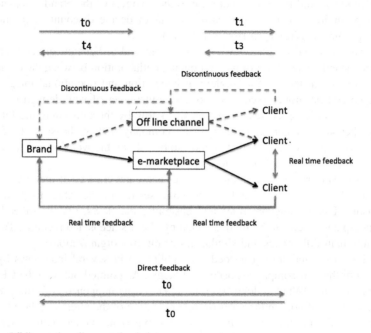

Fig. 1 Off line and on line supply chain

In addition, this study makes it possible to better observe what is the impact of using information technology on collaboration within and across organizations, and the consequent influence on organizational performance.

4 Implications

Several scholars indicates that firms can realize increasing returns from enhanced customer, supplier, and internal integration efforts (Narasimhan et al. 2010). Particularly supply chain integration (SCI) can help firms increase responsiveness to demand and reduce costs through improved stock management, process management and logistics efficiency. Supported by inter-organizational information technology, which enables sharing of large amounts of data, information, and knowledge along the supply chain, SCI has been shown to improve buyer–supplier coordination and performance [47] as we show in our research.

Moreover the role of information technology have proved important for the sharing and management of information from upstream to downstream and vice versa across the supply chain [21, 48]. Both of these aspects require a lot of effort and resources to improve the level of integration of information with partners, and optimize workflow processes. The relationship between Portal.com or Fascioncorp.com and its customers need to grow and deepening long to reach a satisfactory level of integration that leads to a synchronization of the supply chain. This would help to solve several issues of stock outs, system errors, and high rates of return that occur. Then our project of research suggests a number of important managerial implications even in these tough times, managers should dedicate their efforts to develop different marketing channel also through e-commerce intermediaries. It seems mandatory to look for the right partner that it would be able to share risks, investments and profit; at this stage there isn't a specific business model to implement the most suitable e-commerce strategy; our findings doesn't suggest a best practice in that sense, but it is necessary for managers to develop a strategic integration with the intermediaries, not a tactical or a spotty decision, due to the clear opportunity that e-shopping is creating for firms.

Future research, and limitations, on that stream could be conceptualized in a more complex way, particularly understanding how the brands could effectively interact and manage the relationship with the Internet provider.

References

1. Vinhas, A.S., Chatterjee, S., Dutta, S., Fein, A., Lajos, J., Neslin, S., Wang, Q.: Channel design, coordination, and performance: future research directions. Market. Lett. **21**(3), 223–237 (2010)
2. Alptekinoğlu, A., Tang, C.S.: A model for analyzing multi-channel distribution systems. Eur. J. Oper. Res. **163**(3), 802–824 (2005)
3. Rao, S., Goldsby, T.J., Iyengar, D.: The marketing and logistics efficacy of online sales channels. Int. J. Phys. Distrib. Log. Manag. **39**(2), 106–130 (2009)
4. Bakos, Y.: The emerging landscape for retail e-commerce. J. Econ. Perspect. **15**(1), 69–80 (2001)
5. Hong, W., Zhu, K.: Migrating to internet-based e-commerce: factors affecting e-commerce adoption and migration at the firm level. Inf. Manag. **43**(2), 204–221 (2006)
6. Varadarajan, R., Srinivasan, R., Vadakkepatt, G.G., Yadav, M.S., Pavlou, P.A., Krishnamurthy, S., Krause, T.: Interactive technologies and retailing strategy: a review, conceptual framework and future research directions. J. Interact. Market. **24**(2), 96–110 (2010)
7. Braccini, A.M.: Value Generation in Organisations, p. 170. LAMBERT Academic Publishing, Saarbrücken, Germany (2011)

8. Resca, A., Za, S., Spagnoletti, P.: Digital platforms as sources for organizational and strategic transformation: a case study of the Midblue project. J. Theor. and Appl. E-Comm. Res. **8**(2), 71–84 (2013)
9. Seth, N., Deshmukh, S.G., Vrat, P.: A conceptual model for quality of service in the supply chain. Int. J. Phys. Distrib. Log. Manag. **36**(7), 547–575 (2006)
10. Buciuni, G., Mola, L.: How do entrepreneurial firms establish cross-border relationships? A global value chain perspective. J. Int. Entrepreneurship **12**(1), 67–84 (2014)
11. Lee, R.P., Kim, D.: Implications of service processes outsourcing on firm value. Ind. Mark. Manage. **39**(5), 853–861 (2010)
12. Kalakota, R., Konsynski, B.: The rise of neo-intermediation: the transformation of the brokerage industry. Inf. Syst. Frontiers **2**(1), 115–128 (2000)
13. Dikey, M.H., Ives, B.: The impact of intranet technology on power in Franchisee/Franchisor relationships. Inf. Syst. Frontiers **2**(1), 99–114 (2000)
14. Tan, G.W., Shaw, M.J., Fulkerson, B.: Web-based supply chain management. Inf. Syst. Frontiers **2**(1), 41–55 (2000)
15. Grieger, M.: Electronic marketplaces: A literature review and a call for supply chain management research. Eur. J. Oper. Res. **144**, 280–294 (2003)
16. Wang, S., Zheng, S., Xu L., Li D., Meng H.: A literature review of electronic marketplace research: themes, theories and an integrative framework, Information Systems Frontiers. Published online: 5 June 2008
17. Rossignoli, C.: The contribution of transaction cost theory and other network-oriented techniques to digital markets. IseB **7**(1), 57–79 (2009)
18. Wigand, R.T., Picot, A., Reichwald, R.: Information, organization and management: expanding markets and corporate boudaries. Wiley, Chichester (1997)
19. Basaglia, S., Caporarello, L., Magni, M., Pennarola, F.: Team level antecedents of individual usage of a new technology, In: Proceeding of the 16th European Conference on Information Systems, Galway, Ireland (2008)
20. Makadok, R., Coff, R.: Both market and hierarchy: an incentive-system theory of hybrid governance forms. Acad. Manag. Rev. **34**(2), 297–319 (2009)
21. Roberts, E.B., Liu, W.K.: Ally or acquire?. How technology leaders decide, Image (2012)
22. O'Reilly, P., Finnegan, P.: Intermediaries in inter-organisational networks: building a theory of electronic marketplace performance. Eur. J. Inf. Syst. **19**(4), 462–480 (2010)
23. Grey, W., Olavson, T., Shi, D.: The role of e-marketplaces in relationship-based supply chains: a survey. IBM Syst. J. **44**(1), 109–123 (2005)
24. Eng, T.Y.: The role of e-marketplaces in supply chain management. Ind. Mark. Manage. **33**(2), 97–105 (2004)
25. Knemeyer, A.M., Murphy, P.R.: Evaluating the performance of third-party logistics arrangements: a relationship marketing perspective. J. Suppl. Chain Manag. **40**(4), 35–51 (2004)
26. Leuschner, R., Carter, C.R., Goldsby, T.J., Rogers, Z.S.: Third-party logistics: a meta-analytic review and investigation of its impact on performance. J. Suppl. Chain Manag. **50**(1), 21–43 (2014)
27. Daugherty, P.J.: Review of logistics and supply chain relationship literature and suggested research agenda. Int. J. Phys. Distrib. Log. Manag. **41**(1), 16–31 (2011)
28. Ivanaj, V., Franzil, Y.M.: Outsourcing logistics activities: a transaction cost economics perspective. In: XVeme Conference Internationale de Management Strategique, Annecy (Geneve. 13–16 Juin 2006)
29. Morgan, R.M., Hunt, S.D.: The commitment-trust theory of relationship marketing. J. Market. 20–38 (1994)
30. Esper, T.L., Williams, L.R.: The value of collaborative transportation management (CTM): its relationship to CPFR and information technology. Transport. J. 55–65 (2003)
31. Prahinski, C., Fan, Y.: Supplier evaluations: the role of communication quality. J. Suppl. Chain Manag. **43**(3), 16–28 (2007)

32. Mentzer, J.T., DeWitt, W., Keebler, J.S., Min, S., Nix, N.W., Smith, C.D., Zacharia, Z.G.: Defining supply chain management. J. Bus. Log. **22**(2), 1–25 (2001)
33. Svensson, G.: The bullwhip effect in intra-organisational echelons. Int. J. Phys. Distrib. Log. Manag. **33**(2), 103–131 (2003)
34. Sa Vinhas, A., Heide, J.B., Jap, S.D.: Consistency judgments, embeddedness, and relationship outcomes in interorganizational networks. Manage. Sci. **58**(5), 996–1011 (2012)
35. Golicic, S.L., Foggin, J.H., Mentzer, J.T.: Relationship magnitude and its role in interorganizational relationship structure. J. Bus. Log. **24**(1), 57–75 (2003)
36. Flynn, B.B., Huo, B., Zhao, X.: The impact of supply chain integration on performance: a contingency and configuration approach. J. Oper. Manag. **28**(1), 58–71 (2010)
37. Sanders, N.R.: An empirical study of the impact of e-business technologies on organizational collaboration and performance. J. Oper. Manag. **25**(6), 1332–1347 (2007)
38. Rajaguru, R., Matanda, M.J.: Effects of inter-organizational compatibility on supply chain capabilities: exploring the mediating role of inter-organizational information systems (IOIS) integration. Ind. Mark. Manage. **42**(4), 620–632 (2013)
39. Dyer, J.H., Singh, H.: The relational view: cooperative strategy and sources of interorganizational competitive advantage. Acad. Manag. Rev. **23**(4), 660–679 (1998)
40. Barney, J.: Firm resources and sustained competitive advantage. J. Manag. **17**(1), 99–120 (1991)
41. Ray, G., Barney, J.B., Muhanna, W.A.: Capabilities, business processes, and competitive advantage: choosing the dependent variable in empirical tests of the resource based view. Strateg. Manag. J. **25**(1), 23–37 (2004)
42. Benbasat, I., Goldstein, D.K., Mead, M.: The case research strategy in studies of information systems. MIS Q. **11**(3), 369–386 (1987)
43. Yin, R.: Case Study Research. Sage Publications, Beverly Hills (1994)
44. Eisenhardt, K.M.: Building theories from case study research. Acad. Manag. Rev. **14**(4), 532–550 (1989)
45. Voss, C., Tsikriktsis, N., Frohlich, M.: Case research in operations management. Int. J. Oper. Prod. Manag. **22**(2), 195–219 (2002)
46. Fernie, J., Sparks, L.: Retail logistics: changes and challenges. Logistics and retail management, pp. 3–37 (2009)
47. Terjesen, S., Patel, P.C., Sanders, N.R.: Managing differentiation-integration duality in supply chain integration. Decis. Sci. **43**(2), 303–339 (2012)
48. Rossignoli, C., Ricciardi, F., Mola, L., Zardini, A.: Interorganizational networks of e-intermediaries: an exploratory study. In: European Conference on Information Systems (ECIS), Tel Aviv 5–12 June 2014

Comparing Classifiers for Web User Intent Understanding

Vincenzo Deufemia, Miriam Granatello, Alessandro Merola,
Emanuele Pesce and Giuseppe Polese

Abstract Understanding user intent during a web navigation session is a challenging topic. Existing approaches base such activity on many different features, including HCI features, which are also used by classifiers to determine the type of a web query. In this paper we present several experiments aiming to compare the performances of main classifiers, and propose a metric to evaluate them and detect the most promising features for deriving a better classifier.

Keywords User intent understanding · HCI features · Web search

1 Introduction

The success of internet applications is bound to the capability of search engines to provide users with information meeting their expectations. This cannot be guaranteed by merely analyzing the web structure as several existing search engines do. Thus, nowadays, search engines need to incorporate the capability of predicting user intents in order to adapt the order of search results so as to meet their expectation. For this reason, user intention understanding (UIU) has recently become an important research area.

V. Deufemia (✉) · M. Granatello · A. Merola · E. Pesce · G. Polese
Università Di Salerno, Via Giovanni Paolo II, 132, 84084 Fisciano, SA, Italy
e-mail: deufemia@unisa.it

M. Granatello
e-mail: granatellomiriam@gmail.com

A. Merola
e-mail: a.merola10@studenti.unisa.it

E. Pesce
e-mail: e.pesce3@studenti.unisa.it

G. Polese
e-mail: gpolese@unisa.it

© Springer International Publishing Switzerland 2016
T. Torre et al. (eds.), *Empowering Organizations*, Lecture Notes in Information
Systems and Organisation 11, DOI 10.1007/978-3-319-23784-8_12

Some approaches to user behavior analysis in web navigation have highlighted the importance of analyzing user interactions with web pages in order to infer their interest and satisfaction with respect to the visited contents [1, 2]. Other studies have investigated how user interactions with Search Engine Result Pages (SERPs) can be exploited to infer user intent [3–8]. However, such methods for UIU limit their analysis to the results contained in a SERP, ignoring many important interactions and contents visited from such results. On the contrary, the aim of this paper is to show that UIU can be considerably improved by performing additional analysis of user interactions on the web pages of a SERP that the user decides to visit. In particular, we define a new model for UIU that incorporates interactions analyzed in the context of SERP results and of the web pages visited starting from them [9]. The interaction features considered in the model are not global page-level statistics, rather they are finer-grained and refer to portions of web pages. This is motivated on the basis of the results of literature studies, performed with eye-trackers, revealing that although a user might focus on many sections composing a web page, s/he will tend to overlook portions of low interest [10]. Thus, capturing interaction features on specific portions of web pages potentially conveys a better accuracy in the evaluation of the user actions. These and other features are evaluated in our approach by means of a classification algorithm to understand user intents. In particular, to simplify the classification process, we use a two-level taxonomy in which the first level defines three types of queries: *informational*, *navigational*, and *transactional* [11]. On the second level, informational queries and transactional queries are decomposed into several subclasses [12].

In this paper we provide experimental results highlighting the efficiency of the proposed model for query classification, also showing how the interaction features extracted from visited web pages contribute to enhance UIU. In particular, the proposed set of features has been evaluated with three different classification algorithms, namely Support Vector Machine (SVM) [13], Conditional Random Fields (CRF) [14], and Latent Dynamic Conditional Random Fields (LDCRF) [15]. But even though the two-level taxonomy gives us a better precision, it also involves a high dimensionality of results that makes it difficult the comparison between the achieved results. To this end, we introduce a metric to evaluate the performances of the classifiers and detect the most promising features.

The rest of this paper is organized as follows. We present the model exploiting interaction features for UIU in Sect. 2. Section 3 describes experimental results. Section 4 introduces an index to compare UIU classification results. Finally, conclusions are given in Sect. 5.

2 A Model for User Intent Understanding

In this section we describe the model and the features used for the classification process. The model of this work is based on the model proposed in [9].

2.1 Search Model: Session, Search, Interaction

Several approaches and models have been proposed to provide solutions to the user intention understanding problem, but all of them mainly focus on the interaction between users and the SERP. Additional interactions originating from SERP's contents, such as browsing, reading, and multimedia content fruition are not considered by the research community.

The used model aims to extend existing models, by analyzing user interactions between users and web pages during a search session. Our aim is to analyze not only the interactions between users and SERP, but also between users and web pages reached by clicking on SERP's results. We believe that data about interactions between users and web pages may be very useful to clarify the intent of the user, because these interactions are driven by the same motivation behind the initial search query. All user interactions with web pages could be reduced to three main categories, which are the same we consider in our model: *session*, *search*, and *interaction*.

- **Session** A *session* is a sequence of search activities aimed at achieving a goal. When the first query does not provide the desired result, the user tries to gradually approach the target, refining or changing search terms and keywords. All these research activities constitute a session.
- **Search** A *search* activity is the combination of the following user actions: submission of a query to a search engine, analysis of search results, navigation on one or more web page links inside them. During a search activity, a user has a specific goal, generally described by the query itself. This goal is classifiable in a taxonomy, as defined by previous studies [11, 12].
- **Interaction** *Interaction* is the navigation of a web page using a wide range of interactions that include mouse clicks, page scrolling, pointer movements, and text selection. Starting from these interactions, combined with features such as dwell time, reading rate, and scrolling rate, it is possible to derive an implicit feedback of users about web pages [9]. Moreover, several studies have proven the usefulness of user interactions to assess the relevance of web pages [1, 16–18], to classify queries, and to determine the intent of search sessions [8, 19].

This model uses a methodology for tracing interactions between users and web pages. In particular, user interaction analysis is restricted to a smaller portion of a web page: the *subpages*. Indeed, a web page consists of several blocks of text, graphics, multimedia, and can have a variable length. As shown by studies using eye-tracking [10], the user frequently adopts a *E or F reading pattern* during browsing, excluding areas of little interest. Compared to a global analysis of the entire page, the introduction of *subpage-level* analysis gives higher accuracy in the assessment of the interaction.

2.2 A Two-Level Taxonomy

Figure 1 shows the two-level taxonomy used in this work for classifying queries. It is similar to the one proposed in the work [12]. In what follows, we explain the levels of the taxonomy:

- *Informational*: The goal is to learn something by reading or viewing web pages

  - **Directed**: when searching something about a topic;
  - **Undirected**: when the author wants to learn anything/everything about a topic;
  - **Help**: when the author searches some advice, ideas, suggestions, or instructions;
  - **Browsing**: when the authors searches something like news, ...;
  - **Other**: when the topic is not in any of the points above.

- *Navigational*: The goal is to go to specific known website. The only reason of this kind of search is that it is more convenient than typing the URL, or perhaps if its URL is unknown.

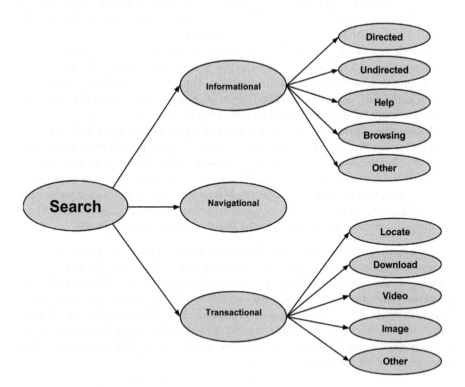

Fig. 1 Two-level taxonomy

- *Transactional*: The goal is to obtain a resource available on web pages.

  - **Download**: when the goal is to download a resource;
  - **Video**: when the goal is to watch a video;
  - **Image**: when the goal is to reach an image;
  - **Locate**: when the goal is to find out whether/where some real world service or product can be obtained;
  - **Other**: when the query is transactional but the topic is not in any of the points above.

2.3 Features

Interaction data extracted from user web navigation have been encoded into features that characterize user behavior. We organize the set of features into the following categories: *query, search, interaction*, and context.

Query These features are derived from characteristics of a search query such as keywords, the number of keywords, the semantic relations between them, and other characteristics of a search or an interaction.

Search These features act on the data from search activities such as: results, time spent on SERP, and number of results considered by the user. The *DwellTime* is measured from the start of the search session until the end of the last interaction originated by the same search session. The reaction time, *TimeToFirstInteraction*, is the time elapsed from the start of the search session and the complete loading of the first selected page. Other features dedicated to interactions with the results are *ClicksCount*, which is the number of visited results, and *FirstResultClickedRank*, determining the position of the first clicked result.

Interaction These features act on the data collected from interactions with web pages and subpages, taking into account the absolute dwell time, the effective dwell time, all the scrolling activities, search and reading activities. The *DwellRate* measures the effectiveness of the permanence of a user on a web page, while the reading rate *ReadingRate* measures the amount of reading of a web page [9]. Additional interactional features are: *ViewedWords*, the number of words considered during the browsing, *UrlContainsTransactionalTerms*, which verifies if the URL of the page contains transactional terms (download, software, video, watch, pics, images, audio, etc.), *AjaxRequestsCount*, which represents the number of AJAX requests originated during browsing.

Context These features act on the relationship between the search activities performed in a session, such as the position of a query in the sequence of search requests for a session.

3 Experiments

In this section we describe the dataset constructed for evaluating the proposed approach and the results achieved with different classification algorithms. In the following, we first provide an overview on the used evaluation metrics and the considered subsets of features, then experimental results are presented.

3.1 Experiment Setup

In order to build the dataset for evaluating the proposed model we recruited different participants to make searches on web. All participants were requested to perform ten searches organized as follow:

- Four guided searches;
- Three searches where the participants already knows possible destination web sites;
- Three free searches where the participants have no idea of the destination web site.

The list of guided searches was:

- The London Metro map image;
- The official video of U2 song Vertigo;
- The e-mail address of an administrative office of Salerno University;
- The size of *Mona Lisa*, the famous painting of Leonardo.

By following this protocol, we had 129 sessions and 353 web searches, which were subsequently manually classified by relying on the intent of the user. Starting from web searches, 490 web pages and 2136 sub pages were visited. All interactions were detected by the YAR plug-in for Google Chrome/Chromium [9].

Evaluation Metrics In order to evaluate the effectiveness of the proposed model, we adopted the classical evaluation metrics of Information Retrieval: accuracy, precision, recall, and F1-measure. They are defined as follows:

$$Accuracy = \frac{\#TruePositive + \#TrueNegative}{\#TruePositive + \#TrueNegative + \#FalsePositive + \#FalseNegative}$$

$$Precision = \sum_{Category(i)} \frac{\#correctlyclassifiedqueries}{\#classifiedqueries} \times \frac{\#categoryqueries}{\#totalqueries}$$

$$Recall = \frac{\#correctlyclassifiedqueries}{\#totalqueries}$$

$$F1 - measure = 2 \times \frac{Precision \times Recall}{Precision + Recall}$$

Feature subsets In order to analyze the effectiveness of the considered features, we have grouped them into several subsets:

- **All**: subset of all the proposed features query, search, interaction, and context;
- **Query**: subset of all the features related to queries;
- **Search**: subset of all the features related to search and context;
- **Interaction**: subset of all the features related to interactions;
- **Query + Search**: subset of the features derived as union from Query and Search. The goal is to evaluate the effectiveness of query classification by using the features considered in other studies [5, 8, 16];
- **Transactional**: subset of all the features related to interactions over transactional queries *ViewWords*, *AjaxRequestsCount*, *ScrollingDistance*, *ScrollingCount*, and *UrlContainsTransactionalTerms*. The goal here is to evaluate the classification of transactional queries by adopting more specific features;
- **Interaction—Transactional**: subset derived by the exclusion of the transactional features from the set Interaction. The goal here is to evaluate the effectiveness of the classification of transactional queries by comparing results achieved with interaction features to those achieved by excluding transactional features.
- **All—Transactional**: subset derived by the exclusion of the transactional features from the set All. The goal here is to evaluate the effectiveness of the classification of transactional queries by comparing results achieved with all features to those achieved by excluding transactional features.

Classifiers We considered three classifiers to evaluate the proposed feature model: SVM [13], CRF [14], and LDCRF [15].

In the context of query classification, SVM assumes that the queries in a user session are independent, Conditional Random Field (CRF) considers the sequential information between the queries, and Latent Dynamic Conditional Random Fields (LDCRF) models the sub-structure of user sessions by assigning a disjoint set of hidden state variables to each class label. They have been configured as follows:

- **SVM** We used MSVMpack [20] as the SVM toolbox for model training and testing. The SVM model is trained using a linear kernel and the parameter C has been determined by cross-validation.
- **CRF** We used the HCRF library[1] as the tool to train and test the CRF model. For the experiments we used a single chain structured model and the regularization term for the CRF model was validated with values 10^k with $k = -1,...,3$.
- **LDCRF** We used the HCRF library for training and testing LDCRF model. In particular, the model was trained with 3 hidden states per label, and the regularization term was determined by cross-validation to achieve the best performance.

---

[1]http://sourceforge.net/projects/hcrf/.

3.2 Results

In order to simulate an operating environment, the set of queries made by users was separated into two subsets, which included 60 and 40 % of web searches, and were used for training and testing the classifiers, respectively.

In order to evaluate the effectiveness of a classifier the features were grouped into several subsets. Each classifier was executed considering each subset of feature once at time. To make a comparison between the behavior of the classifiers we need to compare the results achieved for the different pairs (classifier, feature subset). More specifically, for every classifier we needed to analyze the metrics calculated on the different subset of features. Thus, we need to compare 336 values since we have 3 classifiers, each of which is executed on 8 feature subsets, and for each feature subset we need to calculate 14 parameters. Some of the results for CRF classifier are reported in Figs. 2, 3, 4 and 5.

In order to reduce the effort in the evaluation of the results achieved for the different classifiers in the next section we introduce a metric, which summarizes the performance.

	Informatio nal_Direct ed	Informatio nal_undire cted	Informatio nal_Help	Information al_Browsing	Navigatio nal	Navigatio nal_Down load	Transactio nal_Image	Transactio nal_Video	Transactio nal_Locate	Transactio nal_Other
TruePositive	26	6	0	0	2	0	24	7	0	0
FalsePositive	22	26	9	4	4	0	6	9	0	0
TrueNegative	81	98	130	146	131	149	117	128	151	151
FalseNegative	22	21	12	1	14	2	4	7	0	0
Precision	0,54	0,19	0	0	0,33	0	0,8	0,44	0	0
Recall	0,54	0,22	0	0	0,12	0	0,86	0,5	0	0
F1-measure	0,54	0,2	0	0	0,18	0	0,83	0,47	0	0
Accuracy	0,71	0,69	0,86	0,97	0,88	0,99	0,93	0,89	1	1
Specificity	0,79	0,79	0,94	0,97	0,97	1	0,95	0,93	1	1
Fallout	0,21	0,21	0,06	0,03	0,03	0	0,05	0,07	0	0

Fig. 2 Results obtained with the CRF model on all features

	Informatio nal_Direct ed	Informatio nal_undire cted	Informatio nal_Help	Informatio nal_Brows ing	Navigatio nal	Navigatio nal_Dow nload	Transactio nal_Image	Transactio nal_Video	Transactio nal_Locate	Transactio nal_Other
TruePositive	12	2	0	0	1	0	6	5	0	0
FalsePositive	11	15	4	0	2	5	2	6	1	0
TrueNegative	92	109	135	150	133	144	121	131	150	151
FalseNegative	36	25	12	1	15	2	22	9	0	0
Precision	0,52	0,12	0	0	0,33	0	0,75	0,45	0	0
Recall	0,25	0,07	0	0	0,06	0	0,21	0,36	0	0
F1-measure	0,34	0,09	0	0	0,11	0	0,33	0,4	0	0
Accuracy	0,69	0,74	0,89	0,99	0,89	0,95	0,84	0,9	0,99	1
Specificity	0,89	0,88	0,97	1	0,99	0,97	0,98	0,96	0,99	1
Fallout	0,11	0,12	0,03	0	0,01	0,03	0,02	0,04	0,01	0

Fig. 3 Results obtained with the CRF model on interaction features

	Informational_Directed	Informational_undirected	Informational_Help	Informational_Browsing	Navigational	Navigational_Download	Transactional_Image	Transactional_Video	Transactional_Locate	Transactional_Other
TruePositive	38	1	0	0	0	2	22	8	0	0
FalsePositive	46	16	0	0	0	1	1	2	0	0
TrueNegative	57	108	139	150	135	148	122	135	151	151
FalseNegative	10	26	12	1	16	0	6	6	0	0
Precision	0,45	0,06	0	0	0	0,67	0,96	0,8	0	0
Recall	0,79	0,04	0	0	0	1	0,79	0,57	0	0
F1-measure	0,58	0,05	0	0	0	0,08	0,86	0,67	0	0
Accuracy	0,63	0,72	0,92	0,99	0,89	0,99	0,95	0,95	1	1
Specificity	0,55	0,87	1	1	1	0,99	0,99	0,99	1	1
Fallout	0,45	0,13	0	0	0	0,01	0,01	0,01	0	0

Fig. 4 Results obtained with the CRF model on query features

	Informational_Directed	Informational_undirected	Informational_Help	Informational_Browsing	Navigational	Navigational_Download	Transactional_Image	Transactional_Video	Transactional_Locate	Transactional_Other
TruePositive	36	10	1	0	9	2	23	9	0	0
FalsePositive	33	8	1	0	12	0	1	4	0	0
TrueNegative	70	116	138	150	123	149	122	133	151	151
FalseNegative	12	17	11	1	7	0	5	5	0	0
Precision	0,52	0,56	0,5	0	0,43	1	0,96	0,69	0	0
F1-measure	0,75	0,37	0,08	0	0,56	1	0,82	0,64	0	0
Recall	0,62	0,44	0,14	0	0,49	1	0,88	0,67	0	0
Accuracy	0,7	0,83	0,92	0,99	0,87	1	0,96	0,94	1	1
Specificity	0,68	0,94	0,99	1	0,91	1	0,99	0,97	1	1
Fallout	0,32	0,06	0,01	0	0,09	0	0,01	0,03	0	0

Fig. 5 Results obtained with the CRF model on search features

4 An Index for Evaluating Classification Results

The format of the results shown in Figs. 2, 3, 4 and 5 highlights the complexity of obtaining relevant information, such as "which classifier achieves the best performance?" or "which subset of features performs better?". Often it happens that a classifier works better on a class $L1$, while another classifier outperforms the others on a class $L2$, so we need to find a way for comparing different results favoring immediacy and promptly without losing quality.

The index proposed for evaluating the classifier results is based on the *mean squared error* (MSE), which is defined as:

$$MSE = \frac{1}{n}\sum_{i=1}^{n} (\widehat{x}_i - x_i)^2$$

where $\widehat{x}_i$ is the ith predicted value, while x_i is the ith correct value. For our purposes, we used MSE calculated on the *accuracy* measure. Thus, given the vector of accuracy values $\widehat{a}$, the definition of the *Accuracy Mean Squared Error* (AMSE or $MSE(\widehat{a})$) is

$$MSE = \frac{1}{n}\sum_{i=1}^{n}(\widehat{a}_i - a_i)^2$$

where a_i is equal to 1. We computed a relative AMSE value for each pair *Classifier —SubsetFeatures*.

AMSE is able to gain knowledge about the performance of the classifiers and the subsets of features, and how they work each other. Let

- I = {All, Query, Search, Transactional, Interaction, Query + Search, All-Transactional, Interaction-Transactional}
- J = {CRF, LDCRF, MSVM}

be the set of *SubsetFeatures* and the set of the *Classifiers*, respectively. We designed four AMSE-based values for gaining knowledge about the classifier performances:

- **Global**: it returns the pair *Classifier-SubsetFeatures* with the minimum AMSE

$$min\left(AMSE_{i,j}\right) \quad \forall i \in I, j \in J$$

  It is useful to catch the best performance;
- **Subsets**: it is estimated for each subset of features the classifier that works better.

$$min_{j \in J}\left(x_{i,j}\right) \quad \forall i \in I$$

  so we can easily check which are the best pairs *Classifiers-SubsetFeatures*;
- **FeaturesBehavior**: it computes the average behavior for each subset of features

$$\frac{1}{|J|}\sum_{j \in J}AMSE_{i,j} \quad \forall i \in I$$

  allowing to gain knowledge about the feature subsets working better;
- **ClassifiersBehavior**: it computes the average behavior for each *Classifier*

$$\frac{1}{|I|}\sum_{i \in I}AMSE_{i,j} \quad \forall j \in J$$

  allowing to gain knowledge about the classifiers working better.

The results shown in Fig. 6 highlight that MSVM achieves the best average performance followed by CRF, which has almost the same MSVM value. Notice that, lesser the AMSE value is better the performances are since AMSE is an error.

Figure 7 shows the AMSE values obtained for the different subsets of features. *Transactional* achieves the best performances followed by *Query* and *Query + Search*. Instead, the worst performance is given by the subset *All* whose AMSE value is bigger than each other. Instead the *AMSE global* values in Fig. 8

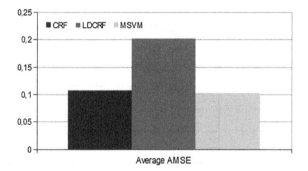

Fig. 6 *AMSE ClassifiersBehavior* values of classifiers

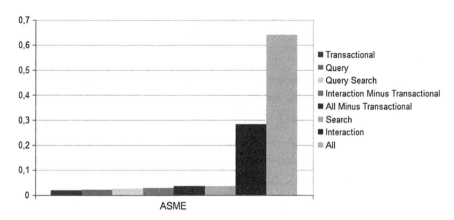

Fig. 7 *AMSE Subset* values for each subset of features

Global		
Classifiers	SubsetFeatures	AMSE
CRF	Transactional	0,01446
LDCRF	Transactional	0,02086
MSVM	Query	0,02105

Fig. 8 *AMSE Global* values for each classifier

highlight that the best pair has been *CRF-Transactional*, while the *AMSE Subsets* values in Fig. 9 highlight that the best performances are achieved by the *CRF* classifier (4 times in the top 8 results).

Fig. 9 Lower *AMSE FeaturesBehavior* values for the considered classifiers

Subsets		
SubsetFeatures	Classifiers	AMSE
All	MSVM	0,58953
All Minus Transactional	LDCRF	0,02903
Interaction	CRF	0,02262
Interaction Minus Transactional	CRF	0,02204
Query	LDCRF	0,02102
Query Search	CRF	0,01475
Search	MSVM	0,02391
Transactional	CRF	0,01446

5 Conclusions

In this paper we have evaluated the performances of several classifiers for web UIU. Based on the results that the interactions of the user with the web pages returned by a search engine in response to a query can be highly useful [1, 16], in this research we aimed to empirically compare the performances of main classifiers, and we proposed a metric for detecting the most promising model features. The proposed index, based on the accuracy metric, has been used to evaluate the best classifier and the best subset of features. The results of the experiments highlight that MSVM classifier given the best average performances followed by CRF classifier. Instead, the *Transactional* features outperformed the others, followed by *Query* and *Query + Search* feature.

References

1. Agichtein, E., Brill, E., Dumais, S.: Improving web search ranking by incorporating user behavior information. In: Proceedings of the International Conference on Research and Development in Information Retrieval, pp. 19–26. SIGIR'06, ACM (2006)
2. Deufemia, V., Giordano, M., Polese, G., Simonetti, L.: Exploiting interaction features in user intent understanding. In: Ishikawa, Y., Li, J., Wang, W., Zhang, R., Zhang, W. (eds.) Web Technologies and Applications. Volume 7808 of Lecture Notes in Computer Science, pp. 506–517 (2013)
3. Kang, I., Kim, G.: Query type classification for web document retrieval. In: Proceedings of the Conference on Research and Development in Information Retrieval, pp. 64–71. SIGIR'03, ACM (2003)
4. Lee, U., Liu, Z., Cho, J.: Automatic identification of user goals in web search. In: Proceedings of the International Conference on World Wide Web, pp. 391–400. WWW'05, ACM (2005)
5. Agichtein, E., Brill, E., Dumais, S., Ragno, R.: Learning user interaction models for predicting web search result preferences. In: Proceedings of the International Conference on Research and Development in Information Retrieval, pp. 3–10. SIGIR'06, ACM (2006)
6. Jansen, B.J., Booth, D.L.: A.S. Determining the user intent of web search engine queries. In: Proceedings of the International Conference on World Wide Web, pp. 1149–1150. WWW'07, ACM (2007)

7. Tamine, L., Daoud, M., Dinh, B., Boughanem, M.: Contextual query classification in web search. In: Proceedings of International Workshop on Information Retrieval Learning, Knowledge and Adaptability. LWA'08 (2008) pp. 65–68

8. Guo, Q., Agichtein, E.: Ready to buy or just browsing? Detecting web searcher goals from interaction data. In: Proceedings of the International Conference on Research and Development in Information Retrieval, pp. 130–137. SIGIR'10, ACM (2010)

9. Deufemia, V., Giordano, M., Polese, G., Tortora, G.: Inferring web page relevance from human-computer interaction logging. In: Proceedings of the International Conference on Web Information Systems and Technologies, pp. 653–662. WEBIST'12 (2012)

10. Nielsen, J.: F-shaped pattern for reading web content. http://www.useit.com/articles/f-shaped-pattern-reading-web-content/ (2006)

11. Broder, A.: A taxonomy of web search. SIGIR Forum **36**(2), 3–10 (2002)

12. Rose, D., Levinson, D.: Understanding user goals in web search. In: Proceedings of the International Conference on World Wide Web, pp. 13–19. WWW'04, ACM (2004)

13. Cortes, C., Vapnik, V.: Support-vector networks. Mach. Learn. **20**(3), 273–297 (1995)

14. Lafferty, J.D., McCallum, A., Pereira, F.C.N.: Conditional random fields: Probabilistic models for segmenting and labeling sequence data. In: Proceedings of the International Conference on Machine Learning, pp. 282–289. ICML'01 (2001)

15. Morency, L.P., Quattoni, A., Darrell, T.: Latent-dynamic discriminative models for continuous gesture recognition. In: Proceedings of IEEE Conference Computer Vision and Pattern Recognition, pp. 1–8. CVPR'07 (2007)

16. Guo, Q., Agichtein, E.: Beyond dwell time: Estimating document relevance from cursor movements and other post-click searcher behavior. In: Proceedings of the International Conference on World Wide Web, pp. 569–578. WWW'12, ACM (2012)

17. Guo, Q., Agichtein, E.: Towards predicting web searcher gaze position from mouse movements. In: Proceedings of the International Conference on Human Factors in Computing Systems, pp. 3601–3606. CHI EA'10, ACM (2010)

18. Kelly, D., Teevan, J.: Implicit feedback for inferring user preference: a bibliography. SIGIR Forum **37**(2), 18–28 (2003)

19. Guo, Q., Agichtein, E.: Exploring mouse movements for inferring query intent. In: Proceedings of the International Conference on Research and Development in Information Retrieval, pp. 707–708. ACM (2008)

20. Lauer, F., Guermeur, Y.: MSVMpack: A multi-class support vector machine package. J. Mach. Learn. Res. **12**, 2269–2272 (2011)

E.Y.E. C. U.: an Emotional eYe trackEr for Cultural heritage sUpport

Davide Maria Calandra, Dario Di Mauro, Daniela D'Auria
and Francesco Cutugno

Abstract Enjoying a painting, a sculpture or, more in general, a piece of art and, at the same time, to receive all the information you need about it: in this paper, we present E.Y.E. C. U. (read "I see you"), a modular eye tracking system which supports art galleries fruition without diverting visitors attention. Every time a visitor lingers on a painting detail, a hidden camera detects her gaze and the framework beams, in real time, the related illustrative contents on the wall region around it, deeply implementing the augmented reality meaning. E.Y.E. C. U. enhances the gaze detection functionalities with an emotional analysis module: as pupil is well known to reflect the emotional arousal, we monitor its size, in order to detect radius variations. Once the visitor has completed her visit, the system summarizes the observed details and the emotional reactions in a report.

Keywords Emotion tracking · Affective computing · Pupil dilatation

1 Introduction

In recent years, with the widespread adoption of mobile devices, museum visitors tend to compensate the lack of information available in the caption aside the artworks, with web researches or dedicated applications usually based on image

D.M. Calandra (✉) · D. Di Mauro · D. D'Auria · F. Cutugno
Department of Electrical Engineering and Information Technology - DIETI,
University of Naples "Federico II", via Cinthia SNC, 80125 Naples, Italy
e-mail: davidemaria.calandra@unina.it

D. Di Mauro
e-mail: dario.dimauro@unina.it

D. D'Auria
e-mail: daniela.dauria4@unina.it

F. Cutugno
e-mail: cutugno@unina.it

© Springer International Publishing Switzerland 2016
T. Torre et al. (eds.), *Empowering Organizations*, Lecture Notes in Information
Systems and Organisation 11, DOI 10.1007/978-3-319-23784-8_13

recognition and retrieval [15]. These solutions satisfy the thirst for knowledge of the visitor but detach her interest from the piece of art which loses the centrality of the visit, as a mobile device interposes between her and the artwork. This scenario gave us the idea to design a software application which supports the artistic fruition without diverting user's attention from the subject of the visit. Thus, a possible solution is just intercepting the visitors' gaze, while they are enjoying the work of art and providing them the contents related to the point of gaze. These last could be soundscapes heard by means of smart headphones [4] or multimedia contents projected on the wall. Moreover, once the point of gaze is known, it can be used to analyse which are the most seen details of each painting, how many users looked at them and for how long time. Then, it could be interesting to know which are the emotional reactions of the visitors while they are enjoying their visit, in order to understand which details arouse pleasure.

In this paper, we present E.Y.E. C. U. (read "I see you"), an emotional eye tracking system which detects the details of the painting observed by the visitor and shows, in real-time, the related deepening contents on the wall around the piece of art; moreover, the *emotional* component computes visitors' reactions while they are enjoying the piece of art. Meanwhile, the logging module stores the information about the points of gaze, the duration of a fixation and which reactions it caused.

Pupil dilation (*mydriasis*) represents a reliable information source in the emotional arousal analysis; this was firstly proved by [8] and we discussed this matter in [2]. In this view, we also monitor the pupillary radius of the visitor to keep track of her emotions during the visit. As we wanted to provide an application working on any expression of art, we generically consider the visual two-dimensional plane beyond the observed object as divided in sections and we aim to detect which section the visitor is gazing; consequently, we can project the multimedia contents concerning the artwork, on the wall region around it, as shown in Fig. 1.

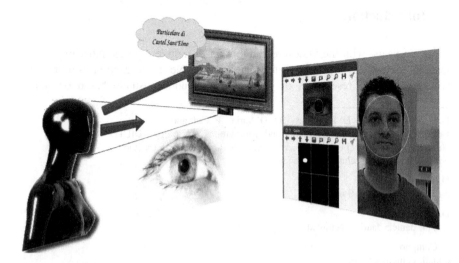

Fig. 1 E.Y.E. C. U

This work represents an evolution of our AutoMyDe [2], presented at itAIS 2013 (http://www.itais.org/itais2013/), in which we developed an automatic mydriasis detector to measure users reactions while they are using a web interface. The mydriatic events were interpreted in terms of cognitive workload.

The paper is organized as follows: Sect. 2 presents the different approaches used to estimate the gaze orientation; Sect. 3 describes the steps needed to detect gaze and to monitor the pupil status; Sect. 4 exposes a case study; Sect. 5 concludes the paper, discussing the obtained results.

2 Point of Gaze Estimation

Before designing a gaze detector, we have to decide if evaluating the points of gaze (PoG) from the eyes movements, from the head pose or both; moreover, we have to establish if users have to wear a device and the precision degree that we want to achieve. In some scenarios, such as the medical diagnosis, patients are usually not allowed to move their head [7] or they have to wear head mounted cameras pointed towards their eyes [11]. In these cases, to estimate the point of gaze means to compute the pupil center position respect to the ellipse formed by the eyelids, while the head position, when considered, is detected through IR sensors in-built on the head of subjects. These systems grant an error threshold lower than 5 pixels [11] due to strict constraints, such as the fixed distance between eye and camera but, on the other hand, they induce users to not natural behaviours. Most remote trackers, such as ones presented in [6], consider the gaze direction determined by the head orientation; these systems do not limit users' movements and do not require they wear a device; they are particularly indicated for scenarios not requiring a high accuracy in identification of details.

To provide a fine-grained remote eye tracker, both head poses and pupil positions have to be estimated, as shown in [16]. Head poses are usually computed by considering 3 degrees of freedom (DoF) [13]: the rotations along the 3 axis of symmetry in the space, $x, y,$ and $z,$ shown in Fig. 2. Once the head pose in the space is known, the pupil center position will refine its orientation.

3 E.Y.E. C. U

We aimed to develop a non intrusive and highly interactive framework which does not constrain users to maintain a fixed distance from the camera, neither to wear an external device. To achieve our task, we designed a remote gaze detector. However, while remote detectors grant non invasiveness, to track the head in its 3 DoF, increases the computational complexity, making interaction slower.

During our analysis, we asked users to perform maximum 15° of head rotations on x axis and maximum 8° on both y and z and to look at paintings of variable size

Fig. 2 Head movements

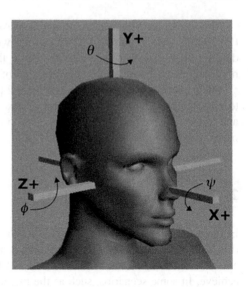

between 50×30 and 180×75 (sizes are expressed in centimeters) from at least 50 cm of distance. Interpreting the nose tip as center of head rotations and dividing the painting in a number of sections between 2 (1×2 matrix) and 6 (2×3 matrix), we observed that the head pose variations in the above cited range did not influence the PoG results obtained only by means of pupil center positions. These considerations allowed us to mediate between precision and real time interaction: instructing users to perform limited head rotations on x and y axis, we estimated wide angular variations along z axis only (1 DoF). Thus, geometrically projecting the nose tip coordinates on the observed surface, we evaluate if they fall in the higher or in the lower half of the painting; then, the pupil center position refines the results, indicating the specific observed section. In this way, in the case of a 2×3 matrix, the nose tip position indicates if users are looking at the first or the second row; the pupil position reveals if users are looking at the first, the second or the third column, depending on its position is respectively at the left, centered or at the right of the eye area.

Once the gaze direction is known, we have to understand if the user is only looking at the detected PoG or she is just observing it; this distinction allows to understand where the focus of the attention is oriented and it is well explained in Sect. 3.4. If the user is interested on a specific detail of the piece of art, we then provide her the related in depth content, by projecting it on the wall.

Pupils are usually easily detected with IR lights because they reflect the infrared, becoming well visible in the eyeball. However, we chose to detect the input stream by means of a webcam. In particular, we used a 720p webcam. We chose to use a common camera, in order to realize an efficient and cheap solution which does not affect users eyes with IR lights.

The open source OpenCV library (http://opencv.org/) has been used to perform image processing.

3.1   The Multithreading Architecture

The usage of classifiers, the image processing and providing multimedia information are not trivial tasks, computationally speaking. Thus, if by one side they are
fundamental operations for our goal, on the other hand they could delay the
interaction, causing a decrease of the usability. For this reason, we considered that
some operations could be executed in parallel, in order to reduce the computation
time. We solved the parallelism with multithreading.

Thus, E.Y.E. C. U. is designed as a multithreading software application: the
visual processing thread works on the video stream, in order to detect the needed
facial features, while the emotional thread monitors pupil size variations; the
reporting thread fills, at regular intervals, a data structure with boolean values
representing the mydriatic events, while the attentional thread populates a buffer
with the detected points of gaze; when the concentration of the PoG belonging to
the same section reaches a given threshold, we consider the visitor interested to it
and the attentional thread starts the timed projection of the deepening content in the
related wall region, as better shown in Sect. 4.

Once the visitor left the detection range of the camera, E.Y.E. C. U. produces a
report indicating the observed sections and the related emotional reactions. E.Y.E.
C. U. architecture is shown in Fig. 3. In the figure, threads are identified by the T,
while the tuple (t, m, g) specifies the mydriatic event m and the gaze direction
g measured at the time t.

3.2   Features Location

As first step we detect the face. To do this, we use the default pre-trained frontal
face detector provided by the OpenCV library. When the application starts, we scan
the entire image; then, we track the detected face in a smaller area. Face detection is

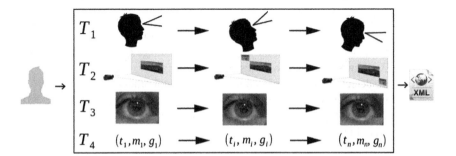

Fig. 3 E.Y.E. C. U. multithreading architecture

performed to constrain the face feature locations to regions inside the facial region, in order to increase both precision and computational efficiency. To obtain the gaze orientation, we firstly need to detect the nose and the eyes: the nose tip will be used to estimate the head position along the z axis; then we search the area of pupils (we actually consider only one eye in computing). Again, the facial features are found using the respective trained classifiers provided by OpenCV; they are Haar-based classifier which extend the set of Haar-like features proposed by Viola and Jones [17]. Once the features have been detected, we computed the detection time: performing the location on images of size 1280×960 pixels processed on an Intel Core i7 with 2.2 GHz, the detection time was about 100 ms. Then, we considered that this performances could be improved by taking advantage from the facial geometry: in particular, eyes are located in the upper half of the face and the nose can be easily found, starting from the facial axis on y axis and from the middle point of the face, for both x and z axis. We observed that the performed optimizations allowed to locate the face, the nose and the eyes in a total average time of 35 ms, reducing the computation time of the 65 %.

3.3 Pupil Detection

The detected ocular region contains eyelids, eyelashes, shadows and light reflexes. These represent noise for pupil detection and they could interfere with the correctness of the results. Thus, the eye image has to be refined, before searching the pupil. The following steps have been executed, in order to perform the refinement:

1. the gray scaled image (Fig. 4a) has been blurred by means of a median filter, in order to highlight well defined contours;
2. the well known Sobel partial derivate on the x axis revealed the significant changes in color, allowing to isolate the eyelids;
3. a threshold operation identifies the *sclera*.

As result, these steps produce a mask, which allows to isolate the eye ball from the source image. Pupil detection is now performed on the source image as follows:

1. we drop down to zero (black) all the pixels having cumulative distribution function (CDF) value greater than a certain threshold [1] (Fig. 4b);
2. we morphologically transform the resulting binary image by means of a dilation process, to remove the light reflexes on the pupil;
3. a contours detection operation identifies some neighborhoods (Fig. 4c).
4. selecting the region having maximum area, the pupillary area is found (Fig. 4d);
5. the center of the ellipse (Fig. 4e) best fitting the pupillary area, approximates the pupil center (Fig. 4f).

(a)   **(b)**   **(c)**

(d)   **(e)**   **(f)**

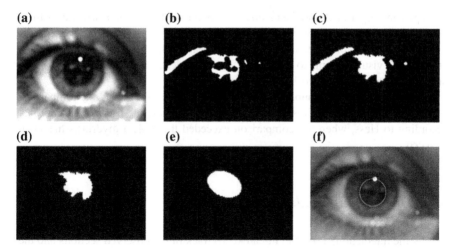

Fig. 4 Pupil detection: main steps. **a** a, **b** b, **c** c, **d** d, **e** e, **f** f

3.4 Focus of Attention

Eye movements, *saccades*, are the fastest produced by the human body: their speed can reach 900° per second and alternate to fixations, which can be interpreted quite differently depending on the context. According to [9], higher fixation frequency on a particular area can be indicative of greater interest in the target or it can be a sign that the target is complex in some way and more difficult to encode. Moreover, more fixations on a particular area indicate that it is more noticeable, or more important to the viewer than other areas [14]. Duchowski [5] reports a mean fixation duration of 1079 ms, during cognitive activities. In order to classify the observed sections of interest, we stored PoG in a buffer of 30 elements (one per frame), working like *history* and we observed that, in the time indicated by Duchowski, the buffer fills the 75 % of its size; for this reason, when the number of PoG belonging to the same section reaches the 75 % buffer size, we consider the user interested to the related section and the projection starts.

3.5 The Emotional Contribute

A wide range of medical studies [8, 10] proved that the brain reacts to emotional arousal with involuntary actions performed by sympathetic nervous system. These changes manifest themselves in a number of ways like increased heart-beat, body temperature, muscular tension and mydriasis. As shown in Sect. 3.1, a dedicated thread monitors the pupillary radius to detect significant variations.

Pupils are larger in children and smaller in adults and the normal size varies from 2 to 4 mm in diameter in bright light to 4–8 mm in the dark [3]. Moreover, pupils react to stimuli in 0.2 s, with the response peaking in 0.5–1.0 s [12]. Hess [8] presented 5 visual stimuli to male and female subjects and he observed that the increase in pupil size varied between 5 and 25 %.

Once we detected the pupil, to calculate the mydriasis we made a comparison between the first stored radius and those computed during the following iterations: according to Hess, when the comparison exceeded the 5 %, a mydriasis has been signaled.

3.6 The Logging Module

During the interaction, a parallel thread keeps track of the observed sections and the related emotional reactions. In particular, at fixed steps of 300 ms, the thread stores the current timestamp, the index of the observed section and a value representing the pupil status. If no section is observed, the section index is −1. If the pupil has normal size, the pupil status is 0, otherwise it is 1. At the end of the interaction, a XML document is built with the collected data. The structure of the XML document is shown in the Listing 1.1.

```
1 <?xml version="1.0" encoding="UTF-8"?>
2 <report>
3     <track idTs="1402674690300" section="-1" mydriasis ="0" />
4     <track idTs="1402674690600" section="1" mydriasis ="0" />
5     <track idTs="1402674690900" section="1" mydriasis ="0" />
6     <track idTs="1402674691000" section="1" mydriasis ="0" />
7     <track idTs="1402674691300" section="1" mydriasis ="0" />
8     <track idTs="1402674691600" section="1" mydriasis ="0" />
9     <track idTs="1402674691900" section="1" mydriasis ="0" />
10 </report>
```

Listing 1.1: Report example

4 A Case Study

In this paper, we analyzed user reactions and the gaze orientation in front of the painting *Borgo di Chiaia* by Caspar Adriaans Van Wittel, located at Diego Aragona Pignatelli Cortes museum, Naples. It is an oil on canvas of size 75 × 174 cm. We imaged the painting as divided in a matrix of 2 rows and 3 columns which identify six sections of uniform size. For each one of the six sections, we prepared a list of

Fig. 5 Case study execution

contents located in corresponding directories. Each time the user lingered on a section for the discussed minimum time, the current content in the related list is projected on the wall region adjacent to the observed area, for a minimum of 3 s after that, if the visitor is still pointing her attention to the contents, these are updated and shown for other 3 s and so on. Meanwhile, the pupil of the visitor is monitored to detect her emotions variations. A real execution is shown in Fig. 5.

5 Results

We tested the system on a sample survey of 23 subjects: 18 adults of age between 23 and 50, and 5 children of age between 4 and 6 years. We asked them to look at the painting, according to the limits exposed in Sect. 3 and to declare which detail they were observing. We considered the test succeeded, when the shown content corresponded to the declared detail.

Experiments registered 75 % of success in adults and 78 % in children: in these cases the projected content referred to the detail that users were observing. System failures were due to a wrong pupil identification: glasses and heavy make-up caused the failure. In 63 % of adult testers, we observed mydriatic reactions; in children the percentage reached 75 %. Results are shown in Fig. 6.

As we stored the indexes of the observed sections, we could count how many times a section has been observed. We represent here the collected data by means of a heatmap, shown in Fig. 7. We built the heatmap using a points distribution function: the higher is the density of the points, the higher is the number of times

Fig. 6 Results

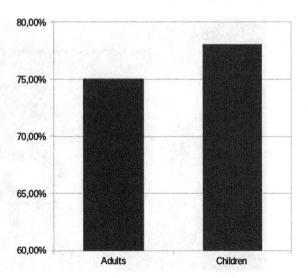

that the related section has been observed. In particular, Fig. 7 is divided in a 2 × 3 matrix representing the six sections in which the painting has been divided. The figure shows that the most observed section has been the second section on the first row: it has been observed by 80 % of users.

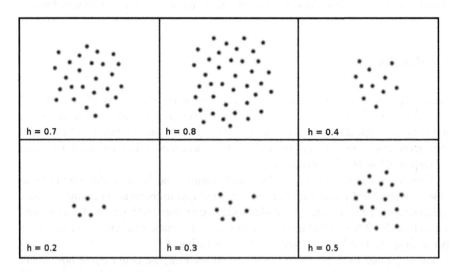

Fig. 7 Heatmap

6 Conclusions

Analysing the software solutions which support the artistic fruition, we observed that most of them divert users' attention from the visit: some require users point their smartphone on the piece of art [15]; others require users type the search key. In both cases, a mobile device interposes between visitor and art.

In order to provide the in depth contents about the object of the visit without deviate users' attention, we realized E.Y.E. C. U., a software application which intercepts users' gaze while they are looking at a painting. E.Y.E. C. U. detects the head movements and the pupil position, in order to understand the observed detail of the painting and then provides the related contents by projecting them on the wall. Just augmenting the reality. As it has been proved that pleasant images cause emotional reactions [8], we even thought to detect pupil dilation, as the pupil is a reliable source of information for the affective computing. In this way we could know which reactions arouse users while they are observing a specific detail.

We tested the system on a real painting, an oil on canvas, and the results showed that E.Y.E. C. U. can correctly detect user's gaze in most of cases. We also observed that people had emotional reactions while they were enjoying the visit, principally the children.

Future works will consist in improving the software application, by reducing users limitations and increasing the precision of the gaze detection. Moreover, we are going to provide audio contents too that could be listened by smart headphones [4] and we are going to enrich the emotional module, by detecting the facial expressions.

Acknowledgment Work supported by the European Community and the Italian Ministry of University and Research and EU under the PON Or.C.He.S.T.R.A. (ORganization of Cultural HEritage and Smart Tourism and Real-time Accessibility) project.

References

1. Asadifard, M., Shanbezadeh, J.: Automatic adaptive center of pupil detection using face detection and cdf analysis. In: Proceedings of the International MultiConference of Engineers and Computer Scientists, vol. 1, p. 3 (2010)
2. Calandra, D., Cutugno, F.: Automyde: a detector for pupil dilation in cognitive load measurement. In: Caporarello, L., Di Martino, B., Martinez, M. (eds.) Smart Organizations and Smart Artifacts. Lecture Notes in Information Systems and Organisation, vol. 7, pp. 135–147. Springer International Publishing, New York (2014)
3. Clark V.L., Kruse, J.A.: Clinical methods: the history, physical, and laboratory examinations. JAMA **264**(21), 2808–2809 (1990). http://dx.doi.org/10.1001/jama.1990.03450210108045
4. D'Auria, D., Di Mauro, D., Calandra, D.M., Cutugno, F.: Caruso: interactive headphones for a dynamic 3d audio application in the cultural heritage context. In: 2014 IEEE 15th International Conference on Information Reuse and Integration (IRI), pp. 525–528 (2014)
5. Duchowski, A.T.: Eye Tracking Methodology: Theory and Practice. Springer, New York (2007)

6. Fanelli, G., Gall, J., Van Gool, L.: Real time head pose estimation with random regression forests. In: 2011 IEEE Conference on Computer Vision and Pattern Recognition (CVPR), pp. 617–624. IEEE (2011)
7. Gómez, E.S., Sánchez, A.S.S.: Biomedical instrumentation to analyze pupillary responses in white-chromatic stimulation and its influence on diagnosis and surgical evaluation (2012)
8. Hess, E.H., Polt, J.M.: Pupil size as related to interest value of visual stimuli. Science 132, 349–350 (1960)
9. Jacob, R.J., Karn, K.S.: Eye tracking in human-computer interaction and usability research: ready to deliver the promises. Mind 2(3), 4 (2003)
10. Kahneman, D., Beatty, J.: Pupil diameter and load on memory. Science 154(3756), 1583–1585 (1966)
11. Kassner, M., Patera, W., Bulling, A.: Pupil: An Open Source Platform for Pervasive Eye Tracking and Mobile Gaze-based Interaction (April 2014). http://arxiv.org/abs/1405.0006
12. Lowenstein, O., Loewenfeld, I.E.: The pupil. The Eye 3, 231–267 (1962)
13. Murphy-Chutorian, E., Trivedi, M.M.: Head pose estimation in computer vision: a survey. IEEE Trans. Pattern Anal. Mach. Intell. 31(4), 607–626 (2009)
14. Poole, A., Ball, L.J., Phillips, P.: In search of salience: a response-time and eye-movement analysis of bookmark recognition. In: People and Computers XVIII—Design for Life, pp. 363–378. Springer (2005)
15. Ruf, B., Kokiopoulou, E., Detyniecki, M.: Mobile museum guide based on fast sift recognition. In: Proceedings of the 6th International Conference on Adaptive Multimedia Retrieval: Identifying, Summarizing, and Recommending Image and Music, pp. 170–183, AMR'08. Springer, Berlin (2010)
16. Valenti, R., Sebe, N., Gevers, T.: Combining head pose and eye location information for gaze estimation. IEEE Trans. Image Process. 21(2), 802–815 (2012). http://www.science.uva.nl/research/publications/2012/ValentiTIP2012
17. Viola, P.A., Jones, M.J.: Rapid object detection using a boosted cascade of simple features. In: CVPR (1), pp. 511–518 (2001)

A Wizard Based EUDWeb Development Process

Loredana Caruccio, Vincenzo Deufemia and Giuseppe Polese

Abstract The pervasiveness of technological media in the daily life of the people has given rise to the end-user development (EUD) research area, which aims to empower end-users to be developers of their applications. The moving towards Web technologies introduced further challenges for EUD researchers. With respect to the significant number of solutions that have been developed, including methodologies and tools, little effort has been produced to support end-users in a proper development process of their applications. In this paper, we propose a wizard-based development process guiding the users towards the construction of own Web applications (Webapps), letting them accomplish complex tasks, such as those related to security and access control.

Keywords End-user development · Wizard-based development process · Web application development · Access control

1 Introduction

In the last decades number of people accessing digital information has increased tremendously, mainly due to the pervasiveness of technological media, such as the new generation of mobile phones that allow users to browse the Web, share contents, and create customized pages on social networks. The familiarity of users with these new technologies yields the need to customize applications to their requirements. In other words, there is the necessity of creating tools capable of supporting

L. Caruccio (✉) · V. Deufemia · G. Polese
Università di Salerno, Via Giovanni Paolo II, 132, 84084 Fisciano, SA, Italy
e-mail: lcaruccio@unisa.it

V. Deufemia
e-mail: deufemia@unisa.it

G. Polese
e-mail: gpolese@unisa.it

© Springer International Publishing Switzerland 2016   173
T. Torre et al. (eds.), *Empowering Organizations*, Lecture Notes in Information
Systems and Organisation 11, DOI 10.1007/978-3-319-23784-8_14

end-users in developing software applications for their needs. For this reason, end-users can be defined as domain developers: experts of a specific domain [6], in which their main goal is more oriented to the development of capabilities available in their setting, than just write software code [2, 3].

The end-user development (EUD) research area aims to empower end-users in developing their own applications [18]. With the growth of the WWW, including new user friendly devices to surf the Web, such as smartphones and tablets, the development of Web applications by end-users (EUDWeb) has received a considerable interest from researchers. However, web-based programming requires dealing with additional aspects with respect to stand-alone programming, like for example, the client/server paradigm, the access control [16], the stateless protocol, and distributed databases. Often, these aspects are known to be difficult even for expert programmers, hence at first glance they appear insurmountable to end-users [26].

A further challenge in EUDWeb is the support of the development process by hiding the software engineering activities that expert programmers usually employ [19]. However, although an end-user can hardly follow a development process like those used by expert programmers, a qualitatively good application cannot be built without a development process with specific steps and activities to be followed.

In this paper we propose an EUDWeb process guiding end-users through wizards in the development of web applications. In this way, end-users can follow a specific development process, which lets them focus on specific tasks with predefined steps, reducing the perception of dealing with a complex work. Furthermore, the proposed process relies on several visual metaphors, which simplify its enactment, by also removing technical aspects, and consequently, the need for programming skills. Finally, particular attention has been given to the access control management that is one of the most complex tasks for end-users, as previously stated.

The paper is organized as follows. Section 2 presents related work by discussing methodological solutions and tools in the EUD area, whereas Sect. 3 describes the proposed wizard-based process for EUDWeb development. Finally, conclusions and future works are included in Sect. 4.

2 Related Work

In the literature there exist many approaches for EUD. In particular, we can find both methodological solutions [10–15] and tools [1, 17, 27–29].

Most methodological solutions are based on the use of the Meta Design paradigm [11–14] in the EUD context. As an example, the Seeding-Evolutionary growth-Reseeding (SER) Model [10] is a collaborative development process where end-users become an active part of it. Another solution following the Meta Design paradigm is the CBEADS framework [15], which requires the development of a Meta-Model of the application and provides a set of tools through which end-users can build and evolve their applications.

Other approaches propose online application development processes that exploit the contents and services available on the Web, such as open API or reusable services [4]. In other words, the development of web applications consists in the combination of data and services provided by web resources into a new integrated service [31]. To this end several programming environments assisting end-users into web-mashup application development have been created [1, 17, 27–29].

Finally, some solutions are based on the WYSIWYG (What You See Is What You Get) paradigm, which allows end-users define all the application's features through a simple composition of user interface elements [5, 7, 22].

Regarding the tools, a first classification of them has been introduced by Rode et al. [25]. In general, many tools exist for developing specific applications as the web and commercial content management [20, 23, 30], or online database management [9, 21, 24].

3 The Wizard-Based Process for EUDWeb Development

In this section we present our wizard-based process for EUDWeb development. It aims to support end-users step-by-step during the construction of general purpose web applications. More specifically, as shown in Fig. 1, we have defined five general steps guiding the users towards the *configuration* and *generation* of web applications. Each step of the process allows users to focus on specific tasks, such as the services to be embedded in the application or the definition of access control policies. Following the development process shown in Fig. 1 the users can generate their own applications and iteratively refine them by moving forward and backwards across steps.

In the following sections, we detail each step of the development process by using a running example concerning the construction of a web application for the management of student information.

3.1 Step 1: What

The first step is indicated with the word *What* and consists of the selection of the application domain. The proposed solution supports the definition of the domain by providing a set of pre-defined management applications.

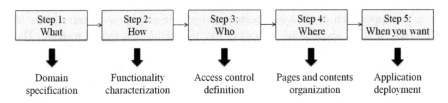

Fig. 1 The step-by-step development process

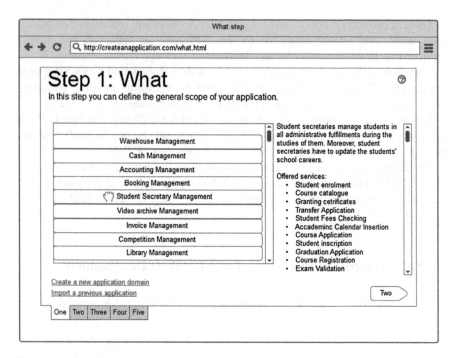

Fig. 2 The user interface for selecting the application domain

An application domain includes the description of the main services offered for the specific application area. In this way, users can read each domain description and select the domain offering the services more suited to their needs. As an example, in Fig. 2 the selection of the *Student Secretary Management* a plication domain visualizes the main purposes of the university secretaries and the list of pre-defined operations. It is worth to note that if the available application domains do not match the users requirements, users have the possibility of defining new application domains or importing an application domain from previous applications.

3.2 Step 2: How

Once the application domain has been specified, the step *How* requires users to define the business services and processes that the application should manage. The proposed solution simplifies the specification of this information through a visual language. In particular, the initial user interface of this step allows users define the services to be embedded in the application by selecting them from a list of pre-defined services or by visually creating them from scratch. As an example, Fig. 3 shows the list of available services for the Student Secretary application. In

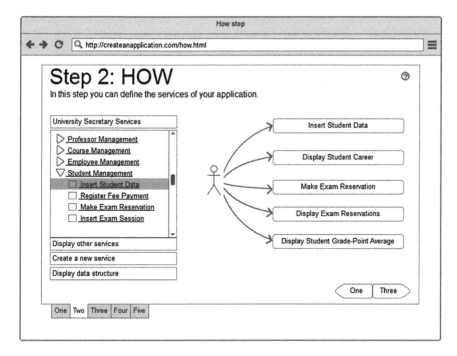

Fig. 3 Selection of the predefined services

particular, the user interface highlights the services for the management of student information. The predefined services can be updated by end-users in order to customize the service-workflow and/or to integrate own business processes.

Figure 4 shows the user interface for visually specifying the services to be included in the service-workflow. As it can be noticed, the user interface is composed of a central workspace, where the user can integrate the application concepts in a linked flow fashion by applying the icon operators.

A *concept* represents a reference data unit that contains all the features of an application domain entity. For example, the Student concept in Fig. 4 has associated all the characteristic elements required by the application domain, e.g., `firstname`, `lastname`, `ID number`, `degree`, `faculty`. The *icon operators* enable the specification of how the application service must work (service-workflow) by linking concepts to operations. The available operators are:

- *Input* It enables the definition of input fields that users have to fill in order to trigger the associated service-workflow. This operator together with the input field names is also used to define the type of each field.
- *Store data* It enables the specification the data to be permanently stored and to define how the concepts coming from the input flow are related.
- *Request data* It enables the request of permanent data from the previous concepts in the flow. It also permits to define conditions on the request, similarly to the WHERE clause in SQL.

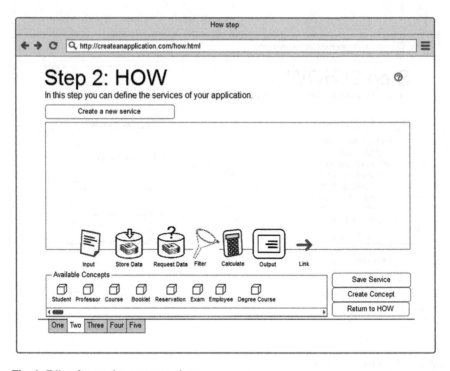

Fig. 4 Editor for creating a new services

- *Filter* It enables the specification of input flow elements to be carried on into the composition process.
- *Calculate* It enables, where possible, the definition of operations on the input flow elements through operators or functions.
- *Output* It enables the specification of the fields to be displayed as output.
- *Link* It enables the definition of the flow that the application service has to follow.

The user interface allows users to apply the selected icon operators and concepts and to add specific details. The latter represent metadata useful for the automatic generation of the application. Figure 5 shows an example of service created for the Student Secretary application. The diagram defines the service-workflow for the exam reservation service. The input form receives information on the student and the exam sessions, and requests user to select the session to be reserved. Once these data are submitted, the student and exam session information are saved in a reservation concept, which is then permanently saved.

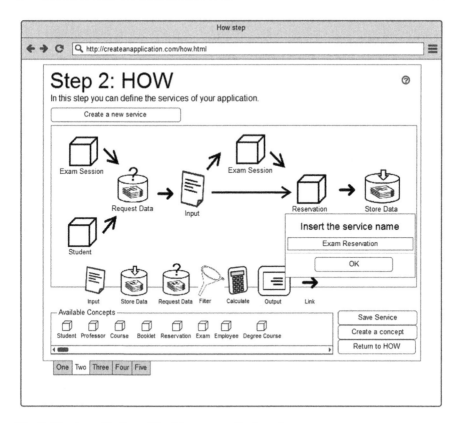

Fig. 5 Visual specification of the "Exam reservation" service

3.3 Step 3: Who

The third step of the proposed development process, named *Who*, allows the specification of application roles and of service restrictions, that is, the specification of access control mechanisms. This task is very relevant for applications running on the Web, since they can be attacked by malicious users willing to access the system and the underlying database.

Since the end-user is a domain developer, s/he strongly knows "who can make what", hence s/he only needs tools simplifying the management of this task. In the third step of the proposed process, end-users can implement access control mechanisms by using the role-based access control (RBAC) model [8]. Figure 6 shows the user interface supporting this activity. Here, end-users can define the roles involved in the application by associating a different color to each of them. Moreover, "padlock" and "key" colored icons are associated to the roles in order to represent role restrictions and access concepts, respectively. The latter are used to identify possible restrictions on the services. As shown in Fig. 7, the user is able

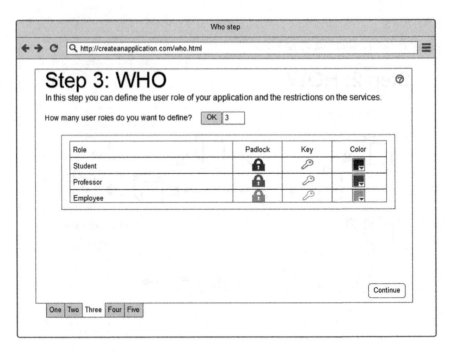

Fig. 6 The definition of user roles

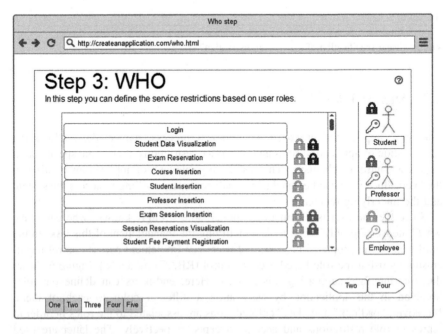

Fig. 7 Specification of access policies for the available services

to specify the restrictions by dragging the colored padlocks on the services defined in the previous step.

3.4   Step 4: Where

The fourth step, named *Where*, enables the end-user to visually organize the application contents and services. The user interface shown in Fig. 8 contains a workspace where the user can define the page flow. A page can be built from scratch or it can be derived through the inclusion of a service. In the last case, the page content is initialized with the elements defined in the service-workflow. A click on a page opens a new interface for content management. As an example, Fig. 9 shows the user interface for specifying the content of web pages. An end-user can select the graphical widgets from the left bar and organize them on the right workspace.

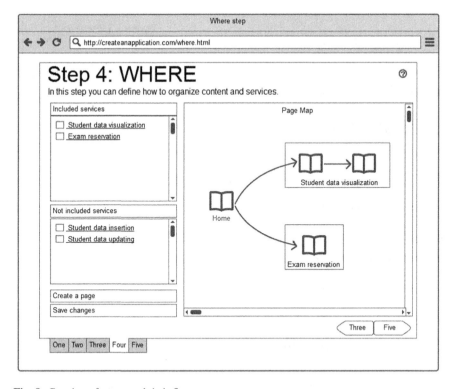

Fig. 8 Creation of pages and their flow

Fig. 9 Content specification for a web page

3.5 Step 5: When You Want

The last step, *When you want*, enables the end-user to perform final checks before generating the application (see Fig. 10). In particular, it is possible to:

- visualize the defined services;
- visualize the application data structure;
- visualize the role-based permissions;
- visualize the page map;
- visualize a demo of the application;
- generate the application.

4 Conclusion and Future Work

The EUD concept for Web application development has been somehow conceived as the possibility for a person of building do-it-yourself (DIY) objects. Expert application developers will continue perform low level programming tasks in order

Fig. 10 User interface for checking and generating the Web application

to satisfy customers willing to have qualitatively excellent objects, with proper attention to details. However, end-users often want to build their own objects, in order to satisfy their tastes, to bring their creativity, and to save costs.

Industry has engaged a task force to make the DIY become a reality; in fact, they have created both tools and semi-finished products to simplify the development work, and to let end-users build their applications through simple compositions. Analogous efforts have been produced by the research community.

In this paper, we propose a wizard-based EUDWeb development process, driving end-users step-by-step towards the construction of the application. In addition, the proposed process enables end-users to manage access control mechanisms, which are mandatory for Web applications, and are particularly complex to deal with.

We are currently implementing tools supporting the proposed process, in order to analyze and empirically evaluate if it is easy to use. Moreover, we would also like to define a visual language for the specification of the application domain, i.e., the *What* step.

References

1. Albinola, M., Baresi, L., Carcano, M., Guinea, S.: Mashlight: a lightweight mashup framework for everyone. In: Workshop on Mashups, Enterprise Mashups and Lightweight Composition on the Web (2009)
2. Cabitza, F., Fogli, D., Piccinno, A.: Cultivating a culture of participation for the co-evolution of users and systems. In: International Workshop on Cultures of Participation in the Digital Age (2010)
3. Cabitza, F., Fogli, D., Piccinno, A.: "each to his own": distinguishing activities, roles and artifacts in EUD practices. In: Smart Organizations and Smart Artifacts, pp. 193–205. Springer (2014)
4. Cappiello, C., Daniel, F., Matera, M., Picozzi, M., Weiss, M.: Enabling end user development through mashups: requirements, abstractions and innovation toolkits. In: End-User Development, pp. 9–24. Springer (2011)
5. Caruccio, L., Deufemia, V., D'Souza, C., Ginige, A., Polese, G.: Supporting access control within a mockup-based EUDWeb. In: Proceedings of 7th International Symposium on Visual Information Communication and Interaction (VINCI), pp. 88–97 (2014)
6. Costabile, M.F., Fogli, D., Mussio, P., Piccinno, A.: End-user development: the software shaping workshop approach. In: End User Development, pp. 183–205. Springer (2006)
7. Deufemia, V., D'Souza, C., Ginige, A.: Visually modelling data intensive web applications to assist end-user development. In: Proceedings of 6th International Symposium on Visual Information Communication and Interaction (VINCI), pp. 17–26 (2013)
8. Ferraiolo, D.F., Kuhn, R.D., Chandramouli, R.: Role-Based Access Control. Artech House Inc., Norwood (2007)
9. FileMaker, I.: File maker pro 13. http://info.filemaker.com/GL_it-IT_FileMaker_Overview_information.html. Accessed 27 Feb 2015
10. Fischer, G.: Seeding, evolutionary growth and reseeding: constructing, capturing and evolving knowledge in domain-oriented design environments. Autom. Softw. Eng. 5(4), 447–464 (1998)
11. Fischer, G.: End-user development and meta-design: foundations for cultures of participation. In: End-User Development, pp. 3–14. Springer (2009)
12. Fischer, G., Giaccardi, E., Ye, Y., Sutcliffe, A.G., Mehandjiev, N.: Meta-design: a manifesto for end-user development. Commun. ACM 47(9), 33–37 (2004)
13. Fischer, G., Nakakoji, K., Ye, Y.: Metadesign: guidelines for supporting domain experts in software development. IEEE Softw. 26(5), 37–44 (2009)
14. Fischer, G., Scharff, E.: Meta-design: design for designers. In: Proceedings of the 3rd Conference on Designing Interactive Systems: Processes, Practices, Methods, and Techniques, pp. 396–405. ACM (2000)
15. Ginige, A., De Silva, B.: CBEADS©: a framework to support meta-design paradigm. In: Universal Access in Human Computer Interaction. Coping with Diversity, pp. 107–116. Springer (2007)
16. Giordano, M., Polese, G.: Visual computer-managed security: a framework for developing access control in enterprise applications. IEEE Softw. 30(5), 62–69 (2013)
17. Google: Google maps Editor. http://www.google.it/mapmaker. Accessed 27 Feb 2015
18. Lieberman, H., Paternò, F., Klann, M.,Wulf, V.: End-User Development: An Emerging Paradigm. Springer (2006)
19. Lizcano, D., Alonso, F., Soriano, J., Lopez, G.: A web-centred approach to end-user software engineering. ACM Trans. Softw. Eng. Methodol. (TOSEM) 22(4), 36 (2013)
20. Microsoft: Visual studio express 2013 for web. http://www.asp.net/vwd. Accessed 27 Feb 2015
21. Microsoft: Visual studio lightswitch. http://msdn.microsoft.com/it-it/vstudio/lightswitch.aspx. Accessed 27 Feb 2015

22. Nestler, T., Namoun, A., Schill, A.: End-user development of service-based interactive web applications at the presentation layer. In: Proceedings of the 3rd ACM SIGCHI Symposium on Engineering Interactive Computing Systems, pp. 197–206. ACM (2011)
23. Open Source Matters, I.: Joomla. http://www.joomla.org/. Accessed 27 Feb 2015
24. Pesce, M.: Gabama. http://www.gabama.com/. Accessed 27 Feb 2015
25. Rode, J., Howarth, J., Pérez-Quinones, M.A., Rosson, M.B.: An end-user development perspective on state-of-the-art web development tools. Technical Report TR-05-03, Virginia Tech Computer Science (2005)
26. Rode, J., Rosson, M.B., Qui, Pérez-Quinones, M.A., et al.: End user development of web applications. In: End User Development, pp. 161–182. Springer (2006)
27. Wang, G., Yang, S., Han, Y.: Mashroom: End-user mashup programming using nested tables. In: Proceedings of the 18th International Conference on World Wide Web, pp. 861–870. ACM (2009)
28. Wong, J., Hong, J.I.: Making mashups with Marmite: towards end-user programming for the web. In: Proceedings of the SIGCHI Conference on Human Factors in Computing Systems, pp. 1435–1444. ACM (2007)
29. Yahoo Inc., Y.: Yahoo's pipes. https://pipes.yahoo.com. Accessed 27 Feb 2015
30. Yes Software: Code charge studio 5. http://www.yessoftware.com/. Accessed 27 Feb 2015
31. Yue, K.B.: Experience on mashup development with end user programming environment. J. Inf. Syst. Educ. 21(1), 111 (2010)

Practicing Mobile Interface Design Principles Through the Use of HCI Design Patterns—A Training Strategy

Giuliana Vitiello, Genny Tortora, Pasquale Di Giovanni
and Monica Sebillo

Abstract One of the main factors behind the rapid development and wide adoption of modern mobile devices is surely the enormous amount of third party applications available for the various mobile platforms. Nevertheless, due to the unique characteristics of the mobile world, designing usable user interfaces for such applications is still a challenging task. Design patterns were conceived to deal with design complexity providing well-recognized and reusable solutions. However, one of the main difficulties arising when design patterns are used by less experienced developers, is the choice of the appropriate patterns for a specific problem. To support novice developers in that choice, we propose MIDE, a tool that devises patterns in the form of ready to use application templates and interface snippets targeted at the Android platform.

Keywords HCI design patterns · Rapid user interface prototyping · Mobile interface development

1 Introduction

Over the last few years, the growing popularity of mobile devices such as smartphones or tablets has certainly revolutionized our lifestyle changing the way we communicate and access information. One of the key factors for the success of these

G. Vitiello (✉) · G. Tortora · P. Di Giovanni · M. Sebillo
Department of Computer Science, University of Salerno,
Via Giovanni Paolo II, 132-84084 Fisciano, SA, Italy
e-mail: gvitiello@unisa.it

G. Tortora
e-mail: tortora@unisa.it

P. Di Giovanni
e-mail: pdigiovanni@unisa.it

M. Sebillo
e-mail: msebillo@unisa.it

© Springer International Publishing Switzerland 2016
T. Torre et al. (eds.), *Empowering Organizations*, Lecture Notes in Information
Systems and Organisation 11, DOI 10.1007/978-3-319-23784-8_15

devices is represented by the wide availability of third-party applications that allow users to perform diverse tasks. In addition, an increasing number of non-professional developers are grappling with the development of mobile applications, exploiting free or low cost development tools. However, those tools do not consider peculiarities of mobile devices that should be carefully taken into account during the application design and development, to offer a satisfying user experience. Among such characteristics we can mention the poor computing power, the different types of interaction modalities, the different level of support offered by current mobile platforms during the development of a specific feature and, above all, the small size of the screen. Those factors have a fundamental impact on the proper design of what is recognized as the most important component of a mobile application, the user interface (UI). In this paper we present a tool that supports Android developers during the design of a mobile user interface providing them with ready to use templates and code snippets. Each template is the result of the adoption of currently well-accepted mobile design patterns. The tool can be used either for the rapid prototyping of pattern-based user interfaces or as a development support tool thanks to its capability to generate executable code.

The paper is structured as follows. Section 2 introduces and discusses some of the major issues related to the development of usable mobile user interfaces. Section 3 analyzes benefits and drawbacks of the use of patterns as a possible means to manage design complexity. The Mobile Interface Development Environment (MIDE) and some details concerning its implementation are described in Sects. 4 and 5. Section 6 presents some results of our experimentation aimed at assessing the tool usefulness during the development of a non-trivial mobile application. Finally, some conclusions are drawn in Sect. 7.

2   Striving for Usability in Mobile Interface Development

Despite their apparent simplicity when compared with traditional complex desktop interfaces, designing mobile user interfaces is often a non-trivial task. In fact, the univocal characteristics of mobile devices entail a series of constraints that are of the utmost importance in order to provide a satisfying user experience. Among such issues we can mention the reduced screen size of such devices, which causes a lack of room for displaying data. Squeezing data to fit the display often results in the loss of relevant information, especially if the meaning of the displayed data depends also on their spatial components [1, 2]. Designers are therefore forced to carefully select what to show at a given time. Moreover, considering that the display is not only used to visualize information but is also usually the primary source for input, the right tradeoff should be reached between data visualization and data input areas. Another common issue is an excessive hardware and software fragmentation within the various mobile platforms that leads developers to implement radically different user interfaces depending on the potential mobile platform on which the application will be executed. This problem is increased also by the fact that the various mobile platforms, such as Google Android, Apple iOS or Microsoft Windows Phone, have their own conventions and guidelines, for the development of mobile applications in general and for the development of the user interface in particular [3–5]. A direct consequence of these issues is often evident during the "porting" operation, i.e., when an application designed for a particular platform, such as Apple iOS, is offered also on another platform with the original user interface and without taking into account the specific design guidelines of the new platform.

A further important issue affecting the "quality in use" of mobile applications lies in the lack of well recognized standards and formal training for development and testing of usable mobile interfaces. This problem is more likely to happen when mobile applications are developed by small teams or by single developers. In those cases a correct usability evaluation of the mobile application can be very difficult since such developers usually have little resources to test their product (for example in a usability laboratory) with a consistent number of potential representative users. In the worst scenario a usability test plan is simply absent.

Usability principles for mobile interface design are not taken into account by the rapid prototyping tools available to novice developers, such as the one supplied with the Android Software Development Kit. In fact, the only goal of such tools is the automatic generation of the UI source code according to the graphical widgets previously chosen by the developer. The goal of the present research is to bridge the described gap and support novice developers with a number of usability oriented design patterns derived from best practices in mobile interface design. The MIDE tool described in the present paper is meant to address this challenge.

3 The Challenges of Using Design Patterns for Novice Developers

A few years after the seminal work by Christopher Alexander [6], who introduced the design pattern concept in the architectural domain, researchers in HCI recognized the approach as especially appropriate to user interface and interactive system design [7–9]. A design pattern is a general reusable solution to a commonly occurring problem, formally documented in a given field of expertise. Its traditional structure (usually known as the Alexandrian or canonical form) is made up of the following sections: Name of the pattern, Problem and Context, Forces, Solution, Examples, Positive and negative consequences, The rationale, The known uses, Related patterns. Design patterns can be used in two different manners, namely as a simple collection of ready to use solutions where each pattern has no relationships with other patterns or combined together to form a complete language for specific domains. Several pattern languages have been introduced, as a lingua franca, by which not only are the interface designers able to share their expertise with one another, but also an effective participatory design process can be carried out, where potential users are actively involved [1, 10]. However, despite their benefits and advantages, the correct usage of design patterns can be difficult for novice developers. In fact, as discussed also in [11], one of the main problems can be the lack of expertise in the identification of the pattern that best suits user's needs. Furthermore, for what concerns pattern languages, important factors such as the developer's background or tight project schedules can constitute a problem limiting the actual usage of the language itself [12]. Such issues are certainly accentuated in the mobile world where the individual application developer might have little knowledge of design principles or have no time to perform a state of the art review of the user interface guidelines for the chosen mobile platform. For example, according to the design guidelines suggested by Google, in the Android platform the action bars that can be used to switch among the various application screens should be always placed at the top of the screen. Putting them at the bottom may originate confusion for the final users resulting in a bad and inconsistent user experience. Moreover, design patterns often represent generic solutions and their adaptation to the real problem can constitute a further element of difficulty, especially when combined with the need to design a user interface consistent with the general look and feel of the underlying mobile platform. Finally, although the solution provided by a pattern should be independent from a specific technology, in practice in the context of HCI there are patterns that provide solutions at a high abstraction level as well as patterns that deal with specific interaction paradigms and technologies, such as the windowing systems commonly available on traditional desktop operating systems [13].

4 MIDE—The Mobile Interface Development Environment

The tool we present aims at helping developers with the design of mobile user interfaces that not only adhere to the Android platform guidelines proposed by Google, but that also reflect the best practices of usability design, dictated by widely used design patterns for the mobile world.

In order to offer effective support to mobile application designers, in MIDE some popular mobile design pattern catalogs [10, 14, 15] are embedded inside a list of common application templates along with a list of the most common features available in current mobile applications. For what concerns, instead, the specific Android design guidelines, MIDE currently supports Google recommendations for the branch 4.x of the operating system. In fact, starting with the version 4 of the platform, Google has put a lot of effort in standardizing the look and feel and provided complete guidelines to develop applications cohesive with that look and feel.

According to the official documentation [3], the common structure of a typical Android interface is made up of the following four elements: the main action bar showing the most important actions available for the specific application, the view control used to select the various application screens, the content area that displays and manages the effective contents of the application and, finally, the split action bar used to provide additional controls. Moreover, Android offers three system themes for the 4.x branch namely "Holo Light", "Holo Dark" and "Holo light with dark action bars". MIDE can be used in two complementary ways: as a step-by-step wizard to rapidly generate the user interface skeleton of a typical Android mobile application or as a collection of commonly used functionalities that the developer can manually compose in order to design the user interface. The general idea is therefore to bring design knowledge closer to non-experts. In the wizard configuration, the developer can choose among a predefined set of application templates. Such templates encompass the general structure of common mobile applications such as an image gallery or a news application. According to the chosen template, the developer can customize the behavior of the proposed interface simply choosing among a proposed set of alternatives. Each alternative is a well-recognized pattern for the specific task. For example in the "Data Entry" section of the Organizer template, for the selection of a single value from a predefined set, the developer can choose among solutions such as Sliders or Spinners. Since these patterns are generally the most used, the choice to use a text field for this task is simply not provided in the available options. Figure 1 shows, for example, the preview panel of the User Registration template along with the modal window that appears when the tool user chooses to download the actual Android code related to his choice.

In the common functionalities configuration a collection of "ready to use" user interface snippets are provided to the designer. In this modality, the user interface of MIDE is divided into two main working areas: the list of mobile functionalities and the panel where the developer can "build" the interface of his/her application simply dragging and dropping the chosen functionalities in the desired order. The proposed

Fig. 1 User registration template

layout and behavior for each single functionality are the result of the application of one or more well-recognized design pattern in a totally transparent manner for the non-expert developer. For example, the "Login" functionality not only presents the traditional set of controls such as the text fields for the insertion of username and password or the buttons to confirm or cancel the action but it also takes into account the need to validate user input or to provide adequate error messages (see Fig. 2).

According to current best practices, the suggested text for those messages will contain only relevant and context related information, avoiding technical details or long sentences that might be difficult to read or have a negative impact on the overall user experience. Moreover, to further simplify developer's choice, the list of available functionalities is divided into the classic interaction categories available in mobile applications such as, Authentication, Showing output, Data insertion etc. After the selection of the desired functionality, two options are available: getting more information about the various patterns that contribute to the realization of that functionality or customizing it to the current context of use. Some details that can be customized are, for example, the visual aspect, the size or the accepted input type of a text entry widget. The last option offered by the tool is represented by the generation of XML files and Java classes forming the actual Android source code of the chosen template or snippet. The user can import and use such code in his favorite development environment. In the following section, we briefly describe some technical choices made during the design and development of the main MIDE modules.

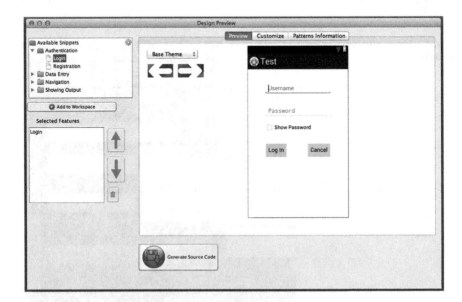

Fig. 2 MIDE common functionalities modality

5 MIDE—Technical Details

MIDE was written using the Java language and exploits several features offered by the Java platform. From a high-level point of view, the whole system architecture can be ideally partitioned into two main modules namely the front-end and the code generation subsystem. The former lets tool users perform operations such as patterns catalogue exploration or personalization of a particular template, while the latter, according to their choices, generates the packages containing the source code along with all the required additional resources that constitute the real mobile UI.

During the system design of the front-end, an important requirement to satisfy was the definition of a template that acted as an underlying common structure for every pattern.

The purpose of such a baseline was twofold. On one side, it simulated both the drawing area of an Android Activity i.e., the software component that actually displays the UI and lets users interact with it, and the several layouts that may define the structure of the interface itself. On the other side, having a shared underlying structure simplified the later code generation phase. However, to actually automate the code generation, we needed, for all the widgets that characterized a pattern, to store additional details such as their ID, the order in which they were added, the list of widgets customized by the user, their position on the screen according to the constraints of the particular layout etc. To simulate, in a desktop environment, the various components and layouts of a typical Android UI and satisfy the abovementioned requirements, we exploited the high flexibility and the customization level offered by the SWING framework.

The common baseline for every pattern is made up of two fundamental framework objects, the *JPanel*, a container for lightweight components such as labels or buttons and the *GridBagLayout*, a layout manager that offers a grid where arrange the graphical widgets. Subsequently, for each pattern, a specific set of SWING widgets (labels, buttons, textboxes, etc.) is added to the Panel. Each widget has been customized to replicate the look and feel of the corresponding Android component. However, to easily store all the additional details useful in the subsequent code generation phase we added an intermediate level of abstraction.

We extended the *JComponent* class, the base class for almost all the SWING components, with customized fields and methods. Starting with the customized *JComponent*, *MyComponent*, we actually instantiate the SWING widget that will constitute the simulated UI. In addition, a reference to every instance of *MyComponent* is stored into an appropriate data structure subsequently parsed by the code generation module. For example, a SWING TextView that simulates the same Android object will be instantiated in the following way:

```
MyComponent  ViewReg  =  new  MyComponent  ("TextView",
"Registration",    null,"wrap_content","wrap_content",12,
"#333333","TextView"+""+(components.size()+1),"0dp","6dp",
0,0,2,this,null);
```

where *MyComponent* is the class that extends the *JComponent* class.

As previously mentioned, the second main functionality offered by MIDE it the automated generation of the Android source code corresponding to the desired design pattern. In the Android platform, there are actually two main ways to create the UI of a mobile application, namely declare and instantiate all the graphic components directly in the application source code or declare them as a set of XML elements. Flexibility and the clear separation of the presentation layer from the code that controls its behavior represent two of the main advantages of the second option. In this context, the core functionality of the code generation module is the transformation of the previously mentioned customized *JComponent* instances into well-formed XML elements that correspond to the graphical elements and layouts. For example, a simple menu icon declared as

```
MyComponent   icon   =   new   MyComponent("ImageButton
Item","search",search_icon",2,0,1,this," ic_action_search
");
```

will be automatically translated into the following XML element:

```
<item
android:id = "@+id/search_icon"
android:icon = "@drawable/ic_action_search"
android:title = "@string/search_title"
android:showAsAction = "always"
/>.
```

6 Evaluation

In order to evaluate the effectiveness of MIDE in supporting non-expert developers during the design of mobile interfaces, we used it as a support tool during the undergraduate course of Human Computer Interaction at the University of Salerno.

The course is held in the first semester of the third year of the bachelor degree in Computer Science. Students' learning assessment is performed with in-class exams aimed at evaluating the knowledge of all the theoretical concepts discussed during the course and with the development of a concrete prototype whose aim is to encourage them to apply, on a real problem, what they learnt. Every year a different topic is chosen and, at the end of the course, students, divided in groups, present and discuss the mobile application they developed.

However over the past years, we noticed that although students usually possess an adequate skills in the use of the most common programming languages, they lack the necessary experience to address usability issues when designing mobile user interfaces.

In the academic year 2013/2014, when we decided to introduce the use of MIDE, there were over 100 students attending our HCI course. At the beginning of the course students were asked to fill out a detailed questionnaire about their degree of experience in the development of mobile applications in general and the design of mobile interfaces in particular.

During the first half of the course, students were gradually introduced to the main factors that influence the design and development of mobile applications. In addition, some introductive lectures on the Android platform were also given in order to provide them with the technical background necessary to fully exploit a modern mobile platform.

Subsequently, we divided students into groups of four or five people and asked them to design an Android application that provides final users with micro-coordination functionalities for small groups of young people that heavily use their mobile devices for everyday activities.

In particular, the application had to offer the following functionalities:

- Login and user account management,
- Ability to create groups of users,
- Shared calendar and notes among the participants,
- Ability for users to share their position or the location of a certain place e.g., a meeting place.

By asking to design a non-trivial application, our aim was to encourage the experimentation among various design combinations and alternatives concerning not only the whole navigation hierarchy but also the choice of the right "data view" to display heterogeneous types of information.

For each of these functionalities, students were asked to perform, first of all, a detailed hierarchical task analysis to decompose users' actions. A mandatory requirement was to take into account, throughout the whole design phase, traditional usability principles and attributes. In particular, according to our academic experience and current research in the field of mobile applications, we asked them to focus on those attributes that mainly influence the usability of mobile applications [16].

Such attributes and the motivations to take them into account are shown in Table 1.

Table 1 Usability attributes in a mobile context

Attribute	Motivation
Efficiency	Once users have learned the application structure, how quickly can they perform tasks?
Errors	How many errors do users make, how severe are these errors, and how easily can they recover from the errors?
Satisfaction	How pleasant is the whole design?
Cognitive load	The importance of context around the user can influence his/her attention on the specific task
	The use of a mobile application can be frequently interrupted as users switch attention among competing activities

Table 2 Describing the application structure

What are the activities users can do with your application?
What is the metaphor behind your system? What were the alternatives?
How are the functionalities divided into functional groups?
Is your design consistent? Why?

Two presentations and reports were also planned to show the progress and changes during the various design iterations. In the first report students had to describe how they expected users would have interacted with their system. Some of the most important questions we asked to answer are shown in Table 2.

During the initial phases of the design, students made the UI prototypes of their application using paper sketches. Such a choice was motivated by the need to facilitate the brainstorming activity among the groups' members, letting them to quickly compare different ideas and design alternatives. The final version of the paper sketches along with a detailed description of the various design choices constituted the subject of the second report.

Subsequently, starting from the provided documentation, we performed a heuristic evaluation to assess critical factors such as consistency of the UI, aesthetic design, etc. In addition, we compared the proposed design choices with the main mobile design principles and the patterns provided by Google to develop Android applications that behave in a predictable and consistent way.

This latter point was particularly critical. In fact, although all the proposed interfaces let users accomplish all the required tasks, the vast majority of them did not have a coherent design among the various applications screens and did not respect the guidelines proposed by Google for its platform. Among the common design mistakes, we can mention a confusing subdivision of functionalities into the three layers proposed by Google (Top Level, Category and Edit views), the wrong use of fundamental elements of the Android user interface such as Action bars or Navigation Drawers and a poor management and recovery of users' errors. These design mistakes are particularly frustrating especially in a mobile environment where users would expect that the application they are using is designed according to the specific interaction patterns and guidelines of the mobile platform they are using.

To mitigate such issues and let students better understand the main weaknesses of the interfaces they proposed, we introduced MIDE and invited them to compare their design choices with the proposals and suggestions provided by the tool.

The first results have been quite encouraging since we noticed a significant improvement in the design quality of the proposed prototypes. At the beginning, students used MIDE as an interactive Pattern catalog. Subsequently, the ability to immediately test the chosen solution on an Android emulator or real device thanks to the on-the-fly code generation was recognized as a valuable feature to rapidly see "in action" the different design patterns.

As a concrete example, we consider the "shared calendar and notes" functionality. It can be decomposed into the following activities:

Table 3 Common mistakes in the initial paper sketches

Task	Issue Type	MIDE
General navigation	The list-view displays only a fraction of information. Not enough details to make a decision	List View + Tap and Hold
Browsing notes list	Several screens to show the set of notes	Carousel Pattern
Creation of a new note or a calendar event	Poor error management	Inline Error Message Pattern

- Visualization of existing notes,
- Creation of new notes,
- Creation of a calendar event,
- Sharing the new resource with other users.

In Table 3, we report a list of some common mistakes we found in the initial paper sketches concerning the interface design for this specific functionality and the redefined solution proposed by the majority of students groups.

7 Conclusions and Future Works

Despite its apparent simplicity, the correct design of a mobile user interface is a complex and challenging task. Design patterns provide widely accepted solutions to recurrent problems and since their first adoption in HCI they represent a valid means to deal with design complexity. However, some of their strengths, such as the generality of the proposed solution, can be a source of difficulties especially for novice developers. The MIDE environment presented in the paper embeds the rationale of the best known mobile patterns into concrete implementations providing ready to use solutions to common design issues on the Android platform. At the moment, the tool supports the most important patterns and the source code it generates is explicitly oriented towards the most common screen resolutions available on the majority of current smartphones.

To assess the effectiveness of the proposal during the development of real mobile applications, we performed an empirical evaluation with undergraduate students. Results show the effectiveness of MIDE not only as a tool to explore a mobile patterns catalog but also as an effective mean supporting non-experienced developers during both the initial design choices and the actual development process.

In the future, we are planning to add new features and templates and to extend the approach to other popular mobile platforms such as Apple iOS and Windows Phone, making MIDE a cross-platform environment. In addition we are developing new patterns browsing strategies to improve the catalogue exploration and facilitate the selection of the solution that best matches developers need.

References

1. Ginige, A., Romano, M., Sebillo, M., Vitiello, G., Di Giovanni, P.: Spatial data and mobile applications: general solutions for interface design. In: AVI 2012, pp. 189–196. ACM, New York (2012)
2. Paolino, L., Sebillo, M., Tortora, G., Vitiello, G.: Framy: visualizing geographic data on mobile interfaces. J Location Based Serv. 2(3), 236–252 (2008)
3. Google Android design guidelines. http://developer.android.com/design/index.html
4. Apple iOS Human Interface Guidelines. http://developer.apple.com/library/ios/#documentation/userexperience/conceptual/mobilehig/Introduction/Introduction.html
5. Microsoft Design Library for Windows Phone. http://msdn.microsoft.com/en-us/library/windowsphone/design/hh202915(v=vs.105).aspx
6. Alexander, C.: A Pattern Language. Oxford University Press (1977)
7. Bayle, E., Bellamy, R., Casaday, G., Erickson, T., Fincher, S., Grinter, B., Gross, B., Lehder, D., Marmolin, H., Potts, C., Skousen, G., Thomas, J.: Putting it all together: towards a pattern language for interaction design. In: CHI '97 Workshop SIGCHI Bulletin, vol. 30 issue 1, pp. 17–23. ACM, New York (1998)
8. Erickson, T.: Lingua francas for design: sacred places and pattern languages. In: DIS '00, pp. 357–368. ACM, New York (2000)
9. Tidwell, J.: Designing Interfaces 2nd Ed. O'Reilly (2010)
10. Hoober, S., Berkman, E.: Designing Mobile Interfaces. O' Reilly Media (2011)
11. Diaz, P., Rosson, M.B., Aedo, I., Carrol, J.M.: Web design patterns: investigating user goals and browsing strategies. In: Pipek, V., Rosson, M.B., de Ruyter, B., Wulf, V. (eds.) End-User Development. LNCS, vol. 5435, pp. 186–204. Springer, Heidelberg (2009)
12. Bernhaupt, R., Winckler, M., Pontico, F.: Are user interface pattern languages usable? a report from the trenches. In: Gross, T., Gulliksen, J., Kotzé, P., Oestreicher, L., Palanque, P., Prates, R.O., Winckler, M. (eds.) INTERACT 2009. LNCS, vol. 5727, pp. 542–545. Springer, Heidelberg (2009)
13. Dearden, A.M., Finlay, J.: Pattern languages in HCI: a critical review. Hum. Comput. interaction 21(1), 49–102 (2006)
14. Neil, T.: Mobile design pattern gallery: UI patterns for iOS, android and more. O'Reilly (2012)
15. Nudelman, G.: Android Design Patterns. Wiley (2013)
16. Harrison, R., Flood, D., Duce, D.: Usability of mobile applications: literature review and rationale for a new usability model. J. Interact. Sci. 1(1) (2013)

A Mobile Application for Supporting Archaeologists in the Classification and Recognition of Petroglyphs

Vincenzo Deufemia, Valentina Indelli Pisano, Luca Paolino
and Paola de Roberto

Abstract In this paper we present a mobile application, named *PetroSketch*, for supporting archaeologists in the classification and recognition of petroglyph symbols. PetroSketch is a virtual notebook enabling users to draw a petroglyph symbol on a white page, or by following the contour of a symbol captured with the camera, and to obtain its classification and the list of symbols more similar to it. The latter is performed by a flexible image matching algorithm that measures the similarity between petroglyph by using a distance, derived from the image deformation model, which is computationally efficient and robust to local distortions.

Keywords Image processing · Computer vision · Cultural heritage · Mobile applications · Pattern recognition

1 Introduction

Petroglyphs are engravings obtained by hitting or scraping stone surfaces with sharp tools made of stone or metal. These symbols were used by prehistoric people to communicate with their divinity or with other men. Basically, we find these carvings as a set of symbols called scenes, which depicts daily life situations. Therefore, the study of the petroglyphs is very important to gain new knowledge and awareness about the periods in which the petroglyphs were created.

V. Deufemia (✉) · V. Indelli Pisano · L. Paolino · P. de Roberto
Università di Salerno, Via Giovanni Paolo II, 132, 84084 Fisciano, SA, Italy
e-mail: deufemia@unisa.it

V. Indelli Pisano
e-mail: vindellipisano@unisa.it

L. Paolino
e-mail: lpaolino@unisa.it

P. de Roberto
e-mail: pderoberto@unisa.it

© Springer International Publishing Switzerland 2016   199
T. Torre et al. (eds.), *Empowering Organizations*, Lecture Notes in Information
Systems and Organisation 11, DOI 10.1007/978-3-319-23784-8_16

Petroglyphs are prehistoric stone engravings unrevealing stories of ancient life and describing a conception of the world transmitted till today. Although they may seem as durable as the rock they reside on, petroglyphs are inevitably deteriorated by natural causes as well as vandalism. As an example, some of them have been destroyed by tourists, while others are disappearing due to acid rain and sunshine. Hence, it is very important to preserve the petroglyphs trying to identify and archive them for future generations.

Research challenges have to be addressed for digital preservation of petroglyphs, including the integration of data coming from multiple sources and the correct interpretation of drawings. The IndianaMAS project is aiming to integrate heterogeneous unstructured data related to rock carvings into a single repository, organizing classified data into a Digital Library, interpreting data by finding relationships among them, and enriching them with semantic information [1, 2]. However, the large number of sites where petroglyphs have been discovered, and the different methodologies they were made, makes their study a complex task. Archaeologists have to deal with a hard and tedious job because they have to report each symbol shape on a notebook paper and search any related information by consulting different books. To address these issues, in this paper, we present *PetroSketch*, a mobile application for supporting archaeologists in the classification and recognition of petroglyph symbols.

PetroSketch is a virtual notebook enabling users to draw a petroglyph symbol on a white page, or by following the contour of a symbol captured with the camera, and to obtain its classification and the list of symbols more similar to it. The latter is performed by a flexible image matching algorithm that measures the similarity between petroglyphs by using a distance, derived from the Image Deformation Model (IDM), which is computationally efficient and robust to local distortions. The classification system has been applied to an image database containing 17 classes of petroglyph symbols from Mount Bego rock art site achieving a classification rate of 68 %.

The remainder of this paper is structured as follows. Background information and an overview of related work in petroglyph classification is given in Sect. 2. A description of the proposed petroglyph classification methodology based on IDM is given in Sect. 3. PetroSketch is introduced in Sect. 4, whereas experiments on a dataset of Mount Bego petroglyph reliefs are reported in Sect. 5. Conclusions are finally drawn in Sect. 6.

2 Related Work

2.1 Rock Art

Petroglyphs are a form of prehistoric art found in many cultures around the world and at many times. There are many theories to explain their purpose, depending on their location, age, and the type of image. Some petroglyphs are thought to be astronomical markers, maps, or other forms of symbolic communication, including a form of "pre-writing". The form of petroglyphs is described by a variety of terms in the archaeological literature. One of the most common forms of rock art around the world is the *anthropomorphic* depiction. They are pictures that resemble humans, but sometimes can represent something else, such as the personification of a spirit or other nonliving thing. Other common images are animals, weapons, and tools.

In this work, we experimented our approach on the reliefs collected and catalogued from Mont Bego, in the extreme south-east of France, which due to the richness of the place in both qualitative and quantitative terms it is ideal for analysis. Archaeologists consider this place as an incredibly valuable source of knowledge, due to the up to 40,000 figurative petroglyphs and 60,000 non-figurative petroglyphs [3]. The figurative petroglyphs represent corniculates, harnesses, daggers, halberds, axes, reticulates, rectangular or oval shaded zones, and anthropomorphous figures. Between 1898 and 1910 Clarence Bicknell realized up to 13,000 drawings and reliefs, part of which were published in [4]. Bicknell identified seven types of figures taking a natural history approach: horned figures (mainly oxen), ploughs, weapons and tools, men, huts and properties, skins and geometrical forms [5]. From 1967 Henry de Lumley is in charge of performing research on the site. Figure 1 shows a picture of a bovine engraving, a Bicknell's relief, and two digitalized reliefs made by de Lumley's team.

2.2 Image Processing of Petroglyphs

The symbol recognition problem is one of the most studied and analyzed research topic in the field of the image processing [6, 7]. But surprisingly, the study of the rock art was only minimally touched by these investigations. Probably, this is due to some unique properties of the petroglyphs (e.g., different petroglyphs may share more or less the same patterns while being different), which make them unsuitable for recognition tasks.

The work presented in [8] aimed to catalogue petroglyphs in terms of lengths of parts of animal bodies, and relations among petroglyphs of several regions. In [9] Takaki et al. proposed new methods to characterize shapes of the petroglyphs and the properties of the group they belong to. In particular, they first extract the skeleton of the petroglyph by applying different image processing algorithms, then the structures are expressed through elementary symbols in order to allow a quantitative comparison. The properties of petroglyph groups are expressed by statistics of simple quantities, such as the numbers of animals and men.

Recently, Zhu et al. applied a distance measure based on the Generalized Hough Transform to find meaningful motifs within large collections of rock art images [10]. They also proposed a tool called *PetroAnnotator*, which allows human

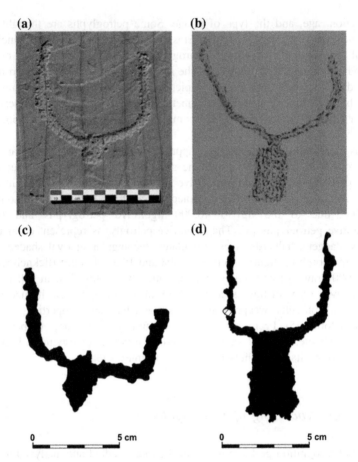

(a)   **(b)**

(c)   **(d)**

0 _____ 5 cm   0 _____ 5 cm

Fig. 1 A picture of a bovine engraving of the Mont Bego (**a**), a picture of a bovine relief made by Bicknell on botanic sheet (**b**), two digitalized reliefs made by de Lumley's team (**c**) and (**d**)

volunteers to "help" computer algorithms to segment and annotate petroglyphs [11]. Finally, in [12] Seidl and Breiteneder proposed an pixel-wise classification for rock art image segmentation and presented some preliminary results.

3 An Approach for Petroglyph Classification

One of the most promising approach to achieve low error rates in the classification of images with high variability is the application of flexible matching algorithms [13]. Among them, the deformation models are especially suited to compensate small local changes as they often occur in the presence of image object variability [14]. These models was originally developed for optical character recognition by Keysers et al. [14] but it was already observed that it could be applied in other areas such as recognition of medical radiographs [15] and video analysis [16]. The image distortion model (IDM) yields a distance measure tolerant with respect to local distortions since in the case two images have different values only for a few pixels, due to noise or artifacts irrelevant to classification, the distance between them is compensated by specifying a region in the matching image for each picture element in which it is allowed to detect a best matching pixel.

These properties motivate its use for petroglyph classification. In the following we describe the steps of our petroglyph classification system.

3.1 Shape Normalization

To recognize a petroglyph symbol regardless of its size and position, the input image is normalized to a standard size by translating its center of mass to the origin. The resulting image $f(x,y)$ is the grid image of the symbol. Then to increase tolerance to local shifts and distortions we smooth and downsample the feature images. In particular, first, to ensure that small spatial variations in the symbol correspond to gradual changes in the feature values, we apply a Gaussian lowpass filter

$$G(x,y) = e^{-\frac{1}{2}(\frac{x^2+y^2}{\sigma^2})}$$

to obtain the smoothed image $g(x, y)$ according to the following equations

$$g(x,y) = f(x,y) \times G(x,y)$$

We then downsample the images by performing symbol removing and resizing (see Fig. 2). This further reduces sensitivity to small shifts and improves runtime performance.

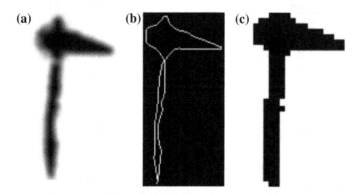

(a)   (b)   (c)

Fig. 2 An example of normalization of an ax petroglyph. **a** The image smoothed with the Gaussian filter, **b** the point removed image, and **c** the image resized at 32 × 32 pixels

3.2   Feature Set

To achieve better performances, instead of directly comparing image pixels, we use derivatives. In particular, for each pixel we consider the horizontal and vertical gradients as features for image matching. Each pixel of a gradient image measures the change in intensity of that same point in the original image, in a given direction. Thus, the horizontal and vertical gradients allow to get the full range of directions.

3.3   Classification

For the classification of petroglyphs we use a deformation model that is robust to distortions and local shifts. In particular, the image deformation model (IDM) performs a pixel-by-pixel value comparison of the query and reference images determining, for each pixel in the query image, the best matching pixel within a region around the corresponding position in the reference image.

The IDM has two parameters: warp range (w) and context window size (c). Figure 3 illustrates how the IDM works and the contribution of both parameters, where the warp range w constrains the set of possible mappings and the $c \times c$ context window computes the difference between the horizontal and vertical gradient for each mapping. It should be noted that these parameters need to be tuned.

The algorithm requires each pixel in the test image to be mapped to a pixel within the reference image not more than w pixels from the place it would take in a linear matching. Over all these possible mappings, the best matching pixel is determined using the $c \times c$ local gradient context window by minimizing the

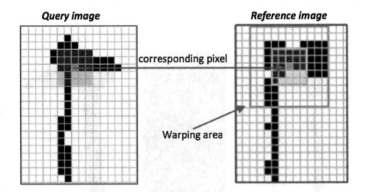

Fig. 3 Example of areas affected by the comparison of pixels with IDM, where $w = 3$ and $c = 2$. The query pixel context (indicated by the *orange area* in the query image) is compared with each equal-sized rectangle within the warping area (*dark-green rectangle* of the reference image). The warping area is calculated by building a $m \times m$, with $m = (w + c) \times 2 + 1$, square around the corresponding reference pixel (*dark-green* pixel) (Colour online)

difference with the test image pixel. In particular, the IDM distance D between two symbols S_1 (the query input) and S_2 (the template) is defined as:

$$D^2 = \sum_{x,y} \min_{d_x,d_y} \| S_1(x+d_x, y+d_y) - S_2(x,y) \|^2$$

where d_x and d_y represent pixel shifts and $S_i(x, y)$ represents the feature values in S_i from the patch centered at x, y.

3.4 Performance Optimization

One of the limitations of IDM algorithm is the high computational complexity, which is even further increased when the warp range and local context are enlarged. Thus, since applying IDM to all the reference images is too slow, we introduce two optimization strategies to speed up the IDM algorithm.

The first optimization is to prune the set of candidates before applying IDM. We use the simple Euclidean L^2 distance as the pruning metric, and the first N nearest neighbors found are given in input to the IDM. In particular, we use the distance:

$$D^2 = \sum_{k=1}^{K} (v_1(k) - v_2(k))^2$$

where $v_i(k)$ corresponds to the horizontal and vertical gradients of the ith image.

The second optimization is the early termination strategy proposed in [17], which relies on the consideration that in kNN classifiers only the k nearest neighbors are used in the classification step. Therefore the exact distance of any image with rank greater than k is not used by the classifier. This means that we can abort the computation of the distance between two reliefs as soon as it exceeds the exact distance of the image with rank r. Since the latter can only be known after all images in the collection have been compared to the query, we approximate it with the distance of the k nearest neighbor identified so far.

4 PetroSketch

PetroSketch is a mobile application developed with the Titanium[1] framework that allows generic users (which in most cases are tourists, trekkers or just archaeology interested people) to support archeologists in collecting and interpreting petroglyph scenes.

---

[1]http://www.appcelerator.com/.

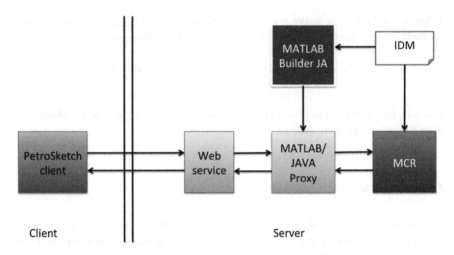

Fig. 4 The architecture of PetroSketch

Figure 4 shows the architecture of PetroSketch. Since the IDM recognition algorithm has been implemented in Matlab environment, we developed a proxy for managing the communication between the server part of the web services and the MCR (MATLAB Compiler Runtime) by using the MATLAB Builder JA.

Figure 5 describes the user interface of the application. It appears as a mobile app where the main part of the screen is occupied by the camera view. We do this choice to focus the user's attention in providing better sketches of the petroglyphs. The remaining part of the screen is employed for managing the menus and the corresponding functionalities. It also provides users with drawing, storing, and retrieving capabilities. In particular, its main functionalities are:

- *Camera*: This item allows users to start the picture acquisition process. It works very similarly to other capture software so we do not need to enter in details. From this phase, it is possible to automatically enter in the drawing mode to trace the borders of the petroglyphs;
- *Pencil Tool*: Here, the user traces the petroglyph borders. S/he can enable this mode for drawing the contours of each petroglyph appearing in the picture or simply choosing the colors or the size of the pencil. Generally, in order to distinguish different single petroglyphs, it is necessary to use different colors for each of them;
- *Album*: The repository of the captured pictures is the Album. Here, photos are stored and previewed. The user can browse the content and choose the one s/he wants to manage;
- *Recognition*: This item allows to begin the recognition phase. By using the previously described approach, the system enables the search and comparison of similar petroglyphs contained within the main remote repository. The image shown in Fig. 5 presents an example where the borders depicted in the center of

Fig. 5 The PetroSketch user interface

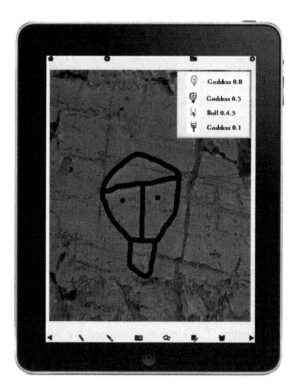

the picture is compared to the remote repository and the final results are presented in the top-right corner of the screen highlighting the most similar together with the similarity values.

5 Experiments

To demonstrate the validity of the proposed approach an experiment focused on measuring the effectiveness of the IDM algorithm on a real dataset has been performed. The considered dataset was extracted from the image reliefs presented in [3] and it is a representative sample of the Mount Bego petroglyphs. Basically, it contains a number of petroglyph reliefs falling into 10 main classes (anthropomorphic, ax, bull, bullgod, dagger, goddess, oxcart, personage, reticulate, stream). These classes were successively refined, with the help of several archaeologists participating to the project, into 17 classes based on the shape of the petroglyphs and additional information, such as the estimated date of the engravings.

The 3-fold cross validation test has been successively applied to analyze the performance of the IDM algorithm on the test set. The difficulty to collect data makes particularly suitable this choice. Generally, in k-fold cross-validation, the original sample is randomly partitioned into k subsamples. Of the k subsamples, a single subsample is retained as the validation data for testing the model, and the remaining $k - 1$ subsamples are used as dataset. The cross-validation process is then repeated k times (the folds), with each of the k subsamples used exactly once as the validation data. The k results from the folds then are averaged to produce a single estimation. In this way all petroglyph reliefs are considered for both dataset and validation, and each relief is used for validation exactly once.

5.1 Settings

The best performance of the algorithm was achieved using the following configuration settings:

1. *Image size*, this value was set to 16 pixels. It indicates the size of the reduced image fed to the IDM. We tried also 24 and 32 pixels but no substantial differences have been found. Thus, we preferred to use the minor size for improving time performance.
2. *Warp range*, together with the local context is one of the parameters of the IDM algorithm. The algorithm obtained the best performance using the value of 3 pixels.
3. *Local context*, this value was set to 2 pixels.

5.2 Results

To evaluate the achieved results we used the k-nearest-neighbor (kNN) classification method [18], which consists in the examination of the first k results produced by the algorithm.

The overall results of the experiment are listed in Table 1. Data are presented in a 20×9 table where the first row represents the classification method, namely 1-NN for the best matching class, 3-NN and 5-NN for the nearest neighbors methods with 3 and 5 considered hits, respectively. The first column lists the 17 classes considered in the experiment. Basically, each data cell indicates the percentage of times a petroglyph relief is correctly classified by considering the first i hits of the IDM algorithm result and by applying the classification method (1-NN, 3-NN or 5-NN). As an example, let us consider the A_{xB} row. As for the 1-NN method, during the experiment the A_{xB} images were correctly associated to the class, namely another A_{xB} image appeared as first hit of the IDM algorithm, only in the 33 %. In the 67 %, it appears either as first or second hit, and finally, it appears in 100 % either as first, second, or third hit. If we consider the 3-NN method, the images of the same classes falling into the first three hits are aggregated using the inverse distance weighting. In this way, the class having the highest distance in the new ordered list is suggested

Table 1 Classification rates of the proposed IDM algorithm

Symbol	1-NN				3-NN		5-NN	
	1st	2nd	3rd	4th	1st	2nd	1st	2nd
Antropomorphe	67	100	100	100	67	100	33	67
Ax_A	33	67	67	100	33	67	0	100
Ax_B	33	67	100	100	33	100	33	100
$Bull_A$	100	100	100	100	67	100	100	100
$Bull_B$	100	100	100	100	100	100	100	100
Bullgod	67	100	100	100	67	100	67	100
$Dagger_A$	100	100	100	100	100	100	100	100
$Dagger_B$	33	67	67	100	67	67	33	67
$Goddess_A$	67	67	67	67	33	67	33	67
$Goddess_B$	67	67	67	67	67	67	67	67
$Goddess_C$	67	67	100	100	67	67	67	67
$Goddess_D$	67	67	67	67	33	67	0	67
Oxcart	100	100	100	100	67	100	67	100
Personage	33	67	67	67	33	67	0	67
Reticulate	67	100	100	100	67	100	67	100
$Stream_A$	100	100	100	100	100	100	100	100
$Stream_B$	67	67	100	100	33	100	67	67
Total	68	82	88	92	61	86	54	84

to be the class that the query drawing image belongs to. In case of A_{xB}, its images are correctly classified in the 33 % considering only the first hit of the result list and in the 100 % considering the two best hits. The same analysis has been performed for the 5-NN classification method.

The last row in Table 1 indicates the average values of the columns. Basically, they erase the differences among classes in terms of correct response percentages and report the average behavior of the IDM associated with the different classification methods.

5.3 Discussion

By analyzing the results shown in Table 1 it is possible to notice that the IDM associated to the 1-NN classification method has a precision of 68 %, slightly worst in case of 3-NN (61 %), and even more worst for 5-NN (54 %). Probably, this is due because even though the most similar relief falls into the same class of the query, allowing the 1-NN classifier to correctly recognize, the other hits are not so different from the query but belong to different classes (two symbols for class are in the dataset). In this way, aggregation of the 3-NN and 5-NN makes the choice of the class more difficult and address it towards wrong classes rather than the class the query belongs to.

Another consideration concerns with the ability of the approach to suggest a number of possible solutions among which to choose the correct class. It is possible to notice that, even if the best classification approach is 1-NN, this is not always true when the algorithm try to suggest a range of possible solutions. Indeed, when considering the most scored two, 3-NN and 5-NN work slightly better than 1-NN (86 and 84 % versus 82 %). Unfortunately, due to the low number of symbols for class, we cannot extend this consideration for the three or four most scored hits. Anyway, for these cases, the 1-NN allows to correctly classify in the 88 and 92 % of cases.

These results highlight the quality of the IDM algorithm in the handling of image deformation but also the natural complexity of the problem faced in this paper. Indeed, in most cases, different classes contain similar reliefs and only reasoned-contextual information may help to correctly classify them.

6 Conclusions and Future Work

In this paper we presented a classifier for petroglyph symbol reliefs robust to distortions and local shifts. The method is based on IDM algorithm [14] to measure the distances between the queries and the reference images, which is an effective means of compensating for small local image. The experimental results show the potential of the proposed method for petroglyph classification with a classification rate of 68 %, which considerably improves a previous distance proposed for petroglyph recognition of about 33 % [10]. These results are achieved on a representative dataset of Mount Bego petroglyphs, which includes all the main petroglyph classification challenges.

The main research challenges for the future will be the investigation of other optimization strategies for IDM and the validation of the results on a larger dataset. In particular, in order to improve the efficiency of the approach we are going to explore the possibility to reduce the number of IDM comparisons by means of a clustering algorithm. Moreover, we intend to investigate the use of a distance with a behavior orthogonal to IDM, i.e., able to achieve good performances for IDM misclassified images. In this way, by applying a suitable weighting scheme it would be possible to exploit the advantages of both techniques.

Acknowledgments This research is supported by the "Indiana MAS and the Digital Preservation of Rock Carvings: A multi-agent system for drawing and natural language understanding aimed at preserving rock carving" FIRB project funded by the Italian Ministry for Education, University and Research, under grant RBFR10PEIT [19].

References

1. Deufemia, V., Paolino, L., Tortora, G., Traverso, A., Mascardi, V., Ancona, M., Martelli, M., Bianchi, N., de Lumley, H.: Investigative analysis across documents and drawings: visual analytics for archaeologists. In: Proceedings of the international working conference on advanced visual interfaces, pp. 539–546. ACM (2012)
2. Mascardi, V., Deufemia, V., Malafronte, D., Ricciarelli, A., Bianchi, N., de Lumley, H.: Rock art interpretation within IndianaMAS. In: Jezic, G., Kusek, M., Nguyen, N.T., Howlett, R., Jain, L. (eds.) Agent and multi-agent systems. technologies and applications. Volume 7327 of Lecture Notes in Computer Science, pp. 271–281. Springer, Berlin (2012)
3. de Lumley, H., Echassoux, A.: the rock carvings of the chalcolithic and ancient bronze age from the Mont Bego area. The Cosmogonic Myths of the Early Metallurgic Settlers in the Southern Alps. L'Anthropologie 113(5P2), 969–1004 (2009)
4. Bicknell, C.M.: A guide to the prehistoric rock engravings in the Italian Maritime Alps. Printed by Giuseppe Bessone (1913)
5. Chippindale, C., Bicknell, C.: Archaeology and science in the 19th century. Antiquity 58(224), 185–193 (1984)
6. Lladós, J., Valveny, E., Sánchez, G., Martí, E.: Symbol recognition: current advances and perspectives. In: Blostein, D., Kwon, Y.B. (eds.) GREC. Volume 2390 of Lecture Notes in Computer Science, pp. 104–127. Springer, Berlin (2001)
7. Tombre, K., Tabbone, S., Dosch, P.: Musings on symbol recognition. In: Liu, W., Lladós, J. (eds.) Graphics recognition. Ten years review and future perspectives. Volume 3926 of Lecture Notes in Computer Science, pp. 23–34. Springer, Berlin (2006)
8. Sher, Y.A.: Petroglyphs in Central Asia. Nauka (1980)
9. Takaki, R., Toriwaki, J., Mizuno, S., Izuhara, R., Khudjanazarov, M., Reutova, M.: Shape analysis of petroglyphs in central Asia. Forma 21, 91–127 (2006)
10. Zhu, Q., Wang, X., Keogh, E., Lee, S.H.: An efficient and effective similarity measure to enable data mining of petroglyphs. Data Min. Knowl. Disc. 23, 91–127 (2011)
11. Zhu, Q., Wang, X., Keogh, E., Lee, S.H.: Augmenting the generalized hough transform to enable the mining of petroglyphs. In: Proceedings of the 15th ACM SIGKDD international conference on knowledge discovery and data mining, pp. 1057–1066. ACM (2009)
12. Seidl, M., Breiteneder, C.: Detection and classification of petroglyphs in gigapixel images: preliminary results. In: Proceedings of the 12th international symposium on virtual reality, archaeology and intelligent cultural heritage, pp. 45–48. Eurographics Association (2011)
13. Belongie, S., Malik, J., Puzicha, J.: Shape matching and object recognition using shape contexts. IEEE Trans. Pattern Anal. Mach. Intell. 24(4), 509–522 (2002)
14. Keysers, D., Deselaers, T., Gollan, C., Ney, H.: Deformation models for image recognition. IEEE Trans. Pattern Anal. Mach. Intell. 29, 1422–1435 (2007)
15. Keysers, D., Gollan, C., Ney, H.: Local context in non-linear deformation models for handwritten character recognition. In: Proceedings of international conference on pattern recognition, vol. 4, pp. 511–514 (2004)
16. Dreuw, P., Deselaers, T., Keysers, D., Ney, H.: Modeling image variability in appearance-based gesture recognition. In: ECCV workshop on statistical methods in multi-image and video processing, Graz, Austria, pp. 7–18 (2006)
17. Springmann, M., Dander, A., Schuldt, H.: Improving efficiency and effectiveness of the image distortion model. Pattern Recogn. Lett. 29(15), 2018–2024 (2008)
18. Cover, T., Hart, P.: Nearest neighbor pattern classification. IEEE Trans. Inf. Theory 13(1), 21–27 (1967)
19. Mascardi, V., Briola, D., Locoro, A., Grignani, D., Deufemia, V., Paolino, L., Bianchi, N., de Lumley, H., Malafronte, D., Ricciarelli, A.: A holonic multi-agent system for sketch, image and text interpretation in the rock art domain. Int. J. Innov. Comput. Inf. Control 10(1), 81–100 (2014)

End User Effects of Centralized Data Control

Peter Imrie and Peter Bednar

Abstract Within distributed technologies there is a need to manage and control the data stored on devices for it to be useful. This control can include limiting what data is stored on the device, applying software updates from different sources and even accessing the private data that is stored on the device. Different approaches have been taken to manage the content on distributed technologies and some of these methods have the potential to negatively impact their usefulness to the end user. In this paper we look at approaches for managing data within the contexts of either the end user or a centralized server and their effects on the usefulness of the support to the end user. Following this we discuss advantages and disadvantages and give examples of technologies that utilize different methods of data control and discuss our conclusions within the context of end user support.

Keywords Data control · Data management · Access control · Categories of support

1 Introduction

Recently the US Navy has announced [1] their new approach to distributing eReader technology to the staff on their vessels. Due to the nature of the environment in which the device is used, there is a desire to manage the connectivity and data stored on the device to ensure it is secure [2]. Although this approach was found to be secure for use within the US Navy the implementation can potentially

P. Imrie (✉)
University of Portsmouth, Portsmouth, UK
e-mail: pch.imrie@gmail.com

P. Bednar
School of Computing, University of Portsmouth, Portsmouth, UK
e-mail: peter.bednar@port.ac.uk

P. Bednar
Department of Informatics, Lund University, Lund, Sweden

© Springer International Publishing Switzerland 2016   213
T. Torre et al. (eds.), *Empowering Organizations*, Lecture Notes in Information
Systems and Organisation 11, DOI 10.1007/978-3-319-23784-8_17

limit the usefulness of the device for the user. Within this scenario the usefulness of the technology to the end user is affected by the very same limitations designed to improve the devices usability [3]. This scenario also demonstrates the need for our on-going exploration of the different approaches to data control and the effects of each from the perspective of the end user.

In this paper we begin with drawing upon the different categories of support that have been previously described [4]. The categories of support can be used to help us to relate the relationships between categories of who controls the data used by the end user with categories of who has access to this data. By discussing the relevant categories (and their relationships) we create a basis for categorising the different methods of content control within the context of who benefits from the control of the data (and potentially in what way). Following this we will discuss a number of strategies for data control as identified by their interactions with a centralized system (not controlled by end-user). These strategies categorise the technologies approach to controlling data. Once we have an understanding of the categories of support and the strategies for data control we analyse key advantages and disadvantages of each strategy/approach to data control and how it affects the end user (from the end user point of view). This is supported with examples of identified type of support. The findings of this exploration are concluded with a brief description of key advantages and disadvantages of each approach including their potential impacts on the end user.

2 Background

Recent events have drawn highlighted issues with the security and control of personal and public data [5–7]. Many users are now paying attention to who has access to their data when using a service or mobile technology. As advances in connectivity are promoting a more centralized approach to data management with 'cloud' technologies and distributed services it is becoming more important to be aware of the advantages and disadvantages of this approach. With the continual development of Internet of Things (or indeed internet of everything) these and similar data control issues are becoming more and more relevant to address and explore from many stakeholder perspectives.

When discussing these advantages and disadvantages it is important to take into account multiple stakeholder views of each point (including the "end-user" or "client" etc.). Usually, disadvantages for one stakeholder would not (purposefully) be implemented unless they were advantageous for another. This means that something (e.g. feature) may be seen by a manufacturer as an enhancement of usability (for the end user). The same feature can be perceived by the end user as negatively impacting the usefulness of "their" device. Within this context the distinction between usability and usefulness is defined by the stakeholder that perceives an advantage of a device "in the context of their own actual use in their own real life situations". If a device is more usable then it may have more possible functionality or potential usefulness, but the usefulness is not guaranteed. A device is more useful if the end user sees these possible functions as an effective solution [3].

2.1 Categories of Control

The controller of the data can be categorized drawing upon the previously developed categories of support as part of a model of infrastructure [4]. The categories described within this infrastructure help to identify key differences between what may on the surface appear to be similar approaches to providing support to the end user while handling data in different ways. The specific categories we will be focusing on are the user controlled services and the information service provider categories as seen within Fig. 1.

2.1.1 Information Service Provider

The information service provider category of support utilizes centralized data control to provide services for the end user. The information service provider has

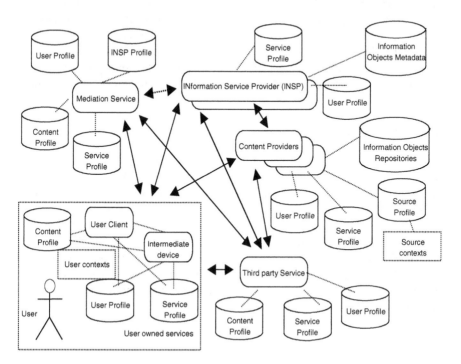

Fig. 1 Categories of support [4]

control over how to respond to an end users request for support. This can potentially allow for prioritizing certain responses that would benefit the information service provider. The information service provider also has access to all data created from the request by the end user and can potentially use this to build on its own service providing capabilities.

2.1.2 User Owned Services

The user owned services category of support uses locally controlled data to keep the control within the context of the user. This includes technologies that remain entirely disconnected with localized data and under the control of the end user e.g. localized chatbots [8], as well as systems that utilize online services on behalf of the end user e.g. virtual personal assistants [9]. A key aspect of this category is the control of the data used to support the end user remains in their control locally.

2.2 Methods of Control

There are a number of different approaches to maintaining access to or control over the data used by the end user. This can include access rights to the data as technologies such as mobile applications require the user to accept the developer's access requirements before it is usable [10]. Data control can be categorised by the method in which the device interacts with a centralized network to provide a service. With the methods of data control on a device categorised we can visualise the differences between similar technologies that differ with who controls the data.

2.2.1 Disconnected Technologies

One approach to data control through managing connections is to create a totally disconnected technology. These technologies have no ability to connect to an outside network and in some instances will have no ability to connect to any other devices at all. For the end user this means that no centralized server will be able to access this data and is most notable on technologies that can use personal data or create data based upon interactions with the end user. The contrast to this is seen in technologies that cannot be managed by the end user despite their disconnected nature. This allows for the creator of the technology to ensure that only the data they intend to use on the device can be operated allowing them to control the device without the need to directly connect to it.

2.2.2 Centralized Technologies

Another example of data control through connectivity management is the approach of making a technology only functional when it is connected to a centralized server. This can be for a number of beneficial reasons, such as distributed processing and using the connection to connect to other users and services, but can also be imposed to ensure that a device can only be used when the (local device specific) data is accessible by the centralized server.

2.2.3 Technologies with Intermittent Connection

It is possible for technologies to have the ability to utilize connections to enhance their functionality but still be able to function (potentially with limited functionality) offline. In these instances the characteristics of usage of the connection can be used to identify who is in control of the data available on the device. For example, end user supporting technologies may have the ability to access the internet and carry out functions on behalf of the end user, but still be capable of providing support to the user when disconnected. In contrast to this a device that is controlled by a centralized server may use connections to update itself and apply changes to the data on the device at the request of the centralized server. It may also have any or all functionality disabled when disconnected.

2.3 Methods of Control Within the Context of Categories of Support

Within the context of the categories of support that we have discussed, we can identify different approaches to data control and categorise them according to which stakeholder has control of the content. This categorization helps to visualise the boundaries between technologies that are supporting different stakeholders but take a similar approach to controlling the devices data. Table 1 shows a table of examples of different methods of control within each category.

Table 1 Methods of control within categories of support

Controller of content	Example of disconnected data control	Example of partially connected data control	Example of fully connected data control
Information service provider	United States Navy's NeRDs	Games consoles, on-board computers in cars	Apple's Siri, possibly Microsoft's Cortana
End user	Localised chatbots	Virtual personal assistants	Remote access media servers

This table uses examples of end super supporting systems to illustrate the differences between each method of data control in relation to the controller of the content. With the different methods of data control show in this table we can examine each approach in detail. Although the categories can seem (superficially) similar between each category of support, the controller of the content can affect the advantages and disadvantages of this type of support for the end user.

Technologies that take the disconnected approach to controlling data tend to be more oriented towards providing privacy and security at the expense of access to a larger selection of services and functionality that would potentially come from allowing an connection to some form of centralized server. Devices that utilize intermittent connectivity have a tendency to focus on being more useful to the end user regardless of who is controlling the technologies content. The device remains usable even in an disconnected environment but has the ability to benefit from services provided by a centralized server. This does however open the device up to the security risks that come connecting to external sources. Devices that require a connection to function have a more strict approach to data control in the sense that they require a primary stakeholder to have access to the device to function. This does allow for tight control over who access and manages data on the device but can even go as far as reducing a devices usability to ensure that data is not being altered in the absence of the controller of the data.

3   Centralized Data Control

Within this section we will discuss how centralized organisations exhibit control over data. This control can be to update and manage software to provide support for the end user by maintaining the distributed technology from a centralized source. In contrast to this, data can be controlled by recording or managing an end users data on a system. This can be to ensure the data on the device is what the centralized organization intended or as a way of gathering data from an end user.

3.1   Control via Required Connection

There are examples of technologies that require a connection to a centralized system despite the fact that a large number of the functions present of the software are capable of working offline with the data stored locally on the device. In some instances this is down to specific attributes of the functionality either requiring an internet connection or even having shared processing.

One example of this can be found in Apples Siri. Siri requires an internet connection to allow the software to pass data to the Apple cloud for all of its functionality [11]. This includes accessing contacts and applications stored locally on the phone. It has been claimed that this mandatory connectivity is due to Apple recording interactions between the end user and Siri [12]. A mandatory connection to the Apple servers has advantages however. Siri can categorise its user with similar users in an attempt to provide a more personalised solution than a generic response to service requests. This can include refining search responses to attempt to provide more useful outputs for the user [13]. With modern advances in mobile connectivity the issue of being disconnected is becoming less significant. The concern with a mandatory connection for this software comes in the form of the privacy of the data. Even with access to an internet connection, users may wish to opt out of transmitting information over the internet and still wish to access the functionality provided by Siri. Microsoft's Cortana could potentially fit into this category as well but the current functionality of the device is unclear [14]. The program itself does have similarities to Apple's Siri and marks Microsoft's take on the same type of supporting technology. Microsoft may potentially use this opportunity to create a competitor to Siri that is still useable by the user when offline.

3.2 Control via Intermittent Connection

Another approach used by some distributed technologies is to utilise connections to manage the device by applying updates to the device from a centralized server. Updates of this type do not require permanent connections, meaning that the systems functionality is retained when it is disconnected. This method of connection allows software to be modified without requiring a new instance of the technology to be created and distributed.

One example of this approach to data control can be found within games consoles. Games consoles are perfectly capable of functioning offline and the end user to play games as they wish but have the capability to connect to a centralized server to play games online. This same connection can be used to update the software on the console, allowing the centralized server to ensure that they still have influence of the consoles themselves. These updates do allow for updates such as improved security but could potentially require people that play games online to allow the centralized server to have access to data stored on the device [15]. This is achieved by including a mandatory update to the consoles software that is required to allow it to play games online but also effects the terms and conditions of which the company has access to the end users data [16]. The end user is left with the choice of adhering to these new terms or losing the online functionality of the console [17]. With recent pushes into the realms of streaming and using consoles for other online activities a lack of connection can be a significant loss of functionality and impact the usefulness of the device.

A second example of this approach to data control is the use of managing on-board systems on cars. As technology is becoming more and more present in our day to day lives, the use of on-board computer system in a car is becoming more important. These on-board computer systems can be updated by the manufacturer to add new functioning or enhancing systems already present [18]. This is currently achieved by either a distributed USB stick [19] or a trip to the cars dealership. While this can provide an advantage to the end user in the form of enhances usefulness and functionality in the on-board computer systems, it does raise some significant security concerns. If a manufacturer can effect a cars on-board computer systems via software on a USB key they it is only a matter of time before malicious hackers can also effect this software. Depending on what systems are linked to the on-board computer systems, this could potentially be a life-threatening risk [20]. Alongside this there is 'considerable interest' in the auto industry developing remote updates for cars [21]. The manufacturers are hesitant to take this method of applying updates to cars after researchers were able to remotely take control of a car and force the breaks on [22].

3.3   Control Through Limiting Access to a Device

One method of controlling the data on a technology is to remove any way for the end user to effect what is stored on the device. This ensures that the system will be used as the creator intended and removes any concern of more data being added to the device or the device being used in different ways. This does however also remove the ability for the end user to personalise the device, meaning that there are imposed limitations on how useful the device will be to the end user.

An example of this can be found in the United States Navy. The US Navy has recently adopted a device named 'NeRD' (Navy eReader Device) to provide its staff access to eBooks in an environment that requires strict control over any data emissions [23]. The devices will be loaded with 300 books ranging from classics to best sellers, and at launch 5 devices will be distributed to each US Submarine. The intention is to function as a replacement for personal mobile devices such as tablets and phones as the crew are unable to use them on-board vessels due to security concerns about the possibility that their data emissions could be tracked. It is also apparent that there is very little space on-board vessels, leaving little room for any entertainment. It has been said that because of this what few books are available are shared amongst the crew until they fall apart [1]. A need for innovation was identified and a solution was created in the form of the NeRDs. While this does give the crew access to the digital media the Navy has prepared, it raises some questions about the effectiveness of this solution.

The device has all of its ports, network access and removable media connections disabled. This means that once the device has been loaded with its books, no more can be added or removed. Even when the device is in a safe environment or with physical access to a secure system the device cannot have its stored books changed. This raises concerns about how future proof this solution is in regards to the changing trends of eBooks. How useful would a library with a total of 300 books be, when all of which are selected by others? The security concerns for this technology are legitimate but the precautions may be overbearing with their restrictions to the point of hindering the usefulness of such a device. It could be argued that the device would be just as secure aboard a vessel even if it had the ability to physically connect to secured navy systems in dockyards, allowing for the device to be managed between deployments. The 300 books that are present on the device are from a library of 108,000 books that the US Navy has digital access to [24]. By removing the devices ability to ever be able to connect to this digital library a huge amount of already available digital media will be unable to be deployed for the crews access on-board vessels.

4   Local Data Control

Within this section we will discuss local data control, where the content is under direct control of the end user. This can be due to a system remaining disconnected while an end user can still manipulate the data stored on the device. This can also be achieved by the system connecting to other sources on behalf of the end user, instead of on behalf of the external source. This allows the technology to utilize these outside sources without changing the focus of support away from the end user.

4.1   Disconnected Data

In some instances an end user has control over their data because the device functions completely disconnected from any centralized server. Users can freely manage and manipulate data on such a device locally and are at no risk of this data being micromanaged by a central source. This allows for the end user to develop a secure private data set on the device to provide a more personalised end user supporting service. An example of a device that provides disconnected data management is the chat bot Kari [8]. As we have previously investigated, Kari can be used well beyond its original intended purpose with the utilization of the data and metadata it creates. Due to the amount of control the end user has over this program it can be manipulated and trained to be a powerful end user supporting tool purely because there are no restrictions to the end users control over its data [22].

4.2   Utilization of Connectivity

Another example of end user data control can be seen in technologies that carry out actions on behalf of the end user. These technologies do have interactions with connected systems and even interactions with centralized servers but do so on the request of the end user, not at the request of the centralized server. This means that a system may be requested to retrieve information by searching online as an extension of the user. One example of this type of system is HAL [9]. HAL is a virtual personal assistant that attempts to use natural language capabilities to hold meaningful and valued discussions with its end user. It has the capability to build up metadata from the data it gathers from the end user to form a locally controlled data library. HAL also has the ability to utilize connections to the internet on behalf of the end user to carry out simple requests such as searching for information the user has requested. The results of which and the data created with the user through discussion are not available to the network it has connected to but is still utilized to support the end user.

4.3 Fully Connected End User Support

It is possible for a service to provide data control to the end user over a connection. This approach doesn't necessarily localise the data with the end user, but gives the end user the ability to manage the data remotely. These services provide support to the end user by distributed data from a remote source or allowing the user to manage the data at the remote source. An example of this can be seen with the PLEX media server [25]. PLEX allows the user to stream media to other devices such as a TV or a smart phone from a user controlled server. The user has direct control over all of the content of this server but requires a direct connection to be able to access the content. This approach allows the end user to access large amounts of media from devices with only a small data capacity and access to the network with the server. Users with this technology will be able to access their entire library of media from a TV with no data storage, but will lose all of its data if the connection is disrupted. A issue with this approach is the concern that the connections may not be fast enough to stream the media at will, resulting in the user waiting on buffering times.

5 Benefits and Limitations

Through discussions around examples of each method of data control within the context of centralized service providers it is possible to identify trends in the advantages and disadvantages of this approach when compared to end user supporting services. Each approach to data management by the centralized organization can negatively impact the usefulness of the device to the end user in some way. This is due to limitations placed on the device to prevent the user from managing the data on a technology without the connection (or lack of connection) that the manufacturer desires.

Examples of this can be seen with limitations such as the loss of functionality when not connected to a network or not updated via connecting to a centralized server. Alongside this disconnected devices can be seen to be restricted by losing their ability to form any connections at all. These limitations are in contrast to potential benefits for the end user when these approaches to content control are within the context of the end user. With disconnected devices, the user has the opportunity to control personal and private data with the intention of better serving the needs of the individual. With devices that can utilize connections the end user has the ability to draw upon content and services that would otherwise be too large to store on the device. This is done as an enhancement to already present functionality and serves to improve the usefulness of the device to the end user. User controlled servers allow devices with no content to utilize connections and become methods of accessing the users controlled media. It is these differences between devices that can lead to the centralized approach to data control being perceived as less useful to the end user. There are advantages for the end user in each centralise approach too, as most approaches are adopted for a purpose that holds some benefit for the end user.

Disconnected devices, even with total restrictions to connectivity and content personalisation, still allow for the end user to use these devices in environments where no other device would be allowed. This approach may be limiting but can allow a large number of users to benefit from technology where there may be no acceptable alternative. Devices that use internet connections for updates via connections to a centralized server may on occasion be limiting as it may require updates before use. This does however go hand in hand with the ability to adapt and potentially remain useful for longer than the expected original product life because of enhancements to the device that are applied remotely. Other devices that require a connection to function may lose all of their functionality when offline, but benefit from the wealth of content built up by the service provider. This could be anything from large volumes of media available for streaming to refined service providing based upon data gathered from actions of the servers entire user base. End users could potentially see benefits from centralized control approaches. However while many approaches can provide usability for the end user—they can also be viewed as directly detrimental to the usefulness of the devices. In effect it is quite possible that some restrictions and limitations purposefully implemented on a device (such as those for organisational security purposes) may result in such a lack of usefulness to completely defy the purpose for why the device was created in the first place.

6   Conclusions

Within the context of distributed technologies the control of the data stored on each device has direct impact on its usefulness to the end user. Devices that function in a completely disconnected environment are shielded from the effects of centralized data control but lose access to the services that come with it. While this does in some situations better fit the need of the end user it can also largely limit the usability of the device. The contrast to this is found in devices with a mandatory connection to a centralized service. This can provide a greater array of services but limits the user's ability to use the device. Although high levels of centralized control can negatively impact the usefulness of a device, there is also the prospect of a win-win situation for all of the stakeholders involved. Some methods of data control via intermittent connections have the potential to enhance the usefulness of a device by allowing information service providers to provide and support services without altering or effecting the end users ability to control and access data.

It has been the intention of this paper to categorise and compare the different approaches to controlling data on distributed devices and their effects on the usefulness to the end user. Each approach has its own advantages over the other approaches and each has its own situations to be used in. To best support the end user careful consideration over how data on a device will be utilized by both the end user and the service provider is required within the context of the technologies intended purpose. This will ensure that the end user has the appropriate amount of control of the data on the device to make it usable, while still receiving the services needed to make the device useful.

References

1. Bayluxe: NeRD. US Navy's own e-reader. http://beyluxe.com/articles/technology/nerd-us-navys-own-e-reader (2014). Accessed 07 July 2014
2. Enis, M.: U.S. Navy launches NeRD, a security enhanced e-reader. http://www.thedigitalshift.com/2014/06/ebooks/u-s-navy-launches-nerd-security-enhanced-e-reader/ (2014). Accessed 09 July 2014
3. Bednar, P., Katos, V.: MCIS2009: 4th Mediterranean conference on information systems. In: 4th Mediterranean Conference on Information Systems, pp. 900–912 (2009)
4. Bednar, P.M., Welch, C., Graziano, A.: Learning objects and their implications on learning: a case of developing the foundation for a new knowledge infrastructure. In: Harman, K., Koohang, A. (eds.) Chapter 6 in Learning Objects: Applications, Implications and Future Directions, pp. 157–185. Informing Science Press, New York (2007)
5. Orlowski, A.: 77 % of Google users don't know it records personal data. http://www.theregister.co.uk/2006/01/24/google_privacy_poll/ (2006). Accessed 08 July 2014
6. Channel 4: Thursday 16 January 2014 UK What GCHQ knows about us—a timeline of revelations. http://www.channel4.com/news/gchq-timeline-revelations-snowden-spying (2014). Accessed 08 July 2014
7. Greenwald, G.: NSA collecting phone records of millions of Verizon customers daily. http://www.theguardian.com/world/2013/jun/06/nsa-phone-records-verizon-court-order (2013). Accessed 05 July 2014
8. Lhandslide Studios: Advanced virtual girl with artificial intelligence. http://www.karigirl.com/ (2012). Accessed 02 July 2014
9. Zabaware Inc.: Ultra hal can hold conversations with you. http://www.zabaware.com/assistant/index.html (n.d). Accessed 09 July 2014
10. Tsavli, M., Efraimidis, P.S., Katos, V.: Reengineering the user: privacy concerns about personal data on smartphones. In: Proceedings of the Eighth International Symposium on Human Aspects of Information Security and Assurance, pp. 80–89 (2014)
11. Apple: Siri. Your wish is it's command. http://www.apple.com/uk/ios/siri/ (n.d). Accessed 15 April 2013

12. Ozer, N.: Note to self: siri not just working for me, working full-time for apple, too. https:// www.aclunc.org/issues/technology/blog/note_to_self_siri_not_just_working_for_me,_ working_full-time_for_apple,_too.shtml (2012). Accessed 22 April 2013
13. Apple: Siri FAQ. http://www.siriuserguide.com/siri-faq/ (2014). Accessed 05 July 2014
14. Microsoft Windows: The most personal smartphone assistant. http://www.windowsphone. com/en-us/features-8-1#Cortana (2014). Accessed 09 July 2014
15. Martin, M.: Xbox One won't play games on day one without mandatory update. http://www. gamesindustry.biz/articles/2013-11-08-xbox-one-wont-play-games-on-day-one-without-mandatory-update (2013). Accessed 05 July 2014
16. Makuch, E.: Microsoft changing Xbox live terms of use. http://www.gamespot.com/articles/ microsoft-changing-xbox-live-terms-of-use/1100-6415826/ (2013). Accessed 05 July 2014
17. Klepek, P.: You must agree to all of Xbox live's new terms of service. http://www.giantbomb. com/articles/you-must-agree-to-all-of-xbox-lives-new-terms-of-s/1100-3846/ (2011). Accessed 07 July 2014
18. Zax, D.: A software update for your car? http://www.technologyreview.com/view/427153/a-software-update-for-your-car/ (2012). Accessed 09 July 2014
19. Ford: How to install Ford SYNC updates in your vehicle. http://support.ford.com/sync-technology/install-updates-sync (2014). Accessed 05 July 2014
20. Vincent, J.: http://www.independent.co.uk/life-style/gadgets-and-tech/researchers-hack-cars-to-remotely-control-steering-and-brakes-8733723.html (2013). Accessed 05 July 2014
21. Bullis, K.: Why your car won't get remote software updates anytime soon. http://www. technologyreview.com/news/524791/why-your-car-wont-get-remote-software-updates-anytime-soon/. Accessed 09 July 2014
22. Bednar, P., Imrie, P.: Virtual personal assistant. http://www.cersi.it/itais2013/ (2013). Accessed 11 July 2014
23. Griggs, B.: Meet the 'NeRD,' the Navy's new e-reader. http://edition.cnn.com/2014/05/08/ tech/gaming-gadgets/navy-nerd-e-reader/ (2014). Accessed 05 July 2014
24. Baker, B.: US Navy develops world's worst e-reader. http://www.naval-technology.com/ features/featureus-navy-develops-worlds-worst-e-reader-4265782/ (2014). Accessed 05 July 2014
25. Plex: What is Plex? https://support.plex.tv/hc/en-us/articles/200288286-What-is-Plex (2014). Accessed 09 July 2014

Risk Assessment to Support Liability Allocation Performed by the System GUI Analysis

R. Cassino, A. Vozella, G. Gigante and D. Pascarella

Abstract Main productive, administrative and social organizations represent interconnected socio-technical systems, namely, complex systems constituted by technical artifacts, social artifacts and humans. The Graphical User Interface (GUI) is a system interaction approach which allows different actors (human, software, ...) of involved organizations to interact with each other by manipulating graphical objects. Often, these complex systems require sophisticated interfaces characterized by dynamic components which can provide information about system behavior. In this paper we present a research in progress, related to the integration of a paradigm borrowed by risk theory, within a tool for the evaluation of software systems through the analysis of visual components of its interface. The idea is to support organizations to define and properly allocate liability among system actors in order to identify recurring errors to possibly evaluate a potential reengineering of the system.

Keywords Systems analysis · Risk assessment · Failure mode effect analysis (FMEA) · Errors liability · Graphical user interface (GUI) evaluation

R. Cassino
Università degli Studi della Basilicata, Potenza, Italy
e-mail: rocassino@gmail.com

A. Vozella (✉) · G. Gigante · D. Pascarella
Italian Aerospace Research Centre, Capua, CE, Italy
e-mail: a.vozella@cira.it

G. Gigante
e-mail: g.gigante@cira.it

D. Pascarella
e-mail: d.pascarella@cira.it

© Springer International Publishing Switzerland 2016
T. Torre et al. (eds.), *Empowering Organizations*, Lecture Notes in Information Systems and Organisation 11, DOI 10.1007/978-3-319-23784-8_18

1 Introduction

Information and Communication Technology (ICT) widely spreads over productive, administrative and social organizations. They represent interconnected
socio-technical systems where interactions are possible among different domains.
Risks of such ICT pervasiveness lie in vulnerability to hazards for systems and
citizens; in fact, malicious attacks and system failures may result is catastrophic
effects. Most of the Critical Infrastructures (Internet, Banks, plants, airports…) are
mainly software related and they are more and more interdependent so a disruption
could lead to a domino effect. Let's think about Supervisory Control and Data
Acquisition (SCADA) applications that get data about a system in order to control
that system. They are used to automate complex industrial processes where basing
only on human control is impractical. A wide variety of applications exist: Electric
power generation, transmission and distribution is one example. Electric utilities
use SCADA systems to detect current flow and line voltage, to monitor the operation of circuit breakers, and to take sections of the power grid online or offline.
Another example is the water and sewage industry. State and municipal water
utilities use SCADA to monitor and regulate water flow, reservoir levels, pipe
pressure and other factors.

Air quality control in specific buildings and facilities is another application.

The manufacturing industry uses SCADA systems to manage parts inventories
for just-in-time manufacturing, regulate industrial automation and robots, and
monitor process and quality control.

Mass Transit authorities use SCADA to: provide and control electricity to
subways, trams and buses; automate traffic signals for rail systems; track and locate
transportation; control railroad crossing gates.

In industry, managers need to control multiple factors and the interactions
among them (Management Information Systems—MIS). SCADA systems provide
the sensing capabilities and the computational power to track everything that's
relevant to operations. Most of these applications require sophisticated interfaces
characterized by dynamic components by which the actors interact with the system.). In particular, suitable GUIs are implemented to let end-users of different
systems interacting with each other.

In case of an accident, understanding the cause and the responsibility at the
whole infrastructure level, requires huge efforts, sometimes thwarted by various
attempts of manual search.

This situation has lead society to be cautious in the adoption of new technology
for GUI, especially targeted to safety critical applications [1].

In this perspective, it would be desirable to have an automatic system to support
organizations to define and properly allocate liability among actors, identifying
recurring errors in order to evaluate a potential reengineering of the system and/or
the use of different solutions.

Usability theory techniques are normally used to drive requirements of GUI for
SCADA systems [2]. Safety assessment approaches, derived by risk theory, have

rarely been applied to the design of Human Machine Interfaces (HMI) of Nuclear Power Plant [3].

On the other hand, several automatic approaches, based on the analysis of the system through its interface, exist in literature. Information on occurred errors on GUI usage can be found in log files which need to be post processed it in order to properly identify the wrong behaviour of the actors and to allocate its liability. An approach that combines different techniques—including formal analysis of models, simulation and analysis of log data—in a model-based environment is described in [4]. The log data at model level can be used not only to identify usability problems but also to identify where to operate changes to these models in order to fix usability problems [5]. On the other hand, a reverse engineering approach is used to automatically recover models of the GUI by dynamically "traversing" all its windows and extracting all the widgets, properties and values [6].

The proposed research integrates two approaches to identify liability in case of system failure:

1. the analysis of the software through the interactions of its graphical user interface;
2. a technique by risk theory based on the analysis of the failure modes (failure mode effect analysis, FMEA).

In particular, through automatic detection of the dynamic components of the interface the corresponding wrong tasks are identified and characterized in details, also in terms of liability allocation.

In this perspective, the innovation of the presented research is twofold:

1. To evaluate the correctness of the interaction mechanisms of a software system by the FMEA, as described in Sect. 2.
2. To characterize and record system malfunctions by the analysis of the GUI screen shots and the interaction with the system actors.

The paper is organized as follows. Section 2 presents an introduction to the risk assessment technique (FMEA); Sect. 3 describes the target application domain of the SCADA systems which represent safety critical applications for the GUI. Section 4 presents the integration of the FMEA module, within a tool for the evaluation of software through the analysis of visual components of the interface. Section 5 shows some conclusions and further research.

2 FMEA Technique by Risk Theory to Support Liability Allocation

The FMEA technique, is generally used to drive software requirements at design stage or to test the system [7]. In scenarios where several operators/controller and several automated support systems interact together for the fulfilment of a task, humans and technology represent a joint (cognitive) system. The term "joint cognitive system" means that control is accomplished by an ensemble of cognitive systems and (physical and social) artefacts which cooperate towards a common goal. Under this perspective, a still open question is that of how to deal with cases in which (as in some recent aviation accidents) conflicting information is provided to operators by humans (controllers) and automated systems, and more generally what kind of priorities should be given to different signals, and when humans may override automatic devices.

The question concerns how to properly analyse and manage the shift of liability due to automation, in order to achieve an optimal allocation of burdens. This will imply reconsidering the role of liability, not only as a tool to redistribute risks and allocate sanctions for errors and accidents, but above all as a means to prevent those accidents and to increase levels of safety and performance fostering the development of a safety culture within organizations. Thus, it will be essential:

1. to identify error tasks and roles of operators and automated tools by the interaction mechanisms of the system interface;
2. to identify violations of the expected level of performance for each task;
3. to consider different kinds of errors (unintentional rule violations, reckless behaviours, intentional violations);
4. to allow automatic recording with all the necessary details of different errors, risks and accidents.

Safety–critical industries and organizations have built paradigms and guidance on a so-called "just culture" to learn from failure with appropriate accountability.

The aim consists in no longer seeing such accidents as meaningless, uncontrollable events, but rather as failures of risk management, and behind these failures are many different actors.

A just culture, then, asks for the sustainability of learning from failure through the reporting of errors, adverse events, incidents [8].

Among the different analysis techniques available in the Risk assessment theory, the one which can support in characterizing the error is FMEA.

Considering that some forms of accountability, and accountability relationships between stakeholders, can be more constructive for safety than others we propose to integrate a module to trace failures in terms of: failure mode description, cause, actor, effects (local and global), detection mode (parameters, time constraints…), associated mitigation actions.

We propose to adopt FMEA techniques to implement a module which can support the identification of run time errors and their complete characterization improving a tool for software system evaluation through the analysis of its graphical user interface.

FMEA is mostly used to drive system component reliability requirement or to assess the system reliability of integrated products. It goes through the following steps:

- Identification of each component and related function/functions;
- Identification of the system boundary;

- Identification of the potential failures and the probability of that failure (occurrence) for each component;
- Definition of the system impact of each failure (severity).

We extend the previous scheme by adding the following features:

- Failure cause, actor, effects (local and global);
- Detection mode (parameters, time constraints...);
- Associated mitigation actions.

A GUI component of a software system allows operators to perform some tasks in a defined process.

A "dynamic" graphical widget is the element of the interface with which it is possible to interact triggering the associated function. Each interaction corresponds to a specific workflow aimed at implementing steps in a process. This workflow may have some constraints in terms of steps to be followed, time to complete the interaction, input to be fed to the system etc. Our approach consists in defining, for each workflow and for each interaction on the GUI, the following information:

- Component Id
- Component Name
- Function
- Potential Failure modes
- Effect of Failure
- Probability of Failure (Occurrence)
- Severity
- Failure cause
- Actor
- Detection mode (parameters, time constraints...)
- Associated mitigation actions

A function is a specific process, action or task that the system is able to perform.

Failure is the loss of an intended function of a device under stated conditions. Severity is the consequences of a failure mode. It considers the worst potential consequence of a failure determined by the degree of injury, property damage or system damage which could ultimately occur.

Occurrence is defined as how often or how likely a failure mode will occur.

Cause is a circumstance that may result in a failure think of the cause as why it would go wrong.

Failure effect is the immediate consequence of a failure on operation, function or functionality, including impact on a customer, both internal and external, if a failure mode is not prevented or corrected.

Then, it is necessary to define the impact that each failure would cause (severity) to the system. In this sense, the next step is to determine the severity of the failures identified in the previous step. Severity is determined in the same manner as occurrence:

- No effect
- Very minor (only noticed by discriminating customers)
- Minor (very little impact on the system, but noticed by average customer)
- Moderate (most customers are annoyed)
- High (causes a loss of primary function; customers are dissatisfied)
- Very high and hazardous (the failure may result in unsafe operation and possible injury/death).

An example will be provided in next section.

3 SCADA and GUI

This paragraph introduces the main parts of a SCADA system and its functionalities, to characterize it as a complex system in terms of heterogeneity of its components and interactions of different actors. A SCADA system performs four main functions: data acquisition, networked data communication, data presentation and control. These functions are performed by four kinds of system components to operate in a cohesive fashion.

The first are sensors (either digital or analog) and control relays which directly interface with the managed system. These report to Remote Telemetry Units (RTUs). These are small computerized units deployed in the field at specific sites and locations. RTUs serve as local collection points for gathering reports from sensors and delivering commands to control relays. These RTU's report to SCADA master units. These are larger computer consoles that serve as the central processor for the SCADA system. Master units provide a human interface to the system and automatically regulate the managed system in response to sensor inputs. These master units use the communications network to control the RTUs in the field.

A real-life SCADA system needs to monitor hundreds or thousands of sensors. Some sensors measure inputs into the system (for example, water flowing into a reservoir), and some sensors measure outputs (like valve pressure as water is released from the reservoir). A real SCADA system reports to human operators over a specialized computer that is variously called a master station, an HMI (Human-Machine Interface) or an HCI (Human-Computer Interface).

The SCADA master station has several different functions. The master continuously monitors all sensors and alerts the operator when there is an "alarm"—that is, when a control factor is operating outside what is defined as its normal operation. The master presents a comprehensive view of the entire managed system, and presents more detail in response to user requests. The master also performs data processing on information gathered from sensors—it maintains report logs and summarizes historical trends. In advanced SCADA systems master can add a great deal of intelligence and automation to system management, making operator job much easier.

The HMI Toolkit is the collection of all of the design elements for the displays (all of the static and dynamic objects) and the related operating console. The toolkit is a separate element, since one set will exists for each control or SCADA system in use.

All aspects of the HMI is intended for a specific set of purposes (primary and secondary) and a set of users (again primary and secondary). The actual tasks to be performed by the users are identified and put on a sequence diagram.

The HMI is conceptually designed to contain the following concepts.

1. Equipment Model -> Models site/equipment and linkage of SCADA values
2. Events -> Conditional expressions or time based events that trigger workflows
3. Workflow Templates -> Configured Templates that contain automated process and manual steps
4. Schedules -> Combines events with workflow templates to initiate workflows

The model of site and equipment stores real time SCADA values for evaluation.

The Conditional Expressions use values stored in Equipment to evaluate expressions.

Events can be triggered based on multiple criteria e.g. Time Based Expression when it uses date/time expression to determine when event should be triggered. Events can be set so one or all criteria must be met. Expressions can also evaluate criteria stored in the workflow process such as a process already running.

The workflow templates contain configured steps and processes which are executed automatically and/or with user interaction. Those steps can be modified by workflow authors and services can be added by administrator. The Workflow Schedule combines workflow template with events, either conditional or time based to determine if a workflow should be generated. When a workflow is triggered, either manually or automatically as part of a conditional or time based event, a series of processes occur an email is triggered, notifying appropriate personnel of the workflow and supplying a work order number if generated Information from SCADA is displayed in the workflow, along with specific information for troubleshooting. Steps guide users through resolution of the issue. They have expiration timers, if steps are not processed in time escalation processes occur (notifications). Besides the logged and recorded information we propose to extend the recorded information by the interactions and the changes on the system interface in terms of screen images for identified failure modes. Table 1 shows an example of FMEA performed for a component on a GUI of a SCADA system.

4   The Proposed Research

In this paper we propose a methodology for assessing the responsibilities of system errors by analyzing the software through the mechanisms of interaction of its graphical user interface.

Cassino and Tucci [9] presents a tool that implements an automatic evaluation system to measure some of the canonical usability parameters of the graphical interface of an application. As described in the cited paper, after the components of

Table 1 Example of FMEA workflow

Component name	Push button
Function	To activate Display RTU# numeric data with facility internal temperature
Failure mode	No activating Display RTU# numeric data with facility internal temperature
	Wrong Activating Display RTU# numeric data with wrong facility internal temperature
Effect of failure (local and global)	Wrong understanding of the state of some temperature sensor
	Worst case effect: wrong decision to go on powering the system with fire which breaks out
Probability of failure	Depending on the reliability of the system
Severity	Can be catastrophic
Failure cause	Error due to: GUI; Communication link; RTU; Sensor
Actor	Humans, automatic system…
Detection mode (parameters, time constraints…)	Inconsistent parameters in the shown string (no values, out of range values, less values then expected…) Visual feedback not matching the expectations…
Associated mitigation actions	Upload pictures for clarification and fast recognition
	To activate deeper control on the specific sensor, RTU, communication link

the GUI are identified, the system determines the type of each element (label, button, link, text-area, menus, etc.) by means of the changes to the interface itself which are activated by interacting with it. An automatic interaction process is implemented. As a matter of fact, the task is carried out by two modules: an automatic interaction module that simulates the input events generation, and a decision algorithm that chooses the interface element to interact with (and what type of input is to generate) and deduces, according to the observed changes in the graphics output, the class of object. Depending on the type of input and on the detected visual feedback, the following typologies of elements are determined:

- Input/output: dynamic element (it is possible interact with it);
- Pause: the system provides a description of the item;
- Press and release of left button of the mouse: the element is a button or a menu item;
- Double click: if the visual feedback is isolated to a neighbourhood of the point with which you interacted, the element is a character and all pixels affected by the change form a group (string);
- Click and double click: the item is a link;
- Insertion of a character: the element is a text field or a text-area.

Now, we extend the interaction analysis performed on the dynamic components of the GUI by the FMEA method to identify and allocate malfunction liability among system actors.

Fig. 1 System model

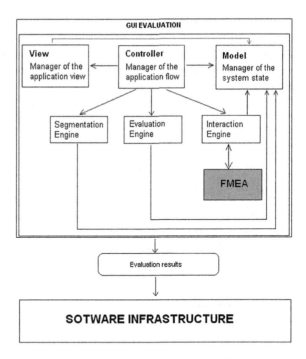

Figure 1 shows the system model designed. The view module includes the functionalities related to the rendering of the system. It sends the controller each user requests and allows the controller to select a particular view.

The controller module defines the flow of execution. Its classes map user requests into actions performed on the model and select a view related to user requests. For each input event, a specific class describes the action to be performed on the model and selects the next view.

The model module encapsulates the application state.

Below a formal description of the FMEA module is provided.

Given a set of workflows on the HMI, we build a set of corresponding nominal (due to correct interactions) visual feedbacks by running the system for GUI evaluation.

For each WFi let G(WFi)j be the corresponding visual feedback j.

Then we generate the corresponding off nominal visual feedbacks by associating wrong visual feedbacks to the specific workflow.

Specifically, for each defined workflow, a list of associated failure modes are identified with all the necessary attributes in terms of actors, causes, effects, parameters, associated visual feedbacks- and recorded in a database. Then:

$$(WFi) \rightarrow [Fk(G(WFi)j), \ldots Fn(G(WFi)j)]$$

With Fk(G(WFi)j) we mean a string made by the description of the Failure Mode k for Visual feedback j of Workflow WFi, the cause of Failure Mode k for Visual feedback j of Workflow WFi, the actor of the Failure Mode k for Visual feedback j of Workflow WFi, the effect of the Failure Mode k for Visual feedback j of Workflow WFi.

We use the tool with the FMEA module to generate for a specific workflow all the set of possible nominal and off nominal visual feedbacks for it, completed with the corresponding information. Each workflow with its related information will be stored in a database.

When an interaction is performed within a specific workflow, the decision algorithm will identify and deduce, according to the observed changes in the graphics output, the class of object according to the observed changes in the graphics output. If this object corresponds to an off nominal visual feedback for that workflow, within the database all the related information about liability and other attributes is already available for further use.

5   An Example

Let us start the example by considering the first following case: a complex interface adopted in a mission control centre to command and control the on board processing of an unmanned vehicle. The interface allows the operator to implement different mission procedures (Fig. 2).

During the execution of a mission a failure occurs. Only the GUI execution trace and the GUI FMEA are available to the operator for processing. The generation of FMEA is completely automatic and independent on the application usage of the GUI.

In a preliminary off-line phase the software tool is executed by giving the GUI under study as input to the View module. The GUI is processed by the segmentation engine and the evaluation engine [9] and the relative hierarchical tree is built (Fig. 3).

The interaction module feeds the tree to the FMEA module. The module identifies:

- For each node the direct child that is the expected next widget to be stimulated in the nominal sequence;
- Any off nominal workflow by considering any combination of widgets different from those represented by the tree.

The identified pair (*parent, child*) represents a record in the FMEA table for which the failure modes are all the combination of *parent* with all other widgets different from *child*.

Let:

- $W_i = \{w_{i1}, .., w_{ik}\}$ a nominal sequence of widgets on the GUI.
- (w_{im}, w_{in}) the current pair parent–child
- $\Delta = \{(w_{im}, w_{ij}) | j \neq n\}$ the set of off-nominal pairs

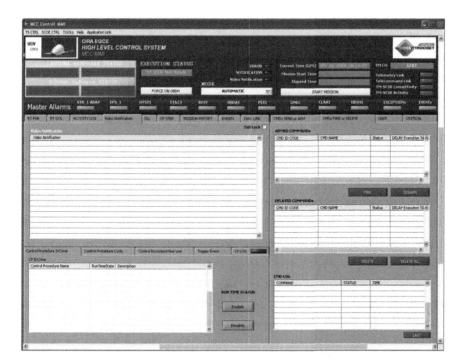

Fig. 2 Mission control center main GUI

The module automatically generates the FMEA table storing it into the database.

In post-processing phase a software program can process the trace log and checks for each pair of stimulated widgets if they are in the failure mode column. In the positive case a possible deviation point from the nominal workflow has been detected identifying also the correct sequence that should have been executed.

Let us follow on the example by considering a second case: The generation of FMEA is partially automatic and dependent on the application usage of the GUI. This means that the FMEA module allows an operator to associate each path in the tree with a specific procedure to be executed by the operators during mission.

Let $\{P_1, \ldots, P_n\}$ the set of procedures to be executed. Each procedure can be described in terms of a sequence of widgets to be stimulated addressing its nominal execution. For each procedure information as actors and the consequence on the system of the failure of each step can be described.

In this case in post processing the software analyser could intercept the deviation point and also other important information as the mission procedure failed, the relative step and the actors involved.

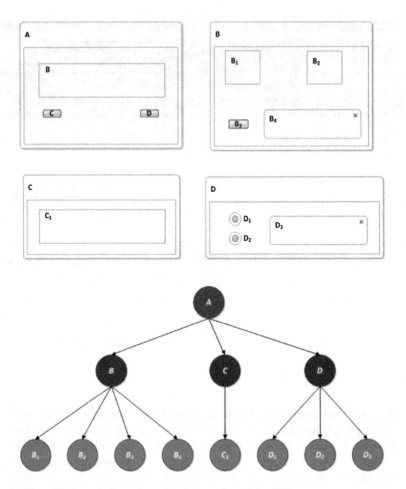

Fig. 3 Hierarchical tree built up from the abstract view of the GUI

6   Conclusions

In the domain of productive, administrative and social organizations, the inter-
connection and the interactions among different actors can expose the system to
serious risks with critical consequences. Supervisory Control and Data Acquisition
(SCADA) applications get data about a system in order to control those critical
system allowing different actors to operate on its Human Machine Interface (HMI).
In case of accident it is not so easy to properly identify liability and failure causes.

   In this paper we propose to integrate a technique by risk theory, FMEA (Failure
Mode Effect Analysis), to support the identification and allocation of liability in
case of critical system accidents within an existing automatic tool for software
system evaluation through the analysis of interaction performed by its graphical

user interface. The visual feedback of the tasks allows identification and characterization of possible failure modes of the system through "this visual approach", so to drive system requirement definition.

Medium term research work will involve the deepening of the integration features between the two control systems, the implementation of the related environment and the following use of this mechanism to analyse errors in system interactions with the GUI at run time, to build statistical data and derive whole system improvement issues.

References

1. Vozella, A.: Promoting trust protecting citizens' rights in digital citizenship. In: AICA 2013 proceedings
2. Vozella, A. et al.: Usability issues for an aerospace digital library. In: AVI 2012 proceedings
3. Orekhova, V.K.: Safety case-oriented assessment of human-machine interface for NPP I&C systems. Integrated HMI safety assessment methodology for safety-critical I&C sytems, RT&A # 03 (26) (vol. 7) (2012)
4. Palanque, P., Barboni, E., Martinie, C., Navarre, D., Winckler, M.: A model-based approach for supporting engineering usability evaluation of interaction techniques. In: Proceedings of the 3rd ACM SIGCHI symposium on engineering interactive computing systems, pp. 21–30. ACM (2011)
5. Melody, Y., Ivory, Marti, A.H.: The state of the art in automating usability evaluation of user interfaces. J. ACM Comput. Surv (CSUR) Surveys Homepage Arch. 33(4) (2001)
6. Atif M.M.: Using reverse engineering for automated usability evaluation of GUI-based applications. Human-Centered Software Engineering: Human-Computer Interaction Series, pp 335–355 (2009)
7. Kraig, S.: Using FMEA to improve software reliability. In: PNSQC 2013 proceedings
8. Sidney, W., Dekker, A.: Just culture: who gets to draw the line? Springer, London (2008)
9. Cassino, R., Tucci, M.: Automatic usability evaluation of GUI: a front-side approach using no source code information. Lecture Notes in Information Systems and Organization, vol. 2, pp. 439–447A (2013)

Cognitive Antifreeze: The Visual Inception of Fluid Sociomaterial Interactions for Knowledge Creation

Lawrence McGrath

Abstract This pilot study investigates the idea generation process of ad-hoc pairs using external visualisations for divergent thought. The study's objective is to examine if pairs' perceived possibility to change the external visualisations of their ideas affects how deeply they explore cognitive categories. The depth of cognitive category exploration is known as cognitive persistence. A 2 x 2 factorial experiment with active middle to upper level management participants was employed. The experiment operationalised the perceived changeability, or fluidity, of visual objects through manipulation of pairs' worksheet template and writing instruments. For the writing instrument, pencils operationalised high perceived changeability, and pens operationalised low perceived changeability. For the worksheet template, blank sheets operationalised high perceived changeability, and pre-printed mindmaps operationalised low perceived changeability. The results indicate that a sociomaterial interaction impacts upon participants' cognitive persistence. This study finds that cognitive persistence is highest amongst pairs using a consistently high perceived changeability pencil/blank worksheet combination. Conversely pairs using a high perceived changeability pencil with a low perceived changeability pre-printed mindmap display the lowest cognitive persistence. The materials pairs note ideas with together influence their need to seize upon an idea. Such seizure reduces cognitive persistence. Fluid visual representations function as an effective cognitive antifreeze.

Keywords Creativity · Dyad · Visualisation · Perceived finishedness · Cognitive persistence

1 Introduction

It is widely known that knowledge creation [1] is crucial to competitive advantage across fields [2]. How to reliably surface effective, efficient knowledge creation is far less well known. This pilot study examines sociomateriality as a means by which to

L. McGrath (✉)
University of St. Gallen, St. Gallen, Switzerland
e-mail: lawrence.mcgrath@unisg.ch

© Springer International Publishing Switzerland 2016
T. Torre et al. (eds.), *Empowering Organizations*, Lecture Notes in Information Systems and Organisation 11, DOI 10.1007/978-3-319-23784-8_19

241

increase the cognitive persistence of creative pairs in an effort to dependably enhance knowledge creation.

2 Literature Review and Hypothesis Development

The research concentrates on whether the degree of perceived finishedness of the graphical representation of a dyad's joint problem solving space influences its tendency to exert cognitive effort on divergent thinking.

2.1 Dyads

Until recently, dyads were largely overlooked in the field of knowledge creation. However, interactive groups formed via the combination of dyads [3] have now been shown to creatively outperform nominal group technique [4] as a function of lowered evaluation apprehension [5]. These findings on group creative process optimisation via dyadic structures create a new imperative to optimise dyadic ideation.

The creativity literature on dyads is sparse, but encouraging. In 1960 Cohen et al. [6] found cohesive, trained dyads to be creatively efficient and effective; and this study positioned cohesion as the key success factor for dyads in creativity. Soon after Cohen, Whitmyre and Funk's work, Janis' influential 1971 work on groupthink [7] began emerging and creativity research on dyads became resultingly sporadic at best. Two years after the second edition of Janis' book Groupthink [8] was published, Pape and Bölle's conclusive demonstration of higher fluency results for ad hoc, untrained dyads than pooled individuals went virtually unnoticed [9].

In the interim between Cohen, Whitmyre and Funk's study, and the onset of the groupthink dialogue Torrance [10, 11] found increased task persistence, participant perceptions of enjoyment, originality of expression and stimulation in dyads. More tellingly, Torrance [11] also discovered increases in flexibility amongst dyads that foreshadows more recent work on co-inspiration [12].

2.2 Need for Cognitive Closure (NFCC)

Kruglanski's lay epistemics concept of need for cognitive closure (NFCC) is highly relevant to group creativity [13, 14]. NFCC refers to "individuals' desire for a firm answer to a question and an aversion toward ambiguity" [15] and consists of tendencies towards urgency and permanence of cognitive closure [15]. NFCC is both a dispositional trait [16] and a situationally-induced state [15]. Eventual cognitive closure on a subject is necessary, yet prematurely reaching closure undermines the effectiveness of cognitive operations such as formal reasoning [17].

Since 1984 "Resistance to premature closure", or "degree of psychological open-ness" [18] has been an integral factor in the world's most recognised creativity test—the Torrance Test of Creative Thinking [19, 20].

NFCC is problematic for both individual and group creativity for a range of reasons. Firstly, creative behaviour requires the processing of a variety of infor-mation [18, 21], particularly via a search of one's own associative memory [22]. "Closure-bound pursuits" [15] bias the associative memory search choices made [22] and exploratory avenues of thought are ignored. This is particularly detrimental to divergent thinking [23] in non-insight problems [13].

The value of criticism and conflict in group ideation are being increasingly recognised [24–26]. NFCC is detrimental to productive cycles of criticism as it increases the propensity of individuals to reject differing opinions on an issue without consideration [27].

NFCC restricts information processing and the systematicity of information processing is concurrently lowered [28]. Contrary to popular belief, the dogged systematic search of associative memory is conducive to creative productivity [29]. NFCC undermines creative processes by muddling associative memory search functions.

2.3 The Dual Pathway to Creativity Model

The Dual Pathway to Creativity Model [29] posits creative performance as a result of two action paths—cognitive flexibility and cognitive persistence. These distinct paths may intertwine and coincide during the creative process; but one of the two acts as the primary enabler of creative output. The concept of flexibility has been used in creativity research since the field has existed [30, 31]; and the measurement denotes the number of idea categories generated during divergent thinking [10]. Using the flexibility pathway to achieve creative output involves "flexible switching among categories, approaches, and sets, and through the use of remote (rather than close) associations." [29].

The second creativity pathway, persistence, involves "hard work, the systematic and effortful exploration of possibilities, and in-depth exploration of only a few categories or perspectives" [29]. The premise of the persistence pathway is that a concentrated search within a category results in the non-original ideas being used up, and with enough time and effort—more original ideas being produced. This pathway is operationalised by the measure of within category fluency (WCF). This is the average count of how many ideas are produced within each idea category. This is calculated by dividing the total number of ideas generated (fluency) by the number of categories used (flexibility) [29].

The Dual Pathway to Creativity Model views creative output as being contingent upon environmental factors such as approach/avoidance behaviours and group dynamics; and is inclusive towards sociomaterial interactions [32]. In presenting their model, Nijstad et al. postulate that higher working memory capacity—one of the most universally-recognised benefits of visualisations [33]—is an enabler of the persistence pathway to creativity. The potential of visualisations to delay NFCC and thus hold open the persistence path to creativity is backed by the finding that working memory aids delay NFCC [34].

2.4 Visualisation

Visualisation consists of the "mechanisms by which humans perceive, interpret, use and communicate visual information" [35]. Above and beyond freeing working memory [33], sociomaterial visual practices bring numerous well-recognised benefits to knowledge creation. Visualisation enables the emergence of knowledge creation [36] through the modalities shown below in Table 1.

The factors listed above are of value during dyadic knowledge creation because dyads rely upon visualisations for a "shared interactional space" [44], this is known as the "joint problem-solving space" [45]. The joint problem-solving space is used as the "unfolding setting for the work at hand" [44].

Individual visualisations have a number of discrete dimensions such as visual impact, facilitated insight, and modifiability [46]. Following Gibson's theory of affordances [47], visual representations invite or discourage specific forms of interaction via affordances, which are the perceived opportunities for action an object or environment provides. Each contribution made by an ideator to a joint problem solving space provides an affordance for their partner to accept, question, discard or build upon it. Non-human agents also have a large bearing on the co-creation of knowledge through the mechanism of affordances. Affordances may be designed, but they are also inherent in the properties of visual markings. For example, as shown in Fig. 1—the basic visual element of the line may be more natural or artificial in nature [48]. Natural lines have more variation and this impacts upon people's perception of, and interaction with them—as can be seen in sketches [49]. This study examines the manner in which joint problem-solving space, writing instrument and dyads entangle [50] to create emergent knowledge.

Table 1 Knowledge creation enablers of visualisation

Visual knowledge enabler	Reference
Assistance of remote association triggering	[37]
Common ground creation	[38, 39]
Explicitation of potential connections between elements	[40]
Freeing working memory	[33]
Internal dialogue development	[41]
Inviting reflection	[42]
Provision of overview for creative sensemaking	[43]

Artificial line

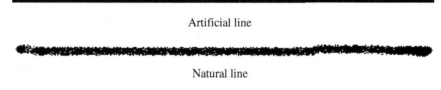

Natural line

Fig. 1 Artificial and natural lines

Rheinberger [51] makes a telling distinction between technical objects and epistemic objects. An idea visually notated in a dyad's joint problem solving space is a transitory epistemic object, yet they are often misinterpreted as factual technical objects—and fruitful opportunities for knowledge creation are missed. Whyte et al. [52] refer to epistemic objects as being fluid and technical objects as frozen. NFCC results in the fluid being prematurely, and often permanently frozen—whilst ideators move onto completely unrelated ideas. Persistence [29] is effectively the overcoming of NFCC [15]. Overly static visual representations which provide no affordance for persistence potentially exacerbate the freezing and seizing of boundary objects' fluidity.

In the current context, visualisations are generated by a combination of human agents, inscription and display devices. A writing instrument such as a pen is an example of an inscription device, while a sheet of paper is exemplary of a simple display device. This study's operationalisation of inscription and display devices is fully listed in Table 2, and shown in Fig. 3. Despite an increasing recognition of the importance of sociomaterial processes and objects [53] both inscriptive and display non-human agents [54] of notation, or notation materials, have gone unexamined in the realm of group creativity. In examining notation materials and their interactions, this pilot study begins to remedy this deficit.

Raw artefacts in the midst of creation by ad hoc groups are relatively low in structure, and high in subjectivity and embeddedness within a group context [55]. Therefore, they are fundamentally epistemic [51], or fluid [52]. This study examines whether consistently fluid notation materials will support emergent sociomaterial objects' development more effectively than the contradictory use of frozen notation

Table 2 Operationalisation of fluid and frozen inscription and display devices

Concept	Operationalisation
Fluid inscriptive non-human agent of notation	Pencil with eraser
Frozen inscriptive non-human agent of notation	Pen
Fluid display non-human agent of notation	Blank A3 sheet of paper
Frozen display non-human agent of notation	A3 sheet of paper with pre-printed mind map template

materials. Complementary sociomateriality in-sync with the group's function is predicted to facilitate persistent creativity [29] in the face of NFCC [15].

Seeber et al. [55] introduce the idea trace phases of controversial initiation, supportive enrichment, steadfast challenge and committed integration. The concept of idea trace phases can also be applied to idea category. Each idea which steps away from the category undergoing supportive enrichment and opens up a new idea category represents at least temporary cognitive closure on the extant category, and the beginning of a new phase of controversial initiation. Through impacting upon NFCC on idea category via degree of fluidity [52], differing compositions of notation materials will affect the level of enrichment, challenge and perceived integration of an idea category's ideas. The perceived modifiability of sociomaterial emergences impacts upon the affordance they create.

2.5 Hypothesis Development

The various actors in the entanglement of writing instrument, display device and dyad are envisaged to create replicable patterns of interaction. Bearing the literature on dyads, NFCC, the Dual Pathway to Creativity Model [29] and visualisation in mind, a hypothesis on the relationship between writing instrument and display device, and their impact upon creativity in a dyadic mind mapping context will be developed below. Figure 2 depicts a conceptual model in which display non-human agent of notation, or display device, is conceptualised to operate via affordance effects [47]. Frozen pre-existing visual templates with vacant affordances for new ideas and idea categories pre-validate any new category initiation. There can be no controversy [55] in satisfying an affordance. In the case of pre-existing mind map templates, individuals sate templates' affordances to supply idea categories to 'empty branches'.

In contrast, when groups create their own mind maps, there are no empty branches. New branches are only created and the first idea noted after a new idea

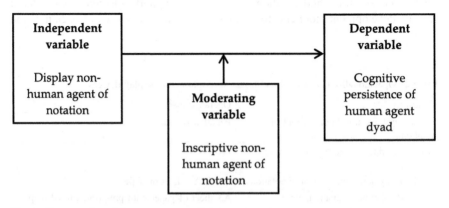

Fig. 2 Conceptual model

category has been cognitively opened by at least one individual. The affordance for individuals then becomes the population of the newly created branch at hand. Prior to a new idea category passing through initial cognition and controversial initiation [55], no empty branch graphically exists to invite supportive enrichment [55]. Once a new idea category branch has been graphically depicted and cognitively opened on a mind map, closely-related, within category ideas will be contributed until within category persistence flags [29], and a new category is opened. Within a highly modifiable joint problem solving space, the cognitive opening and public notation of a new idea category is capitulation to NFCC on idea category and the abandonment of a joint cognitive effort to flesh out the invitation of an at-hand idea category. Display devices operate according to principles of affordance, and their emergent sociomateriality interacts with other agents to develop varying levels of cognitive persistence despite NFCC [15].

Inscriptive non-human agents of notation, or writing instruments, are a fundamental component of emergent sociomaterial processes and objects. Interactions between human agents and writing instruments will impart differing degrees of fluidity [52] upon sociomaterial objects. Fluidity itself is an affordance.

A set of ideas consists of categories [30]. The emergence of idea categories is a result of "structured imagination" [56]. During the attribution of an idea to a category, human agents' "imagination is structured by a particular set of properties that are characteristic of that category" [56]. Central aspects of idea categories derived from naïve mental models [57] define an individual's categories, and multiple human agents subsequently use naïve mental models [58] to compare any new ideas to a prototypical category member's central attributes in order and determine the new item's category membership.

The acceptance of wider deviation from an idea category's central attributes' increases the inclusivity of an idea category. The relatively naturalistic markings of fluid writing instruments are more loosely interpreted than those of comparatively artificial frozen writing instruments [46]. Graphite markings thus lend themselves to the creation of less fine-grained categories than ink markings. Writing instrument markings communicate provisional category norms, which human agents perceive as flexible. Inclusivity of category is expected to result in more persistence [29].

Following the reasoning above, it is hypothesised that fluid non-human display agents of notation and fluid inscriptive non-human agents of notation will interact resulting in the emergence of higher levels of persistence in human agent dyads [29] than is displayed by dyads equipped with frozen non-human display agents of notation and frozen inscriptive non-human agents of notation. In other words, it is predicted that synergies between fluid display devices and fluid writing instruments will enable more persistence in pairs than frozen display devices and frozen writing instruments. This relationship is depicted in Fig. 2.

3   Method

3.1   Research Design

A 2 × 2 factorial experiment was selected to test the hypothesis. The independent
variables are instrument and worksheet used by the dyads, and the dependent variable
is within category fluency. The fluidity of display non-human agents of notation was
operationalised by blank sheets of A3 paper (fluid) and A3 sheets with a pre-printed
mind map template (frozen). The fluidity of inscriptive non-human agents of notation
was operationalised by pencils with eraser (fluid) and black pens (frozen). By
inherent nature of their markings, pen ink produces relatively artificial lines whilst
pencil graphite produces comparably natural lines [48]—therefore pens were used to
operationalise frozen rigidity and pencils were used for the operationalization of
fluidity. The exact materials used are listed in Table 2 and depicted in Fig. 3.

The ideation task was "develop ideas for inexpensive giveaways to remind and
inspire employees organisation-wide of a new strategy". This task was chosen
because of its universal accessibility, and applicability to participants. It is also in
line with Ward's experimental tasks [56].

3.2   Participants

All 58 participants were middle or upper managers from central Europe with at least
10 years of professional experience in departments such as IT, engineering, and

Fig. 3 Worksheets and materials provided

marketing. The participants were from 55 different organisations. Participants' industries were: construction (5.1 %), consulting (6.8 %), education (1.7 %), engineering (6.8 %), financial services (20.2 %), fast moving consumer goods (3.4 %), healthcare (13.6 %), ICT (11.9 %), manufacturing (10.2 %), NGO (1.7 %) and the public sector (18.6 %). Participants had only superficial previous knowledge of each other. The sample was comprised of 79 % males and 21 % females.

3.3 Procedure

The experiment was twice repeated during two separate executive MBA courses on strategic management. The procedure and time of day was identical in both iterations. Participants were told that they would be assigned to dyads, required to generate ideas for a soon-to-be-assigned task using a mind map [59]; and finally select and summarise their best idea [60] using a standardised sheet. Radial mind maps were chosen for their ubiquity [61] and accessibility [40]. To ensure uniform knowledge, mind map use for ideation was briefly explained [62]. Dyads were then randomly formed by the experimenters, and materials assigned to them. Finally, participants were told that there was no minimum or maximum time limit for the simulation, and the ideation task was publicly announced and visibly noted. Upon finishing the activity, participant pairs handed in their mind maps, best idea summary sheet and writing instruments. The time of submission was noted, and participants were each given a short survey to measure control variables.

4 Results

At the outset of the experiment, two participant pairs left the experimental environment, and completed the task at external tables. Their results were removed from analysis.

Mind maps were examined as representative of each group's creative process. Fluency and flexibility require measuring to attain the persistence measurement of WCF. The first measurement taken from all mind maps was ideational fluency [25].

Flexibility was next measured following the work of Seeber et al. [55]. Category coding was begun, and a list of coded idea categories of uniform granularity gradually emerged—for example office stationary, games, and toys. If an idea did not fit into a previously created category, then an appropriate new category was created and added to the category list.

WCF was subsequently calculated using the fluency and flexibility values. The results are reported in Table 3. Neither fluency nor flexibility were significantly different as main factors. The control variables measured by survey had no effect on the result.

Table 3 Factor means

	Condition							
	Blank worksheet with pencil (n = 12)		Blank worksheet with pen (n = 16)		Template worksheet with pencil (n = 12)		Template worksheet with pen (n = 14)	
	Mean	s.d.	Mean	s.d.	Mean	s.d.	Mean	s.d.
Fluency	26	20	17	12	17	12	13	5
Flexibility	8	8	6	3	6	2	4	1
Within category fluency (WCF)	3.79	1.73	2.67	1.13	2.46	1.28	3.04	0.92

n = 54

Fluency, flexibility and WCF differences between the two operational fluidity factors were next examined using one-way ANOVA. The results are presented below in Table 4.

As can be seen, main factor alone played a non-significant role on the fluency, flexibility or WCF of creative output. Univariate analysis of variance was then used to test for moderation of writing instrument fluidity upon display device fluidity. The results are shown below in Table 5.

Univariate analysis of variance shows that the interaction between worksheet and writing instrument for WCF is significant at a level of $p = 0.013$. The univariate analysis of variance general linear model in Fig. 4 shows the powerful crossover interaction between worksheet and writing instrument impacting upon WCF.

Table 4 Factor one way ANOVAs

	Factor							
	Worksheet (n = 54)				Writing instrument (n = 54)			
	ANOVA: Between groups				ANOVA: Between groups			
	df	Total df	F	Sig.	df	Total df	F	Sig.
Fluency	1	53	2.729	0.105	1	53	2.685	0.107
Flexibility	1	53	2.125	0.151	1	53	2.542	0.117
Within category fluency (WCF)	1	53	0.727	0.398	1	53	0.383	0.539

n = 54

Table 5 Univariate analysis of variance moderation test

Source	df	F	Sig.
Worksheet	1	1.419	0.239
Writing instrument	1	0.365	0.549
Worksheet * Writing instrument	1	6.653	0.013

a. R Squared = 0.137 (Adjusted R Squared = 0.085)
b. Computed using alpha = 0.05
n = 54

Fig. 4 Moderating effect of worksheet and instrument for within category fluency (WCF)

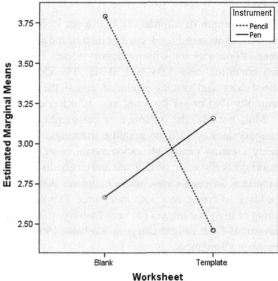

Estimated Marginal Means of Within Category Fluency (WCF)

As seen in Fig. 4, idea generating dyads using pencils with a blank page were approximately twice as persistent as dyads using pencils with a mind map template. A much slighter increase in WCF emerged from idea generating dyads using pens with a mind map template in comparison with pairs using pens and a blank page.

It should finally be noted that although erasers were provided on the end of every pencil in the relevant conditions, none were used.

5 Discussion

The hypothesis that interaction between fluid display devices and fluid writing instruments encourages the emergence of persistence in dyads [29] was supported. As hypothesised, writing instruments' fluidity moderates worksheet fluidity resulting in higher cognitive persistence within dyads. This effect is examined in more detail below.

When the affordance of pre-supplied mind maps to create new idea categories is not present, the cognitive persistence of dyads using fluid, relatively naturalistic markings is increased due to widened category inclusivity. In contrast, when pre-printed mind map branches with multiple contribution affordances are not made available to dyads using the frozen, comparably artificial medium of pen, dyads merely open and close idea categories superficially [48]. These dyads indulged in the claiming of cognitive categories. Frozen ink markings impart very little leeway from central idea category-defining attributes [56] when used freely. To paraphrase

Ward [56], ink rigidly structures imagination and the result is NFCC on idea category.

The strength of affordances is evident in both writing instrument operationalisations. As seen in Fig. 3, each branch of the pre-supplied mind map templates had three affordances for within category ideas. The mean WCF in the template with pen condition was 3.04 (s.d. 0.91). The close mapping between the template affordances and results produced reveal the tempering of ink's rigid category centrality [56] of ink by mind map affordances.

Most notably, the influence of pre-supplied templates decimated the inclusive category leeway [56] of graphite markings. The cognitive persistence of dyads freely creating emergent sociomaterial objects with fluid, somewhat naturalistic markings is shown to be delicate and easily disrupted by the rigidity of pre-supplied templates. In such cases, these templates actually induce NFCC through the affordance to create new idea categories. Graphite markings allow the loose structuring of imagination, yet the very fragility of its framing,which allows for inclusive deviations from central category attributes [56], is easily disrupted by fixed visual template affordances.

6 Conclusion

This study is not without its limitations. This pilot study used a relatively small sample from a limited cultural range, under laboratory conditions. Coding was carried out by a single independent researcher. The current study used only two operationalisations each of display device and writing instrument. Future studies would address these shortcomings and widen the variety of operationalisations, with the aim to include digital variants. Future data collection would include qualitative data to be used in an integrative mixed methods approach [63].

This pilot study opens numerous avenues for further research. More research into the moderation of visual working space effects by notation instrument is called for.

One factor uncovered by this pilot study particularly merits further study: the absence of externally-supplied affordances is not the absence of affordances. Groups with blank worksheets were generating their own affordances as their mind maps emerged. An exploration of differences between personally-generated and externally-supplied affordances would be a useful contribution to affordance theory.

In summary, this pilot study has found the category inclusivity effect of writing instrument to moderate the affordance effect of display devices on idea generating dyads' cognitive persistence [29]. Emergent sociomaterial interactions have thus been shown to be capable of lessening the impact of NFCC in knowledge creation [1]. The fluidity of visualisation components acts as cognitive antifreeze upon NFCC in idea generating dyads.

This study has found the gap-filling affordance of static pre-structured templates to negatively impact the creative persistence [29] enabled by the category malleability effect of fluid, naturalistic markings. However, digital environments are dynamic, and the evident effects of affordances could be dynamically employed to foster creative contributions. For example, mind-mapping software could relatively easily detect the filling of main, category level mind map branches, and create empty new category branches to afford more contributions. At a simple level, mind-mapping software could operate via a programmed rule to automatically add a new sub-branch extending from every single new contribution to a mind map. These vacant sub-branches would de-centrally elicit knowledge. A more sophisticated phased treatment is also technically possible—a model of phased affordances could encourage participants to push themselves to gradually build up and connect layered categories of knowledge in the shared visual working space. A phased model of dynamic—not static, pre-structured—affordances in combination with natural, graphite lines [48] would invite creativity via participants' deep, systematic search of associative memory [29, 64] and idea combination [65].

In general, software design for idea generation, including social media platforms for innovation, should take note of the malleable category inclusivity effect of natural, graphite lines [48] and mimic these. A further application of the finding that natural graphite markings have an advantageous yet delicate function as cognitive antifreeze in the absence of pre-existing structures is in tablet computers' handwriting recognition systems. Handwriting recognition software designed for the support of divergent thought [23] should encourage the retention of user-produced natural lines, instead of transforming users' natural lines into artificial lines by default. Furthermore, automated processes for ordering users' knowledge structures into templates such as stakeholder maps should respect users' existing natural lines as much as possible and produce user line/template hybrids.

Social media platforms for innovation have, at times, suffered under low quality of discussion. The duplicate addition of identical ideas contributes to this problem [66]. The fluid presentation of previously-supplied ideas to potential idea providers could lead to within-category expansion upon them and bolster the idea pool.

The findings of this study are also useful for knowledge managers who can use them to compose sociomateriality in order to elicit or rescind cognitive persistence in dyads in a range of situations. For example, knowledge managers can use the space/medium sociomaterial interaction described as a powerful tool by which to allay the deleterious effects of NFCC on creative output [14]. This sociomaterial effect is especially useful in solving problems prone to eliciting false insights [67] when persistence is needed to push past seemingly satisfactory initial solutions in order to tap into truly creative veins of cognition. Such scenarios can be found in a range of problems from the introduction of new technology into an organisation to resolving thorny programming challenges. Sociomateriality has been shown to matter to the search for creative solutions.

References

1. Nonaka, I.: The knowledge-creating company. Harvard Bus. Rev. **69**(6), 96–104 (1991)
2. McGrath, R.G.: The end of competitive advantage: How to keep your strategy moving as fast as your business. Harvard Business Review Press, Boston (2013)
3. Dew, R., Hearn, G.: A new model of the learning process for innovation teams: Networked nominal pairs. Int. J. Inno. Mgmt. **13**(04), 521–535 (2009)
4. Van de Ven, A., Delbecq, A.L.: Nominal versus interacting group processes for committee decision-making effectiveness. Acad. Mgmt. J. **14**(2), 203–213 (1971)
5. McGrath, L.A.: When pairing reduces scaring: The effect of dyadic ideation on evaluation apprehension. Int. J. Inno. Mgmt. (2015) (In Print)
6. Cohen, D., Whitmyre, J.W., Funk, W.H.: Effect of group cohesiveness and training upon creative thinking. J. App. Psych. **44**(5), 319–322 (1960)
7. Janis, I.L.: Groupthink. Psych. Today **5**(6), 43–46 (1971)
8. Janis, I.L.: Groupthink, 2nd edn. Houghton Mifflin, Boston (1982)
9. Pape, T., Bölle, I.: Einfallsproduktion von Individuen und Dyaden unter "Brainstorming"-Bedingungen: Replikation einer Studie und allgemeine Probleme eines Forschungsgebietes. Psych. Bei. **26**, 459–468 (1984). (in German)
10. Torrance, E.P.: The influence of dyadic interaction on creative functioning. Psych. Rep. **26**, 391–394 (1970)
11. Torrance, E.P.: Stimulation, enjoyment, and originality in dyadic creativity. J. Ed. Psych. **62**(1), 46–48 (1971)
12. Hausmann, R.G.M.: Why do elaborative dialogs lead to effective problem solving and deep learning? In: 28th Annual Meeting of the Cognitive Science Society, pp. 1465–1469. Lawrence Erlbaum Associates, Vancouver (2006)
13. Chirumbolo, A., Mannetti, L., Pierro, A., Areni, A., Kruglanski, A.W.: Motivated closed-mindedness and creativity in small groups. Sm. Gr. Res. **36**(1), 59–82 (2005)
14. Antonio, C., Livi, S., Mannetti, L., Pierro, A., Kruglanski, A.W.: Effects of need for closure on creativity in small group interactions. Euro. J. Pers. **18**(4), 265–278 (2004)
15. Kruglanski, A.W., Webster, D.M.: Motivated closing of the mind: "seizing" and "freezing". Psych. Rev. **103**(2), 263–283 (1996)
16. Webster, D.M., Kruglanski, A.W.: Individual differences in need for cognitive closure. J. Pers. Soc. Psych. **67**(6), 1049–1062 (1994)
17. Lunzer, E.A.: The development of formal reasoning: some recent experiments and their implications. In: Frey, K., Lang, M. (eds.) Cognitive processes and science instruction. Williams and Wilkins, Baltimore (1973)
18. Kim, K.H.: Can we trust creativity tests? A review of the torrance tests of creative thinking (TTCT). Crea. Res. J. **18**(1), 3–14 (2006)
19. Davis, G.A.: Identifying creative students and measuring creativity. In: Colangelo, N., Davis, G.A. (eds.) Handbook of Gifted Education, pp. 269–281. Viacom, Needham Heights (1997)
20. Lissitz, R.W., Willhoft, J.L.: A methodological study of the Torrance Tests of Creativity. J. Ed. Meas. **22**, 1–111 (1985)
21. Thagard, P., Stewart, T.C.: The AHA! experience: creativity through emergent binding in neural networks. Cog. Sci. **35**(1), 1–33 (2011)
22. Nijstad, B., Stroebe, W.: How the group affects the mind: A cognitive model of idea generation in groups. Pers. Soc. Psych. Rev. **10**(3), 186–213 (2006)
23. Guilford, J.P.: The Nature of Human Intelligence. McGraw-Hill, New York (1971)
24. Nemeth, C.J., Ormiston, M.: Creative idea generation: Harmony versus stimulation. Euro. J. Soc. Psych. **37**(3), 524–535 (2007)
25. Gibson, C., Mumford, M.D.: Evaluation, criticism, and creativity: criticism content and effects on creative problem solving. Psych. Aes. Crea. Arts. **7**(4), 314–331 (2013)
26. Hewing, M.: Merits of collaboration with potential and current users in creative problem-solving. Int. J. Inno. Mgmt. **17**(3), 44–71 (2013)

27. Kruglanski, A.W., Webster, D.M.: Group members' reactions to opinion deviates and conformists at varying degrees of proximity to decision deadline and of environmental noise. Interpers. Rel. Gr. Proc. **61**(2), 212–225 (1991)
28. Webster, D., Richter, L., Kruglanski, A.W.: On leaping to conclusions when feeling tired: Mental fatigue effects on impressional primacy. J. Exp. Soc. Psych. **32**, 181–195 (1996)
29. Nijstad, B.A., De Dreu, C.K.W., Rietzschel, E.F., Baas, M.: The dual pathway to creativity model: Creative ideation as a function of flexibility and persistence. Euro. Rev. Soc. Psych. **21**(1), 34–77 (2010)
30. Guilford, J.P.: Creative abilities in the arts. Psych. Rev. **64**(2), 110–118 (1957)
31. Paulus, P.B., Dzindolet, M., Kohn, N.W.: Collaborative creativity—group creativity and team innovation. In: Mumford, M.D. (ed.) Handbook of Organizational Creativity, pp. 327–357. Academic Press, San Diego (2012)
32. Parmiggiani, E., Mikalsen, M.: The facets of sociomateriality: A systematic mapping of emerging concepts and definitions. In: Aanestad, M., Bratteteig, T. (eds.) SCIS 2013, LNBIP, vol. 156, pp. 87–103. Springer, Berlin (2013)
33. Lurie, N.H., Mason, C.H.: Visual representation: Implications for decision making. J. Mktg. **71**, 160–177 (2007)
34. Wollman, W., Eylon, B., Lawson, A.E.: Acceptance of lack of closure: Is it an index of advanced reasoning? Ch. Dev. **50**(3), 656–665 (1979)
35. McCormick, B.H., DeFanti, T.A., Brown, M.D.: Visualization in scientific computing. IEEE Comput. Graphics Appl. **7**(10), 69 (1987)
36. Jacucci, G., Wagner, I.: Performative roles of materiality for collective creativity. In: Proceedings of the 6th ACM SIGCHI conference on creativity & cognition—C&C '07, p. 73. ACM Press, New York (2007)
37. Chambers, D., Reisberg, D.: Can mental images be ambiguous? J. Exp. Psych. **11**(3), 317–328 (1985)
38. Carlile, P.R.: A pragmatic view of knowledge and boundaries: Boundary objects in new product development. Org. Sci. **13**(4), 442–455 (2002)
39. Star, S.L., Griesemer, J.R.: Institutional ecology, translations' and boundary objects: Amateurs and professionals in Berkeley's museum of vertebrate zoology, 1907-39. Soc. St. Sci. **19**(3), 387–420 (1989)
40. Martin, L., Schwartz, D.L.: A pragmatic perspective on visual representation and creative thinking. Vis. St. **29**(1), 80–93 (2014)
41. Ewenstein, B., Whyte, J.K.: Visual representations as "artefacts of knowing". Build. Res. Inf. **35**(1), 81–89 (2007)
42. Knorr-Cetina, K.: Objectual practice. In: Schatzki, T.R., Cetina, K.K., Von Savigny, E. (eds.) The Practice Turn in Contemporary Theory, pp. 184–197. Routledge, London (2001)
43. Larkin, J.H., Simon, H.: Why a diagram is (sometimes) worth ten thousand words. Cog. Sci. **11**, 65–99 (1987)
44. Suchman, L.: Representing practice in cognitive science. Hu. St. **11**(2), 305–325 (1988)
45. Roschelle, J., Teasley, S.D.: The construction of shared knowledge in collaborative problem solving. In: Roschelle, J., Teasley, S.D. (eds.) Computer supported collaborative learning, pp. 69–97. Springer, Heidelberg (1995)
46. Bresciani, S., Blackwell, A., Eppler, M.J.: Choosing Visualisations for Collaborative Work and Meetings: A Guide to Usability Dimensions. Research report, Darwin College (2008)
47. Gibson, J.J.: The Theory of Affordances. In: Shaw, R.E., Bransford, J. (eds.) Perceiving, Acting, and Knowing, pp. 127–143. Lawrence Erlbaum Associates, Hillsdale, NJ (1977)
48. Bradley, S.: Design Fundamentals: Elements. Attributes & Principles. Vanseo Design, Boulder, CO (2013)
49. Tversky, B.: What do sketches say about thinking? In: 2002 AAAI Spring Symposium Sketch Understanding Workshop, pp. 148–151. IAAA Press, Palo Alto (2002)
50. Pickering, A.: The Mangle of Practice: Time Agency and Science. The University of Chicago Press, Chicago (1995)

51. Rheinberger, H.J.: Toward a History of Epistemic Things: Synthesizing Proteins in the Test Tube. Stanford University Press, Redwood City, CA (1997)
52. Whyte, J.K., Ewenstein, B., Hales, M., Tidd, J.: Visual practices and the objects used in design. Build. Res. Inf. **35**(1), 18–27 (2007)
53. Leonardi, P.M., Kallinikos, J.: Materiality and organizing: Social interaction in a technological world. Oxford University Press, Oxford (2012)
54. Barad, K.: Posthumanist performativity: Toward an understanding of how matter comes to matter. Signs **28**(3), 801–831 (2003)
55. Seeber, I., Maier, R., Ceravolo, P., Frati, F.: Tracing the development of ideas in distributed, IT-supported teams during synchronous collaboration. In: Twenty Second European Conference on Information Systems, pp. 1–16. ECIS, Tel Aviv (2014)
56. Ward, T.B.: Structured imagination: The role of category structure in exemplar generation. Cog. Psych. **27**, 1–40 (1994)
57. Murphy, G.L.: Comprehending complex concepts. Cog. Sci. **12**, 529–562 (1988)
58. Lewis, C.M., Sycara, K.P.: Reaching informed agreement in multispecialist cooperation. Gr. Dec. Neg. **2**(3), 279–299 (1993)
59. Buzan, T.: The Mind Map Book: How to Use Radiant Thinking to Maximize Your Brain's Untapped Potential. Plume, New York (1996)
60. Girotra, K., Terwiesch, C., Ulrich, K.T.: Idea generation and the quality of the best idea. Mgmt. Sci. **56**(4), 591–605 (2010)
61. Eppler, M.J.: A comparison between concept maps, mind maps, conceptual diagrams, and visual metaphors as complementary tools for knowledge construction and sharing. Inf. Vis. **5**(3), 202–210 (2006)
62. Eppler, M.J., Pfister, R.: Sketching at work. =mcm institute, St Gallen (2011)
63. Bergman, M.M.: Advances in Mixed Methods Research. Sage Publications, London (2008)
64. Rietzschel, E.F., Nijstad, B.A., Stroebe, W.: Relative accessibility of domain knowledge and creativity: The effects of knowledge activation on the quantity and quality of generated ideas. J. Exp. Soc. Psych. **43**, 933–946 (2007)
65. Harvey, S.: Creative synthesis: Exploring the process of extraordinary group creativity. Acad. Mgmt. Rev. **39**(3), 324–343 (2014)
66. Martini, A., Massa, S., Testa, S.: The inextricable intertwining of the firm, the platform and the customer: the case of a social media platform for innovation. In: Proceedings of the XI Conference of the Italian Chapter of AIS on Digital Innovation and Inclusive Knowledge in Times of Change—ITAIS 2014. ITAIS, Genoa (2014)
67. Simonton, D.K.: Foresight in Insight? A Darwinian Answer. In: Sternberg, R.J., Davidson, J.E. (eds.) The Nature of Insight, pp. 465–494. The MIT Press, Cambridge, MA (1995)

Requirements and Open Issues for ISs Supporting Dynamic Community Bonding in Emergency Situations

Tania Di Mascio, Federico Gobbo and Laura Tarantino

Abstract Studies show that in emergency situations, like in the aftermath of natural disasters, people tend to self-organize into so-called ephemeral organizations and transitional communities based on common problems, common places, etc. Strict interactions among victims, fundamental to strengthen such small communities, may be efficiently supported by a new generation of mobile-empowered disaster management systems based on the social networking approach, with crowd-generated and geo-referenced data. In this paper we discuss how a shift of perspective in the interaction, conceptual, logical and physical models adopted for the social network can efficiently support the dynamic bonding/de-bonding/re-bonding of communities that emerge based on alliances around shared problems and/or objectives.

Keywords Social network · Interaction · Emergency management

1 Introduction

As the European Environmental Agency (EEA) recently reported [13], the impact of disasters due to natural hazards and technological accidents increased in Europe in the period 1998–2009, with nearly 100,000 fatalities, more than 11 million

T. Di Mascio (✉) · L. Tarantino
Università Degli Studi Dell'Aquila, L'Aquila, Italy
e-mail: tania.dimascio@univaq.it

L. Tarantino
e-mail: laura.tarantino@univaq.it

F. Gobbo
University of Amsterdam, Amsterdam, Netherlands
e-mail: f.gobbo@uva.nl

F. Gobbo
University of Milano Bicocca, Milan, Italy

F. Gobbo
University of Torino, Turin, Italy

© Springer International Publishing Switzerland 2016
T. Torre et al. (eds.), *Empowering Organizations*, Lecture Notes in Information
Systems and Organisation 11, DOI 10.1007/978-3-319-23784-8_20

people affected, and economic losses of about EUR 150 billion. In the observed period extreme temperature events caused the highest number of human fatalities, flooding and storms were the most costly hazards, while earthquakes ranked second in terms of fatalities and third in terms of overall losses. EEA observes that the increase in losses can be explained, to a large extent, by higher levels of human activity and accumulation of economic assets in hazard-prone areas and underlines the necessity of measures for risk reduction and management. Although some EU policies have already been adopted or initiated, more effort is needed to implement an Integrated Risk Management approach that includes prevention, preparedness, response and recovery, the four main phases of a cyclic emergency management process [1].

The study discussed in this paper refers in particular to the support that ICT, and Information Systems (ISs) in particular, may provide to response and recovery after natural disasters that cause a massive failure in essential infrastructures and the disruption of the integrity of the affected community.

The subject of social and psychological impact of disasters is widely debated in the literature (e.g., [3, 4, 6, 14, 16, 17, 23, 24, 29]) and it is generally agreed that one of the most relevant effect of a disaster is the relaxation or, in the worst case, the disruption of the social linkages upon which a community is based. Immaterial damages are less evident (though often more relevant) than material ones and may remain unnoticed for a long period of time. It has to be noticed that, in the immediate aftermath of a disaster, the attention of rescuers is usually captured by the material needs of the victims, leaving sociological and psychological needs usually not addressed or addressed by means of standard protocols unable to reach the entire population.

This standard approach for facing emergency is mirrored by the emergency-related ICT proposals, which, in most cases, aim at providing support to rescuers and institutions, mainly offering top down and push communication (from institutions to citizens). Conversely, based on the literature on social recovery and on field evidences (still being) collected after the major moment magnitude 6.3 earthquake that hit L'Aquila and its neighboring territories on April 6, 2009, we are interested in offering a peer-to-peer (among citizens) communication, in order to directly supporting victims and the social dynamics that spontaneously arise in the aftermath of a disaster.

Overall, the L'Aquila earthquake caused 308 deaths and more than 1,500 injured persons. L'Aquila was devastated, both in its residential areas and in the historical center, with massive damages to cultural heritage (churches, monuments, museums, etc.) and fundamental public services (such as the City Government building and even the main hospital). The whole city of L'Aquila was evacuated and the historical center (now the so called "red area") has been isolated. The earthquake made L'Aquila (in particular its city center) a ghost town: all the social areas, the main squares, the churches, the shopping areas were heavily damaged and made inaccessible to the citizens (and so are now). The municipal offices were moved to different locations; factories, commercial areas, public utilities, infrastructures were (and partly are still) unusable. In a handful of seconds more than 70,000 persons (counting just L'Aquila, but the situation in the surrounding villages was not better) lost not only the private sphere of their homes but also all ordinary work and public environments.

The experience of the 2009 L'Aquila earthquake clearly highlights the necessity of online services and multimodal forums able to support social interaction not only in the immediate aftermath of the disaster but also in the medium and long run, to allow citizens to be active agents in the redefinition of their social connections. To have an idea of the length and the pace of the process, one can compare the 2013 and 2014 official figures on the evacuated population [22]: on April 2013, while waiting for the reconstruction of their homes, about 6500 persons were living in self-arranged accommodations, about 250 were still housed in temporary shelters (barracks and hotels), and about 15,000 were housed in more than 20 small new villages built after the quake under the coordination of the Civil Defense and located around the city territory, along an approximately 100 km closed path; in April 2014 the same figures were about 4500, about 150, and about 14,000, respectively.

Based on the experience in the post-earthquake in L'Aquila, our research group launched a number of projects to study and evaluate complementary aspects of ICT support to social dynamics arising in the aftermath of a disaster. While we refer to [5, 6] for discussions on a web 3.0 platform combining mobile computing, social web and semantic technologies, with stress on the role of ontologies, semantic annotation and natural language computing, in this paper we discuss $Emepolis^+$, primarily focused on a major re-thinking of social network models, at interaction, conceptual, logical and physical viewpoint aimed at supporting community recovery.

The remainder of this paper is organized as follows: after discussing in Sect. 2 the social dynamics activated by a disaster, in Sect. 3 we reason on how and to which extent existing ICT and ISs proposals provide support to these social processes, singling out stakeholders and requirements; in Sect. 4 we discuss the features of $Emepolis^+$; in Sect. 5 we discuss the technical choices that allowed us to attain our objectives; finally, in Sect. 6, open issues are discussed and conclusions are drawn.

2 Social Dynamics in the Aftermath of a Disaster

Communities hit by large disaster have to face massive and evident material evidence while also experiencing psychological and social wounds [14, 16, 17]. The disaster causes a sort of "cultural mourning" in the community, i.e., the loss of the world of meanings and social places that constituted the customs, the rituals, and the geography of such a community; victims and witnesses of a disaster tell of a community that is forever changed, no matter how effective the material reconstruction is [14].

Similarly, after a disaster, many "transitional communities" emerge [14], involving groups of displaced people, rescuers, people who shared a particular event, or share a particular problem or common places (e.g., temporary shelters, like tent camps or barracks), etc. These new social communities become very useful in supporting the process of development of new meanings and, ultimately, of a new social order. Figure 1 schematically illustrates the community re-bonding process as described by Gordon [16]: starting from a pre-disaster situation in which social linkages shape the community as a network of inter-connected social subsystems (Fig. 1a), the community then undergoes the sudden tearing of its structure in the area immediately affected by the disaster with disturbance in surrounding areas (Fig. 1b), followed by a first re-bonding—based on newly established linkages and alliances—along the "impact line" in the immediate aftermath of the disaster

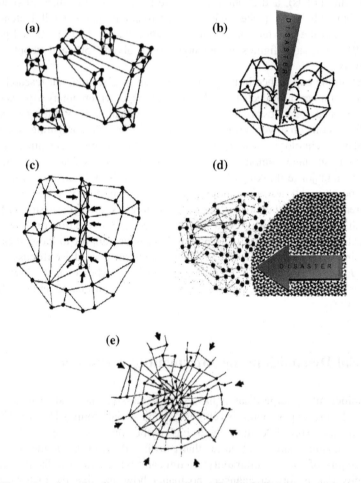

Fig. 1 The community re-bonding process according to Gordon [16], **a** A community in a normal situation. **b** A community when a disaster comes. **c** A community in re-bonding. **d** A community in de-bonding. **e** A commuinity in re-bonding

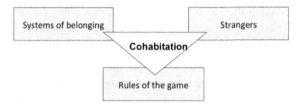

Fig. 2 Cohabitation definition

(Fig. 1c); in this new structure, social ties tend be intense along the impact line and quite loose with the enlarged context, leading to a de-bonding stage (Fig. 1d), after which, gradually, new relationships are built in a second re-bonding stage (Fig. 1e).

As reported in [14], an additional vision useful for analyzing emergency situations is proposed by Carli, focused on the process that allows human beings to achieve cohabitation. According to this vision, cohabitation is made possible by the articulation of three factors (see Fig. 2): (1) development and attainment of systems of belonging to the local community, (2) existence of external entities ("strangers"), fostering self decentralization and opening to the diverse, and (3) writing of the "rules of the game", to define belonging and strangeness. In other words, cohabitation is possible within the framework of a "glocal" model, able to assign value to the local while envisioning the community in a global context. The emergency situation, forcing a massive intrusion of strangers (e.g., rescuers), may become an opportunity to redefine cohabitation through new, possible more advanced, rules of the games.

3   Do Existing ICT Proposals Support Social Recovery?

Summarizing the discussion conducted so far, we can say that the reconstruction of meanings is to be considered a social process that takes advantage of rich and extensive interactions among actors that co-create a shared new universe of legitimate meanings. The adoption of *strategies, techniques and tools to support interaction between individuals* is therefore vital to the process of sense-making.

From this consideration clearly emerges the golden role that ICT and ISs can play in supporting the social dynamics that take place in the aftermath of a disaster. The description of the scenario also highlights basic requirements for an ICT platform able to provide effective support to victims:

- Peer-to-peer communication;
- Sharing of (geo-localized) information and resources;
- Efficient support to intra- and inter- small networks interactions;
- Dynamic bonding/de-bonding/re-bonding of social connections;
- Mechanisms for re-writing the "rules of the game".

It is worth recalling that, as observed by [14], psychological studies recognize four "levels" of victims, who should hence be considered possible stakeholders of ISs supporting the re-bonding process:

- *Primary victims* (people directly hit by the disaster);
- *Secondary victims* (people having tight ties and links with primary victims);
- *Tertiary victims* (rescuers and people that have to deal with primary victims for professional reasons);
- *External victims* (people that live in neighboring areas).

The inclusion among victims of rescuers, professionals, and people apparently non involved in the disaster enlarge the view and identifies a context of use rich of mutual influences among (people belonging to) different groups and interactions that one expects that disaster-oriented ISs take into account and support. It is therefore reasonable to analyze existing proposals under this perspective.

Over the years, many ICT-enhanced support tools, categorized as Disaster Management Systems (DMSs), have been developed (e.g., [8, 20, 21, 25–28, 30]), aimed at supporting institutions, formal organizations, and rescuers in one or more phases of the emergency management process: besides systems mainly useful for prevention and mitigation (like, e.g., NHSS[1]), other DMSs are designed to support also management and coordination of resources and rescuers during response and recovery (e.g., [21, 30]). A notable example is given by the suite of products offered by the Sahana Foundation[2] [8]: in particular, Eden is a configurable platform, allowing easy integration with maps, with the goal of coordinating and improving the efficiency of rescuers activities through organization registry, project tracking, messaging, scenario, and repositories for human resources, inventory and assets, while Vesuvius, focused on disaster preparedness and response needs of the medical community, contributes to family reunification and assistance with hospital triage.

It has to be noticed that most DMSs are oriented to support organized aids (i.e., tertiary victims) and just a few offer citizens (i.e., primary and secondary victims) the possibility to participate in the response/recovery phases by information sharing, whereas the recourse to Internet resources and to virtual spaces is instead expected and natural in a situation in which human relationships cannot take place in their natural physical space. In this sense, an exception is provided by Ushahidi [20, 26], a platform to easily crowd-source information using multiple channels (i.e., SMS, email, Twitter and the Web). Ushahidi enables citizens, besides organizations, to collect and visualize real-time geo-referenced information. However, the ultimate goal is to provide tools oriented to information collection and digestion, rather than supporting people in the reconstruction of a social community.

General purpose social networks, like Facebook and Twitter, certainly prove useful to this aim [18], but the unstructuredness of news feeds and the lack of

---

[1]http://nhss.cr.usgs.gov/.

[2]http://sahanafoundation.org/.

effective tagging/search mechanisms of posts, along with a "friend-centered" rather than "topic-centered" approach, concur to make both interaction and data management inefficient, particularly when posting rate is very high (as in emergency situations). These are exactly the issues we are addressing in the *Emepolis$^+$* project.

4 From a Friend-Based to an Issue-Based Network

The aim of *Emepolis$^+$* is to help local citizens in the reconstruction of their city and in the recovery of their community through a mobile application available for the major mobile platforms (i.e., Google Android, Apple iOS, and Windows Phone). The first test-bed is the territory of L'Aquila. *Emepolis$^+$* was the concrete context where to re-think mobile-empowered social networks from scratch, since it was soon evident that we could not simply rely on existing social networks—as, for instance, Facebook or Twitter—for the interaction and the data management if we wanted to support efficiently the process of community re-bonding.

The current status of the project is the result of two stages of design and development, respectively aimed and supporting: (1) a peer-to-peer exchange of information among citizens through an efficient interaction with news feeds in emergency situations, (2) the flourishing of "alliances" among citizens (the first goal was attained within the Emepolis project financed by Fondazione Italiana Accenture, whose proof-of-concept was preliminarily discussed in [9], under an "interaction in third places" perspective).

With these goals in mind, and according to the indications elicited from the literature and extensive field studies, differently from traditional social networks the focus of *Emepolis$^+$* was not put on user profiles, but rather on the issues posted by the users themselves, which becomes the primary "locus of interaction". In other words, *the information core is in the actual crowd-generated content*, not in the original author who proposed the content itself. Let us explain this view with an example scenario.

4.1 An Example Scenario

In a profile-centered social network (like Facebook), Alice shoots a photo of a dangerous hole in the road caused by the earthquake, with a sharp comment, raising an issue potentially interesting for the community. This issue (actually, a post in the data flow) can be seen only by Alice's friends—in the sense of social network friendship. Bob puts a "like", Charles adds a comment while Dave shares Alice's issues in his wall. The point is that what happens to Dave's copy of the original issues (comments, likes, etc.) forms a *new* data flow which is completely independent from Alice's one, thus preventing the creation of a unitary network of people based on the posted issue (e.g., in an emergency situation, the creation of a

Fig. 3 The example scenario

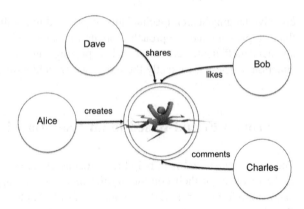

transitional community). This is clearly a severe limit in the model of current social networks with respect to the above-mentioned goals.

What happens if we change the perspective, shifting from user's profiles to user's posted issues? If we consider the example scenario, Alice's issue and the associated photo becomes an *issue node,* with attributes, of the social network. The node is created by Alice, whose *user node* represents the issue author or, better said, *initiator* of the issue node. As depicted in Fig. 3 (which illustrates the scenario without being yet a formal model) Bob's like, Charles' comment and Dave's sharing concur to form a sort of "micro-world" around the issue shaped by the crowd-generated data flow testifying the vigor of the issue itself (similar to the concept of *narrative process* in [7]).

With this new vision in mind, we find it more appropriate a different termi-nology: sharing and likes actions become adoptions with votes. Therefore, issues can be even evaluated and classified so to eventually form "alliances" of users based on the similarities of goals and objectives, favoring the creation of linkages in the re-bonding stages of the process illustrated in Fig. 1.

4.2   Main Interaction Features of Emepolis⁺

According to this scenario, the concept of *issue* is central in our system; the basic idea is that an issue is defined along with a vector of attributes, among which, title, description, and photo. While Table 1 summarizes at a conceptual level the main actions that users (citizens and administrator) can do on issues, Figs. 4, 5, 6 and 7 illustrate them at interface level:

- *Issue feeds* User interacts with issues visualized either as customary news feeds or on a map; Fig. 4 depicts the two cases along with the visualization of the notifications following a user click on the corresponding status bar icon.
- *Issue creation* Creation/modification of issues can be performed through familiar interactive forms; an example of creation is given in Fig. 5.

Table 1 Main action on issues in *Emepolis*⁺

Role	Name	Description
Citizen	Issue opening	User inserts title, description, photo, category, date, status, geo-tagging data
Citizen	Issue adoption	User adopts, possibly voting (5-star model), another citizen's open issue
Citizen	Issue updating	The initiator user modifies issue attributes, system notifies adopters
Citizen	Issue sharing	User creates a message for Facebook, Twitter, g+ , etc. with a referral link to one's issue
Citizen	Issue filtering	User filters issue feed(s) according to preferences, attributes, users, geo-localization options
Citizen	Issue flagging	User sends a message to an administrator when another user's issue/comment is inappropriate
Citizen	Issue comment	User comments an issue
Administrator	–	Besides all above citizens' actions s/he handles flags

Fig. 4 Visualization of issues and system notifications

- *Feed filtering* The issue feed can be filtered according to user preferences (Fig. 6). We notice in particular the possibility of restricting the geographic area of interest around the user; this is, for example, particularly useful in the immediate aftermath of a disaster when users are delocalized into tent camps, barracks, temporary shelters, each with different needs and problems.

Fig. 5 Issue creation/modification

Fig. 6 Filtering options

Fig. 7 Feed selection

- *Issue visualization* When the user selects a particular issue, it is visualized as depicted in Fig. 7, which highlights how the system visualizes possible changes in the status of the problem the issue refers to.

In the next section we discuss how to efficiently support such interaction environment from an implementation point of view.

5 Supporting the Issue-Based Interaction

On the system side, in order to implement the issue-based social network perspective, we decided to reverse the perspective directly into *Emepolis⁺* database design, which influences also the kind of interaction that can be carried on. In particular, we have chosen to use a graph database to model the social network underpinning *Emepolis⁺* on the server side, instead of a relational database.

Actually, there has been much interest, recently, in data store that does not use SQL exclusively, the so-called NoSQL movement (sometimes referred to as NOSQL—Not Only SQL), based on the assumption that a relational data model may not be the best solution in all situations. Besides new proposals, like Google's BigTable [10] and Facebook's Cassandra,[3] based on features from row-oriented and column-oriented

---

[3]http://cassandra.apache.org/.

Fig. 8 The *Emepolis⁺* data model

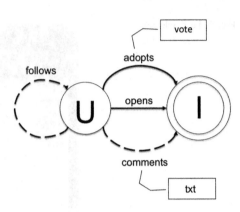

databases, also graph database models are regaining the relevance they had in the 80s and the 90s (we refer to [2] for an extensive survey on graph databases).

This renewed interest in graph database models is motivated by real-life applications where information about connectivity of its pieces is a salient feature, like in *complex networks* that can be found in social networks, information networks, technological networks and biological networks [19]. Classical relational query languages offer little help when dealing with the type of queries needed in these areas, e.g., in social networks, determining distance, neighborhoods, shortest paths, specific subgraphs, betweenness, size distribution of finite connected components [12]. Graph database models, on the contrary, provide special storage graph structures and efficient graph algorithms for realizing specific operations.

In particular, Neo4j[4] is the concrete graph database chosen for the implementation of prototypes of Emepolis and *Emepolis⁺*. In production for some years, it is used for research and industrial purposes, also thanks to its convenient license policy. Its query language Cypher is human-readable and far simpler than SQL if graph traversals are needed. Furthermore, it is easily integrable in a RESTful development environment, as the one used for *Emepolis⁺*client-side mobile application, based on PhoneGap,[5] a framework supporting multiplatform mobile application development.

Thanks to the features of graph databases, *Emepolis⁺* is simply modeled by two types of nodes, issue nodes and user nodes, and four relationships as depicted in Fig. 8 (plain arrows denotes the relationships defined by the original Emepolis project, while dashed arrows denotes the relationships added in *Emepolis⁺*). The user node attributes are user name, password, e-mail, and flag, while the issue node attributes are title, description, category, status, date, coordinates, and photo.

---

[4]http://neo4j.org/.

[5]http://phonegap.com/.

6 Conclusions and Open Questions

In this paper we discussed the main results of the Emepolis and *Emepolis*⁺ projects, aimed at developing a mobile social application able to support the social dynamics taking place in the aftermath of a disaster. At this stage of the work, we have released the Emepolis prototype (depicted in Figs. 3, 4, 5 and 6), which is being evaluated on the L'Aquila territory in cooperation with no profit and no-gov local organization involved in the community recovery, and we are implementing the *Emepolis*⁺ prototype. The main challenge we brought in the design and development of Emepolis and *Emepolis*⁺ is to support the response and recovery phases of the emergency management process, which lead to a spontaneous yet not erratic re-organization of the wounded community. In particular we discussed how a shift of perspective in the interaction, conceptual, logical and physical models adopted for the designed social network can more naturally and more efficiently support the dynamic bonding/de-bonding/re-bonding of transitional communities and organizations that emerge based on alliances around shared problems and/or objectives. In term of *Emepolis*⁺ concepts, this process translates into micro-worlds that arise around issues. It may be noticed that *Emepolis*⁺ can also act as an accelerator of the cohabitation re-definition process, discussed in Sect. 2, by adhering to a "glocal" paradigm.

As to our technical choices, the flexibility offered by graph db-models, their inherent capability of representing connectivity, their ability of keeping all the information about an entity in a single node along with its connections, their natural support to dynamic re-organization, along with their capability of defining data manipulation by means of graph transformations, make them a first choice when looking for a system able to reify the social dynamics typical of the post-disaster.

Actually, the balance between a stable framework of sense-making support and a flexible and adaptive system is not trivial and some open questions have to be solved in future studies. For example, one important problem is related to issue tagging (necessary for allowing users to filter/searching issues). Comfort [11] highlighted that *the vital but elusive characteristic of self-organization is its spontaneity. While influenced by the actions of other organizations or groups, it cannot be imposed by external regulation.* If a free folksonomy (i.e., a tagging system decided by the crowd [15]) might therefore appear as the right solution to the issue tagging problem, an uncontrolled folksonomy may lead to unfocused practices of *Emepolis*⁺ and/or prevent efficient searching mechanisms. On the other hand the adoption of a (dynamically evolving) taxonomy raises the problem of who —and with which criteria—should be responsible for it (presently, for the purposes of the on-going system evaluation, we borrowed possible issue types from the results of the EU-funded project Smart Cities[6]).

Actually, it remains open the role(s) that institutions can have in a system like *Emepolis*⁺, besides being normal users of the application. On the other hand the

---

[6]http://eu-smartcites.eu/.

importance of some kind of monitoring is underlined by Gordon [16], who proposes a view in which rescuers and organized aids not only "bring help" but also favor the active role of primary victims while maintaining a global vision on how the community is reacting and evolving. We believe that an issue-centered social network like *Emepolis*$^+$ can provide valuable support also under this perspective, by offering a sort of reification and "registry" of the dynamics of bonding/de-bonding/re-bonding of social connections.

As a final remark, it is worth observing that the fact that a social network can be a valuable support after a disaster is, on the other hand, already demonstrated by an interesting population-based cross-sectional study conducted in L'Aquila after the earthquake [18], in which authors proved that continual use of social network for at least two years produced a positive effect on mental health and improved the quality of life.

References

1. Alexander, D.: Principles of Emergency Planning and Management. Oxford University Press, New York (2002)
2. Angles, R., Gutierrez, C.: Survey of graph database models. J. ACM Comput. Surv. **40**, 1–39 (2008)
3. Barbini, F.M.: Organization in disaster: The failure of disaster-recovery plans in the aftermath of the AZF explosion. In: 24th EGOS Colloquium. Amsterdam (2008)
4. Barbini, F.M.: Organization in disaster: International cooperation and relief activities coordination during the indian ocean tsunami emergency. In: 25th EGOS Colloquium. Barcelona (2009)
5. Barbini, F.M., D'Atri, A., Tarantino, L., Za, S.: A new generation DMS for supporting social sensemaking. In: De Marco, M., Te-eni, D., Albano, V., Za, S. (eds) Information Systems: Crossroads for Organization, Management, Accounting and Engineering, pp. 105–11. Springer, Heiderlberg (2012)
6. Barbini, F.M., D'Atri, A., Tarantino, L., Za, S.: EagleVox: An innovative information systems to support social sensemaking in the aftermnath of large scale disaster. In: 27th EGOS Colloquium. Reassembling Organizations, Gothernburg (2011)
7. Benini, M., Gobbo, F.: Virtual communities as narrative processes. In: Maggiorini, D., Provetti, A., Ripamonti, L. (eds.) BOF'07—Between Ontologies and Folksonomies: Tools and Architectures for Managing and Retrieving Emerging Knowledge in Communities, CEUR-WS, vol. 312. http://ceur-ws.org/Vol-312/ (2007)
8. Careem, M.: Sahana: Overview of a disaster management system. In: International Conference on Information and Automation (ICIA), pp. 361–366. Colombo (2006)
9. Caianiello, P., Costantini, F., Gobbo, F., Leombruni, D., Tarantino, L.: The adoption of urban public space as a driving force for third places in the remediation of democracy. In: Proceedings of CHI'13 HCI3P workshop (2013)
10. Chang, F., Dean, J., Ghemawat, S., Hsieh, W.C., Wallach, D.A., Burrows, M., Chandra, T., Fikes, A., Gruber, R.E.: Bigtable: A distributed storage system for structured data. J. ACM Trans. Comput. Syst. **26**, 1–26 (2008)
11. Comfort, L.K.: Self-organization in complex systems. J. Public Adm. Res. Theory **4**, 393–410 (1994)
12. Dorogovtsev, S.N., Mendes, J.F.F.: Evolution of Networks From Biological Nets to the Internet and www. Oxford University Press, Oxford (2003)

13. European Environment Agency: Mapping the impacts of natural hazards and technological accidents in Europe—an overview of the last decade. EEA Technical report n. 13/2010, ISSN 1725-2237 (2010)
14. Fenoglio, M.T.: La Comunità nei Disastri: una Prospettiva Psicosociale. Rivista di Psicologia dell'Emergenza e dell'Assistenza Umanitaria 1, 6–23 (2006)
15. Gobbo, F.: Improving flickr discovery through wikipedias. In: Maggiorini, D., Provetti, A., Ripamonti, L. (eds.) BOF'07—Between Ontologies and Folksonomies: Tools and Architectures for Managing and Retrieving Emerging Knowledge in Communities, CEUR-WS, vol. 312. http://ceur-ws.org/Vol-312/ (2007)
16. Gordon, R.: Engineering Aspects of Disaster Recovery. Local Government Guide to Disaster Management. State Government Printing Office, Melbourne (1991)
17. Lanzara, G.F.: Ephemeral organizations in extreme environments: Emergency, strategy, Extinction. J. Manage. Stud. 20, 71–95 (1983)
18. Masedu, F., Mazza, M., Di Giovanni, C., Calvarese, A., Tiberti, S., Sconci, V., Valenti, M.: Facebook, Quality of Life, and Mental Health Outcomes in Post-Disaster Urban Environments: The L'Aquila Earthquake Experience. Frontiers in Publich Health, 2, art. 286 (2014)
19. Newman, M.E.J.: The structure and function of complex networks. J. SIAM Rev. 45, 167–256 (2003)
20. Okolloh, O.: Ushahidi, or testimony: Web 2.0 tools for crowdsourcing crisis information. Participatory Learn. Action Workshop 59, 65–70 (2009)
21. Risk EOS. http://www.riskeos.com/actus/pge/index.php?arbo=0
22. SED Spa per SGE/STM Abruzzo. www.6aprile.it
23. Sellnow, T.L., Seeger, M.W., Ulmer, R.R.: Chaos theory, informational needs, and natural disasters. J. Appl. Commun. Res. 30, 269–292 (2002)
24. Solé, A.: Createurs de Mondes. Nos Impossibles. Editions du Rocher, Monaco, Nos Possibles (2000)
25. Turoff, M.: The design of emergency response management information systems. J. Inf. Technol. Theory Appl. 5, 1–35 (2004)
26. Ushahidi. http://www.ushahidi.com
27. Van deWalle, B., Turoff, M., Hiltz, S.R. (eds.): Information Systems for Emergency Management. Advances in Management Information Systems, vol. 16. M.E Sharpe, Armonk (2010)
28. Wallance, A., De Balogh, F.: Decision support systems for disaster management. Public Adm. Rev. 45, 134–146 (1985)
29. Weick, K.E.: The collapse of sensemaking in organizations. Tha Mann Gulch Disaster. Adm. Sci. Q. 38, 628–652 (1993)
30. White, C.: A real time online delphi decision system, V 2.0: Crisis management support during extreme events. In: International Conference on Information Systems for Crisis Response and Management. Lisbon, Portugal (2010)

Digital Innovation in the Job Market: An Explorative Study on Cloud Working Platforms

Alessandro Ruggieri, Enrico Maria Mosconi, Stefano Poponi
and Cecilia Silvestri

Abstract The evolution of the web has produced a broad change in partnerships and collaboration worldwide due to the centrality of internet, a virtual place where actors from different countries can easily meet and exchange in-formation. This new agency model represents the basis for the development of a new entrepreneurial organization where companies can redefine their idea of business in order to make the web instrumental in the creation of a global social network of actors. This model of cooperation is now possible thank to the creation of the new cloud working platforms that have brought about a revolution in the job market. Main objective of the present work is therefore 1. to analyze and compare, on one hand, three main communities of crowdsourcing (Knowledge or Gig economy) in order to show such evolution, and on the other; 2. to analyze and compare the main platforms of cooperation at distance, in order to identify critical success factors.

Keywords Crowdsourcing · Cloud working · Social network

A. Ruggieri · E.M. Mosconi (✉) · S. Poponi · C. Silvestri
Department of Economics and Management (DEIm), Università degli Studi della Tuscia,
Via del Paradiso, 47, 01100 Viterbo, Italy
e-mail: enrico.mosconi@unitus.it

A. Ruggieri
e-mail: ruggieri@unitus.it

S. Poponi
e-mail: poponi@unitus.it

C. Silvestri
e-mail: c.silvestri@unitus.it

© Springer International Publishing Switzerland 2016
T. Torre et al. (eds.), *Empowering Organizations*, Lecture Notes in Information
Systems and Organisation 11, DOI 10.1007/978-3-319-23784-8_21

1 Introduction

The advent of the digital era 2.0 has introduced many new professional profiles offering the young new job opportunities as for freelancers and company employees (i.e. Community Manager, Search engine optimizer and Web Analyst) [1–3].

The opportunity to be freelancers can be enhanced by the growth of online collaboration portals that are becoming the most peculiar feature of the new economy. Within this frame the above mentioned professional profiles are requested [4, 5].

The essence of the new virtual economy highlights that the evolution of the present social and economical structure is related not only to technology, in the strict sense, but to the way it is being used today [6, 7].

This form of collaborative activity is named to as crowdsourcing and represents a new model of open enterprise, a new way of doing business based on the collaboration with external resources recruited on-line with the help of global communication practices and tools [8–13]. The first definition is ascribable to Howe [14] who defines crowdsourcing as "the act of taking a job traditionally performed by a designated agent (usually an employee) and outsourcing it to an undefined, generally large group of people in the form of an open call" [2].

Furthermore, Brabham [15] points out at its peculiarities and defines it as an "online, distributed problem solving and production model" and leverages online networks to: (1) gather information; (2) distribute large-scale tasks that are easier for humans rather than machines to process (e.g. analyzing photos); or (3) solicit ideas or solutions to existing problems as a challenge that can also be vetted by peers."

In crowdsourcing the companies can externalize their activities to exponentially high number of potential partners by the means of "open calls" [16, 17]. The resulting intellectual capital is formed by the meeting of the actors' skills working together in order to finalize a common project [8, 10, 18, 19].

Presently, crowdsourcing is used as an umbrella term and refers to a form of collaborative work and sharing of knowledge and ideas via web platforms. The ad hoc development of new digital communities represent a new opportunity for those companies willing to develop their projects, where the best ideas proposed, via open calls, become projects, for the implementation of the company business [20, 21].

The most recent progress of the market and of the career on on-line platforms and websites have lead to consider cloud working as a new trend representing an outstanding opportunity to find, among the web collaborators the perfect profile in a due time, reaching professionals with the most needed skills and knowledge, on-demand, avoiding endless research and unsatisfying results.

By the end of 2014 at least 30 workers, out of a hundred, will be working online while 9 companies out of ten will use these on-line platforms to develop and finalize their projects. Evidence of this is offered by the main operators of the field (Odesk) that have investigated the outburst of distance working: 56 % of the new generation of workers has, in fact, expressed a preference for this accepted way of working at distance, the 87 % is willing to work without hour restrictions.

It is a key question then to understand "how" and "why" the most important communities of crowdsourcing are influencing, with their cloud working practices, recruitment strategies to employ the most qualified profiles.

The increasing interest in the literature concerning the subject is not yet exhaustive about managerial strategic aspects of the new phenomenon [22–24]. It is a fact though that the new dynamics of the job market reveal their relevance and centrality in the numberless experiences, on a global scale, relating to the creation of collaborative platforms offering services in the job market, the most successful of which are obviously located in the United States.

In Europe this new phenomenon encounters many difficulties not only because of the different structure of the job market, but also because this recruitment practice is still only intended to work as a simple notice board. It seems necessary then a change of direction, first creating focused studies (literature), so clearly pinpoint the good practices already adopted, and highlight the potentiality and the probability of success prior to the planning of new useful models, so to help professionals to meet the companies needs in cloudworking. According to this perspective, then, the comparison between the most influential platforms represents then a new opportunity.

2 Methodology

Main aim of the present paper describes and discuss the most recent evolutions of crowdsourcing as a management tool for sharing knowledge through the use of dedicated platforms.

Our investigation focuses on the strategic areas of the placement: the publication of profiles, application procedures and payments.

It adopts a qualitative research method approach based on the case study protocol defined by Yin [25].

It represents an exploratory study based on the documentary analysis [26, 27]. In particular, it is aimed at a critical reconnaissance survey of the potentialities offered by cloud working and by the new web community of professionals.

In the final part of the present work, a multiple comparison between the main platforms offering this service is presented.

The platforms considered been selected according to parameters concerning the number of users and sales volume, that in the context of gig economy offer companies and professionals advanced services for a possible collaboration in real time at larger scale. Previous studies [28, 29] and personal experiences complete our survey.

The output of the survey represent a starting point, and possibly the guidelines, for further investigations on crowd working, for political leaders and for all the users of the web that will use electronic resources.

3 Analysis of the Main Types of Crowdsourcing

The main categories of crowdsourcing are determined according to problem solving approaches, classified in the literature as "discovery and management of knowledge".

The premise of this category is that the heritage of knowledge necessary to users (organization or enterprise) exists but is not organized according to specific needs. So an efficient research within an online, well-organized community, can transform it into an available resource. The crowd environment stimulates, by consequence, the on line community to discover new ideas necessary to the companies to implement their projects and business activity.

The difference between this type of crowdsourcing and the so called "common-based peer production", gathering together denominators of specific contents (the most famous example is Wikipedia), is that in this type of platforms information is filtered upstream by the organization managing the platform.

A good example is represented by the master plan Peer-to-Patent Community Patent Review [30] realized by the American USPTO and the New York Faculty of Law. Its goal was to implement the visibility of the state of the art report on knowledge "prior art", instrumental in the recognition of the originality of the invention. Basically, the patents of the organizations involved in the online collaboration were posted online along with other users conducting pre-patent activities to acknowledge the existence of similar inventions in industrial sectors of interest.

Broadcast search is a type of crowdsourcing where information shared by the online community is oriented towards specific problem solving activity. The supply and demand of specific profiles are conducted within the online community where the enterprises require services, as for example the development of the design of new products related to the activity of discovery, such as new chemical formulas. The peculiarity of this type of on-line working environment is represented by the search of knowledge instrumental in solving specific problems. One pitfall here can be represented by the complex nature of a problem that makes the solving problematic.

The Peer-Vetted Creative Production type allows to share information in a working environment where the idea, the solution or the innovative product are popularized among a large audience of users operating simultaneously. Accordingly, the best solution is usually the most widely appreciated. By consequence, a validation process positively informs the new market strategies also taking into account the users' need.

One huge problem for the companies is represented by the management of the increasing overall volume of data. The growth of the number of crowd platforms, identified as Distributed Human Intelligence Tasking type, offers a paid service for the management of small volumes of data. The research helps the companies in the gathering and selection of knowledge so to split the problem in less complex units resulting in more manageable information on the part of the crowd. The most

Table 1 Main types of crowdsourcing (*Soruce* Our elaboration)

Type	Description	Reference
Knowledge discovery and management	Organization of tasks in crowd, through gathering of information in common formats and baskets	Peer-to-Patent—peertopatent.org
		SeeClickFix—seeclickfix.com
		Mobile: Ushahidi (alert of international crisis)
		Mobile: (alert) Peer water exchange peerwater.org
		Mobile: mCollect (alert on prices)
Broadcast search	Organization of tasks in crowd: topic problems	InnoCentive—innocentive.com
		Goldcorp challenge
Peer-vetted creative production	Organization of tasks in crowd: creation and selection of information	Threadless—threadless.com
		Doritos crash the super bowl contest
		crashthesuperbowl.com
		Next stop design—nextstopdesign.com
Distributed human intelligence tasking	Organization of tasks in crowd: analysis large volumes of data	Amazon mechanical turk—mturk.com
		Subvert and profit—subvertandprofit.com
		Mobile: text eagle (microtasks)

widely known example is offered here by Amazon Mechanical Turk and its mobile version, Text Eagle, where softwares are tested, browsers are tagged, and simulation tests for web activities are presented (for online videogames etc.) (Table 1).

3.1 Cloud Working

Communities of cloud working enable the enterprises to employ the most qualified profiles according to their own needs and requirements, and to establish a collaboration without meeting physically and avoiding a long-term commitment.

The basic operating principle of cloud working comes from the e-commerce with the difference that while in the e-commerce users can shop on line, cloud working users can, instead, offer and exchange knowledge and ideas. All that results in a new flexible form of job on demand (Table 2).

Table 2 Comparison between E-commerce and cloud working (*Source* Our elaboration)

	Step 1	Step 2	Step 3
E-Commerce	Search	Select	Pay
Cloud working	Employ	Check	Pay

Table 3 Main crowdsourcing platforms

Platform	Description
Odesk Inc.	American Limited liability company established in 2005, with legal residence in Redwood City, California
Elance Inc.	American Limited liability company established in 1998, with legal seat in Montain View, California. Initially developed as a technology for supporting virtual work, in 2006 sold its enterprise software division and has developed instead its current web-based platform online
Freelancer Ltd.	Australian Limited company established in 2009. It has acquired several online job companies over the years (GetAFreelancer in 2009, EuFreelance in 2009, Freemarket in 2010, LimeExchange in 2010, Freelancer.de in 2011, Scriptlance in 2012, vWorker inl 2012, Zlecenia.przez.net in 2014 e Warrior forum in 2014) becoming the largest crowdsourcing and outsourcing online company

The largest platform in Europe is Twago (Team Work Across Global Offices) established in Germany in 2009 (www.Twago.com). Notwithstanding the fact that it is the largest platform of European crowdsourcing, it has not so far obtained the expected results that would enable it to compete with the other communities in this field.

The cloud working platforms we are considering in the present discussion are summarized in Table 3. In particular, Odesk and Elance will be analyzed separately, ignoring their recent merger, because they maintain separate web domains.

Data available on web platforms show the number of users and of published projects in 2013. While Elance also shows the total amount of projects published since the very start of the company, Freelance only shows the number of projects (competitions included) published in the portal.

All data are reproduced and compared in Table 4.

Data show that the largest platform, Freelancer, although established later than its two main competitors, has acquired several companies, as mentioned above, that have contributed to the enlargement of the present platform.

Table 4 Comparison between the dimension of Odesk, Elance and Freelancers (*Source* Our elaboration)

	Odesk	Elance	Freelancer
Nr. of freelancers	5 millions	3 millions	10.9 millions
Nr. of clients	1 million	1.8 millions	
Nr. of published projects	1.3 millions in 2013	1,214 millions in 2013	5 millions in total[a]
		4 millions in total	

[a]Data referred to Freelancer Ltd. result from the total of acquired platforms

Table 5 Strategies of freelancers and companies (*Source* Our elaboration)

Freelancers	Companies
Publish profile Freelancers register and publish their profiles. In it they describe their specific knowledge, their work experience and establish their own work hours and wage. The web site also proposes some tests proving the qualification of applicants that also less experienced freelancers can show their technical skills to the companies offering the post	**Publish a project** Companies publish their offers (development of a software, writing of an article, design of a logo, etc....) indicating the task, the required skills, workhours and maximum wage
Candidacy in cloud working The platform offers the freelancers the possibility to search among many proposals and opt for the most convenient offer according to their own skills. Freelancers can also be selected and employed directly by the clients	**Employ a freelancer** Several professionals apply and the company, after a careful selection of profiles, decides for a web interview
Payment The employee is paid when the work is done	**Monitoring Activity** An employee monitoring software is used to check the progress of the activity This monitoring software proves with screenshots if the work is being done
	Pay the Freelancer Payment is done at the time of delivery Employers can also give their feedback about the work and the professional activity

These platforms have a social character and are structured as communities where users, professionals or companies, register and collaborate. The main actions carried out by freelancers and companies are synthesized in Table 5.

Internal reports show that the most required knowledge in this market refer to business planning (40 %), 1. for example the development of apps for smartphones and tablets, for the web and of special software for the companies; 2. Design and multimedia (44 %); 3. Marketing and e-commerce and technical support for the administration (70 %); 4. Writing and translation (66 %). Other required profiles are: legal and financial consultants and engineers.

Another phenomenon to put into evidence is that 90 % of the cost for the employment of freelancers is increased from 4 categories, with specific informatic skills, to the present 35 categories. These data bears testimony to the transdisciplinary trend of the last 5 years, also involving fields traditionally not directly related to the ICT.

It is worth noticing that feedback represents a key element in the building of the reputation of a freelancer. In so far that, it has a huge impact on his/her evaluation and on the employer. In order to increase the level of communication of the quality of the activities Freelancer.com presents a dedicated section to launch contests with

Table 6 Comparison between Odesk, Elance and Freelancer commissions (*Source* Our elaboration)

Odesk	Elance	Freelancer		
10 %	8.75 %	Concession	Employers (%)	Freelancers (%)
		Free	3	10
		Intro	3	10
		Basic	3	10
		Plus	3	10
		Standard	0	5
		Premium	0	3

a monetary prize, where candidates make proposals and present their projects to the companies.

A commission is charged by Odesk and Elance that receive a royalty payment at fixed rate, when the project is done, whilst. Freelancer charges separately the employer and the employee (Table 6).

3.2 Volumes of Costs

The high volume of costs related to collaboration on platforms is constantly increasing. In particular, a high volume of costs has been increasing from 2009.

The volume of costs of Odesk has increased up to 9 times the original value in 2009 ("The rise of online work", Odesk, 2013) The costs for Elance have raised from $80 milions to $140 milions in 2011 and gone up to $290 milions in 2013 (elance.com). Freelancers had 500 projects published in November 2009 and 5 milions in 2013. This generated a total cost of 15 billion dollars (freelancer.com) though all freelancers data result from the total of all acquired platforms. It is difficult therefore to estimate the real volume of projects published on the web. The volume of total costs since the start of the activity are included and compared in Table 7.

Within a market that only in 2012 generated a volume of costs of one billion dollars, for which the analysts of Staffing Industry estimate a volume of costs of 5 billion dollars in 2018 [31–34], data show that the three platforms together have contributed with 3.5 billions dollars. Freelancer publishes its yearly results where the EBITDA (Earnings before interest, taxes, depreciation and amortization) is of $1.2 millions in 2013 and of $0.8 milions in 2012. The final growth has then been of 53 % between 2012 and 2013 [35].

Table 7 Comparison of amount of costs of Odesk, Elance e Freelancer (*Source* Our elaboration)

	Odesk	Elance	Freelancer
Total volume of costs	$1+ billions	$1+ billion	$1.5 billions

4 Discussion and Conclusions

Clowdworking offers the employers an opportunity to externalize their activities via web and represents for the employees the chance to manage their working life.

In the US this phenomenon is rapidly growing, on the contrary, in Europe the spreading of this model of cloud working is still delayed by the difficult process of digitalization around the continent, as demonstrated by the volume of investments. Il ritardo è dovuto alla scarsa.

The delay is due to the poor quality of the broadband connection that has revealed a different trend according to the strategies adopted by the different European countries. However, the uneven contribution of each single depends mostly on the existence of a severe and peristent discrepancy in the adoption of digital divide in the member nations [36]. Thank to the adoption of Digital Agenda in Europe, the use of internet has increased of 11 %, due to the digital development in countries with a low number of users, such as Greece, Romania, Ireland, Portugal, Czech Republic and Croatia. The most virtuous among the European countries, such as the Netherlands, Denmark, Sweden and Luxemburg, have now reached the share of 90 % in the use of the web. Besides, the share of the European population of non-users, about 20 %, is still too high. The broadband and high speed internet was in fact available for the 62 % of European users in 2013, more than double the share of 2010, notwithstanding the persistent difficulties in the rural areas of the continent [37].

Due to the recent appearance of web platforms, their present dimensions suggest that the system can easily attract, year after year, a considerable number of users and the propensity of the new generations towards this new employing model shows that in the next future all industrialized countries will benefit of the digital progress introduced.

This study contributes to the literature in two ways. On one hand, it confirms and validates the phenomenon of crowdsourcing and the present change in recruitment strategies of qualified profiles; on the other, it helps identifying the critical success factors of these platforms.

Among the key elements for the development and the affirmation of communities of cloud working we find: motivation, the element that enables a worldwide contact with users; a great investment of resources and time, necessary to support the growth of the community, and great investments on reputation, that is to encourage ethical behaviour instilling a sense of trust in the users.

As for this latest question, the perception users have of the lack of ethical behavior in ongoing business affairs, can seriously damage both the image and the work of the community, causing a possible failure of the project. This is why feedback is necessary for the improvement and success of the network.

The level of performance of a platform is also influenced by the interaction between the actors that offers the employees the chance to get a wider audience and, possibly, a better wage and, on the other, to improve their motivation. In this sense, the variables emerging concern mainly the validation process, on the part of the companies, of skills, past experience and the level of satisfaction or feedback of the profile.

Transparency and credibility are central and instrumental in building an actor's reputation with a consequent increase of validation and wage.

Finally, cloud working, and in general terms the (Knowldege) Gig economy, represents a rapidly growing phenomenon [35, 38], an occurrence that could replace, in the short time, the traditional job market, with the only exception of those activities requiring manual work.

Future research could focus on a benchmarking study in European countries to identify the characteristics and the degree of satisfaction of the advisor to better understand social changes and future developments.

References

1. Xhaet, G.: Le nuove professioni del Web, Hoepli editore (2012)
2. Birdsall, M.: Carsharing in a sharing economy. ITE J. (Inst. Transp. Eng.) **8**, 37–40 (2014)
3. Patel, A., Nordin, R., Al-Haiqi, A: Beyond ubiquitous computing: The Malaysian HoneyBee project for innovative digital economy. Comput. Stand. Interf. **36**, 844–854 (2014)
4. Davies, A., Fidler, D., Gorbis, M.: Report Future Work Skills 2020. Institute for the Future for University of Phoenix Research Institute (2011)
5. Simoni, M., de Ferra, S.: Crescita Digitale. Come Internet crea lavoro, come potrebbe crearne di più. Italia Futura (2012)
6. Freeman, J.: Driving Australia's digital future?: Online engagement and the national digital economy strategy. Telecommun. J. Aust. **62**, 1–79 (2012)
7. Georgieva, L., Zia, I.: Formalisation and verification of knowledge management in digital economy and organisations. Stud. Comput. Intell. **462**, 53–66 (2013)
8. Peng, X., Ali Babar, M., Ebert, C.: Collaborative software development platforms for crowdsourcing. IEEE Softw. **31**, 30–31 (2014)
9. Amtzis, R.: Crowdsourcing from the ground up: how a new generation of Nepali nonprofits uses social media to successfully promote its initiatives. J. Creat. Commun. **9**, 127–146 (2014)
10. Perera, I., Perera, P.A.: Developments and leanings of crowdsourcing industry: implications of China and India. Ind. Commer. Train. **46**, 92–99 (2014)
11. McAfee, A.: Enterprise 2.0: new collaborative tools for you organization's toughest challenges. McGraw-Hill, Boston (2009)
12. Alberghini, E., Cricelli, L., Grimaldi, M.: KM versus enterprise 2.0: A framework to tame the clash. Int. J. Inf. Technol. Manage. **12**, 320–336 (2013)
13. Prunesti A.: Enterprise 2.0: Modelli organizzativi e gestione dei social media per l'innovazione in azienda. Franco Angeli Editore (2010)
14. Howe, J.: The Rise of Crowdsourcing, Wired. 14 (2006)
15. Brabham, D.C.: Crowdsourcing. MIT Press, Cambridge (2013)
16. Trottier, D.: Crowdsourcing CCTV surveillance on the Internet. Inf. Commun. Soc. **17**, 609–626 (2014)
17. Littmann, M., Suomela, T.: Crowdsourcing, the great meteor storm of 1833, and the founding of meteor science. Endeavour (2014)
18. Petrič, G., Petrovčič, A.: Individual and collective empowerment in online communities: the mediating role of communicative interaction in web forums. Inf. Soc. **30**, 184–199 (2014)
19. Chung, C.J., Barnett, G.A., Park, H.W.: Inferring international dotcom Web communities by link and content analysis. Qual. Quant. **48**, 1117–1133 (2014)

20. Sørensen, I.E.: Crowdsourcing and outsourcing: The impact of online funding and distribution on the documentary film industry in the UK. Media Cult. Soc. **34**, 726–743 (2012)
21. Simula, H., Ahola, T.: A network perspective on idea and innovation crowdsourcing in industrial firms. Ind. Mark. Manage. **43**, 400–408 (2014)
22. Aguinis, H., Lawal, S.O.: eLancing: a review and research agenda for bridging the science–practice gap. Hum. Resour. Manage. Rev. **23**, 6–17 (2013)
23. Nevo, D., Kotlarsky, J.: Primary vendor capabilities in a mediated outsourcing model: can IT service providers leverage crowdsourcing? Decis. Support Syst. **65**, 17–27 (2014)
24. Simula, H., Ahola, T.: A network perspective on idea and innovation crowdsourcing in industrial firms. Ind. Mark. Manage. **43**, 400–408 (2014)
25. Yin, R.K.: Case Study Research: Design and Methods. Sage Publishing, CA (1994)
26. Silverman, D.: Qualitative Research. Sage, London (2011)
27. Silverman, D.: Qualitative Research: Theory. Sage Publications Ltd, Method and Practice (2008)
28. Mosconi, E.M., Silvestri, C., Poponi, S., Braccini, A.M.: Public policy innovation in distance and on-line learning: reflections on the Italian case. In: Spagnoletti, P. (ed.) Organizational Change and Information Systems—Working and Living Together in new ways, pp. 381–389. Springer, Berlin (2013)
29. Ruggieri, A., Mosconi, E.M., Braccini, A.M., Poponi, S.: Strategies and policies for avoid digital divide: the Italian case in the European landscape. In: itAIS 2013, X Conference of the Italian Chapter of AIS. Empowering society through digital innovations (2013)
30. Beth, S.N.: Peer to patent: collective intelligence, open review, and patent reform. Harvard J. Law Technol. **20**, 123–161 (2006)
31. oDesk: The rise of online work. oDesk Corp (2013). http://www.Odesk.com
32. oDesk: The Online work revolution and how businesses are reaping the rewards. oDesk Corp (2014). http://www.Odesk.com
33. Elence: Global online employment report, Elance (2014). https://www.elance.com/q/online-employment-report
34. Freelancer: 2013 Annual report freelancer limited. Freelancer (2014). https://cdn2.f-cdn.com/investor/documents/20140227_FLN-FY13_Annual_Report.pdf?v=670d9331bd15f046395c7d3302c5b4de&m=2
35. Rodgers, K.: Using the gig economy to surmount the skills shortage. CIM Magazine-Canadian Institute of Mining Metallurg (2011)
36. Kyriakidou, V., Michalakelis, C., Sphicopoulos, T.: Digital divide gap convergence in Europe. Technol. Soc. **33**, 265–270 (2011)
37. European Commission Digital Agenda Scoreboard. 1–9 (2014)
38. Friedman, G.: Workers without employers: shadow corporations and the rise of the gig economy. Rev. Keynes. Econ. **2**, 171–188 (2014)

Mt.Gox Is Dead, Long Live Bitcoin!

Analysis of the Rise and Fall of a Leading Virtual Currency Exchange Platform

Francesco Bolici and Sara Della Rosa

Abstract In the last decade the intensity and frequency of business and social interactions mediated by digital channels have dramatically increased. Participating in virtual communities, communicating via internet, buying product and services through the web is part of our daily behavior. It is not a surprise the tremendous expansion that virtual currencies are experiencing. Virtual currency exchange platforms (VCEP), specialized in trading virtual currency are becoming increasingly popular. The combination of these two concepts calls for a deeper understanding of their value and models both from an organizational and an information system perspective. We investigate Mt.Gox, one of the most popular VCEP, trading till 70 % of Bitcoin transactions in 2013, and suddenly collapsing as consequence of managerial choices and cyber-attacks. We explore this case study in order to understand the value and the risks associated to the system and the consequences of the breakdown of one of the most important player.

Keywords Virtual currency · E-currency · Bitcoin · Mt.gox · Exchange platform · Exchange market · Hacker · Cyber attack

1 Introduction

In the last decade the intensity and frequency of business and social interactions mediated by digital channels have dramatically increased. Participating in virtual communities, communicating via internet, buying products and services through the web is part of our daily behavior.

F. Bolici (✉) · S.D. Rosa
OrgLab, Department of Economics and Law, UniClam, Cassino, Italy
e-mail: f.bolici@unicas.it

S.D. Rosa
e-mail: s.dellarosa@unicas.it

© Springer International Publishing Switzerland 2016
T. Torre et al. (eds.), *Empowering Organizations*, Lecture Notes in Information Systems and Organisation 11, DOI 10.1007/978-3-319-23784-8_22

The capillarity and diffusion of web services play a crucial role in enabling digital interactions. As a proxy of the growing importance of web activities, we can mention that the number of the existing web pages more than doubled every year from 1996 till 2000, and since then it continues to have an annual increase between 20 and 50 % [1]. At the same time the number of internet users worldwide has constantly increased since 2000, reaching more than 45 % of the world population.[1] Hilbert and López estimated that "in 2007, humankind was able to store 2.9×10^{20} optimally compressed bytes, communicate almost 2×10^{21} bytes, and carry out 6.4×10^{18} instructions per second on general-purpose computers" [2] (p. 60). Considering that, according to Moore law, the capacity storage has a tendency to double every 12/18 months, after 7 years those values will be greatly exceeded. This technological evolution is both the result of a growing demand for more developed services and the enabler of innovative business models and social behaviors.

The *information age* [3, 4] is firmly based on digital interactions, through which overcome the limitations of space and time. Distributed teams, rarely relying on face to face meeting, are increasingly common [5, 6]; externalizing database storage activities, as well as information services, is an established practice [7]; managing customer relationships is progressively shifting on online social networks and digital tools [8]. The large variety of domains in which digital interactions are becoming capillary and crucial also explains the development of virtual currencies as a tool for supporting online trading.

Virtual currency is a form of digital money, and in the last years it is experiencing a significant boost in its diffusion: the weighted value of traded virtual currency has exponentially risen since 2010 to nowadays (see paragraph 2.1). The importance of the topic is clearly proved by the number of financial institutions that in recent years started to analyze the phenomenon. The European Central Bank defined virtual currency as "a type of unregulated, digital money, which is issued and usually controlled by its developers, and used and accepted among the members of a specific virtual community" [9] (p. 5). The European Bank Authority refined its explanation as "a digital representation of value that is neither issued by a central bank or a public authority, nor necessarily attached to a fiat currency, but is accepted by natural or legal persons as a means of payment and can be transferred, stored or traded electronically" [10] (p. 46). According to US Department of Treasury's broader definition, a virtual currency is "a medium of exchange that operates like a currency in some environments, but does not have all the attributes of real currency" [11] (p. 1). The use of virtual currency has become so pervasive that major financial institutions as FED and ECB have raised their attention on the phenomenon trying to identify its characteristics, limits, and risks [9]. Contextually, VCEP, specialized in trading virtual currency, have been developed and released to the market (out of the top 20 VCEP, 4 become operational in 2014 and 10

---

[1]World Bank data retrieved in 2014 at http://data.worldbank.org/indicator/IT.NET.USER.P2.

in 2013[2]). The combination of these two innovative concepts (virtual currency and virtual platforms) calls for a deeper understanding of their value and models both from an organizational and an information system perspective.

We investigate Mt.Gox, a virtual currency exchange platform rising as the dominant exchange platform, trading till 70 % of Bitcoin transactions in 2013, and suddenly falling as consequence of managerial choices and cyber-attacks. Our research aim is to analyze the main factors that lead to the rise and the collapse of Mt.Gox and then to understand the consequences of its break down on the whole virtual currency system.

2 Data and Method

In this section we describe our data collection and analysis approach. Our goal was to investigate the reasons and the consequences of the failure of the main VCEP: Mt.Gox. We describe in turn the setting of our study, considering both the virtual currency and VCEP aspects, the data collected through the case study, and our approach to data analysis. We adopt a case study approach because it represents a good choice to investigate a contemporary phenomenon of business life [12, 13] and it facilitates the exploration of the unexpected while developing conceptual and theoretical contributions [14].

2.1 Setting: Virtual Currency—Bitcoin

While money can support a virtually unlimited number of purposes, its use can be defined according to three main functions, since it can be: a trade facilitator (*medium of exchange*); a measure of value (*unit of account*); and a saving mean (*store of value*) [9]. In any case, money have historically proved to be able to evolve and adapt to new environments and interactions; thus the emergence of an innovative form of money, the virtual currency, can be considered a first answer to the digital world in which more and more transactions are traded.

Even if not all the attributes are in common, virtual currency shares some risks types with the traditional currencies (synthetized in Table 1 below).

Besides the previous list of risks associated with the two kind of currency, virtual currency presents some peculiar risks depending by its own characteristics:

NEWNESS—The first difference is that virtual currency is a new concept (and tool). This means that people and organizations cannot rely on their past experiences in order to use it: while in the last 60 years we never heard of any (or few)

---

[2]See Table 4 for a more detailed VCEP-dataset.

Table 1 Risks types associated with the traditional currencies [17–19]

Market risk	The risk arising from adverse movements in market prices [15]
Credit risk	A borrower default on debts by failing to make required payments [16]
Liquidity risk	Liquidity is associated with the flows among central bank, commercial banks, and market. The liquidity risk refers to the inability of a financial agent to complete these flows [17]
Operational risk	The risk of a change in value caused by the fact that actual losses, incurred for inadequate or failed internal processes, people, and systems, or from external events (including legal risk), differ from the expected losses [16]
Technological risk	Can be an operational risk, but can also be considered as an independent factor when it affects not only one organization, but all the actors using a specific technological solution
Systemic risk	Risk of collapse of an entire financial system or entire market [18]

problem in using or trading Euro or US Dollar, how many of us daily use a Bitcoin or any other form of virtual currency to buy the bread or renting a cloud service?

Being a new tool, it requires some learning attitude in order to understand how it works and how it can be used. Moreover, being in its early life stage, its diffusion is relatively limited, as well as the number of actors/organizations that currently accept it as a mean of payment.

TRUST—The diffusion of a new form of payment and value storage requires a huge amount of trust because virtual currencies are not guaranteed by any institution. There is not government or central bank assuring that the currency will be valid in future or that it must be accepted in every economic transaction. Thus, the virtual currency owner assumes herself the risk that tomorrow the virtual currency will simply disappear or that nobody will accept her digital money.

Besides the trust towards the artifact (currency), the actors should also trust the broker (VCEP) that trades her real money for virtual ones; VCEP that is not recognized by any institution and thus has not any obligation to conforming to any mandatory standard.

ANONIMITY—Most of the virtual currency are designed in order to guarantee (or at least increase) the anonymity during the transactions. While this is often seen by virtual communities as an answer to the control of governments over internet (e.g. As in the case of controlling global internet traffic stated by The Washington Post and attributed to NSA leaker Edward Snowden), anonymity also creates a system in which criminal use of virtual currency is more than just a theoretical potentiality (e.g. As in the case of Feds that were ready to sell Bitcoin seized from the Silk Road as reported in Forbes) [20].

Thus, customers are exposed to higher risks respect to those involved in real money that they compensate with other advantages, like higher level of anonymity and lower costs of transaction [21].

Since it has been launched in 2009 by Satoshi Nakamoto [22] (probably a pseudonym to hide the identity of a group of developers), Bitcoin has been the leader of the e-currency market. Assuring an adequate security level and user confidence has been one of the most problematic issues for the diffusion of Bitcoin.

Table 2 *Source* https://coinmarketcap.com/ (12 pm July 21st, 2014 to 12 pm July 22nd 2014)

Virtual currency	Volume of transactions ($)	Market share (%)
Bitcoin	10.167.800.00	71.8
Litecoin	1.216.550.00	8.6
Dogecoin	231.297.00	1.6
BitcoinDark	228.665.00	1.6
Monero	228.089.00	1.6
OTHER 95 v.c.	2.080.773.00	14.8

For example, some researches focused on the "double spending" problem [23, 24]. Double spending refers to the problem of spending money more than once that has been solved by Bitcoin by verifying each transaction added to the block chain in order to ensure that the input for the transaction had not been spent already. The authors mentioned before focus on the possibility for attackers to successfully double spend Bitcoin in the case of fast transactions, explaining another risk in the Bitcoin system. In 2011, Reid and Harrigan [25] using a clustering algorithm obtained a condensed user graph, and used it to describe the flow of stolen money. Despite the problems related to the security, Bitcoin has been able to take a substantial market share. Nowadays Bitcoin market share is over 71 % (see Table 2).

Being the absolute market leader, Bitcoin can be considered a reliable example to describe virtual currencies [26]. Bitcoin is a decentralized (no third parties are involved in the process of creation, exchange, and supervision of any transaction) private digital currency traded online via a peer-to-peer network. It is based on a Proof-of-work, a principle to artificially impose transaction costs in the absence of a payment system. To prevent double spending there is a consensus on a temporal ordering of transactions. This way, the current owner of a Bitcoin can always be determined. This temporal order is established by what is called a block chain.

Bitcoin, as most of the virtual currencies, showed an extreme volatility but also an astonishing rise in its exchange price in the long term: in 2010 its value was USD 0,0041 while in July 2014 its price was over USD 610 (the highest value ever reached was USD 1124.76 on 29 November 2013).[3]

Considering the ECB [9] classification of virtual currencies schemes on the base of their interactions with traditional money and economies, Bitcoin belongs to the type 3 "virtual currency schemes with bidirectional flow" (Fig. 1).

In order to trade in Bitcoins, a user can buy and sell the virtual currency, exchanging traditional currencies (USD, Euro, etc.), through a virtual currency exchange platform. The VCEP that was mainly used to trade Bitcoin was Mt.Gox,[4]

---

[3]Source: http://www.coindesk.com/ and http://bitcoincharts.com.

[4]As also recognized by ECB (2012, p. 22): "Mt.Gox is the most widely used currency exchange platform and allows users to trade US dollars for Bitcoins and vice versa."

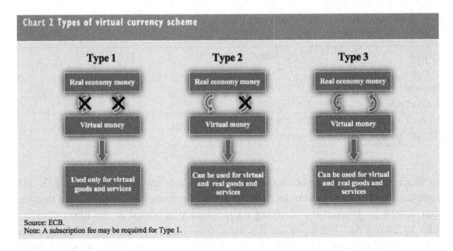

Fig. 1 *Source* ECB (2012, p. 16) Types of virtual currencies schemes

the unchallenged market leader till few months ago, when it was shut down, leading to a loss of $ 450 Million [27, 28].

2.2 Setting: Virtual Currency Exchange Platform

VCEP trade traditional money for virtual currency and vice versa. VCEP are similar to stock exchanges (even if focused only on the currency trade), but without any involvement of financial institutions, including central banks, or governments. This implies that typical financial regulation and supervision are not applicable. Virtual currency is traded on online exchange platforms based on open source communities and regulated by their private developers. Members of these platforms trade with other traders on the exchange. They usually charge a commission for all trades operated through the exchange. VCEP have a function and a value linked to virtual currency with bidirectional flow (as Bitcoin and the large majority of other virtual currencies). Considering their activity, VCEP are mainly brokers, acting in a network value model [29]. Thus, the number of the connected nodes (actors) and the quality of the communication and transaction channels are crucial to deliver value to the market. Higher are both the number of actors trading through a certain VCEP and the quality and the security of the transaction channels, higher will be the value of that specific VCEP (taking advantage of network externalities and trust and reliability perception). In Sect. 2.1 we identified some of the risks connected to virtual currencies, in the following case study we explore how some of those potential risks materialized into reality leading in February 2014 to the collapse of Mt.Gox, the main VCEP platform in the market.

3 Case Study—Mt.Gox: The (Former) Leader in Virtual Currency Trades

In April 2013 Mt.Gox was handling 70 % of the world's Bitcoin trades. In April 2014 Mt.Gox was handling 0 % of the world's Bitcoin trades. An analogy in the traditional financial market would be as New York Stock Exchange for virtual currency suddenly collapses and shut its activities down: unimaginable for most, inevitable (and with unclear consequences) for others.

Mt.Gox was the largest Bitcoin exchange platform in the market, based in Tokyo (Japan). The developer Jed McCaleb launched it in July 2010,[5] and less than 8 months later sold it to facilitate a larger expansion of the platform. The platform quickly becomes the VCEP market leader, trading the large majority of Bitcoin exchanges.

However, during its history several problems emerged: already in June 2011 Mt. Gox experienced a security breach when an hacker was able to steal credentials and money, even triggering the drop of the nominal price of Bitcoin [30–33]; in October 2011 a weakness into the protocol was exposed, leading to the loss of Bitcoins; in February 2013 some funds were lost (and then retrieved 3 months later) during the transaction involving a mobile and online payment network; in March 2013 a technical problem (*blockchain temporary fork*) forced to temporary freeze the deposits and dipped Bitcoin prices of 20 % for a short period of time [34, 35].

On 7 February 2014, all Bitcoin withdrawals were halted by Mt.Gox due to a security issue. On 24 February 2014, Mt.Gox suspended all trading and its website went offline [36, 37]. Nowadays it is still not proved if the collapse was caused by a massive and prolonged theft of Bitcoins or by other reasons. However on 28 February 2014 Mt.Gox filed for bankruptcy protection in Tokyo, claiming that they had lost around 7 % of all Bitcoins in the market (around $473 million near the time of the filing) [38]. In the table below we sum up some other crucial phases (through the company statements) (Table 3).

After exploring Mt.Gox case, we decided to investigate the consequences of its collapse on the whole virtual currency system. Thus we examined Mt.Gox and the other main 19 VCEP trading Bitcoin in USD (we focus only on one currency to facilitate data comparison), collecting data about the volume of transaction and the weighted price of Bitcoin. We specifically focus on two time periods that are just before and after Mt.Gox's collapse: T1 (2014 Jan-Feb) and T2 (2014 Jun-Jul).

As we can see from the Table 4 above, the volume of Bitcoin transactions significantly dipped in the months after Mt.Gox's collapse (−66 %) and all the main VCEP loose a huge number of Bitcoin transactions even if they are increasing their market share, also thanks to the shutdown of one of their biggest competitor.

---

[5]The launch in the market was announced through a forum focused on bitcoin: https://bitcointalk. org/index.php?topic=444.msg3866#msg3866 [Retrieved 16 July 2014].

Table 3 Official news about Mt.Gox

Date	Statement
02-28	Application for commencement of a procedure of civil rehabilitation
03-04	Comprehensive prohibition order judgment announcement
03-14	Announcement of the applicability of US bankruptcy code Chapter 15
03-20	Announcement regarding the balance of Bitcoin held by the company
03-26	Announcement with regard to consultations with investigating authorities on the disappearance of bitcoins
04-16	Announcement of the order for provisional administration, etc.
04-24	Announcement of commencement of bankruptcy proceedings
05-23	Notice of recognition hearing in the US bankruptcy court

Data source www.Mt.Gox.com

Table 4 Virtual money explored in our sample with their volume in USD and market share in percentage (For interpretation of color in the table refer online version)

Virtual exchange platforms	Volume $ T1[6] 2014 Jan-Feb	Market Share %[7]	Volume $ T2[8] 2014 Jun-Jul	Market Share %[9]	Difference between T1 and T2 (%)
Mt.Gox	364.428.055	22.6	Closed	Closed	-
bitfinexUSD	370.254.685	23.0	171.472.551	31.4	-54
bitstampUSD	515.356.681	32.0	140.871.988	25.8	-73
btceUSD	340.139.245	21.1	95.870.713	17.6	-72
lakeUSD	*	0.0	60.374.434	11.1	-
anxhkUSD	75.937	0.0	22.746.513	4.2	29854
hitbtcUSD	590.524	0.0	13.788.713	2.5	2235
itbitUSD	4.204.038	0.3	19.246.032	3.5	358
LocalBitcoins	7.868.207	0.5	11.612.131	2.1	48
1coin	*	0.0	7.710.781	1.4	-
CoinTrader	343.785	0.0	887.307	0.2	158
BitBay	Later	0.0	553.688	0.1	-
Ripple	4.675.639	0.3	327.097	0.1	-93
Kraken	78.391	0.0	227.443	0.0	190
Camp BX	542.308	0.0	167.832	0.0	-69
Justcoin	94.001	0.0	73.228	0.0	-22
bitKonan	73.160	0.0	50.737	0.0	-31
The Rock	98.162	0.0	20.911	0.0	-79
Crypto-Trade	373.577	0.0	10.387	0.0	-97
Vircurex	277	0.0	5.579	0.0	1914
TOT	**1.609.196.672**	**100**	**546.018.065**	**100**	**-66**

Different colors represent the year of platform first transaction: 2011 –light blue; 2013—dark blue; 2014—white

Data source http://bitcoincharts.com/markets/
[a]Volume in currency (USD) from January 27th 2014 to February 25th 2014
[b]From January 27th 2014 to February 25th 2014
[c]Volume in currency (USD) from June 10th to July 9th 2014
[d]From June 10th to July 9th 2014

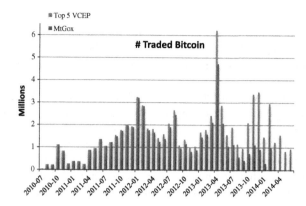

Fig. 2 *Source* http://bitcoincharts.com/markets/currency/USD.html Traded Bitcoin, from July 2010 to July 2014, expressed in Btc on the Top 5 exchange platforms: Mt.Gox, Bifinex, Bitstamp, bct-e, and LakeUSD

In the figure below we can also notice how Mt.Gox market share in trading Bitcoin started to decrease already in 2013 (when some technical problems already threatened its safe and reliable operation), to drop dramatically at the end of the same year till the collapse in February 2014.

Starting from the end of the second trimester 2013, the whole VCEP system was affected by a strong decrease in the number of traded Bitcoin (Fig. 2).

4 Conclusions and Future Research

The virtual currency system is attracting more and more interest, both in business and academia. While the idea of developing *non-traditional* money is not innovative, probably nowadays the environment is readier to embrace the challenge of a new currency system, from a business, social, and technological point of view.

In this exploratory paper we aimed to provide a more accurate look into the phenomenon, focusing on some of the characteristics and potential failures of the system. We identified some of the risks linked to the use of the most common virtual currency in the marker: Bitcoin.

Then we focused specifically on one of these risks: the vulnerability of the Bitcoin brokers (VCEP) and how the severe crisis of a key player could potentially impact the whole system. Thus, we analyzed the collapse of Mt.Gox, market leader in trading Bitcoin, which in 10 months has gone from controlling the large majority of the market to bankruptcy.

In this brief case study, we showed that the potential risks started to materialized well before the February 2014 definitive crisis. Already in 2011 and again in 2013 there were cases of technical problems leading to the freeze of the transactions, as well as issues of poor management of the interdependences with other payment companies. The supposed hacker attack of 2014 and the consequent bankruptcy can be seen as a tipping point for a series of security and managerial issues that emerged along Mt.Gox history.

We have also showed that the collapse of such important VCEP potentially influenced the whole virtual currency system, consistently reducing the total number of trading activities (and probably also impacting on Bitcoin price). However we also showed that the virtual currency system, even being extremely new and thus not very established, does not seem to be doomed, but actually seems being stabilized just after few months from the bankruptcy. Luckily the word did not (and hopefully will never) experience such a shock in the traditional market (an analogy could be the collapse of NYSE), but the system and Bitcoin transactions seem again fully operational (even if for smaller number of transactions and lower exchange rate).

One of the most interesting outcome of our study consists in providing empirical evidences of the fact that (1) the collapse of a dominant VCEP shocked the whole e-currency market (transactions volume before the collapse in T1 was $ 1.609.196.672, dropping to $ 546.018.065 in T2); (2) but nevertheless both Bitcoin and other e-currencies were able not only to survive but to consolidate their positions [39]. The relatively narrow diffusion of virtual currency and their consequent limited impact on real economy is one of the possible reasons for which virtual currencies are able to continue to expand even after a drop of around 2/3 of traded Bitcoin.

This limited (but expanding) environment constitutes a potential limitation for the studies on e-currencies, but it also can be a potential interesting setting were digital trust dynamics [40] and also the robustness of digital systems to internal and external shocks can be tested. One of our further research activity will be focused on the strategies and the organizational changes happened after the "crisis" that were able to stabilize the system.

This paper, through an explanatory analysis provide a better understanding of a very recent phenomenon (Mt.Gox collapsed in February 2014) and draw some research questions that can potentially be deeper investigated when a broader longitudinal dataset will be available. Our analysis further stress, as other contributions did before [26, 41–45], the importance of fully study and identify all the possible risks connected to the virtual currency system in order to anticipate problems and provide right solutions. It is known that Bitcoin is an extremely small part of the economy; any shock, even if could be significant for the players in that specific market, has very few chances to influence the whole economic system. Still this case-study represents the ideal situation to operationally check the characteristics, the value, and the risks of the virtual currency system, in order to avoid that any problem and unexpected consequence could potentially influence a larger setting.

References

1. Bolici, F.: Organizzare in Rete. McGraw-Hill Education, Italy (2012)
2. Hilbert, M., López, P.: The world's technological capacity to store, communicate, and compute information. Science 332(6025), 60–65 (2011)
3. Castells, M.: Materials for an exploratory theory of the network society 1. Br. J. Sociol. 51(1), 5–24 (2000)
4. Brown, J.S., Duguid, P.: Knowledge and organization: a social-practice perspective. Organ. Sci. 12(2), 198–213 (2001)
5. Majchrzak, A., Rice, R.E., Malhotra, A., King, N., Ba, S.: Technology adaptation: the case of a computer-supported inter-organizational virtual team. MIS Q. 24(4), 569–600 (2000)
6. Kirkman, B.L., Rosen, B., Tesluk, P.E., Gibson, C.B.: The impact of team empowerment on virtual team performance: the moderating role of face-to-face interaction. Acad. Manage. J. 47 (2), 175–192 (2004)
7. Lacity, M.C., Willcocks, L.: Global Information Technology Outsourcing: In Search of Business Advantage. Wiley, New York (2000)
8. Choi, J., Bell, D.R., Lodish, L.M.: Traditional and IS-enabled customer acquisition on the internet. Manage. Sci. 58(4), 754–769 (2012)
9. European Central Bank. Virtual Currency Schemes. European Central Bank, Frankfurt am Main (2012). ISBN 978-92-899-0862-7. Archived from the original on 2014-07-15
10. EBA Opinion on virtual currencies. European Banking Authority. 4 July 2014. Accessed 18 July 2014
11. Network, Financial Crimes Enforcement. Application of FinCEN's regulations to persons administering, exchanging, or using virtual currencies. United States Department of the Treasury, March 18 (2013). Accessed 18 July 2014
12. Myers, M.D., Avison, D.: An introduction to qualitative research in information systems. Qual. Res. Inf. Syst. 4, 3–12 (2002)
13. Gerring, J.: Case Study Research: Principles and Practices. Cambridge University Press, Cambridge (2006)
14. Hodkinson, P., Hodkinson, H.: The strengths and limitations of case study research. Learning and Skills Development Agency Conference at Cambridge (2001)
15. CPSS.: A Glossary of Terms Used in Payments and Settlement Systems. CPSS-Committee on Payment (2001)
16. BIS Bank for International Settlements: Principles for the Management of Credit Risk. Basel Committee on Banking Supervision. Basel, September (2000)
17. Nikolaou, K.: European Central Bank Working Paper Series No. 1008 February (2009)
18. Kaufman, G.G.: Banking and currency crisis and systemic risk: a taxonomy and review. Financ. Markets Institutions Instrum. 9(2), 69–131 (2000)
19. Chong, J., Jennings, W.P., Phillips, G.M.: Five types of risk and a fistful of dollars: practical risk analysis for investors. J. Financ. Serv. Prof. 66(3), 68–76 (2012)
20. http://www.forbes.com/sites/kashmirhill/2014/01/16/the-feds-are-ready-to-sell-the-silk-road-bitcoin-kind-of/. Accrssed 20 July 2014
21. Baddeley, M.: Using e-cash in the new economy: an economic analysis of micro-payment systems. J. Electron. Commer. Res. 5(4), 239–253 (2004)
22. Nakamoto, S.: Bitcoin: a peer-to-peer electronic cash system (2008)
23. Karame, G., Androulaki, E., Capkun, S.: Double-spending fast payments in Bitcoin. In: Proceedings of ACM CCS 2012 (2012)
24. Rosenfeld, M.: Analysis of hashrate-based double-spending (2012). bitcoil.co.il/Doublespend. pdf
25. Reid, F., Harrigan, M.: An analysis of anonymity in the Bitcoin system. In: Security and Privacy in Social Networks, pp. 197–223. Springer, New York (2013)

26. Becker, J., Breuker, D., Heide, T., Holler, J., Rauer, H.P., Böhme, R.: Can we afford integrity by proof-of-work? Scenarios inspired by the Bitcoin currency. The Economics of Information Security and Privacy, pp. 135–156. Springer Berlin (2013)
27. http://www.nytimes.com/2014/02/25/business/apparent-theft-at-mt-gox-shakes-bitcoin-world. html. Accessed 23 July 2014
28. http://www.bloomberg.com/news/2014-02-28/mt-gox-exchange-files-for-bankruptcy.html. Accessed 20 July 2014
29. Stabell, C.B., Fjeldstad, Ø.D.: Configuring value for competitive advantage: on chains, shops, and networks. Strateg. Manag. J. **19**(5), 413–437 (1998)
30. http://arstechnica.com/tech-policy/2011/06/bitcoin-price-plummets-on-compromised-exchange/. Accessed 20 July 2014
31. http://bitgear.co/blogs/blog/13602537-archive-huge-bitcoin-sell-off-due-to-a-compromised-account-rollback. Accessed 20 July 2014
32. http://www.dailytech.com/Inside+the+MegaHack+of+Bitcoin+the+Full+Story/article21942. htm. Accessed 20 July 2014
33. http://www.theregister.co.uk/Print/2011/06/19/bitcoin_values_collapse_again/. Accessed 20 July 2014
34. http://arstechnica.com/business/2013/03/major-glitch-in-bitcoin-network-sparks-sell-off-price-temporarily-falls-23/. Accessed 20 July 2014
35. http://www.theverge.com/2013/3/12/4092898/technical-problems-cause-bitcoin-to-plummet-from-record-high. Accessed 23 July 2014
36. http://dealbook.nytimes.com/2014/02/25/trading-site-failure-stirs-ire-and-hope-for-bitcoin/? Accessed 20 July 2014
37. Nagano, Y., Wright, S.: Website of Bitcoin Exchange Mt.Gox Offline. Associated Press, New York (2014)
38. Takemoto, Y.; Knight, S.: Mt.Gox files for bankruptcy, blames hackers for losses. Reuters (2014)
39. http://online.wsj.com/articles/paypal-payments-hub-to-permit-bitcoin-payments-for-digital-goods-1411494837?KEYWORDS=paypal+bitcoin. Accessed 25 September 2014
40. Bolici, F., Giustiniano, L.: Design Science and eTrust: Designing Organizational Artifacts as Nexus of Social and Technical Interactions. Organizational Change and Information Systems, pp. 177–190. Springer, Heidelberg (2013)
41. Androulaki, E., Karame, G.O., Roeschlin, M., Scherer, T., Capkun, S.: Evaluating user privacy in bitcoin. Financial Cryptography and Data Security, pp. 34–51. Springer Berlin (2013)
42. Miers, I., Garman, C., Green, M., Rubin, A.D.: Zerocoin: anonymous distributed e-cash from Bitcoin. In: IEEE Symposium on Security and privacy (SP). IEEE (2013)
43. Moore, T., Christin N.: Beware the middleman: empirical analysis of Bitcoin-exchange risk. Financial Cryptography and Data Security, pp. 25–33. Springer, Berlin (2013)
44. Plassaras, N.A.: Regulating digital currencies: bringing bitcoin within the reach of the IMF. Chicago J. Int. Law **14**(1), 377–407 (2013)
45. Ron, D., Shamir, A.: Quantitative analysis of the full bitcoin transaction graph. Financial Cryptography and Data Security, pp. 6–24. Springer, Berlin (2013)

Research Methods in the itAIS Community: Building a Classification Framework for Management and Information Systems Studies

Francesca Ricciardi and Cecilia Rossignoli

Abstract In this paper, we present a framework for the systematic classification of management research methods. We propose a scalable model based on six classification criteria: Type of Contribution (e.g. theory testing, context-specific description, etc.); Research Paradigm (e.g. positivist, interpretivist, etc.); Research Design (e.g. case study, survey, etc.); Time and Distance Lag Strategies (e.g. longitudinal, cross-cultural, etc.); Information Elaboration Methods (e.g. statistical analysis, text analysis, etc.); and Information Gathering and Preparation Methods (e.g. interviews, secondary data collection, etc.). We suggest that the six-level framework we present here has the potential to allow the systematic and granular monitoring of methodological trends in scholarly communities. In the final part of the paper, the framework is utilized to classify the 62 papers of the itAIS 2011 selected papers collection, and the methodological attitudes of the itAIS community are briefly commented.

Keywords Research methods · Research approaches · Research techniques · Management · Information systems

1 Introduction

Management studies rely on numerous and diverse research methods and approaches. Some of them, such as surveys, were established and accepted long time ago in our scholarly community; whilst others, like configurational studies, emerged only recently and have been much more rarely used so far.

The horizon of the available research methods is wider than many researchers are aware of. Most doctoral students and several faculty are highly specialized in

F. Ricciardi (✉) · C. Rossignoli
University of Verona, Verona, Italy
e-mail: francesca.ricciardi@univr.it

C. Rossignoli
e-mail: cecilia.rossignoli@univr.it

© Springer International Publishing Switzerland 2016
T. Torre et al. (eds.), *Empowering Organizations*, Lecture Notes in Information
Systems and Organisation 11, DOI 10.1007/978-3-319-23784-8_23

one or few research methods [1]. Although this in-depth expertise and "tunnel vision" are often necessary, the evolution of the methodological scenario and the possibilities offered by new, alternative methods may be of great interest both for experienced and young scholars.

But how could the methodological scenario and its evolution be effectively monitored within a community?

Textbooks on business and management research methods can help only partially. In fact, given their didactical purposes, they do not mention many recently developed, peculiar or highly specialized approaches and methods. Moreover, textbooks are influenced by the academic traditions of the country they were written in: for example, a textbook written by USA authors is likely to pay less attention to qualitative—interpretive methods than a textbook written by UK authors; and both are likely not to mention design science research, which is viably rooted, instead, in German-speaking countries [2].

Textbooks, then, especially if taken singularly, do provide a general map of some popular and well-established research design choices that are considered suitable and interesting for Ph.D students, but do not provide a framework allowing a massive classification of virtually all the papers published by a certain journal or by a certain research community in a certain period.

Textbooks aim to thoroughly describe the complexity and nuances of the research design process, and to provide guidelines to address the technical problems implied. But a framework aimed at research method monitoring should be conceived differently. If the aim is classification, categories must be defined very simply and synthetically, so that the room for arbitrary interpretation is minimized. Moreover, the range of categories needs to be much wider than that offered by textbooks, since the model is expected to allow the classification also of new, rare and emergent methodological approaches and methods.

Since we could not find any such synthetic framework in the literature, we decided to take on this challenge.

Our contribution is meant to be as comprehensive as possible, but we are aware that it is impossible to take into consideration all the existing and future research approaches, methods and techniques; thus, we sought to design a scalable framework, where further elements are easy to add or modify whenever needed. Our contribution should be understood as a work-in-progress, a basis for discussion and a tool for catalyzing the debate in our scholarly community.

We built a first draft framework in 2012, by merging the classification criteria extracted from four recent and popular textbooks dedicated to research methods in our discipline [1, 3–5] and a seminal monograph on methods in social science [6]. We created a basket of papers, published in the years 2003–2012 in nine top journals in the management area,[1] and we started to extract papers from the basket

---

[1]Academy of Management Journal; Administrative Science Quarterly; Journal of Management; Journal of Management Studies; Management Science; MIS Quarterly; Organization Science; Research in Organizational Behavior; Strategic Management Journal.

randomly, to check whether our framework allowed to satisfyingly classify each paper into its categories. This led us to identify research techniques and approaches that were not mentioned in our initial version of the framework, and we adapted it accordingly. We went on recursively, by surveying the papers and updating the framework. We found that many categories were missing and that many logical and classificatory issues were raised by each adjustment we introduced into the framework. We also involved six undergraduate and doctoral students in the classification exercises, to test the extent to which different people who had not participated in the process of framework development chose the same categories to classify the same papers. The student's comments on the framework and on the difficulties during the classification process were very useful to identify several weaknesses of the model. We went on until about 300 among the papers included in the basket were classified or reclassified into at least one of the versions of the framework.

In March, 2014, we presented a draft version of the framework at the WOA Conference (Workshop of Organization Studies) held in Udine, Italy. The presentation confirmed that the scholarly community is strongly interested in the development of a synthetic tool allowing to systematically monitor research methods and approaches. Moreover, we collected many constructive comments and suggestions, which proved very useful to further improve the framework.

The version we present here stems from all these discussions and collaborative experiences, along with the valuable suggestions provided by the anonymous reviewers of the itAIS (the Italian Chapter of Information Systems) Conference, 2014.

After a synthetic description of the classification criteria in Paragraph 2, a demonstrative application is provided in Paragraph 3: the 62 papers included in the collection of itAIS 2011 Selected Papers are classified into the framework's categories.

This allows us to test the model also beyond the boundaries of traditional management research. In fact, itAIS papers focus on Information Systems studies, a field in which management issues are cross-fertilized with issues from sister disciplines, such as engineering, computer science, accounting and law.

In the final part of the paper, we comment on the outcomes of the classification conducted, and we describe the further research activities we plan to conduct in order to test, fine-tune and utilize the six-level framework developed.

2 Classification Criteria

The processes of participative discussions on research methodologies that we described above convinced us that it is useful to distinguish high-level classification criteria, operational-level classification criteria, and middle-level classification criteria.

High-level classification criteria should allow to classify publications based on their general orientation and type of approach to science. Operational-level classification criteria should allow to classify publications based on the techniques they have adopted to collect and elaborate information. Middle-level classification criteria should allow to classify publications based on the guidelines they have followed to integrate high-level and operational-level choices.

After analyzing our basket of textbooks and papers, and after the discussions conducted so far, we came to propose six classification criteria. The first two are complementary high-level criteria; the second couple of criteria correspond to two complementary middle-level classifications; and the last couple includes two complementary operational-level criteria. A synthetic list of these six classification criteria follows; each criterion will be more thoroughly described in the following paragraphs.

Classification Criteria adopted:

1. Type of Contribution (e.g. theory testing, context-specific description…)
2. Research Paradigm (e.g. positivist, interpretivist…)
3. Research Design (e.g. case study, survey…)
4. Time and Distance Lag Strategies (e.g. longitudinal, cross-cultural…)
5. Information Elaboration Methods (e.g. statistical analysis, text analysis…)
6. Information Gathering and Preparation Methods (e.g. interviews, secondary data collection…)

2.1 First Classification Criterion: Type of Contribution

All the main textbooks we surveyed agree that a typical purpose for management research consists in contributing to management theory. The word "theory" may have several meanings, but when used without adjectives it usually indicates an explanation of observed regularities [1]. According to this definition, theories identify generalizable cause-effect relationships; in management and organizational studies, the causal relationship is usually understood as nondeterministic, but probabilistic, given the complexity of the phenomena under study.

Most textbooks, on the other hand, agree that a second type of contribution is legitimate in management studies, i.e. the thick, accurate description of a specific, interesting case, which, although not necessarily generalizable, provides the reader with in-depth understanding of a real world context and hints to clear away conventional notions.

But these two categories (explanatory theories and context-specific descriptions) are not sufficient to classify publications based on the type of contribution. Examining our sample of top journal papers, in fact, we found also publications whose core outcome does not contribute either to explanatory theories, or to in-depth understanding of specific cases. For example, several papers provide the reader with construct analyses, taxonomies or maps, which are abstracted and generalized, but not explanatory. Other papers focus on testing the usefulness of a certain type of organizational solution (e.g. a procedure, a norm, an information system) without linking their findings to any explanatory theory.

We then realized that further categories were needed, along with "explanatory theories" and "context-specific descriptions". Thanks to the discussion at the WOA conference and to the anonymous reviewers of previous versions of this work, we identified Gregor [7] as an inspiring source for describing the types of contribution that a management research may provide.

We then adapted the categories identified by Gregor [7], by changing the names of the categories and by merging two of the five categories into one. The first decision is due to the fact that we find some of Gregor's labels quite counter-intuitive for the standard audience of management scholars. The second decision is due to the fact that distinguishing what Gregor calls "type III theory" from "type IV theory" would have made the process of classification quite arbitrary and difficult in our opinion. In fact, in order to decide whether a research belongs to Gregor's type III or Type IV, we should have evaluated the soundness of the cause-effect explanation adopted in the publication under analysis; but we deemed it impossible to clearly define a threshold of explanatory soundness, under which a paper should be classified as a type III, and over which as a type IV.

We then propose the four categories identified in Table 1, in order to classify management publications based on the main contribution(s) they make to the scholarly community.

2.2 Second Classification Criterion: Epistemological Paradigm

Most textbooks insist on the importance of the epistemological underpinnings of research. The dualism between positivism-objectivism, on the one side, and interpretivism-constructivism, on the other side, is often highlighted [6]. Other paradigms are less common in textbooks, but are present in our top journal papers sample: we identified critical realism [1] and design science [8] as recognized alternatives to positivism and interpretivism.

But textbook authors themselves admit that such categories, although didactically useful, raise severe problems if used to classify existing publications, because authors often build upon implicit, diverse, blurred or inconsistent philosophical bases (see e.g. [1], chapter 24). Moreover, there is not a shared view on what each paradigm exactly includes. For example, should the tradition of empirical realism be considered part of positivism? Should a post-modernist study be considered interpretivist? Of course, these are fascinating questions from a philosophical point

Table 1 First classification criterion: type of contribution

Label	Category description
Context-specific description *(corresponds to type II, [7])*	The reader is provided with an in-depth description of a specific case, which is presented as enlightening and interesting per se, and investigated in its context. The interest can stem from (i) the novelty of the described phenomena and/or (ii) the fact that the described phenomena collide with existing theories
Abstracting description *(corresponds to type I, [7])*	The reader is provided with an abstracting definition, measurement and/or description of real world phenomena. Examples include new concepts, constructs, measurement scales, taxonomies, classifications, geographical maps, relational maps, chronologies
Theory building or theory testing *(corresponds to types III and IV merged, [7])*	The reader is provided with an explanation of regularities. *Following a well-established tradition, we further divide this category into the sub-categories Theory Building (a theory is developed but not tested) and Theory Testing (a theory is tested, after having been developed in the same publication or elsewhere)*
Solution building or solution testing *(corresponds to type V, [7])*	The reader is provided with conceptual tools or guidelines on how to solve a certain type of problem or pursue a certain type of goal. *Following the tradition adopted above, we further divide this category into the sub-categories Solution Building (a solution is developed but not tested) and Solution Testing (a solution is tested, after having been developed in the same publication or elsewhere)*

What is the reader provided with?

of view, but may raise unsolvable problems in a process of mass classification of research products.

For this reason, we adopted a simplified criterion to classify publications based on the epistemological paradigm they build upon. Our categories, listed in Table 2, correspond to definitions that should be considered as proxies of the much more complex philosophical concepts they are labelled with.

The textbooks often highlight that some combinations between what we call the Type of Contribution and what we call the Epistemological Paradigm are more frequent or more typical than the others. For example, the combination between Theory Testing (Type of Contribution) and Positivism (Epistemological Paradigm) is very frequent. Nevertheless, the textbooks themselves admit that many alternative combinations can be found in the literature: for example, Theory Testing is conducted also by scholars following the Critical Realism paradigm [1]; Positivism can

Table 2 Second classification criterion: epistemological paradigm

Label	Category description
Positivism	The writing is based on concepts developed by the scholarly community to abstract the key features of social phenomena (e.g. "management commitment", "customer loyalty", "competitive advantage", etc.). These concepts are translated into measurable variables and/or used to develop generalized cause-effect relationships
Interpretivism	The writing is based on concepts developed and used by the subjects under study. It focuses on the meaning that people attach to the social reality they are immersed in. Social action and context are empathically understood by the researcher through the eyes of the people involved
Critical realism	The writing is based on concepts developed by the scholarly community to abstract the pre-existing hidden socio-cultural structures (e.g. prejudices, traditions, legitimated norms, etc.) which influence the beliefs and interactions of the subjects under study. These hidden structures must be identified in order to make it possible to change them, if harmful
Design science	The writing is based on concepts, developed by the scholarly community or by practitioners, aimed to abstract the key features of designable artifacts, which may be adopted and used in organizational settings (e.g. procedures, models, software tools, etc.). These concepts are used to develop generalizable means-ends relationships

What type of concepts is the writing based on?

result also in Context-Specific Descriptions [4]. We suggest that the 16 possible combinations between the four Types of Contribution and the four Epistemological Paradigms provide a sufficiently granular framework of the possible range of high-level methodological choices.

2.3 Third Classification Criterion: Research Designs

The textbooks agree that high-level methodological choices (e.g. positivism versus interpretivism) need to be complemented by consistent operational-level choices (e.g. secondary data collection vs. interviews). The textbooks suggest to follow the guidelines of recognized research designs to manage the intersection of high-level and operational-level methodological choices. Some research designs, such as case studies and surveys, are very popular and cited by all the textbooks. Other research designs, such as experience surveys, are mentioned only in few textbooks [4]. Other, emergent designs, such as the configurational comparative methods, are emerging in conference debates and journals, but are not mentioned at all in our basket of textbooks. Each research design provides a specific tradition about how the research contribution and epistemology should be combined with data gathering and data elaboration techniques. For example, the tradition of surveys suggests to aim at theory testing or abstracting description, to adopt a positivistic point of view,

Table 3 Third classification criterion: research designs

Label	Category description
Literat. review	Specifically aimed to survey the extant literature on a specific topic
Conceptual	Develops concepts, models and theories, based on the researcher's reasoning, without presenting field or experimental research
Ethnography	A qualitative, long-term field research, in which the researchers seek to immerse themselves in the daily life and cultural environment of the people being studied
Action research	The researcher is involved in real-world problems and seeks to both contribute to problem-solving and to extract scientific knowledge from the experience. Unlike Design Science (below) the focus here is on social solutions, such as re-education, conflict resolution, etc.
Case study (single or multiple)	The researcher is concerned with the complexity and particular nature of the case(s) in question (e.g. specific organizations). A very wide range of information gathering and analysis techniques can be implied
Experience survey	A group of people (often practitioners) are presented a problem, and their reactions and/or behaviors and/or comments are collected either separately or in group, either immediately or after a period
Grounded theory	The researcher systematically and recursively analyzes the information from field research to build and validate new concepts, categories, hypotheses and theories
Configurational comparative methods	The researcher selects a sample of cases (e.g. organizations) and translates them into configurations. This allows systematic comparison between different cases through Qualitative Comparative Analysis
Construct/scale development study	The researcher develops and tests concepts, constructs and measurement scales through qualitative and/or quantitative methods of data gathering and elaboration
Social network analysis	The researcher studies social relationships by using network theory and network analysis tools, such as graph theory.
Survey (primary analysis)	The researcher collects quantitative data on a population or sample and statistically analyzes the data for descriptive and/or theory testing purposes. Both cross-sectional and longitudinal (e.g. retrospective, panel, cohort) observational studies are included in this broad category
Secondary analysis	The researcher conducts a statistical analysis on data from existing databases or previous publications. Purposes and methods are analogous to those of surveys based on primary data
Artifact development research	The researcher thoroughly describes an innovative artifact (model, method, procedure, norm, or prototype) aimed to problem solving, its key features and expected outcomes

(continued)

Table 3 (continued)

Label	Category description
Simulation experiment	The researcher uses computer-aided modelling to emulate the behavior of the system being studied, and observes the consequences of induced changes in variables
Natural experiment	The researcher observes individuals exposed to a specific condition in their natural settings: the factors governing the exposure are outside the investigator's control
Experiment	The researcher controls the factors governing the exposure of the subjects to a specific condition, and observes the consequences

to utilize questionnaires or structured interviews for data gathering, and statistical analysis for data elaboration.

Table 3 synthetically lists the Research Designs that we found mentioned in our basket of textbooks and in our sample of top journal papers.

2.4 Fourth Classification Criterion: Time and Distance Lag Strategies

Most textbook include the choices between longitudinal versus cross-sectional, and those between comparative vs. non comparative approaches, at the same logical level of research designs, such as case studies or surveys. From a didactic point of view, this can make sense, because both longitudinal and survey approaches provide the researcher with guidelines and constraints on how data should be gathered and elaborated. But, from a classificatory point of view, we think that longitudinal studies and surveys cannot be included within the same criterion. In fact, what we have called research designs, such as surveys, case studies etc. may be longitudinal or not, comparative or not. Then, we provide a separate criterion for classifying these methodological choices, as detailed in Table 4.

2.5 Fifth Classification Criterion: Information Elaboration Methods

The categories identified in this classification criterion are aimed to identify the established methods for elaborating the information collected in the previous phase of information gathering (see Sect. 2.6). Each Information Elaboration Method can include several techniques: for example, Statistical Analysis includes many techniques, such as multi-variate analysis, structural equation modelling, etc. Given

Table 4 Fourth classification criterion: time and distance lag strategies

Label	Category description
Longitudinal	The elaboration builds upon longitudinal data. Data are longitudinal if the same information gathering activity (e.g. a questionnaire with the same items, or an observation of the same type of activity) has been repeated at least twice within the same case, sample or population, with a time lag separating the different waves of information gathering. The differences between lagged data are taken into consideration for elaboration, without aggregating them, so providing the reader with information about how things have changed in a certain time period or after exposure to a certain stimulus
Cross-sectional	The elaboration does not build upon the differences emerging from repeated observation of the same phenomenon involving the same subjects. Data are aggregated: a "photograph" of the status quo is provided, instead of a "video" documenting how things have changed for each subject under study
Comparative	The elaboration builds upon comparative data. Data are comparative if the same information gathering activity (e.g. a questionnaire with the same items, or an observation of the same type of activity) has been repeated in at least two cases, samples or populations, which the researcher considers interestingly distant from a geographical, cultural, social or organizational point of view. The differences between the data collected in the respective cases, samples or populations are taken into consideration for elaboration, without aggregating them, so providing the reader with information about how things vary from case to case, sample to sample, population to population
Non-comparative	The elaboration does not build upon comparative data. Data are aggregated: subjects to be studied are selected by the researcher because they are considered part of the same sample, population or case type. The focus is on what the subjects under study have in common, instead of what differentiates them

the synthetic nature of this work, we did not include comprehensive lists of techniques for each method. Table 2 lists the categories we propose to include.

2.6 Sixth Classification Criterion: Information Gathering and Preparation Methods

The categories included in this classification criterion are aimed to identify the methods for collecting information and making it usable for scientific elaboration. As the reader can see, Table 6 does not include the full list of all the techniques associated with each method, given the synthetic nature of this work.

Table 5 Fifth classification criterion: information elaboration methods

Label	Category description
Literature analysis	Almost all publications are based also on Literature Analysis, but a publication is classified into this category if literature analysis is the only method for information elaboration mentioned by or inferable from the publication
Text analysis	Includes both implicit analysis methods, coding techniques, language analysis (narrative, conversation, discourse, rhetoric analysis), and hermeneutic analysis
Artifact analysis	The analysis can be conducted both on tangible artifacts (e.g. drawings, working spaces) and intangible artifacts (e.g. software). The techniques vary depending on the nature of the artifacts under study
Direct data analysis	The researcher analyzes simple tables and data sets without the aid of mathematical algorithms or statistical tools, performing intuitive or self-evident data grouping and comparisons
Qualitative comparative analysis	The researcher utilizes Boolean, multi-set and fuzzy set techniques aimed to systematically compare complex cases
Inductive-abductive reasoning	Through systematic or spontaneous processes, the researcher observes regularities and/or conjectures possible causes of observed phenomena. These processes are usually recursive and imply the discovery of analogies. A publication is classified into this category if this is the only method for information elaboration mentioned by or inferable from the publication
Problem solving reasoning	The researcher is involved in practice-related challenges; knowledge is elaborated through problem solving processes, by leveraging methods and techniques such as trial-and-error, requirement analysis, means-ends analysis, lateral thinking etc. Knowledge is generated through the typical problem solving processes, such as trial-and-error, previous solutions recombination, etc. Includes Delphi method
Statistical analysis	This category includes all the methods and techniques for statistical elaboration, such as uni-, bi-, multi-variate analysis, regression analysis, structural equation modelling, trend estimation, factor analysis, etc.
Network analysis	This category includes all the methods and techniques specifically developed for the analysis of relational phenomena, such as those based on graph theory
Spatial analysis	This category includes all the methods and techniques specifically developed to study the topological, geometric or geographic properties of entities and phenomena
Learning and discovery algorithms	The researcher utilizes machine learning/artificial intelligence algorithms to extract patterns from large amounts of data. The systems automatically identifies regularities that had remained hidden. These algorithms are utilized in order to perform tasks such as anomaly detection, clustering, automatic classification. Examples of techniques include neural networks and k-means clustering
Computational modelling	The researchers launches a computer simulation, reproducing the behavior of a system. Includes methods such as agent and multi-agent based modelling

Table 6 Sixth classification criterion: information gathering and preparation methods

Label	Category description
Literature search	Almost all publications are based also on Literature Search, but a publication is classified into this category if this is the only method for information collection mentioned by or inferable from the publication
Text collection	A broad definition of "text" is adopted here: it includes not only written texts (e.g. company reports), but also all the multimedia texts that the researcher may collect to extract complex, unstructured information, such as field notes, audio recordings, photos, videos, web pages, sketches, etc.
Interview(s)	This category includes all the interviews with open questions: structured, semi-structured and unstructured
Survey of existing artifact(s)	The information can be collected both from tangible artifacts (e.g. working spaces) and intangible artifacts (e.g. software). The techniques vary depending on the nature of the artifacts under study
Focus group–group interviews	The moderator/facilitator encourages the interviewees to discuss a topic, and focuses on the joint construction of meaning within the group
Participant observation	The researcher immerses him- or herself in a group for an extended period of time, observing behavior, listening to what is said and asking questions. The focus is on sharing experiences and understanding culture, not on helping the observed group to solve problems
Reflective practice	The researcher is involved in practice challenges and new solution development. Information is informally and implicitly gathered during the problem solving processes, such as trial-and-error, negotiations, work discussions, etc.
Questionnaire and fixed choice interv.	This category includes all types of questionnaires and fixed choice interviews, be they administered by phone, by mail, etc.
Secondary data collection	The researchers utilizes existing structured data, for example from official statistics, company databases, previous publications
Non-participant observation	Includes all the possible techniques for directly observing and recording behavior both in natural and experimental settings. The observer does not participate in the observed phenomenon and minimizes interaction with the observed people
Instrumental observation	This category includes observation mediated by instruments, such as sensors, cameras, software tracking IT users' behaviors, etc.

3 The Six-Level Framework as a Monitoring Tool: Classifying the itAIS 2011 Selected Papers

The Italian Chapter of the Association for Information Systems (itAIS) Conference is held annually since 2003. It focuses on Information Systems seen as an inter-disciplinary field of studies, involving management and organization research, on the one side, and technical disciplines, on the other side. For this demonstration,

Table 7 The itAIS 2011 selected papers classified into the six-level framework presented above

Contrib.	Parad.	Strategy	Inf. gathering	Inf. elaboration	itAIS papers	Tot
Context specific description	INTERP.	Experience study	Focus group	Text analysis	[12]	1
		Case study	Interv.; text Coll.	Text analysis	[13]	1
	DESIGN SCIEN.	Action research	Interview, reflective practice, secondary data	Text analysis, direct data analysis	[9]	1
Abstracting description	POSITIV.	Conceptual	Literature search	Literature anal.	[14]	1
		Lit. review	Literature search	Literature anal.	[15]	1
		Case study	Interv.; text coll.	Text analysis	[16, 17]	2
		Second. anal.	Secondary data	Statistical anal.	[18][b]	1
			Text collection	Text analysis	[19]	1
Theory building	POSIT.	Conceptual study	Literature search	Literature anal.	[20, 21, 22, 23, 24]	5
		Case study	Interv.; text coll.	Text analysis	[25, 26, 27, 28, 29]	5
	DESIGN SCIEN.	Artifact development R.	Problem solving processes	Abductive reasoning	[11]	1
Theory testing	POSITIV.	Case study	Interv.; focus Gr.	Text analysis	[30]	1
			Quest.; instrum. O.	Direct data anal.	[31]	1
		Second. anal.	Secondary data	Statistical anal.	[32]	1
		Survey	Questionnaire	Statistical anal.	[33, 34, [35][a], [36], [37],	5
		Simul. exper.	Literature search	Computat. model.	[38]	1
			Secondary data	Direct data anal.	[39]	1
Solution building	DESIGN SCIEN.	Artifact development R.	Literature review	Problem solving reasoning	[40, 41, 42, 43, 44, 45],	6
			Survey of existing artifacts	Probl. solv. reasoning	[46, 47, 48, 49, 50, 51, 52, 53, 54]	9
			Reflective practice	Probl. solv. reasoning	[55, 56, 57, 58]	4
			Interview; survey of existing artifacts	Text analysis; probl. solv. reas.	[59]	1

(continued)

Table 7 (continued)

Contrib.	Parad.	Strategy	Inf. gathering	Inf. elaboration	itAIS papers	Tot
Solution testing	INTERP.	Experience S.	Focus group	Text analysis	[10]	1
	DESIGN SCIEN.	Experiment	Observation	Direct data anal.	[60, 61, 62, 63, 64],	5
		Natural experiment	Observation	Direct data analysis	[65, 66, 67, 68]	4
		Simulat. exp.	Secondary data	Computat. model.	[69]	1
		Survey	Questionnaire	Statistical anal.	[70]	1

The last column specifies the total number of papers for each category combination. [a]This paper is longitudinal. All the other papers are cross-sectional. [b]This paper is comparative. All the other papers are non-comparative

we considered the volume collecting 62 double-blind peer-reviewed contributions, selected among those accepted for the Conference held in Rome in 2011 (Table 5).

The 62 papers were analyzed and classified into the six-level framework described in the paragraph above. The results were structured as shown in Table 7, starting from the highest-level criterion, i.e. research contribution. Within each type of research contribution, papers are grouped according to the epistemological paradigm criterion; within each epistemological paradigm, they are further grouped according to the research design, and then again according to the information gathering and information elaboration methods. This allowed to identify 26 combinations of the four criteria, characterizing the methodological choices of the itAIS 2011 authors. Table 7 shows that the most popular combinations are those involving Solution Building and Solution Testing contributions through a Design Science paradigm, and those involving Theory Building contributions through a Positivist paradigm. Only one longitudinal and one comparative paper are included in the book; all the other papers are cross-sectional and non-comparative. A wide range of research designs is adopted, along with diverse methods for information gathering and information elaboration. There are also quite original combinations of methodological choices, such as those displayed in [9] (Context-Specific Description through a Design Science paradigm), [10] (Solution Testing through an Interpretivist paradigm) and [11] (Theory Building through a Design Science paradigm). These results confirm the interdisciplinary nature of the itAIS conference, where design-oriented papers presenting or evaluating IT-based solutions come up beside more theory-oriented papers, and novel methodological approaches are experimented.

4   Conclusions and Further Steps

The framework we present here has been enriched by the collaborative contributions of many students and scholars that have been helping us since 2012, by reviewing, commenting, utilizing and testing the categories that we were developing. This process convinced us that a framework for the classification of research methods needs to be multi-level: in other words, it is necessary to organize the categories describing the methodological alternatives into groups, logically ordered from the higher-level criteria to the more operational criteria.

In this paper, we propose a classification framework organized into six levels. This framework was tested by using it to classify about 300 papers from 9 top journals and has proved suitable to classify the 62 paper of the 2011 itAIS selected papers collection. We hope that it has demonstrated a sufficient level of maturity to raise a discussion in our research community. We conceive this six-level framework as a work-in-progress and we will go on eliciting discussion on it and testing it.

As further research steps, we plan to conduct a series of interviews and focus groups to discuss these outcomes, involving expert senior scholars and young researchers and post-docs. Then, some tests will be conducted, in order to assess the extent to which different scholars, independently utilizing the six-level framework, classify the same papers into the same categories. On the basis of the hopefully improved framework emerging from these activities, we will select a longitudinal series of itAIS publications, and we will classify them systematically, in order to monitor whether and how the methodological attitudes of the itAIS community are evolving.

References

1. Bryman, A., Bell, E.: Business research methods. Oxford University Press, Oxford (2007)
2. Winter, R.: Design science research in Europe. Eur. J. Inf. Syst. 17(5), 470–475 (2008)
3. Cooper, D.R., Schindler, P.S.: Business research methods. McGraw-Hill Education (2003)
4. Zikmund, W., Babin, B., Carr, J., Griffin, M.: Business research methods. Cengage Learning, mason (2012)
5. Tharenou, P., Donohueis, R., Cooper, B.: Management research methods. Cambridge University Press, Cambridge (2007)
6. Gerring, J.: Social science methodology: a criterial framework. Cambridge University Press, Cambridge (2001)
7. Gregor, S.: The nature of theory in information systems. MIS Q. 3(30), 611–642 (2006)
8. Ricciardi, F.: Design and normative claims in organization studies: a methodological proposal. In: Baskerville R., De Marco M., Spagnoletti P. (eds.) Designing organizational systems. an interdisciplinary discourse, pp. 21–34. Springer, Heidelberg (2013)
9. Suppa, A., Zardini, A., Sarcià, S.A.: IT helps the Italian Army to implement a performance management system. In: information systems: crossroads for organization, management, accounting and engineering, pp. 85–92. Physica-Verlag (2012)
10. Caserio, C.: Knowledge generating decision support systems: managing the trade-off between generating knowledge and supporting decisions. In: Information systems: crossroads for organization, management, accounting and engineering, pp. 303–311. Physica-Verlag (2012)
11. Spagnoletti, P., Resca, A., Russo, V., Taglino, F., Tarantino, L.: Building theories from IT project design: The HOPES case. In: Information systems: crossroads for organization, management, accounting and engineering, pp. 451–459. Physica-Verlag (2012)
12. Bertini, P.: Focus groups, meaning making and data quality. In: Information systems: crossroads for organization, management, accounting and engineering, pp. 469–478. Physica-Verlag (2012)

13. Angioni, E., Cabiddu, F., Di Guardo, M.C.: Value-co-creation through multichannels distributions: the Nike ID case. In: Information systems: crossroads for organization, management, accounting and engineering, pp. 259–266. Physica-Verlag (2012)
14. Kontos, G., Kutsikos, K.: A service classification model for value co-creation in IT outsourcing services. In: Information systems: crossroads for organization, management, accounting and engineering, pp. 3–10. Physica-Verlag (2012)
15. Cremona, L., Ravarini, A.: Collective intelligence and social computing: a literature review. In: Information systems: crossroads for organization, management, accounting and engineering, pp. 35–41. Physica-Verlag (2012)
16. Lepore, L., Borrello, L., Alvino, F.: ICT and judicial administration: a model for the classification of E-justice innovations. In: Information systems: crossroads for organization, management, accounting and engineering, pp. 339–347. Physica-Verlag (2012)
17. Federici, T., Braccini, A.M.: How internet is upsetting the communication between organizations and their stakeholders: a tentative research agenda. In: Information systems: crossroads for organization, management, accounting and engineering, pp. 377–385. Physica-Verlag (2012)
18. Reggi, L., Scicchitano, S.: Financing public e-services in europe: a regional perspective. In: Information systems: crossroads for organization, management, accounting and engineering, pp. 19–26. Physica-Verlag (2012)
19. Bochicchio, M., Longo, A.: About the relevance of edemocracy in italian regional websites. In: Information systems: crossroads for organization, management, accounting and engineering, pp. 27–34. Physica-Verlag (2012)
20. Coppolino, R., Abbate, T.: Knowledge sharing and innovation: the contribution of innovation intermediaries. In: Information systems: crossroads for organization, management, accounting and engineering, pp. 251–258. Physica-Verlag (2012)
21. Maggioni, I., Ricciardi, F.: Business intelligence for supply chain management: trends from scholarly literature and from the world of practice. In: Information systems: crossroads for organization, management, accounting and engineering, pp. 287–294. Physica-Verlag (2012)
22. Maiolini, R., Naggi, R.: Reducing inertia and forwarding changes: crowdsourcing to reduce uncertainty. a theoretical model. In: Information systems: crossroads for organization, management, accounting and engineering, pp. 315–322. Physica-Verlag (2012)
23. Weiss, S., Aier, S., Winter, R.: Towards a reconstruction of theoretical foundations of enterprise architecture management. In: Information systems: crossroads for organization, management, accounting and engineering, pp. 461–468. Physica-Verlag (2012)
24. Guarino, N., Bottazzi, E., Ferrario, R., Sartor, G.: Open ontology-driven sociotechnical systems: transparency as a key for business resiliency. In: Information systems: crossroads for organization, management, accounting and engineering, pp. 535–542. Physica-Verlag (2012)
25. Dameri, R.P.: The evolution of information systems strategic models: from IT management to IT governance, the FIAT case. In: Information systems: crossroads for organization, management, accounting and engineering, pp. 53–60. Physica-Verlag (2012)
26. Schiavone, F., Agrifoglio, R.: Communities of practice and practice preservation: a case study. In: Information systems: crossroads for organization, management, accounting and engineering, pp. 331–338. Physica-Verlag (2012)
27. Maiolini, R.: How does the management of multiple stakeholders' interests influence decision-making processes? exploring the case of crowdsourced placemaking. In: Information systems: crossroads for organization, management, accounting and engineering, pp. 349–357. Physica-Verlag (2012)
28. Cabiddu, F., Castriotta, M., Di Guardo, M.C., Floreddu, P., Pettinao, D.: Combining exploitation and exploration through crowdsourcing: The case of starbucks. In: Information systems: crossroads for organization, management, accounting and engineering, pp. 359–366. Physica-Verlag (2012)
29. Battistella, C., Nonino, F.: The motivational drivers in open innovation web-based platforms: an explorative study. In: Information systems: crossroads for organization, management, accounting and engineering, pp. 367–376. Physica-Verlag (2012)

30. Ferrari, A., Rossignoli, C., Mola, L.: Organizational factors as determinants of SaaS adoption. In: Information systems: crossroads for organization, management, accounting and engineering, pp. 61–66. Physica-Verlag (2012)

31. De Bernardis, L., Maiolini, R., & Naggi, R.: How teams can achieve success using new technologies in order to help knowledge sharing and organizational learning in communities of practice: a case study in public sector. In: Information systems: crossroads for organization, management, accounting and engineering, pp. 481–489. Physica-Verlag (2012)

32. Francesconi, A., Dossena, C.: E-marketplaces for professional e-services: trust, reputation and performance. In: Information systems: crossroads for organization, management, accounting and engineering, pp. 43–50. Physica-Verlag (2012)

33. Spano, A., Bellò, B.: Managerial and organizational impact of ERP systems in public sector organizations. A case study. In: Information systems: crossroads for organization, management, accounting and engineering, pp. 77–84. Physica-Verlag (2012)

34. Dessì, S., Melis, C., Giudici, E.: Exploring the effectiveness of web ads via Greenwald and Leavitt's involvement model. In: Information systems: crossroads for organization, management, accounting and engineering, pp. 165–172. Physica-Verlag (2012)

35. Neirotti, P., Paolucci, E., Raguseo, E.: The future of work: trends of telework in Italian SMEs between 2005 and 2009. In: Information systems: crossroads for organization, management, accounting and engineering, pp. 323–330. Physica-Verlag (2012)

36. Cavallari, M.: Analysis of evidences about the relationship between organisational flexibility and information systems security. In: Information systems: crossroads for organization, management, accounting and engineering, pp. 439–447. Physica-Verlag (2012)

37. Neirotti, P., Raguseo, E.: Profiting from IT-based capabilities in SMEs: firm-level evidence from Italy. In: Information systems: crossroads for organization, management, accounting and engineering, pp. 527–534. Physica-Verlag (2012)

38. Sabini, L., Valentino, A., Sinha, K.M.: Search phase and the openness effects in MNEs. In: Information systems: crossroads for organization, management, accounting and engineering, pp. 397–406. Physica-Verlag (2012)

39. Calabrese, G.: Change the law: a simulation of the reduction of payment period of trade debts on Italian firms. In: Information systems: crossroads for organization, management, accounting and engineering, pp. 555–562. Physica-Verlag (2012)

40. Diamantini, C., Potena, D.: Data mart integration at measure level. In: Information systems: crossroads for organization, management, accounting and engineering, pp. 123–131. Physica-Verlag (2012)

41. Bianchi, M., Kaklauskas, A., Imoniana, J.O., Orelli, R.L., Tampieri, L.: The evaluation of networks performance in cultural heritage through intelligent systems. In: Information systems: crossroads for organization, management, accounting and engineering, pp. 387–395. Physica-Verlag (2012)

42. Za, S.: New frontiers of managerial training: the LiVES project. In: Information systems: crossroads for organization, management, accounting and engineering, pp. 499–506. Physica-Verlag (2012)

43. Comerio, M., Grega, S., Palmonari, M., Viscusi, G.: Alignment of service science and service oriented computing: a unified interpretative approach to service design and planning. In: Information systems: Crossroads for organization, management, accounting and engineering, pp. 519–526. Physica-Verlag (2012)

44. Baldoni, M., Baroglio, C., Marengo, E., Patti, V.: Supporting the analysis of risks of violation in business protocols: the MiFID case study. In: Information systems: crossroads for organization, management, accounting and engineering, pp. 545–553. Physica-Verlag (2012)

45. D'Aprile, D., Giordano, L., Martelli, A., Pozzato, G.L., Rognone, D., Dupré, D.T.: Business process compliance verification: an annotation based approach with commitments. In Information systems: crossroads for organization, management, accounting and engineering, pp. 563–570. Physica-Verlag (2012)

46. Della Bordella, M., Liu, R., Ravarini, A., Wu, F.Y., Nigam, A.: Sustained competitive advantage using business entities (SCUBE): a practical approach for business agility. In:

Information systems: crossroads for organization, management, accounting and engineering, pp. 11–18. Physica-Verlag (2012)

47. Carullo, G., Ferrucci, F., Sarro, F.: Towards improving usability of authentication systems using smartphones for logical and physical resource access in a single sign-on environment. In: Information systems: crossroads for organization, management, accounting and engineering, pp. 145–153. Physica-Verlag (2012)

48. Francese, R., Passero, I., Zarraonandia, T.: An augmented reality application to gather participant feedback during a meeting. In: Information systems: crossroads for organization, management, accounting and engineering, pp. 173–180. Physica-Verlag (2012)

49. Piccinno, A., Fogli, D.: Representing visual aspects of web services. In: Information systems: crossroads for organization, management, accounting and engineering, pp. 189–197. Physica-Verlag (2012)

50. De Chiara, D., Del Fatto, V., Sebillo, M.: Visualizing geographical information through tag clouds. In: Information systems: crossroads for organization, management, accounting and engineering, pp. 209–216. Physica-Verlag (2012)

51. Cesaroni, F., Baglieri, D.: Technology intelligence: new challenges from patent information. In: Information systems: crossroads for organization, management, accounting and engineering, pp. 267–274. Physica-Verlag (2012)

52. Colantonio, A.: Prioritizing role engineering objectives using the analytic hierarchy process. In: Information systems: crossroads for organization, management, accounting and engineering, pp. 419–427. Physica-Verlag (2012)

53. Barbini, F.M., D'Atri, A., Tarantino, L., Za, S.: A new generation dms for supporting social sensemaking. In: Information systems: crossroads for organization, management, accounting and engineering, pp. 105–112. Physica-Verlag (2012)

54. Sadok, M., Spagnoletti, P.: Managing information security through policy definition: organizational implications. In: Information systems: crossroads for organization, management, accounting and engineering, pp. 409–417. Physica-Verlag (2012)

55. Bianchini, D., De Antonellis, V., Melchiori, M.: Semantics-enriched web APIs selection for enterprise mashup development. In: Information systems: crossroads for organization, management, accounting and engineering, pp. 95–103. Physica-Verlag (2012)

56. Humayoun, S.R., Dubinsky, Y., Catarci, T., Nazarov, E., Israel, A.: Using a high level formal language for task model-based usability evaluation. In: Information systems: crossroads for organization, management, accounting and engineering, pp. 199–207. Physica (2012)

57. Mallamaci, C.L., Saccà, D.: Towards a digital ecosystem to increase effectiveness of technology transfer services. In: Information systems: crossroads for organization, management, accounting and engineering, pp. 275–283. Physica-Verlag (2012)

58. Boella, G., Humphreys, L., Martin, M., Rossi, P., van der Torre, L., Violato, A.: Eunomos, a legal document and knowledge management system for regulatory compliance. In: Information systems: crossroads for organization, management, accounting and engineering, pp. 571–578. Physica-Verlag (2012)

59. Candiotto, R., Gandini, S.: Business intelligence in the taps and fittings sector: organizational and technological aspects. In: Information systems: crossroads for organization, management, accounting and engineering, pp. 295–302. Physica-Verlag (2012)

60. Bianchi, M., Casalino, N., Draoli, M., Gambosi, G.: An innovative approach to the governance of E-Government knowledge management systems. In: Information systems: crossroads for organization, management, accounting and engineering, pp. 113–121. Physica-Verlag (2012)

61. Melonio, A., Tarantino, L., Di Mascio, T.: Towards ICT support for elderly displaced people: looking for natural gestures. In: Information systems: crossroads for organization, management, accounting and engineering, pp. 135–143. Physica-Verlag (2012)

62. Abate, A.F., Nappi, M., Ricciardi, S.: A biometric interface to ambient intelligence environments. In: Information systems: crossroads for organization, management, accounting and engineering, pp. 155–163. Physica-Verlag (2012)

63. Ginige, A., Paolino, L., Romano, M., Tortora, G., Vitiello, G.: ICT for small to medium enterprises: focus on usability for a web-based spreadsheet mediated collaboration

environment. In: Information systems: crossroads for organization, management, accounting and engineering, pp. 181–188. Physica-Verlag (2012)

64. Deufemia, V., Risi, M., Tortora, G.: Hand-drawn diagram recognition with hierarchical parsing: an experimental evaluation. In: Information systems: crossroads for organization, management, accounting and engineering, pp. 217–225. Physica-Verlag (2012)

65. Ardimento, P., Boffoli, N., Caivano, D., Castelluccia, D., Visaggio, G.: Innovation in business processes: pattern-driven process modelling. In: Information systems: crossroads for organization, management, accounting and engineering, pp. 229–237. Physica-Verlag (2012)

66. Battistella, C., Colucci, K., Nonino, F.: Methodology of business ecosystems network analysis: a field study in telecom Italia future centre. In: Information systems: crossroads for organization, management, accounting and engineering, pp. 239–249. Physica-Verlag (2012)

67. Bistarelli, S., Martinelli, F., Roperti, F., Santini, F.: Negotiation of weighted RTML credentials on mobile devices. In: Information systems: crossroads for organization, management, accounting and engineering, pp. 429–438. Physica-Verlag (2012)

68. Casalino, N., Ricci, L.: Organizational aspects and governance of a learning environment aimed at a common curricula for European senior civil servants. In: Information systems: crossroads for organization, management, accounting and engineering, pp. 507–515. Physica-Verlag (2012)

69. Niglia, F., Gagliardi, D., Battistella, C.: Exploring the impact of innovation policies in economic environments with self-regulating agents in multi-level complex systems. In: Information systems: crossroads for organization, management, accounting and engineering, pp. 67–76. Physica-Verlag (2012)

70. Bonazzi, R., Missonier, S., Jaccard, D., Bienz, P., Fritscher, B., Fernandes, E.: Analysis of serious games implementation for project management courses. In: Information systems: crossroads for organization, management, accounting and engineering, pp. 491–498. Physica-Verlag (2012)

Printed in the United States
By Bookmasters